JEWISH ENCOUNTERS

Jonathan Rosen, General Editor

Jewish Encounters is a collaboration between Schocken and Nextbook, a project devoted to the promotion of Jewish literature, culture, and ideas.

>nextbook

PUBLISHED

FORTHCOMING

The Worlds of Sholem Aleichem

JEREMY DAUBER

THE WORLDS OF SHOLEM ALEICHEM

NEXTBOOK · SCHOCKEN · NEW YORK

Library of Congress Cataloging-in-Publication Data
Dauber, Jeremy Asher.
   The worlds of Sholem Aleichem / Jeremy Dauber.
     pages   cm
   Includes bibliographical references and index.
   ISBN 978-0-8052-4278-2
   1. Sholem Aleichem, 1859–1916. 2. Authors, Yiddish—19th century—
Biography. 3. Jews—Ukraine—Biography. I. Title.
   PJ5129.R2Z576 2013   839'.18309—dc23 [B]   2013009267

www.schocken.com

Jacket photograph of Sholem Aleichem, New York, 1907. Courtesy of Beit
Sholem Aleichem Archives, Tel Aviv, Israel
Jacket design by Peter Mendelsund

Printed in the United States of America
First Edition

2 4 6 8 9 7 5 3 1

For Eli

CONTENTS

Contents

Act III. The Spokesman

Act IV. The Wanderer

Act V. The Old Man

The Worlds of Sholem Aleichem

OVERTURE

In Which We Set the Stage

Here's a Sholem Aleichem story, of a sort:

The mid-1990s. My college roommate's wedding. He was a Methodist from rural Ohio, the first person I ever met with a rural free delivery address, marrying a wonderful woman from small-town Iowa. The wedding took place in Hartley, Iowa—the town with a heart, the sign on the way into town attested. I was an usher. A guest, while being ceremoniously escorted to her pew, pointed at my kippah and proudly proclaimed she knew what it was; she had, after all, costumed *Fiddler on the Roof.*

And another:

The very late 1970s. My modern Orthodox day school. A first grade dramatic production. A half-dozen three-foot Tevyes in cotton-ball beards sing "Do You Love Me?" to a bevy of tiny Goldes. No other memory remains, for which I am eternally grateful. My parents claim it was cute.

If you're an American, Jew or no, of a certain generational span—born, say, between the time Sid Caesar first mugged for a television camera and the premiere of *Seinfeld*—there's no talking about Sholem Aleichem without talking about *Fiddler on the Roof,* the stage and screen adaptation of his greatest creation, Tevye the dairyman. Forget Sholem Aleichem: there's no talking about Yiddish, his language of art, without talking about *Fiddler on the Roof.* There's no talking about *Jews* without talking about *Fiddler.*

And it's not just Americans, either. Take a look at YouTube: as of early 2012, a clip titled "Japanese Fiddler on the Roof"—which looks like a rehearsal in a high school gym—had racked up 571,764 views. You can also find significantly less popular but far more professional-looking Hindi and Hungarian versions. Closer to home, high school marching band performances and at least one sock puppet parody nestle side by side with a seemingly infinite number of shaky recordings of high school and community theater productions.

Tevye and his daughters belong to the world, apparently; and as arguably the most popular and powerful representatives of Jewish life to the world at large since the closing of the biblical canon (Superman, as a metaphor, doesn't count), they certainly merit a closer look in their original literary setting. But this book isn't Tevye's story, though by book's end that story will be told. It's the remarkable saga of his remarkable creator, the story of the man behind the show: the man responsible, in his day and ours, for the most compelling picture of the world of our great-grandfathers, a society in dizzying, wrenching transition from the traditional life of centuries past to the modern age. Sholem Aleichem was no Tevye, though, no simple man with a few pithy quotes and some piquant conversations with his Creator; he was really Sholem Rabinovich, a first-class intellect and brilliant writer, who translated the momentous events of his day for an audience looking for nuance wrapped in simplicity.

And he was no detached observer; Sholem Rabinovich did it all. He was an orphan and a devoted family man, a struggling rabbi and a fantastically rich stockbroker; he wore the "Gorky shirts" of the left-wing agitators and left Russia to try his luck in America—when he wasn't attending Zionist congresses. He suffered through family tragedies, personal illness, commercial disasters, World War I, and a pogrom literally at his front door to write some of the most optimistic works of Yiddish literature ever penned—though leavened with a strong dose of skepticism, sadly and honestly earned. His life is Jewish modernity writ small—just as his great creation, Tevye, meets the changing world without ever leaving his daughters and his horse. In the biography of Sholem Aleichem, you'll find a gripping narrative as exciting as any of his characters' stories, complete with a grand romance, financial rise and ruin, a war or two, and at least one revolution.

But his life was his writing. A graphomaniac like few others, he wrote thousands and thousands of letters; his collected works run to twenty-eight volumes—and include around half of his Yiddish output (to say nothing of his efforts in Hebrew and Russian). And it was in that writing that he did nothing less than create modern Jewish literature, modern Jewish humor, a modern Jewish homeland in literature. Before we get to that audacious claim, though, let's leave Sholem Aleichem, as he himself might have phrased it, and return to those first two anecdotes of mine, which, in their own small way, try to nod to Sholem Aleichem's work.

Not because, or only because, both anecdotes revolve around *Fiddler on the Roof*. Both are monologues, a literary form he mastered and used to remarkable effect with characters great and small, Tevye first in their rank. At least one of the stories doesn't, strictly speaking, have an ending—another Sholem Aleichem characteristic, showcasing the fine line between humor and frustration that his stories sometimes, always intentionally, engendered. Their themes—the changing nature of Jewish identity in the modern world, particularly with respect to confronting non-Jewish life and culture, often filtered through the prism of romance, are all solidly in Sholem Aleichem's wheelhouse, as every *Fiddler* viewer knows. And the tone: ironic, yes, but not immune to sentimentality; and ultimately optimistic, with a crowd-pleasing focus on lovers and children. That's Sholem Aleichem, too.

And both stories blur the line between author and literary character: a line Sholem Rabinovich—who, under that cheery pen name of Sholem Aleichem, Mr. How Do You Do, was often buttonholed, petitioned, or even annoyed by his other literary creations—downright obliterated. In a time less attuned to postmodern game playing, his audiences sometimes confused literary persona with actual person; the 150,000 to 250,000 people who turned out for his funeral in New York in 1916—the largest public funeral in New York City then on record—were there to bury Sholem

Aleichem, not Rabinovich. They had good reason for being confused: the author himself, as we'll see, was often an active and willing participant in the obfuscation.

Those men, women, and children who mobbed the New York streets mourned the writer who had given them (and us) a gallery of indelible characters—Tevye, of course, but also the dreaming Menakhem-Mendl, and the cheerful orphan Motl, and the citizens of the little town of Kasrilevke, who had already risen to the level of byword and archetype. You will make their acquaintance in these pages, if you don't know them already, along with a host of other characters who, once met, are impossible to forget. But they were also mourning a culture hero, a symbol: of the man who held it all together, who contained multitudes, who *was* Yiddishland. His comedy was as capacious as the landscape he sketched: whether they know it or not, every Jewish comic of the twentieth century—from your joke-telling uncle to Mel Brooks to Franz Kafka—walks in Sholem Aleichem's comic shadow, which mixes humor, horror, and anger in equal parts. The professor in me knows that all these statements, like any such, are exaggerations; and the book as a whole, of course, presents a fuller context. But I hope, as Sholem Aleichem's life and work unfold, you'll see exactly what I mean.

Because last, but certainly not least, "Sholem Aleichem" himself— the figure Sholem Rabinovich fashioned by will, effort, and imagination, undoubtedly one of his greatest and most influential creations—pointed the way to a new kind of Jewish identity. An identity that mixes tradition and modernity in uncomfortable measure; and which later generations will use—as they use Tevye—as a way of talking about their own beliefs and questions about Jewish life, history, and culture, many of which would have surprised Sholem Rabinovich no end. This book, then, is more than just a life of Sholem Aleichem: it's an afterlife as well—an afterlife that tracks the author's reputation and the history of his greatest work, of Tevye and his daughters, to tell us about American Jewish life and American Jewish history over the last century.

It's fitting, given Sholem Rabinovich's love of disguise, that a good part of that story takes place in the theater. The stage makes its prominent entrance in this book well before Tevye ever treads the boards: Sholem Aleichem's first voyage to America was intimately tied up with the Yiddish theater, and some of his dramatic writings became staples of the Yiddish repertoire. But, as his life was his best performance, it's perhaps fitting that this book's structure will be divided into five acts, complete with scenic epilogue. The acts themselves are the story of the life; the epilogue, a fragmentary afterlife—scenes glimpsed from the century spanning from Sholem Aleichem's funeral to today, with our focus narrowed largely, though not entirely, to the history of Tevye and his daughters, particularly in America. Saying much more would give away the show, so let's begin. But before we do, one cautionary note: think of it as the small print in the theatrical playbill.

Any serious discussion of Sholem Aleichem's life and work runs immediately into a major, staggering problem. Not the questionable reliability of his own autobiographical statements; nor the death of all his contemporaries; nor the tormented publication histories of his works. (Though these are, of course, hardly small problems.) No, the major problem for our purposes is simply put: What do you call the man throughout the text? And in this the book's issues appear in miniature.

Our subject, as we'll see, was raised in, and had deep affection for, two cultures: the Jewish and the Russian. Both employ patronymics. Referring to him, though, as either Shalom ben Nachum, Sholem Nachum's (as the Yiddish might have had it), or Solomon Naumovich results in a character entirely unfamiliar to readers. Using the last name the family employed for official documentation, Rabinovich, offers similar problems and risks seeming overly pedantic; and sticking with just Sholem, especially after he reaches adulthood, seems criminally informal. Using "Sholem Aleichem," on the other hand, is also objectionable: first and foremost, it risks confusing historical figure with literary character—a confusion, as we'll see, that critics and followers alike often fell prey to. (Plus, since the pseudonym as a whole is a well-known Yiddish phrase, simply using the second part of it—"Aleichem"—is grating and inaccurate, like referring to him as "Do You Do"; it just wasn't done, and won't be done here.) On the other hand—and what would a book on a major Yiddish writer be without considering the other hand?—you've got to do *something*. So Sholem Aleichem it is, under protest and through gritted teeth, and I'll take special care, in the sections where I talk about the literary work, to distinguish between Sholem Aleichem the author and Sholem Aleichem the character.

More by way of introduction is, I think, unnecessary: let's get on with the story.

ACT I

The Youth

CHAPTER 1

In Which We Begin Near the Very End

1915–1859

The Bronx, late 1915.

Late at night, the man the world knows as Sholem Aleichem wanders the streets, remembering. He is fifty-six but, to our eyes, looks older: almost seven years of battling tuberculosis has taken its toll, and though he has had periods of good health, he has gotten sicker and sicker while in New York. The noise and chaos of the city have never agreed with him; he has never quite managed to find his footing in its booming Yiddish literary and cultural life—not now, and not when he was last here, almost a decade ago. He misses the warmth of the Italian Riviera; he misses his friends from Russia, separated not only by distance, but by war (the United States has yet to commence hostilities, but he has seen trainloads of refugees and sailed through mine-infested waters; he is well aware of the Great War). A still greater personal tragedy, the death of his oldest son, has just devastated the family, and he has recently composed his will.

Always an insomniac by nature, given to writing late into the night, he leaves his apartment at 968 Kelly Street, right off Westchester Avenue and a block from the 163rd Street subway stop, and walks the neighborhood, a little like his beloved Dickens used to do, spending his time in the past, trying to recall his life's details for his autobiography.

From near the very beginning, he had known his life would make good copy. Twenty years earlier, he'd told his good friend, fellow writer, and sometime competitor Mordkhe Spektor that he would write a lengthy account of his first twenty years; "a man's life [is] the finest novel," he wrote him, "and mine is rich with episodes, characters and types." But life—that rich, varied life—had gotten in the way, and he had put off recording it until 1908, when a grave illness provided him, as he put it, "the privilege of meeting his majesty, the Angel of Death, face to face." Writing an autobiography and making a will were almost the same thing, he once said, and though he composed a few chapters on his sickbed in Italy, he pushed it off as his health improved, preferring, as he so often did, to concentrate on looking forward rather than back. He wrote a critic four years later that he felt so young, so vital, that he would never finish an autobiographical account; there would always be more to the story.

But other factors intervened, which we'll return to in their proper time, and in three short but eventful years that vitality had waned: the work once titled *Step by Step*, with its sense of movement, energy, forward progress, was being serialized in the Yiddish press under the title *From the Fair*. Explaining the choice of name, especially the preposition, he wrote: "A man heading for a fair is full of hope. He has no idea what bargains he will find and what he will accomplish . . . don't bother him, he has no time. But on the way back he knows what deals he has made and what he has accomplished. He's no longer in a hurry . . . He can assess the results of his venture."

Though he was still writing, he had, in his mind, already left the fair behind.

Sholem Aleichem, as it turned out, had spoken truthfully—he never did finish his autobiography. *From the Fair* was the last major project he worked on; a partial outline of it was on his writing desk the day he died. What we do have only covers up to the year 1881, when he was twenty-one—just a year past his original estimate. He'd planned to write more. Papers found in his archive provide a long list of chapter titles, indicating plans to treat at least the following decade's events: his dramatic marriage (in a chapter titled "The Hero Steals Away the Princess"), his early Yiddish publications, his attraction to Zionism. But he didn't follow his outline precisely in the part of the work we have, so we simply don't know what he would have decided about the book's intended scope. Maybe, emulating the Russian writers he so admired, he would have simply given a portrait of the youth who became father to the man, of the artist as a young scamp.

Looking back across the gulf of years, fame, and illness, Sholem Aleichem depicts himself as a child of endless imagination, creative, sympathetic, unbowed and eternally optimistic despite a string of hardships and sorrows. Readers could (and have) easily taken the self-portrait as a quintessential Sholem Aleichem character, the germ of those engrossing children's stories that fostered his international reputation as a masterful chronicler of childhood. But what gave the readership such jolts of familiarity rings, to use a much more recent coinage, of truthiness rather than truth: the long view is never a friend to autobiographical accuracy, and, as an artist, it's hardly clear that Sholem Aleichem was much interested in presenting the unvarnished facts to begin with. The life he fashions conforms to his fiction, which itself used fact as a springboard for literature: the birth of Sholem Aleichem, not Sholem Rabinovich.

Take this passage from the memoir's very first section:

" 'Write your autobiography'—the real story, not an invented tale—is easier said than done . . . That's why I chose a special form of autobiography: memoirs in the form of a novel. I'll talk about myself in the third person. I, Sholem Aleichem the writer, will tell the true story of Sholem Aleichem the man, informally and without adornments and embellishments, as if an absolute stranger were talking, yet one who accompanied him everywhere, even to the seven divisions of hell."

Even in the brief passage, contradictions abound. A sentence asserting that literary adornment will be avoided is itself adorned with a flowery passage about Gehenna's gates, and a proclamation of honesty reinforces the great masquerade of the writer's career (he calls himself Sholem Aleichem, not Rabinovich). And more sleight of hand follows: most famously in the author's description of his bosom friend Shmulik the orphan, a master tale-spinner whose stories of mysticism and adventure enchant the young Sholem, enrich his imaginative life, and ultimately inspire him to become a writer. Shmulik may be an invention, or a composite, or a real individual retroactively imbued with almost unearthly gifts; but the one thing he shouldn't be is taken at face value. All forgivable, as Sholem Aleichem has insisted on the novelist's, not the memoirist's, prerogative, but great care is in order—as it always is with the master tale-spinner who entered immortality under a name that was and wasn't quite his own.

Such care suggests stepping back from personal history to Jewish history for a moment. By 1859, the year of Sholem Aleichem's birth, both Russia and its Jewish population had begun to take cautious steps toward modernity. Tsarist Russia had, to put it mildly, a fraught relationship with that Jewish population, in no small part because they hadn't been under Russian rule for very long. Yiddish-speaking Jews had migrated east from German-speaking lands several centuries before; but for most of the intervening time the land they had settled in had been the Polish-Lithuanian Commonwealth, broadly speaking (names, rulers, and borders came and went in this part of the world almost with abandon). Under relentless pressure from expansionist neighbors, three partitions of Poland between 1772 and 1795 gave Russia a large chunk of the commonwealth and its tsarina, Catherine the Great, a Jewish problem. About a million Jewish problems, to be more precise, and growing: in 1764, there were about 750,000 Jews in Poland and Lithuania; a century and a quarter later, close to 5 million Jews lived under tsarist control.

Recounting the dark history of the empire's "solutions" would take a book of its own, but three of the most important ones stand out for the purposes of our story. The first was a highly successful effort to limit Jewish residence in Russia's traditional interior by establishing an almost 400,000-square-mile "Pale of Settlement" stretching from the Baltic to the Black Sea; Jews could only reside in cities "beyond the Pale" under certain very clearly delineated circumstances, like engaging in a medical profession, or if they'd graduated from a university. This last was difficult, since—the second solution—Jewish entrance to universities and to professional training was restricted through rigorously applied quotas and systematically discriminatory entrance examinations. By the early 1880s, no more than 10 percent of the student body of *gymnasia* (high schools) and universities within the Pale could be Jewish, though the Jews often constituted over half the population of towns; beyond the Pale, the percentages dropped still further—in Moscow and St. Petersburg to as low as 3 percent. Finally, and perhaps looming most largely in the Russian-Jewish psyche, was the effort by Nicholas I (reigned 1825–1855) to use the assimilating force of the military by conscripting young Jews—sometimes as young as twelve, six years younger than non-Jews—into the tsar's army in special "cantonist units." The hope was that they, like other minorities, would shed their specific identities for the majority one during their service—service which, it should be noted, included the subsequent twenty-five-year term required of all military recruits.

The particulars would wax and wane through Sholem Aleichem's life (he died in 1916, never seeing Russia ruled by anyone other than a tsar), but his early, formative years coincided with the rule of Alexander II (reigned 1855–1881), who had begun a careful process of liberalization: he abolished the institution of serfdom and, closer to home for the kingdom's Jewish community, stopped drafting children and allowed certain groups of "useful" Jews to settle outside the Pale, affording new possibilities for a lucky few to enter Russian society as never before.

Which begs the question: Why would a traditional Jew want anything to do with Russian society in the first place?

Lovers of *Fiddler on the Roof* may remember its blessing for the tsar—"May God bless and keep the Tsar . . . far away from us!"—but the total rejection of Russian government, society, and culture the joke implies was actually the subject of an increasingly complicated culture war within Jewish society. By the eighteenth century's end, the Enlightenment had blazed its way through Western Europe, and the Jewish question was at its heart. If, as its proponents held, governments and kings should rule based on rationalist principles, then that meant they should withhold judgment on matters of faith—since, after all, there was no way of really *proving* who was right. Which meant that Jews could be emancipated, as citizens with full social and political equality—assuming, that is, that they acted like good, upstanding citizens who just happened to be, as a contemporary locution had it, of the Mosaic faith.

What that meant wasn't always specified or clear—and, from a current perspective it seems drastically unfair that the Jews had to conform to someone else's constantly shifting target of acceptability, with no guarantee of acceptance even if they did. But it was a previously unimaginable possibility of acceptance, and some Jews seized on it, changing their dress, behavior, reading and speaking habits, and social and professional ambitions, to model more closely those of their non-Jewish neighbors. (Some of them also changed their religion, but that is—at least until we get to Tevye's daughter Chava—a different story.)

The excitement of this "Jewish Enlightenment," or Haskala, made its way eastward, and eventually reached Jewish Eastern Europe—and the Poltava province of the Ukraine, where the Rabinovich family lived. But the situation was quite different in tsarist Russia than in cosmopolitan Berlin: in the latter, modernization and urbanization had already begun to lower the walls of difference between Jews and their neighbors, while no such process had occurred in the Pale of Settlement. Instead, government policies had reinforced, if not hardened, classic prejudices. And second, the language spoken by Jews in the German lands—Yiddish—was fairly close to their neighbors' German, which meant it wasn't too difficult for the community to learn the majority language. In the Pale of Settlement, the opposite was true for the 98 percent of its Jews whose native language was Yiddish: though there are plenty of Russian, Ukrainian, and Polish words in Yiddish, this hardly meant that the lingua franca of Eastern European Jewry was closely related to those Slavic tongues, and few Jews had more than a rudimentary knowledge of their neighbors' languages.

Nonetheless, the enthusiasm of their Western counterparts was hard to entirely ignore, and a small but devoted and ever-increasing coterie of intellectuals became *maskilim*, or advocates of the Haskala. Mostly male and mostly highly educated in traditional settings, they were also mostly ostracized by their religious communities when their inclinations were discovered—communities that instinctively mistrusted both deviation from tradition and the state authorities the maskilim intended to enlist in their efforts.

One of Sholem Aleichem's earliest stories features a Hasid ripping a Haskala journal to pieces, then burning it, then dancing on its ashes; but that was nothing. When the author Y. Y. Linetski's family discovered his Enlightenment tendencies, they made him divorce his young wife—and then remarried him to a deaf and mentally handicapped girl, to ensure he couldn't lead her astray with his blasphemous ideas. It's no wonder that marriage, suitable and unsuitable, arranged and for love, became one of the great subjects for these writers. Not only was the idea of romantic love a symbol of all the other new, modern ideas the maskilim carried with them, not only is it a classic, timeless subject, but it's also a metaphor for winning someone over to your side, your point of view: certainly this idea comes up again and again in the Tevye stories, as we'll see.

These maskilim wrote for themselves and for a skeptical audience, trying to convince others of the rightness of their cause: polemicizing for their own values and satirizing those—Hasidim, particularly—whom they felt to be foolish, retrograde, or corrupt. Enlightenment values of purity and classicism were their watchwords; and so they preferred writing in Hebrew, the classic, literary language of the elite (this preceded any efforts to revive Hebrew as a spoken language), and eschewed their native Yiddish, regarding it as a corrupt "jargon," an impure version of German that could therefore bear no pure values or ideas. Modern Hebrew literature can be said to really begin as a result, and one of its many fathers, the proto-Zionist writer Abraham Mapu, was a particular favorite of Sholem Aleichem's father, Menachem Rabinovich.

In *From the Fair*, Nochem Vevik (as he was often called) is depicted, foreshadowing his son, as containing within himself the multiple facets of a Jewish society in transformation: a philosopher and lover of this new Hebrew literature, a well-respected communal leader (a young Sholem would often eavesdrop on the gatherings of the local intelligentsia in their home), but also a pious householder, a prayer leader, and a Tolner Hasid. Crucially, the father's combination of traditional observance and more modern sensibility meant that the son—unlike so many of his contemporaries—had few of the wrenching emotions of guilt, betrayal, and anger associated with the decision to take up this new Jewish way of writing, emotions that shadowed so much of those contemporaries' work.

This hardly inoculated either father or son, it should be said, from the shadows and tragedies of everyday life.

CHAPTER 2

In Which Our Hero Is Born, Spends His Early Years, and Faces Personal Tragedy

1859–1872

At the time of Sholem's birth on March 2, 1859, and during his early youth, Nochem was a well-to-do merchant with, as his son puts it, a "pack of businesses"; among other endeavors, he served as a real estate agent; supplied beets to sugar mills; handled freight on barges on the Dnieper River; traded in wheat, lumber, and oxen; and ran the rural post office to boot. He also owned a dry goods store where his capable but strict wife, Khaye-Esther, kept a careful eye both on the wide variety of groceries and other sundries and on her eight children, of which Sholem was the third. Khaye-Esther doesn't come off quite as well in the memoirs as her husband does: Sholem Aleichem asserts she wasn't quite as gentle as other mothers, and that she often used to slap the children. Observers, however, saw her echo in his energy, intelligence, and articulateness.

Sholem was born in Pereyaslav, a small- to medium-sized town on a tributary of the Dnieper River near Kiev. (In the kind of historical irony that would probably elicit a rueful smile from Sholem Aleichem, the town had been home to the Cossack leader and vicious anti-Semite Bogdan Khmelnitsky centuries before, and thus now contains both a Sholem Aleichem Museum and a Museum of Cossack Glory. It also, it should be said, houses a Museum of Bread and a Museum of Decorative Towels.)

The family left the town, though, when Sholem was only two, and moved closer to Kiev, to the village of Voronkov—where, as the author would later put it, he and his family "spent their happiest years, the golden era of their childhood."

Voronkov was smaller than Pereyaslav—"as small as the fine print in the prayer books," Sholem Aleichem would later remember. It was there he first attended school, the traditional *kheyder*, fastidiously trying to keep his clothes clean of the thick mud that coated the roads and much of everything else a good part of the year. It was there he "met" that mysterious and probably fictional storytelling inspiration, Shmulik; there where he amassed the raw stuff of small-town Eastern European Jewish life that he would later transmute into the image of the shtetl, often by removing its Christian presence and proximity. (To take just one dissonant real-life example: According to his brother, a young Sholem would pelt the charity box of the nearby wooden church with dirt and stones, offering mock prayers to the Virgin Mary until the old church warden would chase him away. Needless to say, hardly the image of Jewish-Christian shtetl relations we imagine, much less of the almost purely Jewish locale appearing in Sholem Aleichem's fiction.)

And it was in Voronkov, too, that his father was ruined. The reversals took place in Sholem's early adolescence and stemmed, at least in large part, from an unscrupulous business partner, who cleaned Nochem out by renewing jointly owned real estate leases in his own name only. Nochem refused to sue for his losses, unwilling, as his granddaughter put it, to "drag a Jewish name through a Christian court." Sholem Aleichem would later filter this trauma through the crucible of his imagination: Shmulik and Sholem's Voronkov adventures in *From the Fair* revolve around the search for a hidden treasure, rumored to be buried locally by a "Jew-hating general" who had despoiled the Jews of their possessions. The treasure motif would recur in his literary work, an all too reasonable fantasy for a young boy who saw, from an early age, how easily fortunes could be made or lost.

Remembering the old Jewish maxim "Change your place, change your luck," Nochem decided to return to Pereyaslav in 1871—in the process, of course, wrenching Sholem from his beloved childhood home. The parents left first, postponing the children's departure until the end of the school term; when Sholem and his siblings finally arrived, they discovered their new home to be a small, unprofitable inn. All the furniture from the Voronkov house had to be squeezed into a single room; meals now consisted of gruel and beans. At night, Sholem Aleichem writes, their parents would lock the bread away in a cupboard so the starving children wouldn't get into it.

A tragedy far greater than their poverty, though, was the death of Sholem's mother during a cholera outbreak in 1872, soon after his bar mitzvah, rendering him an orphan by the cultural standards of Jewish Eastern Europe. Later in life, Sholem Aleichem was markedly superstitious, and a notable experience from Khaye-Esther's final days must have contributed at least in some small part: Immediately before she sickened, she dreamt she'd lit the Sabbath candles—and her neighbor who had died of cholera the previous week appeared and blew them out. (The neighbor's name: Frume Sarah—shades of the avenging ghost in the story of Tevye's Tsaytl.)

Perhaps the natural sense of a boy's abandonment led to his mother's more equivocal depiction in the memoir; perhaps it was what happened next. Quick remarriage was the order of the day when there were children to be raised, and Nochem would prove no exception to the trend; he packed Sholem and five siblings off to their mother's Hasidic parents in the nearby town of Bohuslav while he traveled to Berdichev to find a new wife. Bohuslav, in the adult writer's recollection, was a place of tradition—the stories his ascetically inclined, mystically oriented grandfather used to tell him were of Jewish history and the world to come, as opposed, he writes, to Shmulik's princes and treasures. Sholem Aleichem depicts the Jewish holidays in Bohuslav with a festive folksiness that would often be described, incompletely, as a hallmark of his work. Like Voronkov, Bohuslav is consciously depicted as a fairly idyllic existence—better to highlight the contrast to Sholem's return to Pereyaslav upon his father's remarriage.

In wooing Khane, Sholem's soon-to-be stepmother, Nochem seems to have misrepresented both his financial station and the number of children she would have to care for (the siblings in Bohuslav were actually referred to, only somewhat jokingly, as "contraband merchandise"; the term became a family nickname). This hardly endeared her charges to her when she discovered the truth, and she became, according to Sholem Aleichem's daughter, "a combination of the proverbial shrew and the wicked stepmother," physically abusing her stepchildren and begrudging them even their meager portions of food while Nochem did nothing to alleviate the situation. Making matters even worse, a rival inn, more luxurious, had opened nearby and was attracting all the moneyed guests. Sholem's stepmother sent him out to try to convince potential lodgers to stay with them instead, and when he failed—as naturally he often did—she berated him bitterly, with the ornate curses that were a hallmark of Yiddish linguistic creativity.

Yiddish curses can, and often do, play off a fellow conversant's statement. If one were to say the word "yell" to Sholem Aleichem's stepmother, for example, she might have responded with the phrase "May a toothache make you yell"; the word "drink" might have elicited the wish that leeches drink your blood. Turning trauma into comedy, as he would so often do, Sholem Aleichem's first literary production in Yiddish would be an alphabetical list of his stepmother's curses. In Curt Leviant's felicitous translation, the *alef-bays* goes something like: "A—abusive, addlepate, aggravator, animal, ape, apostate, argumentative, ass; B—backscratcher, bandit, bathhouse flunky, beggar, boaster, broom, bum"; and so on.

It's not surprising that Sholem Aleichem, who would be later acclaimed for his ability to mimic the widest swath of an increasingly diverse Jewish society, presents his self-proclaimed first literary steps as imitations. In *From the Fair*, the young Sholem is portrayed as a talented mimic, occupying the center of attention for his uncanny ability to represent the one-eyed family maid and her nose-whistling new husband at their wedding, or the way his grandmother prayed or said grace when he thought she wasn't looking. In his youth, he once wrote a fellow writer, it was almost "a sickness with me . . . to point out the ludicrous in everything and everyone," and not just at home—the memoirist has his parents confess to his *kheyder* teacher, a less amused victim, that it's not just him; "the rascal imitates everyone like a monkey."

Any punishments he received at school, though, seem to have been less important than the reception he got at home. Here's the end of the story of his stepmother's curses, his graduation from acted to written imitation. Not only, he relates, was his father delighted with what his son had been hunched over writing and rewriting, but his stepmother was mollified as well—"a strange, frenzied laughter overtook her; she almost got apoplexy from the shrieking." And Sholem Aleichem claimed that, recognizing his talent, she trod more lightly from that day on. If the story's ending strikes us as smacking a bit of wish fulfillment—literature can bring the new family together in their shared admiration of the artist—it certainly sets a pattern for Sholem Aleichem's future, where his imaginary landscape created a kind of unity that was often less apparent in a turbulent, modernizing Jewish world.

CHAPTER 3

In Which Our Hero Gets—and Gives—an Education

1872–1877

Sholem Aleichem's graphomania was evident from the start. As a child, lacking reserves of clean, white drawing paper, he substituted the whitewashed walls of neighboring houses, scrawling on them with charcoal—and every morning the maids and domestics would wash off the previous day's activity, cursing the child as they did so. Though his list of his stepmother's curses was in Yiddish, he had, like his father and many of his contemporaries in the Haskala, the Jewish Enlightenment, inherited the sense that real, literary, modern writing took place in other languages. And in his early years, following in his father's footsteps, that meant writing in Hebrew.

In those days, because of the Haskala's classical orientation—and the comparative underdevelopment of the Hebrew language—a love of Hebrew meant a love of biblical Hebrew, and of works, like those of the writer Abraham Mapu, whose language derived largely from it. Early on, Sholem developed a love of, and great familiarity with, the Bible that would last a lifetime; he would come to learn it practically by heart, and in later years would often both carry a pocket Bible and keep one by his bedside. His own literary activity developed accordingly: he attempted his own biblical commentary as he entered *kheyder*, Jewish primary school, and, at the age of ten, wrote a work on the Bible and on Hebrew grammar that his father cherished. (Nochem showed it to a friend, who responded that the content was irrelevant, but the handwriting was beautiful; Sholem Aleichem would later call this "his first criticism.")

Whether his *kheyder* education helped or hindered him in all this was a different question. This system of elementary schooling that Sholem, like almost all his Eastern European Jewish contemporaries, attended was the bête noire of most reformist, modern Jewish writers. It was castigated for its rudimentary pedagogical methods, its ignorant teachers, and their constant resort to, and often reliance upon, corporal punishment. The results of the *kheyder* system, according to the authors, were generations of ignoramuses and occasional successes despite themselves: Sholem Aleichem, hardly an intellectual slouch, claimed he "didn't understand a word of the Talmud discourse" prepared for him to give at his bar mitzvah. He also claimed other archetypal experiences: a teacher, for example, with "an extra bone in his thumb which, when he poked it into your ribs, back, or temple, made you see your great-grandfather in the world to come."

Occasionally, but only occasionally, they'd find echo in his later work. There's a 1908 feuilleton, or satiric sketch, titled "Preserves," for example, that presents a violent *kheyder* rebbe who cares about nothing but his tuition fees; and an early work, "Poem from the Kheyder," compares the educational system to the dark, cold season, its chill—in the form of the baneful rebbe—creeping its way even into the narrator's dreams, and ending with the hope that the institution, like the season, will give way to a brighter spring. (Incidentally, the poem was later reworked into a popular music-hall song under the title "I Don't Want to Go to Kheyder.")

Whether these charges were true or exaggerated in the smarting hindsight of poets and memoirists is not our concern here; it is indisputably the case, though, that the *kheyder* prized the study of Jewish subjects and texts disproportionately—often almost exclusively—at the expense of what could be referred to as "secular studies," and even that study of Jewish subjects was deeply circumscribed. This was a path that Sholem—whose memoir speaks of his desire to seek the treasures of a wider world—found ultimately limiting. His father firmly agreed. Disgusted with Sholem's earlier teachers because of their lack of commitment to Hebrew and biblical grammar (a hallmark of the Jewish Enlightenment's influence), he had agreed—apparently to some family controversy—to transfer the young Sholem's education to Moshe David Ruderman, whose progressive credentials included the fact that his son attended the secular district school. By his midteens, Sholem was reading the most advanced literature, poetry, and philosophy of the Hebrew Haskala; a decade later, he would write a warm letter to one of the authors acknowledging his "old debt to you for your pleasant, sweet speech, which was my finest recreation in my childhood years when I conducted a romance with the holy tongue."

The leading lady in Sholem's romance with Hebrew, though, with the possible exception of the Bible, was Abraham Mapu's Hebrew novel *Love of Zion*, set in biblical times and crucial to the formation of many an early Zionist. Sholem devoured it one Saturday, and immediately set about composing his own work, *Daughter of Zion*, in the same flowery biblical Hebrew. Tragically or not, this work of juvenilia never saw the light of day: his stepmother caught him writing it at night—the only time he could write, after school and chores at the inn—and created a scene, bemoaning the waste of kerosene. Though his father confiscated the work, he seemed proud of the achievement, and would stand up to his wife more directly after Sholem's next literary production: proudly displaying *The Jewish Robinson Crusoe* to the intellectuals who frequented the inn, he told his wife Sholem had more important things to do than chores for her, and apparently even commanded her to stop harassing and browbeating him. And apparently she did (excepting the occasional grumble about the cost of ink and paper).

The Jewish Robinson Crusoe speaks volumes about Sholem's engagement with broader cultures—especially the Russian one around him. A year earlier, at fourteen, Sholem had left the world of Jewish education, registering, with his father's approval, in the three-year course at

Pereyaslav's Russian district school; he would study there between 1873 and 1876. Certainly his Jewishness—and that of his friend and fellow student Elye Barkhash—was a live issue there. Sholem would have stood out—for missing class every Sabbath, for leaving the room whenever the local priest taught his lesson. And difficulties ensued: some of the other students, in a hazing ritual, pinned him to the ground and smeared his lips with lard. Though he would receive a scholarship from the Ministry of Education for his excellent academic performance at the end of his first year, the school's director told him that as a Jew he would merely receive a 120-ruble stipend, rather than the tuition-free scholarship his performance merited. He reminisced, in a letter to Barkhash decades later, that their teacher, while "no enemy of Israel, nonetheless used to good-humoredly inform us that Jews were physiologically incapable of truly internalizing Russian culture." All of this may well explain why Sholem, at least by his own account, never particularly enjoyed the school; but he became enchanted by the Russian and other non-Jewish literature he learned to read there.

This was, after all, the wake of an extraordinary period of Russian literary creativity. Turgenev, Pushkin, and Lermontov were acknowledged masters; *The Possessed* was published the year before Sholem entered the district school, and *Anna Karenina* appeared the year after he graduated. And, of course, the Western canon was open to him through Russian translation; in *From the Fair*, Sholem Aleichem name-checks as influences—among others—Byron, Shakespeare, Dickens, Swift, Thackeray, Goethe, Heine, and Cervantes. (He'd later write a friend that reading *Don Quixote*, he "grew sick with laughter and the female innkeeper thought I had gone out of my mind and wanted to send for the doctor. Sadly, I'm not exaggerating!") Though he undoubtedly received a more intensive formal Russian education than many of his fellow Yiddish writers, like them his education was also marked by a healthy dose of random autodidacticism: one of his characters in an early novel remarks, not unfondly, of his unsystematic, not always comprehending reading in an old library where the books had simply been purchased by the pound.

But perhaps the young Sholem Aleichem's most notable literary encounter was with his celebrated fellow Ukrainian, "our own Gogol," as he would put it. (In fact, Gogol came from Sholem's own Poltava province.) As a Ukrainian rather than a Russian, Gogol might have suggested to Sholem Aleichem that there was room as an ethnic minority to make a success of oneself in the majority culture. The budding author first sought to imitate him in superficial ways: not too many years later, Sholem would wear his hair long and brushed down like Gogol's, and the latter's portrait would come to adorn his study. But it wouldn't be who the author of the brilliant comedy *The Government Inspector* and the absurdist masterpiece *Dead Souls* was that made such an impact; it was, of course, what he said, and, especially, the way he often said it. Gogol was a master of *skaz*, a written form that attempted to reproduce the oral monologue. Take, as just one example, "Ivan Fyodorovich Shponka and His Aunt." There, the narrator, telling the story of the titular characters, warns his audience up front that he has forgotten the story's ending ("You must know," he confides in us, "that my memory is incredibly poor"), and so, after numerous pages in which we lose ourselves in the story's masterful details, we come to an abrupt end—because our teller has run out of things to say.

Gogol's forays into absurdism and storytelling impossibility undoubtedly appealed as well—one of his masterpieces, "The Nose," provides a climactic situation that can only work on the page (and brilliantly so): running into your own detached nose, but, humiliatingly, having it dressed in a uniform that outranks your own. And the way Gogol employed the supernatural, as he did so effectively in "The Overcoat," to provide a haunting sense of the moral imbalance of the universe—all of these techniques were to find strong resonance in the mature Sholem Aleichem's literary style. And, finally, it was apparently a passage from Gogol's *Dead Souls* that inspired Sholem to craft the pithy formulation that has characterized (and unfairly confined) his sensibility ever since. The passage, in his very free translation, that he kept among his personal papers reads: "It seems we are fated . . . to observe the great, tumultuous life with open laughter and hidden tears." Laughter and tears, inextricably bound: it would be a central part of Sholem Aleichem's legacy through his lifetime and the century after his death.

More prosaically, mastering Russian language and literature also helped the young Sholem acquire the personal independence every teenager yearns for. Sholem began giving private Russian lessons at sixteen, and was sufficiently successful at it to get enough money to move out of the family home, after obtaining his father's permission. (The first thing he bought with his earnings: boots to navigate the mud, which he kept as scrupulously clean as possible.) Though in previous years the decision might have been made solely on financial grounds, things had recently been improving in the Rabinovich household. During Sholem's last year at school, Nochem had switched businesses; no longer a struggling innkeeper, he now operated a tobacco store with a wine business in the cellar, providing the family with a comfortable living. (In another classic teenage activity, Sholem used to sneak wine out of the cellar with Elye Barkhash.) One might speculate that his relationship with his stepmother also contributed to his decision to move; certainly he could now study— and write—late into the night without disturbing anyone or hearing complaints about paper, ink, or kerosene.

In *From the Fair*, Sholem Aleichem links his reading and writing Russian literature to another, more charged, display of independence: his first desecration of the Sabbath. One Saturday afternoon, he recounts, he found a piece of chalk in his pockets and began, almost despite himself, to scribble a Russian rhyme on one of the wooden fences in the area. Writing, and writing Russian, in other words, was not only Sholem's ticket to salvation but his passport to trouble: discovered by his pious Hasidic uncle, Pinny, reported to family and even to the local authorities, who had agreed to his release from Saturday classes precisely because he would not write on the Sabbath, he faced both ostracism and expulsion. But thanks to his scholastic excellence, he reports, he came out of it unscathed, with only his teacher's mocking nickname of Author to show for it. Every modernizing Jewish intellectual had his own tale of the first time he desecrated the Sabbath. But Sholem Aleichem's own version isn't just about the departure from tradition; it's about the arrival of an author.

S holem Aleichem graduated at seventeen with top marks in Russian language, arithmetic, geometry, and geography (though his grades in handwriting and drawing were slightly less stellar), and, like other upwardly mobile, Haskala-oriented types, looked to the system, specifically to university, to make him into the very model of a Russian citizen of the Mosaic faith: a doctor, perhaps, or an attorney. But of all his options, Sholem chose, along with Elye, to attend the Government Jewish Teachers Institute of Zhitomir, and even received a government scholarship to do so. His decision to continue working in the Jewish community in one form or another, rather than simply abandoning it in the name of personal advancement, again illustrated his strong grounding in his father's Haskala: his desire to use the knowledge he had acquired, in Hebrew and Russian alike, for social and communal reform.

But the optimism and faith that characterized the Haskala philosophy met its first real challenge as Sholem ran afoul of the bureaucratic system that, ostensibly, provided his meritocratic salvation. All Russian men, including Russian Jews, were required to give army service at specific times. Unfortunately, as the institute's head, Chaim Gurland, wrote Sholem, he would be eighteen at the time of his matriculation, and therefore required to report for military service after his third year of the four-year course; completing the course would be thus impossible, and so he could not be admitted. The only options—immediately rejected from further consideration—were "chicanery" or forging a changed birthdate. It struck Sholem, he remembers, "like a bomb, like thunder on a bright sunny day," seemingly rendering years of work in vain at a stroke.

Trying to make ends meet, the seventeen-year-old took up tutoring more extensively, teaching Russian not only in Pereyaslav but in other small towns in Kiev province. It was a hand-to-mouth existence, Sholem Aleichem later recalled, featuring "one angry landlady after another, mer-

ciless cockroaches, biting bedbugs, rats and other disgusting creatures."
After an undistinguished and unsuccessful semester, though, his fortune changed: during a fruitless attempt to become a magnate's tutor—
spending the last of the tutoring money he'd saved up on suitable clothing
in his efforts—he met a distant relative. Quite distant: Joshua Loyeff's
late mother was the sister of the first wife of the father-in-law of one of
Nochem's children. But the two hit it off—Loyeff was a fellow fan of both
traditional Jewish literature and Abraham Mapu—and Loyeff asked if he
would be interested in tutoring his younger half sister, from his father's
second marriage. Through his intervention and after an interview with
the patriarch at a Bohuslav inn, he was invited to join the household of
the wealthy Jewish magnate Elimelekh Loyeff, in the village of Sofievka,
as his private secretary and tutor to his daughter Olga.

Skipping ahead a bit: In a few years, the young writer would make a
literary splash with *The Trial of Shomer*, a pamphlet conducting a "mock
trial" of a best-selling author (real name Nokhem-Mayer Sheykevitch)
who specialized, according to Sholem Aleichem, in romantic fantasies fit
only for daydreaming serving maids, tales that resolutely—and, in the
critic's mind, fatally—failed to match the realities of Jewish life in Eastern Europe. Certainly the tale of a poor but dashing tutor who romances
his young student over her father's objections would be exactly the kind
of story the young critic would reject out of hand as unrealistic and overly
sentimental. It is testament to the unconventional life of Sholem Aleichem
that it seems to be exactly what happened.

CHAPTER 4

In Which Our Hero Suffers the Ecstasies
and Agonies of Love

1877–1880

It was a literary romance from the start. Much of the tutoring seems to have consisted of reading novels and plays together, both classics by Shakespeare, Dickens, Gogol, and Tolstoy and contemporary potboilers by authors like Eugène Sue, whose *Mysteries of Paris* would inflame the imagination of a generation of Eastern European Jewry. All these works were to be found in Elimelekh Loyeff's capacious library, filled not only with the latest works in Hebrew, German, French, and Russian, but also boasting a full representation of a new phenomenon: modern Yiddish writing.

Fifteen years earlier, in 1862, the Hebrew-newspaper publisher Aleksander Zederbaum had explored the possibility of expanding his *Hamelitz's* neurasthenic sales by adding a weekly Yiddish supplement titled *Kol Mevaser* (Voice of the Herald). The tail was soon wagging the dog: the supplement became better known than the original, thanks to its resident genii, the maskilic writers S. Y. Abramovitch—better known by his pseudonym Mendele the Book Peddler—and Y. Y. Linetski. Their works, like *The Little Man* (1864) and *The Polish Lad* (1867), took on what they saw as the corrupting influences in Eastern European Jewish life: wealth, Hasidism, superstition, and immorality cloaked in piety. They weren't the only ones writing in Yiddish, or even the truly popular Yiddish writers—Isaac Meir Dik had been so successful writing Yiddish romances that he could make a living doing it—but they opened up a new field for writers, especially writers interested in combining literary effort and social activism. Sholem's first significant exposure to these writers probably occurred in Loyeff's library; over the next decades, he would develop relationships—and, in the case of Abramovitch, an almost familial bond—with most of them.

At the time, though, Sholem's self-described astonishingly prolific output of "long, heart-rending novels, impassioned dramas, and complicated tragedies and comedies"—he would later claim he wrote more in those three years than in any ten after becoming a professional writer—was produced not in Yiddish, but in Russian or Hebrew, following standard Haskala practice. Olga served as an admiring audience for the works, which were almost immediately consigned to the fire as the next ones proved their predecessors' inferiority. But Sholem's appeal for Olga wasn't purely literary. She wrote, in a fragment of a memoir, "On that evening in September 1877 when he came into our house, my fate was sealed. He entered with my father and brother, looking very young, his blond hair long and wavy, one lock occasionally drooping over his forehead. His skin was very fair; his head large, his neck short and fairly thick. He wasn't exactly handsome, but he was different from any young man I had seen before." He may have been a trifle on the short side, but he had piercing blue eyes and a smile that could, in later years, entice anyone into a conversation. The dashing older man—he was eighteen and a half when he arrived, and she hadn't quite turned thirteen—would provide formal lessons for a few hours, and then the two would stroll in the garden or the orchard, watch the peasants work in the fields, or be driven to other estates close by.

The backdrop certainly didn't hurt, either. Sholem would later call Loyeff's house "a second home" and describe the roughly three years he spent there, from 1877 to 1879, as "the best, the finest, and the happiest years" of his life. Loyeff was an *arendator*, an estate manager, leasing farmland from two noblemen and supervising its agricultural activity, selling the grain and sugar beets produced using the newest, most scientific methods. Local Russian farmers used to say, "If you want to learn how to manage a farm, go to the Jew Loyeff." (His practice of going from peasant hut to peasant hut during cholera epidemics administering medicine with his own hands must have helped his local reputation.) Success paid off, for Loyeff and his young employee. Sholem Aleichem ate on silver and china in the family's elegant dining room; he had a large, bright room of his own; there were servants everywhere to wait on his every need. The romance could proceed idyllically.

Sholem himself was a stranger to love. Yes, he writes in his memoir of brief lovesick fancies and what he imagined to be a romantic entanglement with a girl he calls "the cantor's daughter," its climax occurring on the holiday of Simchat Torah when she kisses his hand, instead of the Torah. (As recounted, the story's end displays Sholem Aleichem's ironic and explosive tendencies as a writer: not only, it transpires, had she never actually loved him, but she had been in love with a non-Jew all along— with whom she absconds, something far more serious than the simple depredations of unrequited puppy love.) But he had never had a real romance before meeting Olga. Like any good literary romance, though, this one didn't run smooth.

He had to negotiate his draft service, for one thing. But the combination of a high draft number and, especially, of Loyeff's influence—he moved Sholem's registration venue to a place where he had greater sway, and almost certainly paid a signicant bribe—seems to have done the trick: he was released from service in 1879. Far more consequentially, though, Loyeff eventually caught wind, via a visiting cousin from Berdichev, of the romance brewing between his tutor and his daughter. There's an old Yiddish saying that "a guest for a while sees a mile," and Aunt Toibe, as the cousin was called in the family, took one look at the pair sitting close together, laughing and sharing from the same plate, and drew the obvious conclusion. Trouble ensued.

From the available evidence, it doesn't seem like Loyeff opposed

Sholem's suit because he was poor, or had few prospects. From the first, he had insisted that the tutor be treated like a member of the family, and his taking on the trouble and presumed expense of negotiating Sholem's draft status certainly suggests his sincerity in that regard. In addition, the two seem to have genuinely bonded over a mutual love of Hebrew literature and storytelling. Loyeff comes off remarkably well in Sholem's memoir, in fact, characterized as "a rare sort, an original, a Jew like no other . . . an exemplar of a Jewish landowner," farmer, and intellectual; he even, according to the memoir, had Sholem's old talent for mimicking others and shared Sholem's penchant for telling tall tales. It's not impossible to suggest that Sholem saw him as a second father figure—which made Loyeff's anger and disappointment all the more crushing.

Loyeff seems to have objected to what he felt was the dishonesty, the implicit betrayal of trust, of this occurring under his roof without his knowledge. "It was he, her father," Sholem Aleichem wrote, "who was supposed to introduce such a young man to her. And she must not choose him herself, without having consulted her father! This is what vexed him more than anything else." The sentiment echoes, years later, in Tevye's own bafflement and anger: *"What kind of decided to get married already?"* Regardless of the reasons, the young tutor had to go. Emerging from his room one winter morning, Sholem Aleichem found no one present, only an envelope marked for him; it contained nothing but his accumulated pay, and a sleigh waited outside for his departure. He wrote to Olga, sending the letters through the offices of a friendly local postmaster, Malinovsky—until it was established that the postmaster was friendlier to Loyeff than to Sholem, and was alerting the paterfamilias to the correspondence. No responses were forthcoming.

With his earnings, Sholem made his way to Kiev to seek his fortune in the big city. Illegally: he had no residence permit, and so lived in regular fear of raids by the authorities rousting unauthorized residents. (If caught, he would be returned to his hometown in chains, forced to travel there on foot in convoy.) A brief, disastrous stint as a legal secretary followed—he naïvely handed over his nest egg to his employer, a thief with a gambling problem—and was forced to borrow money from his family to return home to Pereyaslav. Depressed, alone, bankrupt, Sholem Aleichem made the fateful, unhappy decision, at the very end of 1880, to become a rabbi.

This may require some explanation. The tsarist Russian authorities, while willing to grant the Jewish communities some degree of self-governance, needed individuals who could report births and deaths, register marriages, and fulfill other official functions—mostly to make sure that the taxes were paid on time and that the military quotas, which were assigned by community, were properly filled. These figures were often linked to places like the Zhitomir teachers' institute, which Sholem had just missed attending; it was an elected position, though the existence, time, and place of elections were all set by the government. It's easy to imagine that the "crown rabbi," a figure combining the qualities of an Internal Revenue Service agent and draft board chairman, wouldn't be the most popular person in town; to make matters worse, the positions were generally filled by representatives of the modernizing movement, adding a patina of suspicion on top of the general antipathy. One friend's reaction: "No decent man, he said, could shake his hand, since a Certified [i.e., crown] Rabbi was nothing but a hypocrite, a bootlicker, a Tartuffe, a tool of the rich and a henchman of czarist bureaucracy."

But it was even worse than that. True, Sholem won election to the crown rabbinate of Lubny, a town in Poltava province, fair and square; through a combination of the support of an elderly leading citizen and a crackerjack speech—Sholem Aleichem always did have the gift of gab—he was chosen by acclamation at the close of 1880. But in doing so, he of course displaced the previous incumbent, who happened to be the son of his old teacher Moshe David Ruderman—and who was now, thanks to Sholem, out of a job with a family and mouths to feed. It was hardly the fate he had dreamed for himself; as he said, borrowing a phrase from Chekhov, he felt like "one who had eaten soap."

Sholem Aleichem died before reaching this point in his memoir, but a story he wrote the year before his death might shed some light on his feelings about his time in Lubny. A warning before proceeding, though, here and through the book, in talking about the stories this way: Whatever's read there—even and perhaps especially if it uses "I"—is hardly dispositive evidence. Anything Sholem Aleichem sets down on paper, including his own name, is suspect.

A reform-minded crown rabbi, elected to a small town in Poltava province, begins to "stick [his] head into the community pot," settling disputes and giving advice. After he chides some leading citizens for their behavior, one insists on telling him what he claims is a true story: needing a tenth man for his son's bris, he offers a stranger eternal life to help him out. The narrator cossets the amenable stranger with food and luxuries for days, then sticks him with an enormous bill. The guest drags the narrator to the crown rabbi—who sides with the narrator. The narrator stops the dejected guest from paying up: "What do you think I am, a highwayman? . . . I wanted to show you what kind of man our rabbi was, that's all!" Not to be outdone, though, the crown rabbi responds with a story of his own. A traveling man leaves money with a rabbi over Yom Kippur for safekeeping, with several fine townspeople witnessing the transaction. At holiday's end, the rabbi denies any transaction took place—and the townspeople back him up. Before the traveler collapses, the rabbi produces the money. His explanation: "I just wanted to show you the kind of leading citizens we have in our town." That's the last word—of the story-rabbi, the narrator-rabbi, and of the story itself.

It's of course unlikely such an event ever occurred: it's based on an old joke, one which Sholem Aleichem had already mined for a different story ten years before. Still, there's something about that hostile dynamic that seems to ring true about a young man's progressive, or radical, social beliefs and the willingness to speak truth to power in a fragile position (he was elected, after all, and money talks) and his use of the gift of gab, of wit and literature, to do so. This wouldn't have made him a lot of friends, though, and that crown rabbi, at the end of "A Tale for a Tale," is left alone with the cold comfort of getting the last word.

CHAPTER 5

In Which Our Hero Finds
the Two Loves of His Life

1881–1884

While Sholem was serving in Lubny, modern Jewish history began. It started with a bang, in this case a literal explosion: the assassination of Tsar Alexander II on March 1, 1881 (by the old Russian calendar), by bomb-throwing revolutionaries, members of the Narodnaya Volya, or People's Will. The revolutionaries called for rebellion; the country was in chaos; the government, reeling, looked for a scapegoat to help them consolidate their hold. And they found the Jews. The fact that the assassination was conceived and carried out by non-Jews (though one Jewish member was involved in the plot) was less relevant than the fact that growing anti-Semitic sentiment, ironically catalyzed in some part by the Jews' increased presence in Russian life thanks to Alexander's liberal reforms, meant a dark seam of anger and hatred existed, ready for manipulation.

One result was the first major wave of pogroms in Jewish history. Starting in Elizavetgrad on April 27, after Easter week, over two hundred and fifty separate events occurred during the next fifteen months in places like Kiev, Warsaw, and especially the town of Balta. Most attacks were aimed at property rather than people; but dozens died in anti-Jewish violence that many Jews believed was organized at the highest levels of government (there's no evidence that this was the case, however). None of this—the blame, the violence—surprised the liberal Jewish intelligent-sia. What came as a shock was that the liberal *Russian* intelligentsia—those whom the rationalist, optimistic Haskala proponents had counted on to recognize their own changing behaviors and the promise they represented—failed utterly to support the Jews or decry their attackers. They remained almost entirely silent both about the pogroms and during the establishment of the anti-Semitic "Temporary Regulations" (better known as the "May Laws," having been passed in May 1882), which pro-hibited Jews in the Pale from living or owning property outside of towns and townlets, owning mortgages there, or doing business on Sundays and Christian holidays. Other restrictive legislation would be passed over the next years. Though some farsighted thinkers had been predicting the fail-ure of the implied bargain of emancipation in Russia for several years, the events of the early 1880s, for most Jewish intellectuals and modernizing Jews, provided a definitive answer to the Russian Jewish question. The specifics of what was to be done, however, were much less clear, and the history of modern Jewish life is the history of the answer to that question of specifics: the embrace of emigration, or of Zionism, or of revolution.

Though Sholem Aleichem would come in his own way and his own time to embrace each of these to varying degrees, at this point, in solitude and under strain in Lubny, he had embraced the doubtfully comforting answer posed by certain Haskala writers before him: that his only com-munity was the imagined one of like-minded readers and thinkers, and that his existence was bound up in joining that community. As early as the late 1870s, he'd been sending correspondence to Russian journals—and to the weekly Hebrew newspapers and journals that were cropping up over the newly liberalizing tsarist empire. An 1879 letter from "Sholem Rabinovich" in the Hebrew *Hatsefira*, his first published correspondence, savaged a previous writer who had slandered Pereyaslav maskilim as igno-ramuses who couldn't string together a few sentences in Hebrew or Rus-sian. (Even from the first, Sholem was thinking about his father.) Most of his Hebrew and Russian correspondence, though, gave the "editors, thank God, something to light their ovens with," as he would later put it.

Now, however, he began to write articles in earnest—and to get them published. His first-ever published article, also written in Hebrew, appeared at the end of 1881 in *Hamelitz*. Signed "the youth in the legions of Judah, Sholem Rabinovich, government crown rabbi," its topic, "Education and Its Relation to Military Service," showed Sholem Aleichem, at this transformative time, weighing his Enlightenment orthodoxies against his communal sentiments. The article was written in response to a maskilic suggestion that rabbis should prevent Jewish shirking of military service—which most Haskala proponents saw as an essential step in emancipation—by refusing to marry those who had failed to complete their army obligations. Sholem Aleichem (who, let us not forget, had escaped the service himself) dismissed the idea out of hand; in a typical literary turn, he suggested an emphasis on education and professionalization—which was in large part, he argued, the crown rabbi's responsibility. Indeed, he tweaks his own Lubny for failing in this regard, building a beautiful and expensive new synagogue while poor children remain unclothed and uneducated. The year's events may well have suggested recalibration: though Sholem Aleichem may never have been the most radical of reformers, his own sympathetic nature and current history meant thinking about Jewry as the poor people he knew and cared for, not as political abstractions.

Sholem Aleichem promised in the article to write more on the education question, were the editor to publish it. In a footnote, the latter indicated his willingness to do so, and so two further articles followed in the beginning of 1882, one a continuation of the first theme, the second on reform of the *kheyder* system. Striking what would become his ongoing, nuanced balance between traditional and modern life, he suggested mandating the inclusion of progressive and secular elements—while simultaneously maintaining religious aspects. The publications began what he later termed his composition of Hebrew articles "by the pound." Though he would dismiss these a quarter century later, perhaps unfairly, as "foolish," "contentless," and "talentless," they had several positive effects close to home. First, they made quite an impression on Sholem's Hebraist father; overjoyed, he predicted great fame for his son—as a Hebrew writer. But, far more important, they led to a reunion with his beloved.

Olga Loyeff hadn't forgotten about Sholem. Quite the opposite. She'd resisted all her parents' attempts to marry her off—in that day and age an impressive feat of perseverance. It's likely that her maskilic cousin, Avrom Markovich Yampolsky, read Sholem Aleichem's pieces in *Hamelitz* and alerted her that her beloved had resurfaced; at her request, Yampolsky wrote to the publisher and received Sholem's Lubny address, allowing the couple to write each other directly.

The wedding took place in Kiev on May 12, 1883, on the Jewish holiday of Lag Ba'omer. It says even more about Olga that she was willing to marry Sholem against her father's wishes; undoubtedly, there are echoes of her behavior in the portrait Sholem Aleichem would craft of Tevye's strong-willed daughters. And also, perhaps, in the portrait of their acquiescent father: a reconciliation between Loyeff and his daughter was soon effected, and Sholem and Olga were invited back to the Loyeff estate, which allowed Sholem to leave his position as Lubny's crown rabbi in August. They spent the end of the summer at Sofievka, and moved that November to Belaya Tserkov (now known as Bila Tserkva, about fifty miles south of Kiev), where they would remain for the next three years.

Two months after his wedding, Sholem made his debut as a Yiddish writer.

Yiddish had always exercised a certain lure for him. In *From the Fair*, he fondly recalls his father entertaining a crowd one Saturday evening in Voronko, his own idiosyncratically modern equivalent of the Hasidic *melave malke*, by reading aloud from a book of Yiddish stories, and thinking that "God willing, when he grew up and became an adult, he too would write a book that would make Jews laugh and good naturedly curse the author." Availability, the opportunity for others to read his work—that was a powerful incentive to write in Yiddish. So was the ability to "write the way you think": writing Hebrew, he knew, meant thinking in Yiddish and then translating for the page.

But there were downsides, too. Yiddish, as we said earlier, was considered common jargon, not fitting for enlightened discourse; his father may have read it on Saturday night to a crowd, but that didn't mean he wanted his son writing it. And his attachment to other languages was real. He would continue to write in Hebrew and Russian throughout his life, both in his literary work and his correspondence, with great success: a translation he did of a story of his from Yiddish to Hebrew was so good most readers believed it must have been done by the editor of the journal. That editor, the noted Hebrew critic David Frishman, wrote Sholem Aleichem that "in my private opinion, you're not a Jargonist but a Hebraist." And, for that matter, Sholem Aleichem wrote a relative in 1879 that despite his many hours learning Russian, he preferred writing Hebrew, "our holy tongue, mother of all languages."

But Yiddish was beginning to exercise a more concrete appeal: because the circumstances for publishing Yiddish writing—for that availability— were changing. Yiddish writing had developed in fits and starts since Aleksander Zederbaum had started *Kol Mevaser*; though the 1860s had seen the weekly journal succeed, launching Linetski and Abramovitch/ Mendele's literary careers in the process, the paper had closed in 1872 due, in part, to the publisher's own financial difficulties. By the late 1870s, Zederbaum had returned to the newspaper business, and, after relaunching *Hamelitz*, he ventured back into Yiddish. This time, the *Yudishes folksblat* (The Jewish People's Paper) was a full-fledged Yiddish paper, a supplement no longer. Founded in 1881, a moment when questions of politics and literature were particularly charged, the weekly "political-literary newspaper" was at this point the only Yiddish newspaper in Russia; its place of publication, the cosmopolitan St. Petersburg, spoke to its own paradoxes, its attempt to maintain an elite approach to literature and culture while relying on the use of the Yiddish language—and the occasional dip into sensationalism—to sell papers.

Zederbaum was a practitioner of what we would now call cross-promotion: in a response to an article in the Hebrew *Hamelitz*, he recommended checking out a relevant case described in the *Folksblat*. The article was written by Sholem Aleichem, and a quarter century later, he recalled getting his hands on the *Folksblat*'s first issue and his astonishment at "the simplicity of the idea . . . a newspaper published in such a simple language, that was available to all Jews, even to women!" Two years later, his own work appeared there—and in Yiddish—for the first time.

That first Yiddish appearance showed how much Sholem Aleichem was willing to draw from the stuff of life to make his art, and the value of one's native language in expressing raw—not to say uncrude—emotion. "Two Stones" was dedicated to Olga and appeared in the *Folksblat* in July 1883, though it was written before their wedding; it's the tale of an impoverished young tutor, Shlomo Rabovski, whose three-year developing romance with the daughter of a well-to-do businessman is conducted over their shared love of European literature. Life does not, however, imitate art entirely, to say the least: the story takes a (melo)dramatic turn when, after the daughter declares her love for her tutor, the father has him locked away and convinces the daughter he has abandoned her. Distraught, the daughter commits suicide by jumping into the river, and the young tutor, driven insane by witnessing it, follows soon after. The two stones of the title are the young lovers' headstones. Add the characters' clichéd, stock dialogue to the melodramatic plot, and it's no wonder Sholem Aleichem insisted it be stricken from the editions of his collected works that appeared during his lifetime.

"The Election," published two months later, draws on a different realm of Sholem Aleichem's experience, as it concerns a freethinking crown rabbi up for reelection whose candidacy is opposed by the traditionalist powers that be (the town, after all, is symbolically named Darkness). Far more interesting than the actual sketch, though, is the name signed to it. Perhaps the young writer knew he was treading on politically sensitive ground and didn't wish to create local controversy; regardless, he decided to make a change—though the installments of "Two Stones" had been credited to the fairly transparent "Sholem Rab-ovitch" and "Rabbiner Sholem Rabinovich," "The Election" bears the authorial credit, for the first time, of "Sholem Aleichem."

Pseudonyms were hardly uncommon in those early days of Yiddish writing: a way for writers like Abramovitch to save themselves from the embarrassment of letting their enlightened friends know they were stooping so low—even for the public good of educating their jargon-reading audience. Did Sholem, as he later claimed, take on the pseudonym to hide from friends, neighbors, and family? Was it the fear of his father's Hebraist disapproval? Or the concern that his father-in-law would see him as a writerly dilettante, not the businessman he wanted him to be? (His father-in-law certainly seems more fearsome—and, as we have seen, inflexible—than the fairly mild-mannered Nochem, who, in the end, told his son he was proud of his son's literary and artistic success, even if it took place in "a weekday tongue of cooks and serving-girls.")

Whether one, any, all, or none of these reasons, one thing is almost certainly true: the actual pseudonym itself, "Sholem Aleichem"—peace be unto you, how do you do—which would later be taken by readers, critics, elegists, popularizers, and even the author himself as a symbol of his ability to stand in for, as one admirer put it, "the sweet familiarity, the informality, the utter lack of side, that is associated with the Yiddish-speaking masses of Eastern Europe," was designed as nothing of the sort. It was one of numerous pseudonyms he would use at the beginning of his career; it was a literary tip of the hat to a series of sketches by the famed Yiddish writer Linetski (which featured stories called both "The Election" and "Sholem Aleichem"); and it was a jeu d'esprit by a young man who loved to play with language. But to credit Sholem Rabinovich, at the very outset of his career, with the almost mythic, world-encompassing sensibility he would develop seems prophetic, not historical.

This said, "Sholem Aleichem" was developing an independent existence from the very beginning. In the author's next work, a series of "Intercepted Letters" published in the *Folksblat* between October 1883 and July 1884—the first writing he'd later be willing to consider his debut—the letters in question are intercepted "by mail, and they were printed, word for word, by the heretical Zederbaum in his journal *Folksblat*, through some sort of shlimazl named 'Sholem Aleichem.'" And the shlimazl keeps getting into the act. Later, one of the letter writers, overhearing others laughing over the intercepted correspondence, is nonplussed to hear their suggestion that "Sholem Aleichem" may be some sort of fiction; by the tenth installment of "The Intercepted Letters," a character has actually gone looking for Sholem Aleichem in Belaya Tserkov (where, remember, Sholem Rabinovich was actually living), but can't seem to find him.

And it gets even more complicated than *that*. Sholem Aleichem begins to create what we might now call "sock puppets," literary cutouts, to publish letters in the *Folksblat* to push the joke even further. One letter, signed Gamliel ben Pedahtzur, a pseudonym taken from a minor biblical figure, attests to seeing a character sailing away in the balloon, trailing intercepted letters of his own behind him; and in an exchange of letters between "Sholem Aleichem" and a Lithuanian writer in Warsaw (both sides, of course, written by Sholem Aleichem), the latter recounts his embarrassment at being mocked by others for imagining one of the intercepted-letter writers to be a real person—but then recounts his relief when the latter actually shows up at his door! Whether anyone was taken in by this mystification seems to be beside the point; more important is the exultant sense of literary possibility, of fresh, freewheeling creativity in this aspect of the work, so at odds with the standard Haskala critique present in much of the rest.

Purporting to represent a correspondence between "Reb Leibele from the other world" and "Reb Velvele from this world"—a standard literary device of the time—the "Letters" use Reb Leibele's postmortem perspective to rehearse a standard series of maskilic complaints: society privileges wealth over merit, the poor are maltreated, Hasidic rebbes are frauds, punctilious observance untethered to morality is rewarded, while true moral goodness by modernizing types goes unheralded. Sholem Aleichem tells us in his memoir that back in his Pereyaslav days, a habitual visitor to his house dared to say that "I have no use for piety—honesty is what counts"; and this is the essential ethic of Sholem Aleichem's first significant work—not rejecting tradition, but centering it around human behavior. But there were newer political trends on notice in the "Letters" as well, reflecting more recent events.

In this post-1881, post-pogrom world, the characters of "The Intercepted Letters" put no faith in their neighbors. Instead, throughout 1884, thirteen years before the first Zionist conference (but the same year as the first convention of the proto-Zionist Hibbat Zion movement), they come out strongly for a Jewish homeland centered in Palestine. One of the characters makes it the centerpiece of a sermon he delivers to an astonished audience; another sends in a (not terribly distinguished) poem with the title "Palestine" to the *Folksblat*. In another series he wrote for the *Folksblat* concurrently, a "Correspondence Between Two Old Friends," Sholem Aleichem and his "correspondent" discuss the fate of a third friend, the allegorically named Israel. Israel, it emerges, has squandered his patrimony and become subject to anti-Semitic legislation and, ultimately, violence; Sholem Aleichem suggests, in the strongest terms, that Palestine is the solution to the problem. But, he adds, the solution depends on unified, communal action—which he knew to be an unrealistic possibility. From the very beginning of his career, Sholem Aleichem's rueful realism provided ironic counterbalance to his rampant optimism. A poem written at 1884's end, "To the New Year," notes that "we're rich with advice . . . we've got lots of 'projects.'" The people to carry out those projects, on the other hand—those are what's missing, as the year, and the years, ebb away.

His anxieties weren't just political, though. A postscript at the end of one of the "Intercepted Letters" asks why one character always ruins his letters' powerful effect by including some comic elements at the end. And another "sock puppet" letter addressed to Sholem Aleichem, by one "Baron Dragon," excoriates Sholem Aleichem for writing satire rather than serious material, and hackneyed Haskala satire at that. Even when he tried for pathos through poetry—as in 1884's "Sabbath Eve," the lament of a recently widowed, impoverished coachman's wife, or "A Jewish Daughter," whose parents force her to marry a Hasid she despises rather than the student she loves—the tears are simply laughter transformed. At least, so suggests the protagonist of another contemporary poem, "They Ask Me Why I Weep," who explains that his lament emerges not from a genuine tragic sensibility, but, rather, a thwarted sense of merriness.

Sholem Aleichem, constantly criticizing his own work in his own work, asking himself why he weeps, has no one to throw down the gauntlet to him but himself: Can comedy be successful literature? What can the subject of that comedy be? Can it touch on, and address, issues of the day? And can ordinary individuals be its basis? The next ten years, through remarkable transformations and numerous writings, would be devoted to Sholem Aleichem's search for answers.

ACT II

The Man of Business

CHAPTER 6

In Which Our Hero Gains a Fortune, and an Enemy

1884–1887

It wasn't only his literary career he was worrying about.

He was a magnate's son-in-law now, after all, and the understanding—at least on his father-in-law's side—must have been that his writing would be a harmless sideline to a career in the family business. Elimelekh Loyeff ran an estate noted for high yield and excellent management, which meant deep involvement in all aspects of production—including exercising a fairly strict, patriarchal control over his newest employee. The son-in-law chafed. "My father-in-law doesn't give us any money to make any deals," he wrote his brother, "and I can't ask him for it," for reasons he declined to elaborate.

The solution to his problems, he suggested, is to find another position out from under his father-in-law's thumb, and he did so quickly, wangling a position inspecting the sugar estates of Lazar Brodsky, the Kiev Jewish magnate so wealthy his name was a byword among Yiddish-speaking Jewry. By July 1884—a month after his previous complaint—he was proudly writing about his weekly inspection trips to southern Russia's Yekaterinoslav province, and his faithful return to Olga and their newborn daughter, Ernestina, in Belaya Tserkov every Sabbath. Just like "a real Hasid" shuttling between family and rebbe, he joked. But the rebellion, such as it was, was short-lived: Loyeff put his foot down, vigorously opposed to his son-in-law working for someone else, and Sholem returned to working for him, continuing to publish in the *Folksblat* throughout. Liberation would come soon, though—unexpectedly, and marred by tragedy.

In early 1885, Olga grew ill, seriously enough that she had to travel to consult with doctors. Loyeff had already lost two sons; in both cases, he had received the dreadful news by telegram. In a heightened state of nervousness about his daughter's illness, he received another telegram— and, thinking it was notice of her death, collapsed and died. The telegram concerned a shipment of grain. Loyeff's death—and his predecease by his two sons—meant his daughter inherited a fortune, 220,000 rubles by one account (over $2.6 million in 2010 dollars). Tsarist law mandated that a wife's property was transferred to the husband; at a stroke, the former starving student was transformed into one of the wealthiest Jews in Eastern Europe.

No one could say he didn't embrace the possibilities the money offered. In September 1887, he moved his family to Kiev, to a luxurious apartment on Teatralnaya Street, lavishly decorated with Gobelin tapestries, Chinese porcelains, Irish linens, a black concert grand piano, living room furniture imported from Vienna, and a live-in cook and nursemaid. The "city of churches, guardian of the Russian soul" had only been reopened to limited Jewish residency a quarter century earlier, after their expulsion by Nicholas I in 1827; sugar merchants and industrialists lived side by side with upwardly mobile students enrolled in universities—and the illegals, speculators and brokers trying to strike it rich in and around Kiev's commodities exchange, established in 1873. Business was booming and the city boomed with it, doubling its population from 1864 to 1874, and then doubling again between then and 1897. If you didn't have a permit and didn't want to risk the convoy, you could live in one of the suburbs, like Podol or Demiyevka, and get day papers, but you might miss out on something, whether it be a jackpot deal or a chance to be part of the city's cultural ferment.

Take theater, for example. Kiev had two repertory theaters and an opera company, where they played Gogol, Ostrovsky, Shakespeare, Molière, Ibsen, and new modern plays by Gorky, Chekhov, and Hauptmann. Sholem Aleichem's daughter doubted her parents missed a single new production in any of the three houses. And the community of Jewish literati—both old-line masters of the Hebrew Haskala and intellectuals newly interested in Yiddish literature—provided an exciting and congenial framework that the fledgling author had only found previously in the pages of journals like *Hamelitz*. Kiev's Jewish population may have been small—thirty-two thousand in 1897, ten thousand less than Berdichev's—but it was his kind of community. Technically, the four of them—Sholem and Olga's second daughter, Liali, was born in 1887—were living there illegally, but given their assets and lifestyle they were hardly the type to be stopped and searched.

But with wealth had come responsibilities, too: liquidating the family estate, serving as guardian of his wife's nieces. (His first task had been to bargain with the Bohuslav *khevre-kadishe*, the local burial authorities, who demanded the unearthly sum of 30,000 rubles—over $350,000 in 2010 dollars—before allowing Loyeff's interment in sacred ground; it was a scandal so great it was written up in Kiev's Russian newspaper.) And he had to maintain the lifestyle to which he had become accustomed: thus his decision to found a company of his own to speculate in wheat, sugar, and stocks and other financial instruments.

For someone who had already gambled big—on romance, on Olga—and won so spectacularly, financial and commodity speculation, particularly betting that prices would rise in the teeth of a roaring market, must have seemed natural. In addition, Sholem Aleichem was already a man who loved the life of the imagination and loved to communicate, and the exchange, that place where abstractions assume the power of real things (it's not the commodities themselves that change hands, after all), and are argued over, talked through, and bargained out, must have held a special appeal. But it all took time away from writing.

Sholem Aleichem's literary output for 1885 consisted almost entirely of "The Counting-House: A Drama in Two Flowery Letters, Eighteen Business Letters, and Twenty Telegrams." Again purporting to be gathered by Sholem Aleichem from his stack of intercepted letters, the mischievous figure *Folksblat* readers were getting to know proudly insisted that he hadn't added even "half a word; I didn't even want to add a long 'Preface' with a short poem at its end, as the fashion is with our authors, because I'm no author, simply an anthologizer, that is, practically (saving the comparison!) an editor . . ." Like most of Sholem Aleichem's jokes, this one was barbed; and the barb bit deeper into his own flesh than anyone else's. He *was* anxious about being an author, as the business of the countinghouse threatened to encroach more and more on the business of writing works like "The Counting-House." And the next two years' writing, largely autobiographical, pseudo-autobiographical, and quasi-autobiographical, laid many of those anxieties bare.

Sholem Aleichem's first published book, *A Journey Around the World: A Very Pretty Tale*, appeared in 1886. The teenage narrator's tale of his failed search, along with his small-town friend Aryeh-Leyb, for like-minded, Haskala-oriented spirits in the wider world—despite painfully sacrificing their traditional observance and small-town sensibilities, they find little embrace of their ideals, their passion, and their writing—reads like an attempt to describe a path not taken, to write something close to a standard Haskala pseudo-autobiography. Though its broad-minded comic strokes—the country bumpkins getting rooked by the city slickers, responding to any challenge by reading poetry aloud from the latest Haskala journals—suggest, especially as the story grows to encompass poverty, sickness, and death, reform-minded Haskala literature's incapacity to deal with the pain of everyday life of Eastern European Jewry, its ending is especially, and personally, telling.

The novel concludes with an extensive excerpt from Aryeh-Leyb's diary, which not only echoes a scene from the author's own life—a love interest between a daughter and a private secretary—but records the diarist's efforts to become a professional writer. But Aryeh-Leyb is no author, though the elegant evidence of the diary suggests he may be a writer. It is the world's opinion that matters, and a wide variety of editors eviscerate him for his callowness, his works' incomprehensibility, and his overweening ambition at too young an age. The final pages of the novel boast what may be the most vicious rejection letter in the history of rejection letters: the writers of *Hamelitz*, exhausted by Aryeh-Leyb's constant stream of inferior product, inform him that "from this day forward your letters will no longer be opened; all of your work will be thrown away unseen, or cast into the fire; since you have earned such bitter enemies among the editors that they would have broken your bones had you shown up here in person . . . but to ensure that we can get rid of you once and for all, we will present you a formal announcement, to wit: 'We, the undersigned members of the editorial board, swear to you by all that is holy, that you cannot write, that you will never be a writer, that as long as you live, not a word of yours will be published anywhere, and if you might possibly think that you have an ounce of talent, allow us to tell you, again and again, that you are entirely and terribly mistaken!'"

Hamelitz had been the first venue to publish Sholem Rabinovich's work; and by the time this final installment appeared Sholem Aleichem was a practically omnipresent contributor to the *Folksblat*. But—fairly transparently—the anxiety lurks nonetheless. Perhaps it was exacerbated by a new fear that had grown along with his fortune: that his growing literary profile stemmed from a source other than his writing skill. As he wrote a friend, "Our elevated aristocracy, the mercantile class . . . value my finances more highly than my literary talent." What's more, he was well aware of the obstacles to honest self-assesment new money could bring. One of his *Sketches from Berdichev Street*, another series he published in the *Folksblat* at the time, tells the story of a contractor who, after coming into wealth, begins acting like "a big shot, a millionaire, the way all the millionaires on Berdichev Street did then," with servants, a countinghouse, a beautiful carriage, and, most important for our purposes, the flattery of others. "No one knew his virtues," writes the narrator, "but everyone said his powers were limitless." Wealth leads to the dishonesty of others, which, as the sketch goes on to illustrate, leads to foolish personal judgment, which leads to ruin.

At the same time he was anxious that his peers failed to value his talent properly, he was complaining that they were hardly aware of it. He complained, in that same letter to his friend, that his literary pseudonym was "a terra incognita" for his Kiev merchant neighbors, even as he presented, in his imagined work, the precisely opposite picture of a figure whose readership was growing increasingly curious for personal information about him. (He offered to provide them answers about life, work, and family if they wrote him; given that the address he provided for them to do so was located on Tic-Tac-Toe Boulevard, though, the offer may have been somewhat disingenuous.) And even, he asserted, the people who were familiar with this figure dismissed his work as simple "foolery," not realizing the serious craft and motivation that animated it.

Like many another speculator, he decided to face these uncertainties and challenges by doubling down. If he (or his persona) were unknown, or worse, not taken seriously, he would have to engage even more explicitly in other kinds of serious, highbrow literary activity, thrusting his persona directly into the center of it all. And, in doing so, he could address his growing concerns about the future of the Yiddish literature and culture in which he was already playing a foundational role.

If you were a Yiddish reader in the 1880s—and almost all Jews in the empire were Yiddish speakers, and over half were literate in Yiddish—the chances were pretty good you were reading Shomer. Shomer, the pen name of Nokhem Meyer Shaykevitch, was one of the most prolific and successful writers in the history of Yiddish literature; by the time he died in 1905, he had racked up about two hundred novels, and by this point he had written at least fifty of them. Shomer's popular success came from his masterful ability to give the people what they wanted—and what they wanted was sentimental, melodramatic fiction packed with juicy murders, star-crossed lovers, wild plot twists, and far-flung settings with, at least arguably, no redeeming educational or literary value whatsoever.

This gave the Haskala writers hives: Why were people reading this trash when they could be reading elevating fiction and nonfiction like the kinds that were being written by, well, themselves?

This had been a topic of surpassing interest to Sholem Aleichem from the beginning of his literary career. In "The Intercepted Letters," he'd already begun mounting attacks on novelists who "cook their novels like potatoes, by the dozens" and foist them on "the blind masses" who spend their precious time and money on unedifying material; in *A Journey Around the World*, his narrator insists he's not writing "one of those truly interesting novels in eighteen parts with an epilogue and with two Hebrew poems," then continues with a long, parodic paragraph stuffed with the overwrought melodramatic writing he despises, complete with storm winds, swaying trees, and dark clouds. It wasn't just the prose styling that was the problem, of course. To Sholem Aleichem and to others, Shomer's romances were actively dangerous: they filled people's heads with romantic illusions that cruel life tended to crush, even—perhaps even particularly—as the traditional system of arranged marriage was starting to weaken under the claims of romantic love.

Another short novel Sholem Aleichem published at the time, 1886's *Children's Game*, provides a very different view of romance than the one in Shomer's novels. Though the plot starts Shomeristically—a Romeo-and-Juliet tale of Boris and Rosa, the children of two childhood friends turned business partners turned rivals—Sholem Aleichem soon turns his attention to the go-betweens attempting to help the young couple: Berte the divorcée and the son's school friend Ayzenshtot. The former, unlucky in love herself, has assuaged her own sorrows by immersing herself in Shomer-type romances; the latter is crushed by poverty and his own unrequited feelings toward Rosa. Despite Ayzenshtot's skepticism, the two disastrously support an elopement in the name of romance: with disastrous results, as the generally feckless Boris is easily persuaded by his mother to throw the poor, pregnant Rosa over for a better and wealthier match. Romance and literature lead the intermediaries astray to ignore the harsh realities of life, and suffering is the only result.

The rejection of romance reached its height in Sholem Aleichem's next novel, whose subtitle said it all: *Sender Blank and His Highly Esteemed Family: A Novel Without a Love Story*. In telling the story of the conventional male ingénue Markus, the narrator insists it will not end in romance, and indeed it doesn't. Markus simply fades away, echoing the novel's progress itself: though *Sender Blank* begins with its titular character at death's door, it transpires that he's hardly in danger at all—a bit of indigestion after eating some fish, and a patriarchal whim to gather the family, is the cause of all the chaos, and as he improves, everyone just sort of . . . disperses. Yiddish, like Russian and German, uses the same word for "romance" and "novel," *roman*; and the combination of Sholem Aleichem's rejection of Shomer's romantic sensibility and his impish narratorial strategies—undercutting the suspense, apologizing for digressions, refusing to include a cracking love story or a big finish—result in an attack on the novel similar in degree, if not yet in quality, to those of the comic writers like Cervantes and Sterne that he so admired. That same year, he wrote that "one has to be naïve, like a young child"—or like Shomer, he might have added—"to believe that the plot of a novel is its most essential element." Rather, what really matters is plausible characters, psychologically authentic portraiture: in his words, "the positive and negative effects of human nature." No wonder *Sender Blank*'s narrator fantasizes, in detail, about people packing up those other novels and sending them off by the wagonload!

Sholem Aleichem wasn't the only one taking on Shomer. Simon Dubnow, later one of the most eminent Jewish historians of the modern era and a future friend of Sholem Aleichem's, called Shomer out for his badly written, inauthentic tales in the Russian-Jewish journal *Voshkod*; a partial Yiddish translation of his critique was published in the *Folksblat*, which between 1887 and 1888 played host to all sorts of arguments, mostly critical, about the merits of Shomer and his ilk. It was the beginning of a new chapter in the story of Yiddish: an emergent sense that Yiddish literature could and should be *literary*, with ideological and aesthetic dos and don'ts. And Sholem Aleichem was at its forefront: at least if one were to judge by its established archenemy, who, in letters to the editor and prefaces to his own numerous works, singled out the young Sholem Aleichem for special attention, characterizing him as "clownish" and "prattling" and wondering aloud why the editors devoted so much space to someone so untalented.

It may be the case that any publicity is good publicity, but the criticisms must have stung nonetheless, regardless of who issued them. What unquestionably rankled, though, was an anonymous piece in the *Folksblat* in late March 1888 full of rapturous praise for Shomer; especially aggravating was Sholem Aleichem's strong suspicion that the piece was written by the *Folksblat*'s publisher himself, Yisroel Levi. Levi, who referred to Yiddish as "garbage," had been angering Sholem Aleichem for years with his increasingly willful disregard of the language. A case in point that struck particularly close to home was his constant practice of changing his writers' language, adding Hebraisms incomprehensible to most of his readers to suit his own, yeshiva-oriented taste—most egregiously in the special supplements where many of Sholem Aleichem's longer pieces were published.

Sholem Aleichem had previously written friends about how "heartbreaking" it was to see "how our dear *jargon* is being ruined" in the *Folksblat*: now, annoyance and sadness gave way to outrage. After reading the piece, he wrote a friend and fellow anti-Shomerist contributor to the *Folksblat*, Y. Kh. Ravnitski: "He says that Shomer is no less than a kind of Turgenev, Zola, Dickens, etc.! And his *types* are such good, true types—taken straight from Jewish life (?!?!?!)." Outrage wasn't the same as defeatism, though; not even close. If the *Folksblat* wouldn't be native ground for a new kind of Yiddish literature, the newly wealthy, endlessly ambitious Sholem Aleichem would have to create one himself.

And take out Shomer at the same time.

CHAPTER 7

In Which Our Hero Publishes a Trial, and Endures the Trials of Publishing

1888

In 1888, Sholem Aleichem decided to put Shomer on trial. At least on the page.

Over the previous fifteen years, Russians had become increasingly fascinated with the phenomenon of the public trial, and their writers took the hint, setting scenes in and around courtrooms in their novels and dramas. Sholem Aleichem took this a step further: in *The Judgment of Shomer, or, The Jury Trial of All of Shomer's Novels*, he plays court stenographer for a proceeding purporting to return an indictment on eight counts against Shomer, following a commission's examination of over fifty of the author's novels. (He had done his homework, searching far and wide for Shomer's writings to be fully prepared—and armed.) The charges read:

1. Almost all of his novels are, pardon the expression, stolen from foreign literatures.
2. All his novels are of the same cut.
3. This so-called novelist does not provide a realistic, authentic picture of Jewish life.
4. As a result, his novels have no connection to the Jews whatsoever.
5. These romances ignite the imagination, but provide no ethical direction, no moral.

6. They contain obscenity and cynicism.

7. They are very poorly constructed.

8. The author appears to be an ignoramus.

The cry of the modern literary artist, shaped by the Haskala: the champion of creativity, of realism, of ethical utility, of decorum, and of craft. The defense's response? Befitting a polemic, it's given limited space, essentially boiling down to (1) if people like it so much, how bad can it be?; and (2) people have to make a living, don't they? Shomer's attorney ends by throwing his client on the mercy of the court, beseeching: "Leave the public alone to choose what material it wants to read. The audience, I repeat, is like a little child. It will grow up."

The work's end, though, surprises. The opening charges had been accompanied by the suggestion that "it would be a great act of charity if he and all of his fantastic and uncouth novels were expunged from our literature by means of serious, clear-headed criticism." But the jury is instructed, after the proceedings, to consider three options—guilty, innocent, and guilty with extenuating circumstances (the last meaning, according to the judge, to treat Shomer with "mercy, compassion, and pity"), and, after fifty pages of damning indictment, the verdict returned is the last: extenuating circumstances apply.

Why, at the last moment, did Sholem Aleichem hold his fire? True, the court's sentence—the finding that "Shomer is not a belletrist, a poet, an artist, a moralist, a philosopher, a satirist, or an aesthete," along with an insistence he never reprint any of his old novels—is no slap on the wrist. But it hardly seems to fulfill the promise Sholem Aleichem had previously made to "do away with Shomer . . . cut him up, atomize him, destroy all traces of his bones, innards, and arteries."

Was it the grudging respect of a populist at heart for a massively successful writer? After all, prolific as Sholem Aleichem had been over the previous few years, he wasn't even close to matching Shomer's output or his reach. *The Judgment* contains several portraits of groups of women moved to tears by Shomer, seemingly reflecting his actual readers' responses; maybe this was Sholem Aleichem's way of sitting up and taking note, envious of—and trying to learn from—that ability to connect with his public. Or was it that he saw a bit of Shomer in himself? Chiding the author for the speed with which he produced his works, treating them "as if churning out a new novel every day was some kind of business transaction," not realizing that "each and every book [must] be carefully chiseled . . . [that] before the author publishes each book, he must first go through it carefully, think about it ten times over, improve it, correct it, freshen it up and rework it so that it reaches the level of a work of literature," could easily be seen as a case of protesting too much. Though Sholem Aleichem would later insist on multiple, careful revisions of his works, at this point in time, by his own admission, he would hardly even give his writing a second look before sending it to press, much less rewrite it. The result, as he ruefully acknowledged, was a tendency to fall into caricature. Showing mercy to Shomer let him off the hook a bit as well.

Sholem Aleichem certainly put himself front and center in the third point of the jury's decision, though: "Every new work that is published by Shomer immediately must be submitted to the critics, who will go over it in detail." *The Judgment* is literally Sholem Aleichem's attempt to set himself up as judge and jury; to establish the critical rules of the game, with himself as chief arbiter. And more: he would not only be in charge of Yiddish literature's present, but its past, and its future. In *The Judgment*, the secretary reading Shomer's indictment prefaces it with a potted version of modern Yiddish literary history, thus allowing Sholem Aleichem to create a Yiddish canon. The list not only includes the usual suspects of Abramovitch/Mendele and Linetski, but names Aleksander Zederbaum, the *Kol Mevaser*'s editor and publisher; Sholem Aleichem knew well how central editors and publishers were to Yiddish literature's past—and its future.

Criticism, literary history, and publishing, past, present, and future; all were linked, and would merge in Sholem Aleichem's next endeavor. By using his own resources to publish what, according to his critical principles, was the best literature, he could establish new entries in the canon he had begun to sketch in *The Judgment*. (Naturally, canons are determined by what you exclude as well as what you include.) The works themselves could be authored by canonical figures from the dawn of modern Yiddish literary history—since that dawn was only about a quarter century back—and blend unobtrusively with work by newer authors, most notably himself. And by publishing congenial criticism, both his own (pseudonymously and otherwise), and of like-minded individuals, he could cement his principles as the new standard. The result, *Di yudishe folksbibliotek* (The Jewish People's Library), would be nothing less than Sholem Aleichem's dream of the Yiddish literary ideal.

Sholem Aleichem had been thinking of getting into the journal business for some time. As in his other literary efforts, he first turned to Hebrew: contemplating a takeover of the struggling Hebrew journal *Hayom*, or possibly founding one of his own. But given the hash of things Levi was making at the *Folksblat* with his Shomerism and negative attitude to Yiddish (with the inevitable result: readership fell by two-thirds), and, far more important, his own increasing love for and support of Yiddish, his plans changed. By March of 1888, he was telling prospective contributor Linetski about his plan to publish an occasional anthology "for the honor of jargon"; to reach out to all lovers of Yiddish, regardless of what language they had previously written in. He'd pay well, in advance, and on time—unlike his friend and now competitor Mordkhe Spektor, "who pays with promises" (and whose literary miscellany *The House-Friend*, the competition, would print the first Tevye story a few years later). And, he tells a less-established writer, Yankev Dinezon, he'll try to cast his net widely and speak for as broad a community as possible in an increasingly partisan time: the proposed journal, for example, won't "have an ideological bent; it won't be pro-Palestine, or anti-Palestine, or anti-anti-Palestine, but rather a simple Jew, a Jew like *I* am." The emphasis is in the original: as Sholem Aleichem goes, so does the community, and vice versa.

The work went quickly, but took its toll: by June, he wrote a friend he had "gone grey in two months, like a dove." (The birth of his third daughter, Emma, couldn't have made things easier.) The *Folksbibliotek* was in proofs by late July, and he figured his "little bundle of joy" would be published by around mid-September. It had cost him a thousand rubles (about $12,000 in 2010 dollars) out of pocket for honoraria, but it was worth it: it "will definitely make a good impression on my readers," he wrote, "and a bit of a racket among my critics, who, unfortunately, cannot bear my talent." Production took longer than expected, perhaps due in part to a newly visible aspect of Sholem Aleichem's professional personality, soon to become an essential feature: dogged perfectionism. Long letters went to his friend Ravnitski, who'd agreed to participate in the editing process, replete with attention to technical details: ways of numerating pages, heading formats, how to deal with proofs for correction.

Still, September's end saw an announcement in the *Folksblat* proclaiming publication would occur at the beginning of the next month. But then more bad news intervened: in mid-October, he learned his niece and ward Manya had become critically ill with tuberculosis, and he had to join her in Yalta in mid-November, further delaying the final necessary revisions. She died several weeks later, at the age of nineteen—the first, but hardly the last, time the disease would afflict Sholem Aleichem's family. The volume would finally be ready in January 1889; when it was complete, Sholem and Olga went to Warsaw to visit Yankev Dinezon—who'd become intimately involved with the *Folksbibliotek*'s production and sale—and just to breathe; the new publisher had promised his wife he would take a few months off before starting the next volume, for the sake of his health.

Had it been worth it? He had had to compromise on at least one of his dreams: making the book accessible to a wider public by pricing it, as he memorably phrased it to one prospective contributor, "cheaper than borscht." As delays had mounted, the price had risen, and it ended up costing about $15 in today's money. How that relates to the price of borscht is a judgment call, perhaps; but looking at the volume today, you feel readers got their money's worth. Reading the volume feels like touring the skyscraper of which *The Judgment* was a blueprint: Sholem Aleichem putting his ideas into living, voluminous practice (the miscellany clocks in at 477 pages plus a 94-page supplement).

Criticism comprises a significant and central section of the massive volume, and the editor gets in his own (pseudonymous) innings. Writing as "S. Book-Gobbler," he savages what's now available "On the Literary Marketplace," with its poor imitators of recent highbrow successes, its wanting allegorists, saccharine poets, poor translators of Russian literature, and even its unfunny joke-book writers. "Book-Gobbler" concludes, as Sholem Aleichem had been saying for years, that a two-pronged solution was necessary. "We must shoot with two pistols," he wrote, both "give the people proper material to read, to instill taste and sentiment within them," and to get rid of the old "shmattes," terrible works like those reviewed. The criticism, and *The Judgment*, took the second approach; and in the miscellany's lead section, "Belles-Lettres," Sholem Aleichem did his part for the first. Leveraging his ready cash, wagering that the gossip that someone was paying advances for Yiddish would raise eyebrows and his profile, he reached out boldly, wangling contributions from the old masters.

"Who's paid you cash before now to write in jargon[?]," he wrote Yehuda Leib Gordon, and despite the esteemed Hebrew poet's bewilderment that his correspondent, a fluent Russian writer and "master of our literary language, Hebrew," could "give [himself] up to cultivating the jargon," he provided a poem for the *Folksbibliotek* nonetheless. Money talked. A few years back, Sholem Aleichem had written Abramovitch, who was now increasingly seen—in part thanks to the former's efforts—as Yiddish literature's highbrow founder, a fawning letter on the occasion of his literary jubilee. He had presented himself as an ardent admirer and potential disciple "stubbornly and diligently" following in his footsteps and dedicating his time "on the altar of our people's muse"; Abramovitch, besieged by petitions from Yiddish writers and busy trying to make his own living in Odessa, paid little if any attention. He had also failed to answer the first letter asking him to contribute to the *Folksbibliotek*, but then changed his mind—possibly the result of the new rate he was offered of twenty kopecks a line.

The money didn't make *everything* easier, though. Linetski came to

Kiev at Sholem Aleichem's expense to discuss a proposed contribution; he took one look at the young man's study and asked if there was any justice in the world when he, the great Yiddish writer, had to beg for travel money while his host lived so luxuriously. Seeing an opportunity, Linetski demanded high rates—which he received—and editorial control—which he did not. (The editor got his piece, though: a sort of sequel to the famed *Polish Lad*.) Sholem Aleichem's ruthless, perfectionist insistence on doing things his way, a youthful confidence assuredly aided by his sense of the golden rule—i.e., that he who has the gold makes the rules—loomed throughout the editorial process. He carved a massive work by Dinezon down to a few pages; not even Abramovitch escaped the knife. And his edits to a third writer led to one of the most famous literary arguments in Yiddish literature, one that would illustrate the divergent futures of Yiddish.

I. L. Peretz, whose *Folksbibliotek* contribution, the poem "Monish," would mark the beginning of one of the most celebrated careers in Yiddish literary history, was then so unfamiliar with Yiddish literature he apparently confused Mendele and Sholem Aleichem, Sholem Rabinovich with Sholem Abramovitch; he was, at the time, a Hebrew poet of middling fame and a lawyer who, due to his recent disbarment, was looking for sources of income. When a friend told him about the *Folksbibliotek* and its wealthy publisher, he saw an opportunity, but Sholem Aleichem felt the poem's ironic tone and German-inflected language would have puzzled and alienated much of the anthology's potential audience in other parts of the Pale—Sholem Aleichem's native Ukraine, for example. When he asked for revisions to make the poem more generally palatable, Peretz's discomfort was palpable. "Your wish and goal (as far as I understand it)," he wrote, "is to write for the sake of the audience that speaks jargon of jargon-land: I, for my part, write for my own pleasure, and if I take any reader into consideration, he is of the higher level of society." Peretz's artistic credo, even complete with elitist caveat, is hardly unfamiliar to modern readers of literary fiction. But it was deeply foreign to highbrow Yiddish literature of the time, with that Haskala-influenced polemical ethos (which meant reaching audiences), and particularly to Sholem Aleichem, who had his own interest in being broadly accepted and loved. He made the changes without Peretz's approval nonetheless, marking the beginning of a charged relationship between two men who would grow to become among Yiddish's most influential writers, each championing a different vision of what that literature should be.

But the real glimpse of Sholem Aleichem's own literary future wasn't in the editing job he did. It lay in the miscellany's supplement, where his own novel appeared: a work that marked the culmination of the first phase of his career and the harbinger of far greater things to come.

CHAPTER 8

In Which Our Hero, Writing About
an Artist, Becomes One

1888

What should the new Jewish literature look like? Sholem Aleichem knew his own literary contribution to the *Folksbibliotek* would have to live up to the lofty ideals he had propounded throughout the volume. Which would be a challenge.

Obviously, it couldn't be a "romance," at least as Shomer and others understood the term. Abramovitch had put it pungently when he counseled him not "to write romances. . . . In general, all Yiddish romances are worthless. They make me want to vomit." Abramovitch was preaching to the choir, as *The Judgment* had shown; but his further observation, that "if there are romances among our people, they are entirely different from those that exist among other peoples," and that a Jewish writer "must understand this and write differently," was easier said than done. He'd have to grapple with one of his most serious charges against Shomer: the latter's failure to "provide a realistic, authentic picture of Jewish life," not just life in general. And that wasn't a problem limited to Shomer. Even Haskala novels, with their starkly sketched, melodramatic characters, had failed in this respect. He agreed wholeheartedly, as he would write, that "the Jewish people has its own character, its own Jewish spirit, with its special customs and rules, which are quite different from those of other peoples. These very national traits of ours, which remain forever genuinely Jewish, must display themselves in a Yiddish novel if it is to be truly drawn from life." But how to put that on the page?

It wasn't as though he hadn't tried before. His *Sketches from Berdichev Street*, published over the previous two years, had presented a satiric but richly texured milieu of everyday Jewish life; its narrator, one Sholem Aleichem, confesses his love for the street—and, presumably, for writing about it—"with his whole being, without clevernesses, flattery, compliments," despite all its faults. But there was a problem with regular life: the regular people who lived it. As early as 1884, "Baron Pipernoter" blames Sholem Aleichem's readers for not living the kinds of lives that are worth writing about: "they don't live," he writes, "they dream, they sleep." As the decade continued, what may have started as Haskala-influenced elitism, after years of watching readers gobble down Shomer's works (while, perhaps, underappreciating his own), blossomed into full-fledged frustration. "These are my readers?" he complains in the last entry of *Sketches from Berdichev Street*. "For them I give up my strength, my brain, my time?"

Entirely unexpectedly, though—particularly for a man under thirty—whatever energy does emerge from the works comes from looking backward, not forward. In a series published the year he was working on the *Folksbibliotek*, *Sketches from Zhitomir Street*, the narrator, "Sholem Aleichem," visits his old stomping grounds and is shocked to find how much has changed. Over fifteen or twenty years, the street has become unrecognizable, and childhood friends are hard to find—not because they've moved, but because they've Russified their names. New opportunities to acculturate mean, for many, a firm break with their past; the narrator tries to renew old relationships, but they'll have none of it. The scene's climax occurs when the author turns this satiric gaze on himself. Identifying one "Solomon Naumovitch," a name Sholem Aleichem himself had used more frequently these last years, he shakes his head: whatever's become of "Sholem Reb Nochem's," the little student with a good head who was expected to become a small-town rabbi or a slaughterer? The ironic—and yet emotionally charged—juxtaposition of the imperfect but somehow still sympathetic past with the unsatisfying present; the notion that progress, and success, aren't all they're cracked up to be; the jolt that personal autobiography gives, the touch of autumnal memory—all of this seemed to be key.

The one thing lacking was a sense of fun. Sepia tones, even if necessary, would hardly have been sufficient for the playful, disruptive young writer who had populated his early fiction with dead letter writers and mischievous sock puppets. A studied insistence on rendering regular life realistically makes the work, in fact and by definition, quotidian, both for the author and, judging from their book-buying choices, the audience. What kind of extraordinary, yet plausible, Jewish work of literature could be created that would ironically juxtapose the past and the changing present, and, for good measure, include doses of playfulness, disruption, along with the occasional self-referential or autobiographical excursion?

As it turned out, this was, in essence, the recipe Sholem Aleichem would follow for the rest of his career: when the elements were blended properly, with a little seasoning here and there of monologue, an indelible character sketch, or a sly take on contemporary politics, he would find his way to the audience who he felt eluded or misunderstood him, making their sense of change, of uncertainty, his own—and very much vice versa. But for now, he was a young writer taking a leap, trying not to rely on the tricks that had afforded him a certain measure of success in favor of tools that would force him to rise to another level.

Abramovitch pushed him. A warm correspondence had developed out of their *Folksbibliotek* discussions; they exchanged portraits, and the normally saturnine Abramovitch gushed that he saw "a good, wise, honest man" there. Sholem Aleichem, for his part, placed Abramovitch's portrait on his desk and began asking himself, when he wrote, whether the result would please the watching writer. One change certainly did: by his own admission, Sholem Aleichem started to slow down. Abramovitch, characterizing his own writing style as like a woman's painful, laborious childbirth, compared Sholem Aleichem by contrast to a hen who runs clucking about the room and quickly lays an egg; the latter cheekily admitted that though Abramovitch insisted that writing is something "one must sweat over; one must work, polish every word," "we young guys, we never have time and rattle-off the whole work, standing up . . . not stopping at every thought, at every word, separately, to work and polish as you do."

The admission appeared in an open letter prefacing Sholem Aleichem's new *Folksbibliotek* novel—a letter dedicating the novel to Abramovitch. The letter famously provides Abramovitch a nickname of his own; it's addressed to his kind *zeyde*, his "grandfather," and Sholem Aleichem signs it as a devoted *eynikl*, a grandchild. At the time, he was twenty-nine, and Abramovitch fifty-eight—but by dropping a generation from the mix, Sholem Aleichem pulls off the hat trick of canonizing himself through a direct, familial link with the recognized paterfamilias of Yiddish literature, defusing any potential father-son tensions, and presenting a young, enthusiastic, energetic image that renders him easily forgivable for any excited trespasses against others or literature. But it was an image belying the autocratic editor, the seasoned feuilletonist, and, most important, the new craftsman: Sholem Aleichem, despite his statements, had been sweating over and polishing *Stempenyu*, telling friends that he was rewriting for the first time, that this was "my *first* novel . . . an *artistic work*, on which the entire future fate of my literary activity depends."

The rewrites helped: if *Stempenyu* isn't a cornerstone of his literary reputation, as the young Sholem Aleichem hoped it would be, it's a major step toward those works' composition. It revolves around two major figures: the title character, a prodigiously talented, ne'er-do-well violinist, a married Jewish wedding musician who refuses to be tied down; and Rokhele, who struggles with her attraction to Stempenyu and the difficulties in her own marriage. As the novel progresses, Stempenyu attempts to break free of his wife's attempts to domesticate him, ultimately unsuccessfully; and Rokhele, whose barely developed romantic sentiments toward her husband are stunted by her in-laws' constant, passive-aggressive hovering, manages to put Stempenyu behind her, communicate with her spouse, and begin what promises to be a happy marriage.

Ensuring we know he's practicing what he's preached, Sholem Aleichem throws in a dig at Shomer to praise himself by contrast. "Readers who are used to 'highly interesting' modern romances," he writes, "have suffered enough from this novel, which has no tearful scenes, no assignation. No one has shot himself, no one has poisoned himself, we have met no counts or marquis. We keep seeing only ordinary people, musicians and everyday Jewish women." But romantic ordinariness, in the novel, takes specific cultural form, fulfilling the author's aspiration to treat romance *Jewishly*. In an essay in 1889, a year after *Stempenyu* appeared, Sholem Aleichem wrote that "a Jewish young woman is not the same as any other young woman . . . [she] knows she must first love God, then her parents, then her husband and children . . . a Jewish heroine . . . contains her desires, forgets her caprices, abandons her passions for someone else." That's Rokhele in a nutshell. Her attitude toward Stempenyu quickly progresses from disgust to obsession (he haunts her dreams), but their climactic rendezvous—on Monastery Street, no less; talk about the conflating of eroticism and non-Jewishness!—dissolves in guilty renunciation of her desires, and of desire. Her ambivalent "victory" over her passion, though, seems to be rewarded by a true one: a reconciliation with her husband that leads to a child. The ostensibly virile Stempenyu, it should be noted, bursting with musical and romantic energy, is childless.

Anticipating readers' yawns, Sholem Aleichem takes the offense by preemptively imagining their reaction: "'A dull story!' says the reader, apparently quite dissatisfied, for he's been raised on those modern romances," he writes before the novel's epilogue. But *Stempenyu* isn't dull; it pulses with energy. Not because of Sholem Aleichem's effort to play out a Jewish romance, though. (Abramovitch's criticism was on target: despite warm congratulations on the transformation in his writing, he opined that "novel writing is not for you . . . Your descriptions of life are a pleasure to read[, but] when you play out a love plot nothing comes of it.") *Stempenyu* works not because Sholem Aleichem is right that ordinariness is exciting. It's because of the work's two extraordinary elements: a decidedly non-quotidian artist-hero whose main enemy is bourgeois ordinariness, and a virtuosic display of musician's argot that leaps off the pages of the novel, plausible and absorbing simultaneously. Insisting "that *Stempenyu* is by nature a *Jewish* romance, and so it can't tolerate any Germanisms or Slavicisms—the essence is only *Yiddish*," Sholem Aleichem forges deep links in the novel—and thus in the emerging history of Yiddish literature—between Yiddish language and Jewish culture. (Remember that in Yiddish, the word *Yiddish* means both "Yiddish" and "Jewish," an often fruitful blurriness generally lost, by necessity, in translation.)

Sholem Aleichem came by that musical slang honestly: he had always been interested in music, if without extensive training, deeply envying those with the talent to play the violin. (He himself had limited technique; as an adult, he would sometimes play the piano for his family, generally playing by ear, something melancholy.) His father's inn seems to have been a regular stopping place for visiting cantors, choristers, and musicians, probably because it was cheaper than the competition—and his father didn't always insist on their paying for meals. Local klezmer musicians lived near the *kheyder*, and the young Sholem could hear the music wafting from their houses on his way to school or even, in the case of one Yisroel Benditsky, playing at family weddings. And as a wandering tutor, Sholem claimed to have met "a kind of Stempenyu" who gave him violin lessons: a physically prepossessing, uneducated, enormously talented musician and composer named Abraham the Klezmer, a womanizer with a "poetic nature" (though, unlike Stempenyu, with a happy and good-natured wife).

Sholem Aleichem would claim two sources for Stempenyu's name: it was a love-potion seller's name in Abramovitch's work, and it was well known as that of a remarkable Berdichev fiddler. Or so, he proudly claimed, he had confirmed on a recent information-gathering trip to Berdichev, where he—imagine!—discovered his novelistic efforts accorded in almost every detail with the information he had gleaned from Berdichev's elders and klezmer musicians. How much Sholem Aleichem's tongue was in his cheek is impossible to determine, but the novel takes this imagined combination of love spirit and folk legend—a Jewish type, far enough off society's radar to express new and daring emotions, but near enough to remain a plausible character—and whittles him down to size. The means: his shrewd businesswoman of a wife, who holds him to his marriage contract and then, as a moneylender, enforces plenty of others. Cold cash and careful husbandry end up being Stempenyu's enemy, the artist's snare, as much as domesticity, if not more.

This ends up being the autobiographical story behind the story for Sholem Aleichem: the uneasy, anxious energy hidden in commerce that lurks under the love affair with music and art. And he wasn't wrong to be anxious. Yes, he had created a community of like-minded writers and thinkers supporting his vision of the Yiddish literary future, Abramovitch first among them, and he could boast to his brother that his home in Kiev had become "a gathering place for maskilim and intellectuals . . . known to every arrival in the city." But he had made enemies in the process. Linetski, still smarting from his treatment by Sholem Aleichem—which he believed stemmed from the latter's allegiance to Abramovitch—and asserting that *he* was the rightful "grandfather" of Yiddish literature, helped to found an Odessa-based group sometimes called the *Sitra akhra*, or "Darkside." These "Odessa bandits that call themselves litterateurs," in Sholem Aleichem's phrase, published a miscellany the following year, the *Little Waker*, sharply criticizing Sholem Aleichem and his literary *zeyde*.

Even worse, though, was the painful break with his friend, fellow Ukrainian Jew and *Folksblat* contributor, and now rival publisher Mordkhe Spektor. Recognizing that they were kindred spirits from their *Folksblat* contributions, the two had conducted a warm correspondence about the "new" Yiddish literature. Spektor had even visited the young married couple in Belaya Tserkov, where they had addressed each other by their various literary pseudonyms and spent hours talking, as Sholem Aleichem would later write, of "youthful projects, elevated but foolish ideas, pure and godly sentiments, serious and true as God himself." Spektor would almost become a member of the family—a rarity for Sholem Aleichem, who preferred not to mix writerly friends and family friends. And, in an intriguing and playful turn of phrase, he even referred regularly to Spektor as his "wife" in correspondence.

Spektor was in dire financial straits in 1888: he had lost his editorial job at the *Folksblat*, and had sunk thousands of rubles into unsuccessful efforts to publish another Yiddish newspaper. He had pinned his hopes on his own literary anthology, *The House-Friend*, whose first volume featured a contribution by Sholem Aleichem. And then he heard, like everyone else, the rumors about how "the Kiev banker," as Sholem Aleichem was sometimes then called, was showering Abramovitch with gold, paying Frishman a ruble a line for poems, and throwing massive banquets for his contributors—a dear friend turning competitor in a limited market. The details may have been false, but Spektor's complaints echoed within the small Yiddish literary community nonetheless—including (or so Sholem Aleichem believed) in the pages of the *Folksblat*. Sholem Aleichem, who never boasted the thickest skin, lashed out: reacting to Spektor's claim that he'd paid a thousand rubles for a poem, he offered to give him the finger a thousand times, and dismissed his former "wife" in a letter to a friend as a "nothing . . . not worth your pen and ink." There would be a reconciliation, but the sensitivity, the aloofness, the bridling hostility, were symptomatic of another side of Sholem Aleichem's personality, one less on public display.

Shomer left Eastern Europe for America a year after *The Judgment* and the *Folksbibliotek* appeared, and Sholem Aleichem always claimed credit, perhaps because Shomer, in his subsequent, still-prolific writing, railed constantly against him and his *Judgment*. (Shomer died around the time that Sholem Aleichem's plans to take his first trip to America became public, and the latter, in a not atypical barb, would joke that he'd now forced Shomer to peddle his product in the Other World.) But it wasn't a total victory for Sholem Aleichem. Not on the critical front: besides Abramovitch's concerns, the rising critic David Frishman tweaked Sholem Aleichem for sounding—of all things—too much like the antiquated, if talented, Abramovitch. (He wrote about *Stempenyu* "that if it were a lady, I would say she seemed a bit on the elderly side.") And Shomer himself would later level a particularly intriguing if entirely unsubstantiated charge: that Sholem Aleichem's novels of the period were significantly edited by "real" talents like Abramovitch and Ravnitski, with the young writer paying lavishly for the privilege. The charge seems more reflective of an easy caricature—a wealthy, spoiled author, willing to buy his way into respectability—that was hardly warranted by the facts; but it was, as we'll see, a psychological gambit that struck close to home, in outline if not in details.

And as for Sholem Aleichem's hopes for the *Folksbibliotek* itself? Despite his prediction in early 1889 that the whole run would sell out over the next few months—and his certain pleasure in a former opponent of Yiddish's inquiry about submitting to the *Folksbibliotek*'s second volume—one of the miscellany's own features tells the tale. In the "Register of All of the Yiddish Books Published in TRMH (1888–1889)," compiled by Sholem Aleichem under the delightful pseudonym "Solomon Book-Eater," the editor himself has a very respectable three of the seventy-eight works listed, numbers 52–54 on the list (*Sender Blank*, *The Judgment*, and *A Bouquet of Flowers*, which we'll get to in a bit). The ironies of alphabetical order put Shomer right next to him—with the next twenty-four works, going right through to number 78! If that wasn't smarting enough, the sales figures would have done it: the *Folksbibliotek* would go on to sell 3,200 copies that year, a seemingly respectable tally until it's compared to the 96,000 that Shomer's works sold.

Sholem Aleichem can be generally credited with winning in the battle of intellectual opinion. Shomer's name is forgotten to all but recondite specialists; his works are even more obscure. But Shomer's brand of potboiler would flourish in the Yiddish newspapers, and the battle for the soul of Yiddish was still, the *Folksbibliotek* notwithstanding, very much to be decided.

CHAPTER 9

In Which Our Hero Loves His People,
Mourns His Father, and Dreams of Zion

1888–1890

Sholem Aleichem was sick: afflicted with, he wrote, "a damned illness." Its name? It "can be called, it shouldn't happen to you, 'feuilletonmania.'" How else to explain that he kept publishing in the *Folksblat* as it continued to inveigh against the author and his new *Folksbibliotek*? But he needed to write, and, outside of the occasional miscellany, Levi's paper was the only game in town. That said, something else was driving him, too. "I feel a kind of bond exists between me and the people, that is, between all the people who read *jargon*," he wrote. "It seems to me like I need them and they need me. Perhaps this is just the power of imagination, a fantasy, and enough—but there it is." Fantasy then, perhaps; but the later life of Sholem Aleichem—the tremendous connection he would make with Jews of all sorts and stripes—would turn it into prophecy.

The sobering reality at the time, though, was that the only game in town was looking increasingly tenuous. Sholem Aleichem claimed that the trouble with the *Folksblat* started when he turned Levi down for a thousand-ruble loan; things could only have gotten worse when, in response to Levi's request for more material, Sholem Aleichem had an artist draw a picture of a fig (the Russian equivalent of an extended middle finger), placed it in the middle of a large sheaf of paper, and sent the entire thing, labeled "manuscript," to Levi via registered mail. The former illustrated the financial constraints that would cause the paper to close in 1889; the latter might explain why, when Sholem Aleichem explored buying the *Folksblat* himself and recasting it as a more upscale, literary production, the publisher apparently chose to shut it down instead. Faced with his own graphomania, his sense, fantastic or no, of his own literary indispensability, and the rapid drying up of other options, he decided to publish another volume of the *Folksbibliotek* despite its cost in "blood, time, and health."

His editorial attentions were as exact and punctilious as ever: and he wrote a friend that his own literary contribution to the volume, the novel *Yosele Solovey*, "cost me a half year of work and, it seemed, several years of life" between composition and revisions. All this meant spending precious funds and even more precious time away from his business: he famously claimed that writing *Yosele Solovey* cost him 30,000 rubles, apparently meaning that, entranced in literary work, he failed to provide appropriate oversight for the brokers investing his money. But if his schedule—writing from early in the morning until about noon at a standing desk built specially for him, then breakfasting, dressing, and going to the market, to return later in the day for revisions and rewrites—prevented full attention to business, he also felt it weakened his novelistic efforts. He put it sedately in the novel's dedication, apologizing for insufficient revision: "There is no time. One is, alas, no more than a frail human being, and only half a writer at that, or more accurately, half a businessman, and half a writer, as is usually the case among Jews." Writing privately, wry frustration boiled over into anger: "I am pregnant with so many thoughts, so much imagery, that I must be made of iron that I do not come apart at the seams, and ah me, I have to run in search of a ruble! The market be damned! The ruble be damned! That a Jewish writer should not be able to live on his writing alone, but have to run in search of a ruble!"

Despite his divided attentions—or perhaps because of them—the novel is far more similar to *Stempenyu* than to almost any of his earlier works. Like Stempenyu, Yosele Solovey—literally "Nightingale"—is an artist-hero of mythic dimension with folk antecedents: here, a vocal prodigy who grows up to become a remarkable cantor. Yosele, whose enraptured audiences believe he must have some sort of instrument or songbird hidden in his throat, is very loosely inspired by the true story of the cantorial prodigy Joel David Loewenstein-Straschunsky, better known as the Vilner Balabeysl, the "Little Master" of Vilna—who, according to legend, ran off with a Polish singer and lived to regret it, losing his voice and his sanity, wandering from shtetl to shtetl before dying young, alone, in an asylum. (When a friend to whom Sholem Aleichem had sent a draft complained the singing descriptions were too over the top, Sholem Aleichem simply replied that he'd clearly never heard the stories about the Vilner Balabeysl.)

Yosele's genuine romance with Esther—not one, the narrator takes great pains to point out, based on "romantic novels"—dissipates in his fame, fortune, and bad company: he marries the rich and decadent Perele and becomes a songbird kept in a gilded cage. As in *Stempenyu*, the culminating scene shows virtuous adherence to convention prevailing over romantic emotion: Yosele returns home too late, and when he implores Esther to go off with him, she refuses, and he goes mad. But despite the similarities, Sholem Aleichem was right to be convinced that the novel was "as far from *Stempenyu* as *Stempenyu* was from my previous works"— but not, as he suggested, because of its variety of admirably sketched characters or its discovery of "the poetry that lies within us, in Yosele's soul." It's because he created an incomparable advantage for himself in designing Yosele's story over Stempenyu's: he began the novel with Yosele's childhood, allowing him to play to what would become one of his greatest, and most acknowledged, strengths.

Several years prior, his story "The Penknife" had appeared in the *Folksblat*, about a young boy who wants his own knife so badly he steals one— and then suffers the consequences of his conscience. A child's consuming guilt over a theft, petty or otherwise, has been a staple of Western literature since Augustine confessed to stealing pears almost two millennia ago; and Sholem Aleichem, who would become a great chronicler of the fervid emotions of childhood, tracks the escalating course of guilt as the offending penknife is discarded, removing the possibilities both of capture and of restitution, the resulting psychic conflict leading to the child's fever and delirium. Though the fever breaks, the story ends in a fashion paradoxically both powerful and inconclusive: he remains uncaught, but guilty. Critics have read the story in manifold ways; Sholem Aleichem, in his memoirs, provided his own interpretation by recalling an incident from his teenage years—impossible to know if true or false—that clearly is meant to serve as a "model" for the story. Regardless of interpretation or origin, "The Penknife" was arguably Sholem Aleichem's first and only major pre-*Stempenyu* literary and critical success: the Russian-Jewish critic Simon Dubnow, soon to become a friend, reviewed the work favorably, giving the young writer needed encouragement and inspiration—and planting the hint that Sholem Aleichem had a particular skill when it came to telling stories of children (different, we should note, from children's stories).

A good part of *Yosele Solovey*'s energy and delight comes from Yosele's childish dreams of cantorial success, of traveling the world and singing for an audience, of sheer liberation: he's off to join the circus. This lets Sholem Aleichem provide a rogue's gallery of colorful mountebanks who populate the synagogue fairway (including the fantastically named rival cantors Mitzi and Pitzi), and Yosele's moves from one cantor or manager to another, and from the rural backwaters to the city, allow for the unspooling of a colorful Eastern European panorama. But the novel keeps returning to Yosele's imagination, the vivid imagination that will tragically loom so large in his final descent into madness, once he realizes what he has lost, since for Sholem Aleichem loss is the feature that looms largest, for good and for ill, in both childhood and artistry.

And speaking of loss: Near the end of the novel's first section, Yosele, in love with Esther and looking forward to making his fortune, looks tenderly back at his hometown as he's about to leave: "Everything took on a festive appearance. The people, the streets, and the houses appeared to him bright and joyous. Mazepevka, with its dark, muddy alleyways, its squalid, lopsided hovels, its gloomy, burdened inhabitants, appeared in his eyes like a Garden of Eden, where everything blossoms and shines, thrives and rejoices." The passage, written as the impressionists were creating their masterworks, doesn't just suggest the way a creative artist like Yosele—or his creator—renders reality subjectively, according to his own moods. It's an early look at the way that people leaving their small Eastern European towns on their way to the big city gaze nostalgically back at their *shtetlekh*—even if the thought of crossing the Atlantic, or heading to Palestine, hasn't entered their minds. Sholem Aleichem's first steps as the writer most responsible, directly and indirectly, for the creation of Eastern European nostalgia are taken in the service of what scholars call internal migration, not emigration; and they echo the journeys Sholem Aleichem had made, though they would come, in time, to symbolize those that lay ahead.

B ut a second loss had been animating Sholem Aleichem's life and work recently, one much closer to home: his father's death, from esophageal cancer, in January of 1888. A Hebrew note on a page torn from a calendar reads: "His memory will not pass from my heart until the last day. These are the words of his young son, who is writing this with a sorrowful soul and a broken heart." By the time of his death, Nochem Rabinovich seems to have approved of his son's course: insisting his son reconsider his refusal to submit his picture to the *Folksblat*, he wrote that "you are the head of all writers of our time . . . it seems right and proper that all the readers should know and recognize who it is that lights the darkness of their way, and blows a spirit of life into the jargon literature." But Nochem clearly viewed him as head not only of the fellowship of Jewish writers, but of the family. His ethical will—which Sholem would read every year, much as he would direct his descendants to do with the one he'd write himself—was directed only to Sholem, his younger son, because "God has given you wisdom and understanding a measure above all of your brothers."

The will encouraged him to pursue his own Jewish path and asks him to support his father's orphaned family, despite his stepmother's "crimes" against Sholem and his siblings.

But it's impossible, from this distance, to know precisely what emotions, what unresolved guilts or lack of them, remained. The evidence is necessarily inconclusive: the portrait of a sickening father betrayed by his briefly wayward child in "The Penknife," written before Nochem's death, or of the father abandoned by his artist son in *Yosele Solovey*, written immediately after it, might be projection—or simply the exercise of artistic imagination. His increasing literary activity in his father's beloved Hebrew after a sustained quieter period may be the shouldering of perceived filial duty—or simply a matter of coincidental timing, given changing publication opportunities. Or, as we'll see, a sign of his increasing interest in another aspect of Eastern European Jewish life. What *is* clear is that Sholem would serve as the custodian of his father's memory, chiding a brother for not visiting Nochem's grave enough, practically dictating the terms of his next visit to the cemetery, brusquely offering to pay his travel expenses, even reminding him not to forget his prayer shawl and phylacteries.

One literary project, though, was a clear result of Nochem's passing: a small, privately printed and circulated collection of prose poems titled *A Bouquet of Flowers*. In an article in the *Folksbibliotek*, Sholem Aleichem had suggested—perhaps mindful of his own poetic efforts—that poetry, particularly lyric poetry, was "a sort of snare, heaven forfend, a kind of grave which is covered with flowers and golden tinsel on top to fool the weak poet," in which the unwary writer will be captured, struggling mightily but producing nothing but half-baked versification. Perhaps that's why he chose to produce prose poems, "poetry without rhyme . . . in the style of Turgenev and Guy de Maupaussant, an original thing which *jargon* has neither heard nor seen." It didn't work: his assessment to his daughter, a decade later, that "I am no master of writing poetry; I love prose, simple, good, honest, prose," seems more on target.

But there might have been another reason he combined prose and

Sholem Aleichem's future wife, Olga, describing her first glimpse of her young tutor in 1877, wrote: "He entered with my father and brother, looking very young, his blond hair long and wavy, one lock occasionally drooping over his forehead. His skin was very fair; his head large, his neck short and fairly thick. He wasn't exactly handsome, but he was different from any young man I had seen before." (*From the archives of the YIVO Institute for Jewish Research, New York*)

Sholem Aleichem with his father, Nochem Rabinovich, in 1885. The father would revere the son for his intellectual and creative accomplishments, even if he might have preferred they take place primarily in Hebrew. The son, in turn, would serve as the family custodian of his father's memory. (*YIVO Institute*)

Sholem Aleichem and Olga in 1883, at the time of their wedding. Though their married life would have its share of tribulations, theirs would be a lifelong romance. (*YIVO Institute*)

With son Misha in 1893. (*YIVO Institute*)

In Kiev, in 1889, with Olga and their daughters (left to right) Ernestina, Liali and Emma. Sholem Aleichem dearly loved his "republic," as he called his family, and strove to have them around him as much as possible. (*YIVO Institute*)

Sholem Aleichem and Olga lived in this house in Belaya Tserkov as newlyweds, between 1884 and 1887, as the writer adjusted to becoming a businessman and a man of wealth.

The St. Sophia Cathedral in Kiev. The "city of churches" welcomed Jews only under very specific circumstances. Sholem Aleichem lived there illegally. (*Library of Congress, Prints & Photographs Division*)

A few of Sholem Aleichem's literary idols. *Clockwise, from top left:* From Nikolai Gogol, he learned the power of rendering ordinary speech on the page; Ivan Turgenev taught him about portraying generations in conflict; Anton Chekhov shared his discomfort with neat plots and simple endings; and Charles Dickens crafted vast panoramas and shared his work from the reader's podium. (*Library of Congress, Prints & Photographs Division*)

With a few of his Yiddish contemporaries. (Seated from left to right) S. Y. Abramovitch, also known as Mendele the Book Peddler, was Sholem Aleichem's self-proclaimed "grandfather" and one of the first to show him that Yiddish could be a vehicle for expressing his literary ambitions. The noted Hebrew poet Hayyim Nachman Bialik would become a beloved friend. Fellow writer and Zionist Mark Rabinovich published under the name Ben-Ami. (*YIVO Institute*)

Mordkhe Spektor, an occasional cherished friend and occasional literary competitor, published Sholem Aleichem's first Tevye story in 1895. (*YIVO Institute*)

I. L. Peretz (center), whose first foray into Yiddish appeared in Sholem Aleichem's *Folksbibliotek*, became one of the few writers in Yiddish literature whose reputation would rival his. Yankev Dinezon (right), a friend and contributor to the *Folksbibliotek*, would become Peretz's closest colleague and confidante. (*YIVO Institute*)

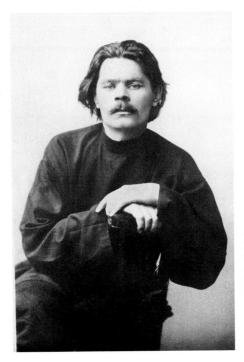

Maxim Gorky's fiery progressivism and uncompromising prose inspired a generation of Russians. (*Library of Congress, Prints & Photographs Division*)

Sholem Aleichem was among those so affected; he placed the writer's portrait in his office and adopted his style of dress, particularly the "Gorky shirt." (*YIVO Institute*)

The republic expands: The family in 1910. (Seated left to right) Numa, Emma, Sholem Aleichem, granddaughter Tamara (on his lap), and Misha. (Standing left to right) I. D. Berkowitz, Ernestina, Olga, Liali, Michael Kaufman, and Maroussia. (*YIVO Institute*)

I. D. Berkowitz, Ernestina's husband, was a Hebrew and Yiddish writer who would become an essential aid to his father-in-law's literary enterprise. (*YIVO Institute*)

The author in one of his favorite spots to convalesce, though the climate was actually hindering his recovery: Nervi, on the Italian Riviera, in 1911. In this classic pose, he holds one of the little notebooks in which he did most of his writing. (*YIVO Institute*)

poetry in this novel way, suggested by, intriguingly enough, a previous poetic effort. Published a year before his father's death, "An Open Response" bridles at his previous poetic efforts, which he dismisses as doggerel. Swearing off poetry (in rhymed stanzas, it should be said), Sholem Aleichem promised faithfully to involve himself in prose, where he would write "seriously, without joking about." The only problem is that the poetic (and comic) muse comes to him whether he will or not: and so he recognizes, invoking a doctrine many of his critics would ascribe to him over the next century, the inevitable mixture of laughter and tears.

Years later, after the notorious bloody pogrom in Kishinev, Sholem Aleichem would come under attack for publishing light and comic stories at such a serious time; he responded by pleading a particular constitution that "when it comes to writing, it may be that no matter how tragic the subject, the scenes I see, through tears, make me laugh . . . What shall I do, when laughing is a kind of illness for me, God save us, from childhood on?" Still, there's little sign of any laughter in *Flowers*: treating thematically apropos subjects like the selfishness of the rich, the wretchedness of poverty, the dark ironies of misfortune, the ravages of age, false friendship, and death's omnipresence, it delivers its observations in a dolorous tone that renders the poems as difficult to read as they may have been therapeutic to write.

One instructive exception, though, is a brief sketch called "The Western Wall"; in it, a *kheyder* rebbe eagerly asks a Jew returned from the land of Israel if he had seen that remnant of the Temple, and bursts into tears upon receiving a positive answer. Though Sholem Aleichem's ironic sensibility peeks through—the *kheyder* students have taken advantage of their teacher's emotional distraction to sneak out and go ice skating—the rebbe's powerful reaction genuinely seems to echo Sholem Aleichem's new engagement with an old enthusiasm: Palestine. Since "The Intercepted Letters," Sholem Aleichem had been speaking positively about what couldn't yet, strictly speaking, be called Zionism, but his interest through the middle years of the decade—as the Hibbat Zion movement sought to found communities within Israel—waxed and waned, his natural positive inclinations often conflicting with his psychological and aesthetic assumptions.

When his friend Ravnitski asked him, for example, to contribute a novel with Zionist tendencies to an 1886 anthology, he responded: "Writing to order is no damn good! I can't tell someone to believe when I have little faith myself . . . I want your idea to be adopted no less than you do. But what shall I do when I know my people Israel so well that I can't believe they will take it to heart? . . . I, loving my people with *warm* heart and *cold* reason . . . tell the truth." Sholem Aleichem's skepticism of the possibilities of unified Jewish action extended to this new movement, as it did to everything else; but his aesthetic—his understanding of his own personality and writerly capabilities—played a major role, too. He asserted it was impossible to believe he could simply satirize one side of the debate, that his satirical consciousness would work in alignment with a particular ideology. Instead, that constitution of his sees the foolish side of everything; containing multitudes, he stood beyond—and above—such partisanship. "I am no assimilator and I am no Palestineist," he wrote in a later letter; "I am a Jew and love Jews, as I am a person and love people." (This a week after he'd asked: "Is it my fault that in every thing and in every person I always see the worst side of things?")

But the late 1880s saw a change in his perspective. Maybe his greater literary activism and critical engagement allowed him to see himself involved in other kinds of activism. Maybe the increasing activity and tangible successes of the Hibbat Zion movement were inspirational. Or possibly his recollections of reading Mapu in his father's house struck especially strong in the wake of the latter's death. One definite element, though, was the "great language debate" of 1889—probably because it grew, in no small part, from his own actions in publishing the *Folksbibliotek*. Unsurprisingly, the *Folksbibliotek*'s positions on Yiddish—to say nothing of its own existence as an avowedly highbrow Yiddish document—had thrown new fuel on the long-standing debate between Hebrew and Yiddish in the Eastern European Jewish literary community, particularly in the Hebrew press.

Sholem Aleichem's credentials as a lover of Yiddish were, of course, unassailable. ("Jargon is my love, my second passion, my idée fixe," he wrote Ravnitski; "I hear two Jews, two women speaking jargon—I'm there.") But certain Hebraists, writing in *Hamelitz* and *Hatzefira*, assailed him for precisely that reason, castigating the young businessman for using his wealth to "lure away" Hebrew writers to the problematic path of Yiddish. One writer, A. L. Levinski, offered a subtler critique. Arguing he had nothing against Yiddish—opining, in fact, that after hundreds of years of service to the Jewish people, it "has also become sanctified and become a 'Hebrew language'"—he focused his concern on how Sholem Aleichem's activity limited Hebrew's own capacity to generate figures like the young publisher himself, linguistic and cultural activists. It was a zero-sum game, in short, and the evident implication was of damage to the Hebrew, and thus the Zionist, cause (the *Folksbibliotek*'s positive articles on the subject of Zionism notwithstanding). Sholem Aleichem's response in *Hamelitz*—in Hebrew, naturally—twitted Levinski (who would later become a close friend) and others for calling the *Folksbibliotek* writers Hebrew writers, given their lack of recent Hebrew activity; far more important, though, he suggested that the revival of Yiddish was a national obligation aside from its instrumental worth as a popular language. His attachment to Hebrew was profound, but the two languages, he felt, were "complementary and not antagonistic."

His sense of national obligation seems to have applied to matters other than Yiddish. Seemingly caught up in the movement's increasing momentum, Sholem Aleichem sent 25 rubles in 1888 to Leon Pinsker, the founder of Hibbat Zion, and asked to be enrolled as an official member; by the next year's end, he was leading the organization's Kiev branch, conducting its correspondence, organizing its funds, and raising money to support the new community of Gedera. The year after that, he attended the movement's first meeting in its new government-sanctioned form in Odessa as a Kiev delegate, along with leading figures in the movement like Pinsker, Ahad Ha'am, and Moshe Leib Lilienblum. His primary work of fiction for that year, the 1890 novella "Zelig Mechanic" (or "Zelig the Tailor"), endearingly reflected his current preoccupation.

Zelig, a humble tailor from the small town of Mazapevke, becomes enraptured with the idea of going to the land of Israel. Zelig, a man who thinks he knows more than he does and who doesn't always get straight to the point, is hazy about the new political stirrings and the precise details of emigration procedures. But, fired by dreams of Holy Land, of messiah, and of "cabbages, garlic, cucumbers, our own fig tree. Camels. And mules!" he heads to the big city to register for emigration tickets, despite the fact that his somewhat more sensible wife doesn't quite understand his enthusiasms. Arriving, he finds no quick solutions, no easy journeys—just a man collecting money to support the fledgling Palestine communities, with no payoff but the satisfaction of doing "a bit of a mitzvah." Zelig donates and happily returns home; when a fellow traveler assumes he has "struck lucky in Yehupetz," Zelig doesn't contradict him.

A slight and overly didactic story—unsurprising, given its clear instrumental purpose of encouraging financial support for Hibbat Zion. But "Zelig Mechanic" is far more important to Sholem Aleichem's story than as a simple illustration of his Zionist leanings. It's Zelig, not Stempenyu or even Yosele, who's the prototype for an archetypal Sholem Aleichem character: a quick enthusiast, a man of the people with dreams above his station, a filter for the tenor of the times (with a more grounded wife to serve as a foil). Like most Eastern European Jews—like most of us— Zelig learns, thinks, and feels imprecisely, knowing great things are afoot but failing to focus properly on the details. This isn't completely his fault: communal and conventional wisdom tends to act like a game of telephone in Sholem Aleichem's work, spreading misinformation or generating tempests in teapots as a matter of course. But it's in acting on those thoughts, and getting tripped up on the details, that reality becomes the stuff of magnificent comedy.

The *Folksbibliotek*'s second volume appeared in the first half of 1890. At the end of the summer, Sholem Aleichem and his wife visited Odessa once more, full of plans for the third; they stayed at the nicest hotel in town and threw a banquet for Abramovitch. People talked about that banquet for years. One story that made the rounds was that after the banquet Sholem Aleichem took the assembled guests to the city's richest tobacconist and treated them all to ten-ruble cigars. A more likely story was that the guests stayed out all night discussing Yiddish literature; and when the dawn broke, Moshe Leib Lilienblum, a member of the local burial society, groaned, "Oy, vey, it's already broad daylight! Time to go bury Jews!"

If Sholem Aleichem had known what was coming next, he might, for a moment, have envied Lilienblum's charges.

CHAPTER 10

In Which Our Hero Loses His Fortune and Gains His First Great Character

1890–1894

In June of 1890, Sholem Aleichem was still the generous Kiev donor, sending money to support a Jewish writer's widow and orphans; three months later, he was in Paris hiding out from his creditors, his inheritance and profits wiped out.

What happened? True, the fall of 1890 was a period of financial crisis; the Baring panic had spread from Britain to Russia and played a large part in Kiev's stock market crash in October. Sholem Aleichem's problems had predated the crash, though. By the beginning of that month he'd written Simon Dubnow that his "shattered friend, who has progressed so stormily through a stormy life, has stumbled and is lost . . . lost through the world of gold and paper . . . I beg you to remember what we spoke about in Boyarke. Already then matters had stood badly. The one step I made, to extricate myself from my undefined and uncertain position, had hastened the end. Two–three greater failures, two–three horrible busts—and I'm down in flames. Seized by a fire of debts and obligations . . ." Sholem Aleichem summered in Boyarke, so the letter means he was already in precarious financial shape then; and another letter reveals that he'd given a friend a thousand rubles to hold for him in case he went bust—apparently seeing the writing on the wall.

Probably the explanation is exactly what Sholem Aleichem claims it is, the same malady he'd diagnosed in "The Counting-House" and *Sketches from Berdichev Street*: overconfidence, insufficient hedging against risk, excessive borrowing, and false and ignorant friends who occasionally lured the tyro businessman into disastrous deals. Written at the height of his financial success, the former begins with Reuven Shnel's inheriting a fortune, and chronicles his eventual ruin thanks in no small part to his ignorant speculations and investments; in the latter, Meyerbeer spends profligately and ignorantly, not even knowing his own bank balance, and, in overextending himself, "what God has given, God takes away." Literary prescience wasn't enough to achieve personal wisdom, though; or, if it was, it wasn't enough to save him. A not unfamiliar story, to those writing—and reading—at the beginning of the second decade of the twenty-first century.

The collapse dislocated Sholem Aleichem in every sense. Geographically, first of all: moving his family from Kiev to Odessa, where his friends Ravnitski and Dubnow could watch out for them, he fled the country to escape his creditors, staying in Czernowitz and Vienna as well as Paris. (He was briefly jailed in Czernowitz, but for reasons totally unrelated to his debt; he'd signed a hotel register with the single name "Solomon" at the moment the local gendarmerie were looking for an identically named con man.) With his mother-in-law's financial help, though, he managed to settle his debts and return to his family in Odessa in the spring of 1891, staying there until the fall of 1893. But it had deep psychological impact, too. The few surviving letters from the period amply show his disbelief, his utter inability to get his footing. "Your friend Sholem Aleichem still lives," he wrote Ravnitski, "he still lives, though his life is no life, and if it weren't for my love of my one and only heart's beloved in the world, that is my wife, and my daughters and my only son—if it weren't for that, I would have long since made an end to my life, because my life has become repulsive to me!"

And Sholem Aleichem's life, of course, was inextricably connected to his literary efforts. For the moment, publishing was out: plans for the

Folksbibliotek's third volume were shelved. (It would never see the light of day.) Sholem Aleichem had always been worried about his reputation, fearing the literary community saw him as a bankroller, not a litterateur. "What will the 'world' say? How will my friends take it, the sincere and insincere ones?" he wrote anxiously. Perhaps this was an opportunity to establish his reputation as a Yiddish writer without the specter of his wealth intervening; unfortunately, the prospects for making a living writing Yiddish literature, particularly his kind of elevated Yiddish literature, weren't very good. The only forum that had paid well had been his own *Folksbibliotek*, and the *Folksblat*'s 1890 closing had left no regular Yiddish periodicals publishing in this period.

So, for the first post-bankruptcy years, the road back to Yiddish writing for Sholem Aleichem lay squarely through restoration of his family fortunes. In the true gambler's (or, perhaps more charitably, speculator's) spirit, he tried to make back his losses through further investment on the Odessa exchange: his niece Natasha Mazar begged him to take her nest egg to invest, and eventually his mother-in-law followed suit. Rokhl Yampolsky had been Elimelekh Loyeff's second wife, after a divorce in her early twenties from a man her father had forced her to marry. A formidable and complex woman without formal education, she insisted on traditional observance in the face of her daughter and son-in-law's modernizing ways—an insistence that complicated Sholem Aleichem's home life when his speculations failed and he lost her nest egg, requiring her to remain in their household for the rest of her life. (Natasha lost her dowry, too. She would eventually marry a widower twenty-five years her senior—it ended up being a very happy marriage, despite Sholem Aleichem's attempt to sabotage the match.)

This is not to say the Odessa years had no compensations, particularly on the literary front. Abramovitch became a regular guest at their house, along with other friends and Hebrew writers like Ravnitski, Levinski, Lilienblum, and Dubnow. That Hebraist atmosphere—along with the absence of Yiddish venues—encouraged Sholem Aleichem to start writing in Hebrew again, publishing in journals like *Hamelitz* and *Pardes*; he also wrote sketches and short novels for Russian newspapers like the *Odesski Listok* and *Voshkod*. But the financial problems remained; and in grave straits and with a still-growing family—his first son, Elimelekh (Misha), had been born in October 1889, and a fourth daughter, Miriam (Maroussia), was born in 1892—Sholem Aleichem increasingly began to focus on turning his literary efforts to financial benefit. His primary plan—though there were a few other fruitless initiatives—was to try to return to the way things had been, by producing a third volume of the *Folksbibliotek*.

Of course, he could no longer simply fund it himself. He had to go the more traditional publisher's route of issuing a prospectus, including a few samples of what the reader could expect to see in the volume (all written by Sholem Aleichem, under his "own name" and various other pseudonyms). Advertisements supported part of the publication cost—one, from an insurance company, was ironically accompanied by an article Sholem Aleichem had written about the value of providing one's family with financial security—but it wasn't enough, and Olga sold her last pieces of jewelry to pay the printer. This was more than just another shot at literary success; it was a lifeline.

Making things that much more difficult, at least in Sholem Aleichem's mind, was that in the intervening years, a copycat had come on the market: in 1891, his old contributor Peretz had published his own miscellany, its title *Di yudishe bibliotek* (The Jewish Library) a near copy of Sholem Aleichem's *Di yudishe folksbibliotek* (The Jewish People's Library). Sholem Aleichem stayed furious for years: three years later, he wrote a friend that Yiddish literature seemed fated to have one insane person in it at all times, and that Levi had given way to Peretz. The addressee: Mordkhe Spektor, with whom Sholem Aleichem had reconciled. (Apparently, he didn't see the irony in complaining to Spektor despite having done the same thing to *him* several years before.) He attacked Peretz throughout the prospectus, from its opening (a grieving letter from the *Folksbibliotek* itself twitting Sholem Aleichem for abandoning it, asserting that such foul treatment could hardly be based on its merits—after all, others have stepped into the breach and gone around imitating its good name) to its "correspondence" from supportive *Folksbibliotek* readers (who complain of picking up a similarly titled anthology and finding it lacking Sholem Aleichem's touch and imprimatur); to its scathing review by "Criticus the Second" of Peretz's recent book of Yiddish poetry, castigating it for its obfuscatory introduction, its unclear theme, and its clunky style.

But Sholem Aleichem knew that he couldn't simply accentuate the negative; he had to deliver the literary goods. Two particular works stand out. The first, a "folk song" called "Sleep, My Child," would become so popular it received the highest compliment a folk song can be paid: less than a decade later, it appeared in a seminal collection of Yiddish folk songs as a traditional, unattributed lullaby, an organic part of the Eastern European Jewish landscape. But the other was the appearance of Sholem Aleichem's first great character, born of personal travail and financial desperation: Menakhem-Mendl, the ever-striving, never succeeding businessman.

Well, reborn, actually.

Five years previously, a character by that name had written the *Folksblat* editors to complain about all the space Sholem Aleichem was getting for his "Intercepted Letters," insisting his own work was much better; in response, the "editors" berated him for his foolishness in thinking he or his would-be counterpart authors were better than Sholem Aleichem. Menakhem-Mendl, in other words, starts out as a failed writer, asserting that writing is in itself a kind of business, which is itself a failure: who'd try to make a living *writing*? Sholem Aleichem's own words must have stung, five years later, when trying to make a living writing was his goal by necessity; perhaps that sting, along with more recent preoccupations, suggested a different approach. Menakhem-Mendl, the character who thought he was the smartest writer in the *Folksblat*, was a perfect means to explore the psychology of all of the investors—Menakhem-Mendl's author included—who thought they were buying into a sure thing, an ever-increasing bull market.

And this is, essentially, the plot of "Londons": Menakhem-Mendl uses the part of his dowry he manages to get his hands on to speculate in futures (and isn't that the perfect choice of subject for the time?), insisting confidently to his wife that he's sure to make a fortune. "On Londons you can make your fortune in a day," he says in his first letter, then loses his shirt just as quickly when the market crashes: "I should have made my move a day earlier," he writes in the last exchange. "The man they called the Rothschild of Kasrilevke has become a big joke." His wife, of course, knew it all along; she's constantly insisting he put aside his foolishness and return home to her and their three children. But returning home is the one thing, in the long series of adventures Sholem Aleichem will come to share with his readers, that Menakhem-Mendl refuses to do. Because that, you see, would be the death of hope. But that lay ahead. "Londons" was designed as a one-shot story, not the beginning of a series; Sholem Aleichem gives a list of works slated to appear in the *Folksbibliotek*'s projected third volume, and Menakhem-Mendl isn't among them. Maybe he just thought his readers would be more excited by sequels to earlier works like "The Intercepted Letters" and *Sender Blank* (from early on, he certainly understood the sequel's appeal). Or perhaps he was simply more interested at this date in anatomizing folly than in insisting on its redemptive value.

The story's structure, it should be said, illustrates that folly in its purest form: all the "classic" Menakhem-Mendl stories take the form of letters exchanged between husband and wife, and Sheyne-Sheyndl isn't shy about sharing her opinions of Menakhem-Mendl's castles in the air. Here's a selection from one of her "Londons" letters, in Hillel Halkin's brilliant translation:

"From Sheyne-Sheyndl in Kasrilevke to her Husband Menakhem-Mendl in Odessa. To my dear, learned, and illustrious husband Menakhem-Mendl, may your light shine! First, we're all well, thank God. I hope to hear no worse from you. Second, you write like a madman. Forgive me for saying so, but I hope to hear no more of your Odessa than I understand about your blasted shorts and hedgerows! You're throwing rubles away like last week's noodles. Money-shmoney, eh? I suppose it grows on trees over there. I'll be blamed, though, if one thing doesn't stump me: what kind of cat in a bag can you trade in but not see?"

Sholem Aleichem had long known the comic effect gleaned from juxtaposing the formal salutations (and occasionally meaningful postscripts) that were the fruit of formal letter-writing books, or *brivn-shteler*, with highly incongruous content. There are several such letters in "The Counting-House," notably between a husband and wife; and those letters, like that of Menakhem-Mendl's earlier incarnation, boasted postscripts beginning with the phrase "I forgot the main point." But with Menakhem-Mendl, Sholem Aleichem began to achieve a new mastery of crisp idiom and popular slang, following through on his claims for Yiddish in the *Folksbibliotek*'s first volume. If it wasn't quite accurate, as Sholem Aleichem insisted years later with tongue firmly in cheek in prefacing a Menakhem-Mendl collection, that "Menakhem Mendl is no hero of a romance and especially not a made-up figure. He is, alas, an ordinary Jew, with whom the author is personally and closely acquainted [and] has gone through life with him for almost twenty years," Sholem Aleichem was certainly working from life, echoing characters and language he had seen and heard around the Kiev and Odessa exchanges.

In Kiev, it was literally "around" the exchange: for Jewish businessmen, spending time on the exchange rarely meant stepping inside the actual *birzha* at 1 Institutskaya. Rather, "the more substantial brokers among them traded with agents of firms on the stock exchange in a nearby café, which was operated by an Italian, Semodenni. For perhaps 99 percent of the Jewish brokers, Semodenni's *was* the *birzha*." And these secondary brokers would often trade with those who couldn't even get in to Semodenni's and were forced to stand out on the street. Sholem Aleichem, who never had a seat on the exchange himself, was generally to be found in Semodenni's, which is mentioned by name in the Menakhem-Mendl stories—though he talked to everyone, of course, to get material for his work.

But if inspired by life, Menakhem-Mendl, like all literary characters and more so than most, is a creature composed entirely of language, of the words he puts down on paper, which make his appearances in other Sholem Aleichem works feel slighter rather than the opposite. Among the most notable of those appearances was in Sholem Aleichem's first full-length play *Yaknehoz*, published in 1894, a year after he'd returned to Kiev with his family and renewed his commercial pursuits, focusing on the stock exchange and the commodities market, particularly on sugar. The transition hadn't been easy, as one particularly troubling episode illustrated. When the family moved to Odessa, they had lent their furniture to a merchant on the understanding they would retrieve it upon their return. When they came back, though, he denied it had ever been theirs. Both parties knew the matter couldn't be taken to court, "since they had lived in Kiev illegally before the move, and had no right of residence now. The first thing the court would do would be to banish the entire family, on foot under convoy, to Pereyaslav." To establish that right of residence (also necessary for the growing children to attend *gymnasia*), Olga Rabinowitz had gone to school to learn dentistry while the family had lived in Odessa, which would provide her family, though not her husband, protective rights—as well as, crucially, a steady household income, allowing them to live something like an upper-middle-class lifestyle. With Olga working, Sholem Aleichem's mother-in-law took care of most of the household management—with an iron fist. In the meantime, Sholem Aleichem's return to the Kiev exchange, and his encounters with the personalities there, would form much of the basis of *Yaknehoz*.

Technically speaking, the play's title is an acronym, standing for the correct sequence of five blessings said during the holiday kiddush when the holiday's first night falls on Saturday night, the Sabbath's end. But, in its own way, the word serves as a multivariegated introduction to Sholem Aleichem's world. First, it moved from elite heights to the vernacular, from its first Hebrew/Aramaic appearance in the Talmud to Yiddish: it eventually took on the Yiddish meaning of "small, essentially insignificant or even non-existent things." According to the dean of Yiddish linguists, Max Weinreich, the Yiddish equivalent of a snipe hunt was sending someone to borrow a *yaknehoz* from a neighbor. But it's also a centuries-old pun: by the late Middle Ages, the word's similarity to the phrase *yog dem hoz* ("hunt the hare") had given Haggadah illustrators the excuse to doodle exciting hunting scenes beneath details of holiday blessings. Sholem Aleichem's *Yaknehoz* combines these several aspects: the flow of high financial currents through low settings, and the delight with language's ins and outs—to say nothing of the word's punning connotations. As Weinreich writes, "Profits on the stock market run like the hare, here today, gone tomorrow."

But that first meaning also lurks. Few if any of Sholem Aleichem's Kiev investors are concerned by their absolute ignorance of what their Yaknehoz shares represent, exactly what commodity they're trading and buying: all that matters is that everybody's doing it. The frenzy gets so great that, in one of the play's high points, a multiply married housewife who's received her latest dowry in Yaknehoz shares comes looking to get in on the action. A whole round of Menakhem-Mendls inhabit *Yaknehoz*, eager to sign up for another round of speculation, and so it's hardly a shock when Menakhem-Mendl, fresh from his Odessa misadventures, shows up himself. Intriguingly, everyone on the exchange seems to know about Menakhem-Mendl's travails, and his writings; great enthusiasm attends a reading out of one of Sheyne-Sheyndl's letters. But her imprecations and dire predictions—"Don't fly so high," she warns, "and you won't crash so low"—go unattended: Menakhem-Mendl, cursed with the optimist's ability never to learn that things *do* happen the same way twice, continues to deal with Yaknehoz, to his dismay. The inevitable crash, increasingly invested with Sholem Aleichem's rueful experience, contains the sobering possibility—as subsequent events would suggest—that Sholem Aleichem hadn't learned Sheyne-Sheyndl's lesson, either, at least not totally, even as "Menakhem-Mendl" would become a byword describing a kind of ne'er-do-well, unfortunate *luftmentsh*.

Yaknehoz almost didn't see the light of day. Kiev businessmen, objecting to their portrayal as card-playing gamblers, lobbied the local censor to forbid publication. The censor charged blasphemy, on the fairly specious reasoning that the play's character Shmuel Pasternak regularly mangled biblical verses; the motion was denied, probably because Pasternak doesn't actually do so. What he *does* do is give comically relevant interpretations of passages, or issue ironic claims that Slavic sayings are taken from the Talmud—as a much, much more famous successor of his, created later that same year, would do to far greater literary and comic effect.

Aside from his speculations on the exchange, Sholem Aleichem tried a variety of different jobs to support his family, which involved a great deal of time on the road and yielded little success. Still, his mood had changed. The shift was presaged in a short feuilleton published in Mordkhe Spektor's *House-Friend* in 1894, a work utilizing the setting he now spent much of his time in and which would come to occupy greater and greater prominence in his work: the railroad. Although the train station, that great site of modern literature and harbinger of modern sensibilities, had had minor cameos in some of his early novels—*Sender Blank* ends at a train depot—"Mazapevke Station" features Sholem Aleichem himself, buttonholed by admirers for the brief duration of his train's stop. Though there's bitter satire there—Sholem Aleichem castigates the fans who eagerly profess to be waiting for another edition of the *Folks-bibliotek* but are either unwilling or collectively unable to pony up the cash required for that to happen—the sketch ends with the train moving on, and Sholem Aleichem with it. Perhaps leaving old ideas and old fans behind, but moving on.

The trains, not coincidentally, were also a place he could get his writing done. Though he would later write of his ability to write "in every time, every place, in all sorts of circumstances: in a salon, a kitchen, a train compartment, a restaurant, even traveling with a coachman or lying in bed," an autobiographical sketch written the same year suggests that the last few years had been an exception. "To 'The Dove'" tells the story of "a Yiddish writer, a sort of humorist but really a big fool, named Sholem Aleichem," a writer of bad poetry and humorous feuilletons who got rich and became the subject of such flattery he ended up believing everyone's compliments, tried to do too much, and lost everything. In a mordant pun, he writes that *Sholem Aleichem* has become *Olev-hasholem* (may he rest in peace), a goner who had suffered from serious writer's block. But now, he wrote, "behold, a year or three have gone by, the clouds have parted, the heavens have lightened, the air has freshened, and Sholem Aleichem has begun to revive once more . . . like a man who, when he awakens from an illness, little by little restores his previous appetite, all his senses and pleasures return to him once again."

The restoration of appetite was accompanied by the resumption of ambition. "Jargon and the jargonists," he complained to Ravnitski, "have fallen asleep on us," and he wanted "with God's will, to wake them up, but not, as is usually the case, to wake them politely—excuse me, excuse me, time to get up—no! I want to wake them up with a crash, a thunder, a whack in the head, so that they fall out of their beds." Though he was talking about the *Folksbibliotek*'s third, ultimately never-published volume, it was, in the conflicting and ironic currents that characterized his work and life, a small story about a superficially unimportant, deceptively ordinary man that made more noise, over the next century, than any thunderous proclamation or polemical stance of his ever would.

CHAPTER 11

In Which Our Hero Meets a Dairyman

1894

Like most upper-class or upwardly aspiring Russians, Sholem Aleichem and his family summered outside the city, and, since shortly after their marriage, had done so in Boyarke, an hour's train ride from Kiev. Though Sholem Aleichem had originally been skeptical, preferring to remain in Belaya Tserkov, he soon changed his mind, and the family would spend their summers there almost every year between 1884 and 1905, generally from mid-May to mid-August.

Boyarke had many advantages. It was naturally beautiful; one of Sholem Aleichem's narrators describes being charmed by its fictional counterpart, Boiberik, its "green forests, the fresh air, the tweeting birds, and the neat summer houses, each of which looked like a well-dressed bride on her wedding day." Its fruit gardens and woods allowed the writer to take advantage of his propensity to rise early and feed the birds; it boasted recreational possibilities, baths, pools, free concerts and plays; rents were quite reasonable (one could rent a dacha for the whole season for as little as 150 rubles); there was plenty of time for him to write (Olga, after her training, gave free dental care at a clinic for the peasants); and Jews were allowed to live there—there were none of the anxieties that had marked their first years in Kiev. Sholem Aleichem would lie on a hammock strung between two pine trees, umbrella over his head, or take his notebook and pencil and talk to other residents—everyone, even the local non-Jews, knew the way to his dacha—listening for interesting turns of phrase that might find their way into a future work.

Yes, there were downsides: the incredible inconveniences and travails of moving a household, for one (it was an hour by train, but a day by wagon, and the furniture—the dachas were rented unfurnished—had to go by wagon). And in truth, it wasn't all luxury: dachas were generally four or five rooms with a separate shed for a kitchen, though in lean years the one they rented might be even smaller. They had no lighting or plumbing (they used outhouses), water was drawn from a communal well, and when it rained "a miniature lake would form in the middle of the living room." But Boyarke turned out to offer an additional compensation. That same narrator also writes of "salesmen swamp[ing] our cottage offering all sorts of dainties," including "chickens, eggs, vegetables, and dairy-products," and in the summer of 1894, Sholem Aleichem met a particularly interesting specimen of the type: the local dairyman, Tevye, who delivered butter, cheese, milk, and cream to the summer crowd.

On September 21, 1894, the day after Rosh Hashanah, Sholem Aleichem wrote Spektor that though he didn't want to make any promises until the story was completed, he was certain he had a new offering for the *House-Friend*'s next volume. He wrote: "The story will be called 'Tevye the Dairyman,' composed in Boyarka, that is to say, I heard the story from Tevye himself as he stood in front of my dacha with his horse and cart, weighing out butter and cheese. The story is interesting, but Tevye himself is a thousand times more interesting! I convey the story in his own words, and am spared the effort of describing him since he describes himself."

Sholem Aleichem was playing his usual games: yes, there was a real Tevye, and, according to Sholem Aleichem's daughter, he did fascinate her father, who "loved to talk with him, often chuckling at a remark he made, something in Hebrew, which we did not understand but was evidently very funny to my father. Occasionally during the conversation, my father would take out his little notebook and jot down a few words." Maybe a few of the original Tevye's turns of phrase, if that's what Sholem

Aleichem was indeed jotting down, made it into the stories; thirty years later, a Soviet Yiddish theater troupe would play in Boyarke and meet the dairyman, and were so amazed by the "Tevyeh-like expressions which rolled spontaneously off the unsophisticated tongue" that they gave him money for a new cart and dairy equipment. But the original Tevye's relationship to his literary counterpart was probably akin to what Kenny Kramer's was to the *Seinfeld* character: an inspirational canvas on which creators of genius sketch their own comic imaginings.

He settled on terms with Spektor, and sent him "Tevye the Dairyman— the Story of His Sudden Rise, Described by Tevye Himself and Dictated to Sholem Aleichem Word by Word" in two parts during November. (He had to wait for the copyist to produce a clean copy, a regular part of his composition process. Sholem Aleichem went through a lot of copyists, dissatisfied with their propensity to pitch their own stories to him, lose his manuscripts, or ask about his personal life.) Spektor wasn't impressed by the story, and told him so; its author replied: "Please don't be offended— the world will certainly like it. I don't know whether this is because the world knows more than you do, or because it knows nothing at all." He was right, to put it mildly. The story appeared in the new year in the *House-Friend*'s fourth volume, and that July, Sholem Aleichem, when he invited Ravnitski to join him in Boyarke, added getting "dairy products from Tevye" to the attractions.

And the appeal wouldn't just be limited to his houseguests. Sholem Aleichem's daughter would later write that the Tevye stories "were popular enough to reach the summer residents in Boyarka, and Tevyeh learned that he was 'written up in the gazettes.' At first he resented it and complained . . . that the stories had brought him great embarrassment, for wherever he went among the summer people they called him the Milky One and laughed at him. But in time he began to enjoy his fame and admitted it was good for business, too. Some people became his customers merely to be able to tell their friends in town that in Boyarka they were served by Tevyeh, the Milky One." Sholem Aleichem, who from the beginning had built his own literary identity by playing games with the thin line between the actual and the imaginary, the real person and the invented persona, couldn't have failed to notice that the world was following suit: readers loved seeing the "real" thing, even if fiction had created it.

Tevye, in various incarnations, will be with us through the rest of the book, through both Sholem Aleichem's life and afterlife, so a few more general words might be in order. Modern readers—especially after *Fiddler on the Roof*—tend to think of Tevye's story as all of a piece, with a beginning, middle, and end, focused around Tevye's travails with his beautiful, strong-willed daughters. That's not strictly true. Sholem Aleichem published each Tevye story separately, over a twenty-year period, and the stories' emphases change dramatically as the author's interests and experiences did. During this period—and it's worth emphasizing that this is a conscious artistic decision—Tevye lives and ages in real time along with Sholem Aleichem, his prime and perhaps only audience, referring and reacting to historical events that have occurred since their last meeting. Tevye, as the years progressed, meant different things to Sholem Aleichem and to his readers.

And so the first story, unsurprising given the period and circumstances of its composition, is another story about money. Not marriage, but money, the ebbs and flows of fortune. The brilliance of "Tevye the Dairyman" (which would be revised, and reappear some years later, under the title "The Jackpot") stems from Sholem Aleichem's transposition of these matters from the countinghouses and financiers of Kiev to the *yid fun a gantz yor*, the common Jew. In this case, a rural Jew: Tevye, at the story's beginning, isn't even well-off enough to be a dairyman—for that, you need enough capital to buy a cow. Instead, he's engaged in the arduous work of hauling logs from the forest; by his good fortune, he manages to meet a few lost ladies from the rich dachas, who, rewarding him with their pocket change, allow him to irrevocably change his class and fortune. Tevye's daughters? Never seen in the story; but they're mentioned, all seven of them, in passing.

Fiddler on the Roof viewers may be wondering where the extra daughters got to; we might blame it on the vicissitudes of adaptation, except that even in Sholem Aleichem's own later stories, a few of them disappear in Tevye's accounting. (The historical record doesn't help and is equally muddled; Sholem Aleichem's daughter says the original Tevye didn't have daughters, people who met him decades later claimed he had two.) Maybe Sholem Aleichem, who wrote the individual stories years apart, didn't necessarily refer back to every detail and forgot; maybe he just ran out of daughter-related stories to tell. The reason to *start* with seven daughters is clearer, though: an old Yiddish saying that *zibn tekhter is keyn gelekhter*, seven daughters is no laughing matter, because, of course, of the seven dowries the father must come up with. Sholem Aleichem seems to have tossed in the detail to simply indicate the kind of financial woes that Tevye has, clothing the proverbial in actual flesh, blending the worlds of imagination and reality. Certainly Tevye's description, which appeared in the story's first version, was realistic enough: "Tevye is a healthy Jew," Sholem Aleichem writes, "with broad shoulders and thick, dark hair; his age is hard to guess; he wears heavy boots . . . In a word, Tevye is one of those village Jews who eat good dumplings with cheese, live to ninety, and have no need for eyeglasses or false teeth, and know nothing of hemorrhoids or other Jewish troubles or misfortunes."

Sholem Aleichem also notes in his introduction that "Tevye is always ready to talk." Inspired by Gogol, Sholem Aleichem wanted monologues, talking Jews: knowing that the Jewish world existed not just in books but in the voices of its people, he wanted to meet the challenge of creating high literature that echoed those voices—but not, as he had criticized Shomer, by writing dialogue for shopkeepers that "can only be the product of a talented humorist, a cheerful satirist like Shomer." Good writing, Sholem Aleichem felt, wasn't good if it was implausible: a shopkeeper didn't talk like Shomer, and so, in a story, shouldn't. Tevye had to talk like a Tevye, a Jewish character who spoke unmistakably—but plausibly—Jewish. How? Tevye, according to the introduction, "likes an honest saying, a parable, a bit of Torah"; he studs his speech with quotations from the Torah, the liturgy, and the occasional Talmudic source—and some trickiness results.

Tevye and his author, from near the very start, play high off against low: that is, Tevye quotes something from its high-status original source in Hebrew or Aramaic, then provides a Yiddish translation or conclusion to the verse, prayer, or saying. The "problem" is that the Yiddish translations don't actually match the originals. Take a famous example from "Tevye the Dairyman," also in Halkin's wonderful translation. Tevye says to the wealthy family whose members he's saved: "What's my work? For lack of any better suggestions, I break my back dragging logs. As it says in the Talmud, *bemokoym she'eyn ish,* a herring too is a fish." Halkin maintains the high/low interplay by only translating the Yiddish, meaning English-language readers have a roughly analogous experience to the one Yiddish readers had. That said, most Yiddish readers would have recognized the statement's first part, too; it's the first half of a famous rabbinic saying. Tevye is basically right in calling it a Talmudic saying (it comes from *Ethics of the Fathers* 2:6), but the phrase as a whole—*bemokoym she'eyn anashim hishtadel lihyos ish* ("In a place where there are no men, try to be a man")—is quite different from what Tevye's saying.

No critic reading the stories ever thought *Sholem Aleichem* had gotten it wrong, naturally; as we've seen, Sholem Aleichem's own knowledge of the Bible was prodigious, and though he wasn't a rabbinic scholar, most of Tevye's quotations aren't from particularly recondite parts of the Bible or Talmud—they're generally either phrases that had become bywords or regularly recited parts of the liturgy. But many critics and translators, particularly in mid-twentieth-century America, were quite convinced *Tevye* had gotten it wrong—that he was intended as a Mr. Malaprop whose charm and humor came from his simplicity and ignorance. As we'll see, that had as much to do with the interpreters as with the character, if not more: though Tevye himself isn't as learned or clever as he believes himself to be—hardly unusual for Sholem Aleichem's characters, for their author, or, for that matter, for anyone—Sholem Aleichem's characterization that "he's neither a great scholar nor an ignoramus when it comes to the fine print" seems right. And so the odds are good that he's using the texts ironically, sensing the mastery born of comic diminution: in this case, reflecting on the grandness of the rabbinic text's suggested action, and juxtaposing it with his small but noble efforts to maintain dignity and family in a difficult situation, faced by wealth and society, high versus low. In *Yaknehoz*, Shmuel Pasternak wasn't blaspheming when quoting these texts, but he wasn't being religious, either; he was trying to be witty, though, from the play's evidence, amusing no one but himself. Tevye uses the Jewish texts for the most religious of reasons: to explain his situation, to himself if no one else, to give himself fortitude and hope.

"Hope" was the title of a tiny essay Sholem Aleichem had published in the *Folksblat* eight years before, in 1887. In that small allegory, Reason accuses Hope before the divine court of deceiving humanity by leading them astray with dreams. Hope, brought before the court in chains by Reason and Despair, ultimately blames God, who gave it the power to give people the wish for happiness but not the power to help them achieve it. Shattering its shackles, it returns to earth, since the Hope-deprived population is suiciding at an enormous rate. God, acquiescing in the outcome, tells Reason to mind its own business: people can't live without hope, after all. Menakhem-Mendl, in these first appearances, experiences an entire, self-contained cycle of optimism and disappointment: "Londons" and *Yaknehoz* begin with excitement and end with ruin. But Tevye? Here, in this first appearance, he prays for divine assistance with his situation, and the story ends with his receiving it, or something very like it. There would be other stories with Tevye, other disappointments, but from the very beginning, the seed had been sown, in Sholem Aleichem's mind as well as in his readers. Here was a character who stood for something like hope.

ACT III

The Spokesman

CHAPTER 12

In Which Our Hero Returns to Zion and Other Old Preoccupations

1895–1899

Over the next three years, Sholem Aleichem, working hard to support his family, wrote little; practically his sole work of published Yiddish fiction for the next three years, another Menakhem-Mendl story, showcased what were becoming usual financial concerns. But he hadn't stopped writing, or—impossible for Sholem Aleichem—stopped hoping: his optimism, excitement, and dedication had simply been transferred elsewhere.

The Zionist movement had been gaining momentum over the course of the decade; Theodor Herzl's *The Jewish State* appeared in 1896. It wasn't that the ideas were new—Leon Pinsker, whom Sholem Aleichem had met in Odessa, had put forth many of them in his *Autoemancipation*, published a decade and a half before. (Sholem Aleichem would later call it "the first stone of that great structure which our people created afterwards.") But Herzl's drive and energy—his insistence on setting dramatic goals and making bold gestures and public moves—were hugely enchanting, particularly to a dreamer by nature like Sholem Aleichem. "Dr. Pinsker poured out his bitter heart quietly, reasonably, without fuss or clamor," he wrote, but "Herzl demanded publicly, to the whole world, a ready-made Jewish state."

Here's Sholem Aleichem's description of Herzl: "Doctor Herzl is a young man, thirty-seven years old [a year younger than Sholem Aleichem], one of the outstanding German writers, one of the editors of the leading newspaper in Vienna, 'Neue Freie Presse,' a man of culture, a true aristocrat, an orator and a diplomat, and a man of wealth as well. At first Dr. Herzl was little interested in Jews, till the anti-Semites started digging under us. Then he came to see that things were really bad for the Jews, and he took to thinking about it. Two years ago he published his book, *Der Judenstaat*, where he shows, proof positive, that Jews can and should set up a state in Eretz Yisrael. This book caused a sensation among Jews and Christians, and it made Dr. Herzl world famous."

If this sounds a bit more didactic than Sholem Aleichem's usual prose, it's the context: a thirty-page Yiddish pamphlet he published with the well-known Hebrew publishing house Ahiasaf, describing the First World Zionist Congress held in Basel, Switzerland, in 1897. The prevailing sense of ideological urgency, so similar to that of his early Haskala days, may have led him to adopt not only their tone, but their old rationale for using Yiddish. "The First Jewish World Congress has been written up in all the most important Russian and foreign newspapers," he wrote, "so that it is only right to put it forward also in our poor Yiddish language, for our people, in Jargon." Whatever the rationale, the pamphlet sold twenty-seven thousand copies (compared to Herzl's own Hebrew pamphlet, which sold only three thousand); numbers in Shomer territory, assuredly testifying to its author about the enormous audience out there thirsting for news of the day, even when delivered or mediated secondhand.

Sholem Aleichem hadn't attended the conference himself—he remained in Kiev, possibly for financial reasons—so much of the text is dedicated to others' reports of the events, but his sensibility shines through, an essential part of the work's appeal. Take his comments on emancipation: "A light had dawned for the Jews. Rejoicing. Great rejoicing. And as usual with the Jews, when they are let off the leash for a while, they became puffed up with pride, thinking that they really and in fact had become equals with everybody else, from tip to toe, until something like this happened: the nations had second thoughts and repented the marriage bond into which they had entered, and the Jew grew to be a bogeyman in their eyes." Or his caustic characterization of objectors to Zionism: "Some will say, 'So you've had a congress! Psha! Not worth a pinch of snuff! A lot of talk, speeches, speeches! That's where it will all end!' Others will make fun of the whole affair. 'What do you think about it? About those Zionists, that want to bring the messiah down!' And some will fly into a rage, as though someone had upset a good business deal for them. 'Atheists! Disbelievers! Want to hold back the Redemption!' So here we are, reckon it up, and draw your own conclusions." We can almost hear Sholem Aleichem's future monologists and narrators, who take on Dreyfus, America, the first Russian Revolution, and the First World War with their own skeptical, ironic sensibility—the wellspring, perhaps, of a specific kind of Jewish humor. Zelig Mechanic, created seven years before, had been the foil, the common man who simply absorbs the zeitgeist; Sholem Aleichem would begin to realize the importance of creating figures who would opine on it.

Buoyed by the pamphlet's success, Sholem Aleichem continued to write explicitly Zionist material into 1898, publishing another two pamphlets with Ahiasaf—each with its own idiosyncratic twists. "Why Do the Jews Need a Land of Their Own?," before providing its standard Zionist answer, opens with a stand-up comic's take on the matter, a Jewish shrug and a raised eyebrow: "What do Jews need a land of their own? Some question! . . . It's as though they were asking you what do you want a home for? Naturally everyone should have a home. What else? Stay outside?" "To Our Sisters in Zion," dedicated to his four daughters, stresses women's particular role in Zionism by providing a quick survey of celebrated women in Jewish history; but it takes the time—and courts the controversy among Zionism's Hebraist supporters—to champion old "Yiddish" culture in comparison to acculturated ignorance. "There is little these [pious Yiddish-reading] women know of the history of the Jewish people," Sholem Aleichem writes. "Yet they know more than our 'ladies' do. I mean those who 'with respect beg to inform that they suffer from nerves.' They read novels, travel to the spas, take the 'cure'—what do these ladies know of Yiddishkeit, Jewish history, anything outside 'nerves,' novels, social calls, concerts, dining out, card games?" The essay's chastisement of Jewish ignorance, though addressed to women, would suggest an increasingly important theme in Sholem Aleichem's thinking and fiction: the idea that Jewish knowledge, an efflorescence of Jewish culture and cultural memory, could be the factor that unites Jews into a Jewish nation, rather than the specific acts and prescriptions of religion or the abstract principles of Jewish faith, increasingly ignored by Jews in this changed and changing modern world. Jews needed a land of their own, his Zionist works clearly state; but they need their own culture and history as well.

Though that idea was well within mainstream Zionist thinking, Sholem Aleichem's writer's need to express things his own way—idiosyncratically, suffused by his own comic sensibility—created friction with movement representatives. Witness the fate of his "Zionist novel" *Messianic Times*, which began publication that same year, part of a project established to produce Zionist materials in Yiddish. Sholem Aleichem's offering was killed by Ezra Press after only two installments for "too much witticism and too much feuilleton style." You can see what they meant: Sholem Aleichem tweaks the Everyshtetl Mazapevke's inhabitants for falling in love with breathless, fantastic descriptions of messianic transformations rather than the practical, actual account of the First Zionist Congress, comparing them to the children and the childish games they play right outside the synagogues and houses of study where the adults' discussions occur. But, much like in his writings about financial speculation, the author manages to indict himself along with his readers: Is there anyone more of a sucker for a good story, or more sympathetic to the illusions of childhood, than Sholem Aleichem? This constant shift between satire and sympathy, alienation and inclusion, was a central part of Sholem Aleichem's developing style, but his ability to embrace the multitudes of human—and Jewish—experience was less appealing to the more strictly doctrinaire editors at the press.

Luckily, another venue sprung up that was congenial to both Zionist sensibilities and literary wit. *Der Yid* (The Jew) was founded in 1899 by Sholem Aleichem's old friend Ravnitski and published by Ahiasaf with an eye to blending highbrow writing and bulletproof elite, Hebraist credentials with popular appeal—meaning, of course, the sixteen-page bimonthly (later a weekly) would be published in Yiddish. If that wasn't appealing enough for Sholem Aleichem, Ravnitski, highly influenced by the Zionist thinker Ahad Ha'am, intended the paper to demonstrate the essential connection between Zionism and cultural revival; though Sholem Aleichem grumbled about the paper's name, preferring something like "The Jewish World" or "The Jewish Paper," and constantly pushed for more literary poems and more criticism, he was an enormous supporter of what he called "the first serious Yiddish journal." He became a regular contributor from *Der Yid*'s first issue, and between news features, reports on Zionist congresses, and far-flung correspondents' reports, the paper printed some of the period's Yiddish literary masterpieces—including that first contribution of Sholem Aleichem's, which brought together, for the first and last time, two of his greatest characters.

Tevye and Menakhem-Mendl's meeting, in "A boydem" (translated as "Tevye Blows a Small Fortune"), can be considered the meeting of two modes of Jewish life entire: the urban commercial figure and the rural dairyman, the rootless traveler and the family man. But even more important is how the story encompasses two modes of Jewish hope: the optimism of the speculator, who puts his trust in himself and in business, and that of the believer, who puts his faith in God and Jewish destiny. Sholem Aleichem, the Zionist and businessman, saw both within himself, and recent events had probably accentuated his natural bent of thinking.

In 1898, probably late July or early August, he had managed to arrange the sale of a large Russian estate, earning a substantial sum for his efforts. True, most went to pay off his even more substantial debts. Still, it was enough to allow him to send his brother some money for the coming holidays—a telling illustration not only of his constant need to be the generous one, the provider, but also to suspect that a single swallow would make a summer. Though the story had apparently been in the works for some time—he had written Spektor about a new Tevye piece as early as 1896—the optimism created by gains that might or might not prove to be temporary was certainly on his mind as he prepared "Tevye Blows a Small Fortune" for publication. Tevye, remember, had ended his first adventure on a high note, "when God looked my way and did me a favor for a change, so that I managed to make a little something of myself and even to put away a few rubles." Meeting up with Menakhem-Mendl, though, who "got hold of me and filled my head with such pipe dreams that it began to spin like a top," dreams like making a good match for his eldest daughter and donating to charity, Tevye hands over his nest egg, and Menakhem-Mendl does what he does best: loses it all.

Tevye, telling Sholem Aleichem the story in retrospect, asks: "Why does a Tevye, of all people, get involved with a Menakhem-Mendl? Well, the answer to that is: because. Fate is fate." Menakhem-Mendl is introduced as Tevye's relative, and we're meant to notice the resemblance: "A black day it was that you became a businessman," Tevye thinks to himself, and we've heard that sentiment before, from Sheyne-Sheyndl's lips. And yet the two aren't alike, exactly, and Tevye's resignation to his fate isn't the same as Menakhem-Mendl's frantic, explosive collapses. Tevye *isn't* really a businessman, or a business dilettante, if that's a better characterization of Menakhem-Mendl; he doesn't invest and lose the money himself, but needs someone else to do it for him. That could have been for logistical or commercial reasons. Maybe Sholem Aleichem felt Menakhem-Mendl's cameo appearance would delight regular readers. (Reading the story reminds me of the comic book crossovers I loved so much when I was little: finding Spider-Man in an X-Men comic book suggested the existence of a Marvel *Universe*, to use the company's phrase, not just an individual set of adventures, that these characters had their own lives that were going on all the time, and we had just happened onto a window into them.) But just maybe there's something about Tevye that Sholem Aleichem didn't want to adulterate by having him conform to Menakhem-Mendl-itis: ensuring he retains some kind of untouched possibility for hope without folly. When you come down to it, the reason Tevye loses his money is because he puts his trust in the wrong man, which is not entirely unadmirable, and even, in its own way, nobly foolish. How Tevye deals with others—particularly his daughters, and with God—will be, in its own way, the focus of the rest of the stories, and the thing that makes him great.

Equally significant about the story, though, is that it's a full-fledged sequel, a continuing adventure in the lives of these set characters, who are now revealed to have their own conventional ways of behaving, speaking, and writing. Sequels and series, both structured and occasional, would become an increasingly important part of Sholem Aleichem's output as time went on. This partly resulted from artistic concerns: there were simply more stories Sholem Aleichem wanted to tell with these newly versatile, potent characters. But something more seems to be happening: another step toward Sholem Aleichem's greater populism, the further development of his brand. At a time when financial concerns were obviously paramount, the logic of sequels becomes compelling—audiences will be willing to pay for more adventures from beloved characters; why not produce them? If Tevye and Menakhem-Mendl weren't yet the archetypal characters they would become, at least their successful reception indicated they were on their way.

Case in point: Pitching the next installment of the Menakhem-Mendl stories to Ravnitski in February 1899, he explicitly sells it as a sequel. "Write me, if you remember in the *House-Friend* (the previous annual), when they printed my 'Stocks and Bonds'—a correspondence between Menakhem-Mendl to Sheyne-Sheyndl and Sheyne-Sheyndl to Menakhem-Mendl—about the Yehupetz stock exchange. I have also completed another 24 such letters—an illustration of the Yehupetz brokers.—Does that sound good to you, or not?" It did; and though "Millions" begins with Menakhem-Mendl's flat declaration to his wife that "I'm through with investing," that's not, of course, the same thing as being out of business. This time it's a variety of things: a middleman trading commodities, buying and selling loans, urban real estate, country property, lumber, sugar mills, gold mines, and sundry other proposals. Menakhem-Mendl's power continued to stem from his essential inability to change—in this installment, he writes his wife in all sincerity that "you must be wondering how I became involved with a business about which I didn't know a blessed thing, even though it's quite elementary"—but a few months later a different sequel revealed a stock character transformed.

With the publication of "Today's Children," the third Tevye story, Sholem Aleichem shifted Tevye's focus from money to marriage—and made a quantum leap in discovering how to balance his preoccupations with larger questions of Jewish character and immediate questions of Jewish politics. "Today's Children" is the first of the stories whose outlines are well known to fans of *Fiddler on the Roof*, since its plot—Tevye plans to marry off Tsaytl to the butcher Leyzer-Wolf, but stops when he hears of Tsaytl's own arrangement with the tailor Motl Kamzoyl, and uses a ruse to convince his wife, Golde, that the other world is smiling on the new match—is rendered largely faithfully in the play and the film.

Sholem Aleichem had been balancing love and marriage since the beginning of his career, as a brace of one-act plays illustrated. "A Doctor for a Bridegroom" (1887) satirized marriage à la mode, boasting an ignorant parvenu couple whose plans for their daughter seem to shift according to fashion and whim; a more modern son, who claims his sister will only marry a doctor; a matchmaker who'll marry anyone to anybody as long as he earns his commission; and, finally, the daughter herself, entering late in the scene and offering the revolutionary suggestion that grooms should talk to their brides about marriage themselves. Sholem Aleichem not only champions modern romantic love—no surprise there, biographically or ideologically—but does it in a woman's voice. The next year's more complex "The Bill of Divorce" starts along standard maskilic lines, picturing a new generation that married for love and an older one, in the form of the wife's monstrous mother, trying to disrupt the marriage for unreasonable reasons—here, anger over deeply unflattering portraits of her in Yiddish newspapers created by her son-in-law's friend. But, since the two are already married, as the friend points out, there's nothing the parents can do—assuming the couple summons the strength to fight off these marital threats. People fail because they're human, not because of their generational identity.

Sholem Aleichem's own experiences, in fact, illustrated how such matters didn't easily fall along generational lines: he himself, champion of romance and temporary victim of paternal interference, had attempted to arrange marriages for his wife's nieces in the late 1880s. A Tevye in reverse, he even suggested a strategem to get around the problem with "today's Jewish daughter . . . [who] will in no way agree to marry herself through a matchmaker or even through the groom himself, if he comes to see and to be seen," proposing the prospective groom visit the house as his own guest, thus providing a natural way for the young couple to meet, all unbeknownst to the prospective bride. (He even suggested, seemingly unironically, that the optimal matches should have their own money and not be writers!) Caught between different impulses—paternal, authoritarian, conservative, and modern, romantic, radically impulsive—it all went into transforming Tevye's stories into a series exploring generational conflict like no other in contemporary Western literature.

The scholar Ruth Wisse has remarked that though many novels of the period focus on the quarrel between generations—Turgenev's *Fathers and Sons*, a book Sholem Aleichem was sure to have read, even places the issue squarely in its title—most focus on sons, not daughters, and, far more crucially, the Tevye stories are the only ones told from the fathers' perspectives. And, what's more, sympathetically so: the stories' brilliance lies in figuring out just how much sympathy the fathers can muster for the children's new ideas, pinpointing precisely just how much they will—and can—change in response. Later readers would confuse Tevye with Sholem Aleichem, and nothing could be further from the truth: Tevye is a rural Jew with little education and less worldly experience (different from wisdom, of course), and Sholem Aleichem an educated, elite cosmopolitan. But the difference between the two diminishes when it comes to living the emotional complexities of conflicts posed by their rapidly changing worlds—emotions Sholem Aleichem no doubt experienced in the jaw-dropping, whipsawing series of changes in his religious, economic, and educational state.

Tsaytl's name in Yiddish means "little time," and "Today's Children"—the Yiddish phrase has the same valence as "kids today"—reflects its author's increasing desire for his characters to mirror, and respond to, a changing world. Sholem Aleichem had written in *The Judgment* that a "writer of the people—a true artist and poet—is a mirror in which the rays of his epoch and generation are reflected." Shomer and his transgressions were certainly still on his mind a decade later: a sketch he published that same year in *Der Yid*, "In the Book Store"—a delightful five-page parody of Shomer's stories complete with attempted poisonings, evil wealthy exploiters trying to take advantage of poor servant girls, abandoned wives, poor suitors returning à la *Count of Monte Cristo* as wealthy counts, and mixed-up genealogies—tells the tale. (At sketch's end, everyone dramatically kills themselves—including the author and the reader.) "Today's Children" was another way to rebut Shomer: another plausible Jewish romance. But this Tevye story was, perhaps for the first time, where he fully began to become both an artist and poet and a writer of the people.

CHAPTER 13

In Which Our Hero Reads the Newspapers in Yiddish and Becomes a Media Star

1899–1903

A new century was dawning. Sholem Aleichem's natural excitement and optimism—his daughter recalls her parents creating a kind of "time capsule" to celebrate their marriage and family at the turn of the century—would give way to financial concern, particularly as he devoted more and more of his time to writing. A telling anecdote of the family's precarious finances at the time: Sholem Aleichem's second son and final child, Numa, was born in 1901. Right after the birth, Sholem Aleichem went out for a walk and disappeared. The family was in a tizzy: as he had no personal residence right in Kiev, were he picked up by the police, he would be deported, and of course they couldn't contact the authorities. The reason for his vanishing act? As they found out later, he'd gone in search of a loan from a friend or acquaintance to pay off the midwife and the doctor. By the winter of 1902, he was writing Spektor frantically: "I need money, and need it now, today, yesterday I needed it—and you promise me a world to come of earnings. *Gevalt*, my dear brother, what should I do? I need, I need, I need!"

The problem was one of venue. After the *Folksblat* folded, the tsarist government had refused to issue publication licenses for Yiddish newspapers or journals for a decade. (To avoid the ban, *Der Yid* was published in Cracow, in Galicia, and thus officially outside the heart of the empire.) But with 5 million or so Yiddish speakers clamoring for material, the government was flooded with petitions, and everyone felt they would have to relent sooner or later. Sholem Aleichem, the erstwhile publisher, was trying to get into the act, hoping to use some of the money from his business windfalls in the late 1890s to publish a newspaper inside the empire proper, perhaps from Warsaw; he would have similar dreams for years, but nothing would come of them.

There were cracks in the walls, though, heralding a change in Sholem Aleichem's fortunes and a new age for Yiddish. Spektor's promise of earnings resulted first from Sholem Aleichem's decision to collect and "polish up all of my works . . . at a price amenable to all, and get a little something for myself out of it" and to include his "*real* autobiography, merrily and artistically written" for good measure. Talks, conducted via Spektor, began with the Tushiya Press by mid-January, but Sholem Aleichem's financial pressures meant he needed a deal, and ready money. On February 23, he wrote: "Quick, brother, tell me in two words: is it possible, I'll get money *soon* and *how much* and *when*? . . . Because I tell you again, the noose is around my neck, and is pulling stronger all the time, and slowly I'm strangling, and God knows what will become with [signed] Your best Sholem Aleichem." By April, he claims he's having trouble coming up with money for future rent, and is so beside himself that he, the graphomaniac, can't write—"You understand: *I* can't write!" He had just received a telegram from Ben-Avigdor, Tushiya's head, that money was being wired to him at a Kiev bank, but without detailing which one, and he had just visited all the banks and post offices, with no success.

But it wasn't, or wasn't only, the collected works that promised ready money; in the interim months, Spektor had come up with another opportunity. Tushiya had jumped into the Yiddish publishing fray, and had gotten permission to publish two weekly Yiddish newspapers in Warsaw, the *Froyenvelt* (Women's World) and the *Folkstsaytung* (People's Paper). Spektor was involved in editing both, and in mid-March he had traveled from Warsaw to Kiev specifically to invite Sholem Aleichem to contribute to both papers—contingent on signing a non-compete clause forbidding him to write for *Der Yid*. Ahiasaf, *Der Yid*'s publishers, pleaded with him to stay when they heard the news of the switch, even sending him some money to try to change his mind, but Sholem Aleichem was immovable, if for no other reason than, as he gleefully wrote to Abramovitch, Tushiya paid "cash money!" He even managed to wangle an advance out of them, and by early May, except for some holdover commitments, he had left Ahiasaf and begun writing for the *Folkstsaytung*.

Within a year, the Russian Ministry of Internal Affairs, bowing further to the pressures of those petitions—part of a general liberalizing trend, about which more later—allowed Shabtai Rapaport and Shaul Ginzburg to publish *Der Fraynd*, the empire's first Yiddish *daily*, in St. Petersburg, the heart of the regime; another daily, *Der Tog*, opened there a year later. Sholem Aleichem was naturally delighted, figuring he'd be able to earn over double the money he was getting from the *Folkstsaytung* writing for a daily. "Hurrah! That He has sustained us and brought us to this time!" he wrote Spektor, quoting a traditional blessing. He cabled Ginzburg accepting the latter's offer to contribute to the new paper, but pleaded that his name not be mentioned in the prospectus—there was still that non-compete clause, after all—though he was certain the *Folkstsaytung* would allow him to contribute to the paper in the end (which is what happened; Sholem Aleichem would write for both papers, as well as the *Tog*). Tellingly, he also asked Ginzburg for an advance.

A new age was beginning, an age of the popular press. Sholem Aleichem, wooed by the *Fraynd*, predicted that one day "purely literary journals will kneel before the 'daily literature,' almost like in America. Remember the words I speak in prophecy." The day came even sooner than he imagined. *Der Yid* closed in 1902; the *Folkstsaytung* before 1903 was out; the *Froyenvelt*'s last issue was in December 1903. By contrast, the *Fraynd*'s circulation would hit 100,000 by 1905; two years earlier, the combined circulation of all Russian Jewish periodicals had been a fifth of that. And an age of the popular press meant an age of Yiddish. A feuilleton Sholem Aleichem published early in 1903, "Jewish Newspapers and

Gazettes," depicted an abandoned Hebrew bemoaning her sunken lot; all her champions—Isaiah, Judah Halevi, Mapu—have vanished. Yiddish tries to comfort her, but is precisely the wrong person to do so; even the traditional Hebrew publishing companies and journals are publishing Yiddish books, pamphlets, or supplements.

And if anyone was poised to bestride the age, it was Sholem Aleichem. The year 1903 marked his twentieth anniversary as a Yiddish writer, and the young upstart had become the celebrated master. Tushiya's Yiddish arm, the Folksbildung (People's Education), did end up issuing his collected works, in four volumes, giving Sholem Aleichem the occasion—as would be the case with future collections—to prune and rewrite. Not a problem, since his voluminous output would need to be cut regardless for reasons of affordability and readability. The last few years had been particularly voluminous; with more and more paying venues to place work in, he had issued a regular torrent of material. As a result, 1903 had marked another turning point for Sholem Aleichem: the first time he could give up his business activities and attempt to make a living through writing alone, even if it meant selling off some furniture and moving to a more modest apartment. It was liberating: he felt "new born, with new, brand new strength," he wrote Spektor. "I can practically say that I'm just beginning to write." But it wasn't just the volume (and quality) of the stories that was solidifying Sholem Aleichem's position as the popular writer of the age. Like many another celebrity after him, Sholem Aleichem had begun to tour.

He had begun his public career around the turn of the century by giving readings at Zionist benefits in Kiev, Belaya Tserkov, and Berdichev; he described his performances as a kind of "compote" that would sweeten the overly dry speechifying that generally characterized the events. "God has given me the talent, as people recognize," he would write years later, "to read my work publicly—reading, I make the audience roll with laughter, while at the same time, I evoke more than one tear and more than one sigh over the horribly tragic and highly comic fate of my unfortunate brethren in the Russian ghetto."

Those first readings were also a chance to partner with and support a new friend and fellow artist, M. M. Warshawsky. Warshawsky, a lawyer Sholem Aleichem knew from Kiev, had a side effort in what we'd now call folk poetry: he authored the famous Yiddish song "Ofn Pripetshik." This kind of effort—to unearth, catalog, codify, and work in the veins of "folk culture"—wasn't just popular among Jews. In fact, some of the Jewish effort was clearly designed to counter increasingly ugly strains of Russian and Polish nationalism based on the concept of an inherent folk culture—that is, equating the "true" members of a state with "genuine" participants in a specific, rooted ethnic culture. Others, like Jews, need not apply. A possible counterargument was to insist on equality through demonstration of a vibrant and thus legitimate folk culture of their own; in recent years, an appeal to collect folk songs had generated much discussion in the Yiddish press, as did a noted concert of Yiddish folk songs in St. Petersburg in 1899. Sholem Aleichem's deepening interest in folk culture—a way to maintain his self-proclaimed bond with his people—could naturally combine with his long-term interest in music. Music, he claimed, was a deep and broad Jewish interest—"What Jew doesn't understand singing?" he wrote—and Warshawsky's songs, he felt, "reflect, as in clear water, the entire life of the Jewish people, with all the Jewish joys and sorrows." And so the evenings had cultural and aesthetic import for him as well. But finally, and certainly no less importantly, the tours helped him realize that such evenings could be profitable.

An early version of the money tour in the summer of 1902, visiting Jewish cities around the Pale to support the *Folkstsaytung*, was distasteful; Sholem Aleichem only agreed to do it because he had no financial choice. But it unquestionably gave him greater exposure and publicity. Helping the process along, the spread of photography meant newspapers were printing his picture. That summer he wrote his daughter Ernestina perturbed that a group had recognized him on the street from his photograph and forced him to hide in his hotel. (He also complained about the impossibility of buying back unflattering photos once they've been circulated, a complaint preceding the Web's invention by almost a century.) As throughout his literary career, his relationship with his readers, ideal and actual, was accordingly fraught: *Folktsaytung* sketches from 1903 featured devastating portraits of a simpering, ignorant, philistine reader who assaults him with a repetitive, annoying monologue ("My Reader") and an annoying, intrusive wealthy lover of his works who refuses to put his money where his mouth is to support publishing them ("My Fan").

As the years went on, he'd get more used to it, coming to embrace his celebrity and his public persona: by 1905, though still complaining about the circulation of badly reproduced photographs, he'd brag about receptions in one town ("What can I say about my reception in Brisk? It was a full-fledged triumph. Ovations without number. An accompaniment to the train station. Etc., etc.") and the hysteria in another (when his train was delayed, he writes, the unrest grew, the crowd shouting his name; eventually, he had to be paraded in the marketplace "so everyone could see and be convinced that Sholem Aleichem was no myth, no fantasy, but a reality"). Sholem Aleichem was becoming, thanks to appearances that had transformed from benefits into something more like rock concerts, a figure that hovered between reality and fantasy.

Of course, it came down to the writing, in the end; and the writing flowed in these years, copiously, for the waiting press and readership. There was the graphomania; and the delight in publishing; but anxiety, too. Sholem Aleichem understood the vagaries of the business, first and foremost that the papers might not always want what he was selling. Having learned to be leery of bubbles, he was aware of overconfidence about the market for his work; the diagnosis comes through in a novella he published in 1903, "The Merry Company," which told of an odd group drawn together by their involvement in various get-rich-quick schemes. One—a writer—articulates his scheme: consider the size of the Jewish reading public; multiply that number by the price of books; and sit back and count your money. If that wasn't enough, even Menakhem-Mendl got into the act. That year's "An Honorable Profession" returns our luckless hero to his earliest authorial roots, and the key, that clueless businessman writes to Sheyne-Sheyndl, is volume: "The paper wrote that it liked my writing and wanted more. If it was as good as the sample I sent, it would print it and pay me a kopeck a line . . . I sat down and figured out that in summer, when the days are long, I can knock out a thousand lines per day. That's a ten-spot right there—and there are thirty days in a month! Not bad, a starting salary of 300 rubles . . ." Menakhem-Mendl might not understand that the bubble would soon burst, but Sholem Aleichem could fear that it would: so better to write while the iron was still hot.

Sorting through Sholem Aleichem's work of these first few years of the twentieth century, then, isn't easy; the voluminous writing went in several directions, and untangling them will take a few chapters. But over and over again, in their separate ways, they all spoke to his attempt to make sense of Jewish life while creating specifically Jewish art: a grounded, deeply rooted set of works that spoke to an image of Jews, not as they were now or even had been, but how they saw their changing selves in their own imaginations and reflections.

Take, as a matter of introduction, two immensely popular folk stories Sholem Aleichem wrote, assuredly influenced by those debates around folk culture. "Folk stories," like Warshawsky's "folk poems," is a misnomer: Sholem Aleichem used the trappings of folk culture to create modern, complex, twentieth-century works of art. The first, flaunting its folk ties, appeared as a stand-alone volume, a "stylized chapbook" under the title "A Story Without an End" (though later, and better, known as "The Enchanted Tailor"). The eponymous tailor Shimon-Eli, we learn, had the impressive power to "take an old caftan and turn it into a cloak; then the cloak into a pair of trousers; of the trousers he could make a shirt; and of the shirt something else again." "Don't think that's such easy work," the narrator tells us, and he's right: the power of transformation—of folk material into modern literature, of Sholem Rabinovich into "Sholem Aleichem," of the Jews into Sholem Aleichem's picture of them—is hard and dangerous work.

Transformation is the story's central metaphor. Shimon-Eli, acquiescing to the insistence of his "Cossack of a woman" that they transform their lives by buying a milk-producing nanny goat in a nearby town, stops en route at a tavern operated by his cousin, who's annoyed by Shimon-Eli's sense of intellectual superiority. Returning home the same way after a successful purchase, the cousin plies Shimon-Eli with liquor . . . and somehow, the latter's triumphant return home is spoiled; he has, somehow, brought back a billy goat. Angrily returning to the next town (having once more stopped at the inn), Shimon-Eli calls the sellers to rabbinical court . . . to find that the billy goat has transformed into a nanny goat. Heading home, he consults his cousin at the inn, proposing dark magic may be at work . . . a sentiment only strengthened when the goat, once again, is revealed to be a billy goat. Shimon-Eli, increasingly terrified, haunted by old wives' tales of demonic beasts, goes mad; the town, less superstitious but no less suspicious, forms a mob to attack the other town, whom they suspect of fraud; and the goat itself escapes.

Compare the second "story without an end," written a few years later. "Eternal Life" features a student narrator venturing into the real world for the first time; at a "strangely solitary" tavern, he discovers a grieving family surrounding a woman's corpse. The young man offers his sleigh to take the body for burial preparations, and when they gratefully accept, offering him promises of eternal life, he suddenly "grew in stature before my own eyes, becoming what some people call a hero." Hubris, though—whether it's Menakhem-Mendl's sense of his business infallibility, Shimon-Eli's belief in his intellectual prowess, or this narrator's moral certitude—is the bubble that, in Sholem Aleichem's modern versions of these tales, is always burst. En route, the peasant-driven sleigh gets lost, he forgets the deceased's name (along with her husband's), and begins to fancy the corpse will awaken and speak. But unlike in a true folktale, the horrors visited upon Sholem Aleichem's heroes are perpetrated by humans, not ghosts and demons. The narrator, as he fears he might, does indeed lose his senses, but for a different reason: when he arrives at a town, his own offer of eternal life to the townspeople in return for assisting him with the body elicits reactions ranging from shrugs to skepticism to outright suspicion. The local burial society, with a threatening smile, rolls him for almost all the money he has on him (shades of Sholem Aleichem's own experience with his father-in-law), the police get involved—he's toting around a corpse, after all, with no burial papers—and he passes out during the interrogation. By the end, the wised-up narrator says: "Whenever anyone mentions Eternal Life, I run."

Sholem Aleichem lived up to his promises: neither story has much of an ending, if by an ending you mean a grand, punchy, neat conclusion. Both sort of peter out. But that discomfort, that uncertainty, is exactly the point. A traditional townsman the narrator meets asks him, "You are a young man representing Eternal Life? . . . See to it that people are prevented from dying of hunger and cold and *you* will win Eternal Life." Maybe the young, maskilic Sholem Aleichem would have ended the story there. But by this point his idealism had been tempered by experience and artistic growth; and the darker, more skeptical side of his work had reached its maturity. Depriving his audience of the ending, the betrayal of the writer's promise—to tell us how it all turns out, or, at least, what it all means—yanks away our security blanket as readers: the province of the best horror stories.

But the stories' sense of creeping terror and madness, the almost existential horror of a world haunted by ordinary evil, would also lead—as Sholem Aleichem's cyclical sensibility rotated around and around—to the necessary embrace of comedy and optimism. "'What is the moral of this tale?' the reader will ask," he wrote, in a revision to the ending of "The Enchanted Tailor" a decade after its first publication. "Don't press me, friends. It was not a good ending . . . And since you know the author of the story—that he is not naturally a gloomy fellow and hates to complain and prefers cheerful stories . . . let the maker of the tale take his leave of you smiling, and let him wish you, Jews—and all mankind—more laughter than tears. Laughter is good for you. Doctors prescribe laughter."

CHAPTER 14

In Which Our Hero Spends the Holidays with Us, Visits a Town He Has Created, and Fails to Get a Word in Edgewise

1900–1907

Maybe the best place to start talking about Sholem Aleichem's twentieth-century literature is with a story that puts time on notice right up front: a spooky little story called "The Clock," published in the new century's first year. The clock, an ancient inheritance that has proudly kept the time for generations, suddenly begins striking thirteen times rather than twelve; attempts to fix it result in its making bizarre sounds. The decision is finally made to weight the mechanism further—and the clock soon collapses under the extra weight. Sholem Aleichem was notably superstitious, claiming to see spirits around the house, and he particularly hated the number thirteen; but "The Clock"'s genuine uncanniness—like in "The Enchanted Tailor," or "Eternal Life"—isn't from intimations of the supernatural. Rather, it's from the sense that the old, metronomic order has come loose; that attempts to fix it merely reveal its strains and stresses; that the weights of the modern condition, all the attempts to modernize, synthesize, harmonize, are simply cues to destruction. A disturbing proposition, to say the least. If the previous year's Tevye story, with its emphasis on the children of today and a daughter named "Little Time," suggested the uncomfortable pull of progress, Sholem Aleichem was also well aware of the impossibility of stasis.

He found a natural platform to explore these questions of time, progress, and tradition: the Jewish holidays, which were, and remain, powerful markers of Jewish time and historical and cultural memory. Though he himself didn't keep a strictly observant household, he combined, not unusually, that lack of ritual observance with strong feelings about religious traditions and customs: so, for example, he always celebrated the Seder with great gusto, and prepared the house fastidiously and energetically for the Passover holiday. Others shared his sentiments; so it seemed, at least, from the frequent special theme or holiday issues of journals and newspapers—meaning that a designated "holiday story," using widely known customs and traditions to make symbolic points, had an excellent chance at publication. Certainly an additional argument in their favor for the cash-strapped author. Looking at Sholem Aleichem's Jewish year in holiday stories over those first few years is remarkedly illustrative.

Start with Passover, probably the Jewish holiday most naturally disposed to discussing changing Jewish history and fate. Sometimes the stories, following the line in the Haggadah, suggest continuity, that every generation, including those of his characters', is the same as those before them: 1903's "Home for Passover," for example, equates Fishel the *melamed*'s travails to return to his family—including crossing the torrential river Bug—with the Exodus and traversal of the Red Sea. But the story's triumphant ending, which echoes the comforting and comfortable promises of a traditional Jewish reading of history, isn't the only kind of Passover story Sholem Aleichem tells. "Discomforting" may be the best word for 1900's "In Haste," a Passover story featuring Menakhem-Mendl; the story is shocking in how quickly it alters a basic convention of a by now well-established character. He's still a failed businessman (this time in matchmaking); but this story sees him actually returning home to wife and family. But in doing so, he finds no promised land: mocked by his fellow townsmen, scorned by his wife and mother-in-law, the Seder is ruined. Probably realizing the character's success relied on iron-clad adherence to the formula, Sholem Aleichem kept the story out of Menakhem-Mendl's "canonical" adventures, but the story's real danger issues not from its variation, but from its insistence that the promised homeland may not be all it's dreamed to be.

If the future looked worrisome, the solution might lie in sketching the past. "Four Goblets," a 1900 revision of a sketch he had published in the *Folksblat* a dozen years before, expands the original satiric narrative (a wine seller's boast of how he rooked Passover customers seeking to fulfill the Seder ritual of drinking four cups of wine by passing off homemade productions as expensive foreign vintages) by placing it in the childhood recollection of an adult narrator, the distance allowing meanness to be replaced with fondness (the wine seller is revealed as incompetent at best and as a kind of folk trickster at worst) and providing an opportunity for an older, more uncertain author to smile at human frailty. But the past's consolations, as it turns out, reflect uneasily on the present condition. The episode's real power, the narrator suggests, lies in its demonstration of children's (and adults') familiarity with and knowledge of the many details of Passover law and custom; he explicitly contrasts them to today's children, whom he characterizes, using the language of the Haggadah's Four Sons, as "those who are unable to ask." Despite—or perhaps because of—their acculturated and cosmopolitan educations, he argues, they have only the vaguest idea of what Passover is. Two years later, Sholem Aleichem used the language of the Four Questions to castigate parents for failing to teach Jewish history and culture, writing, "Why have you taught us all languages, old and new, but there's one language you've forgotten to teach us—our own Jewish language? The language in which the Torah was written, the language in which the prophets spoke, the language in which there is, they say, a fine, great, rich literature?"

Passover wasn't the only holiday Sholem Aleichem pressed into service on this point: 1901's "What Is Chanukah?" sees the Yiddish writer "Solomon Naumovitch Sholem Aleichem" attending a card party to celebrate the holiday at the house of an extremely Russified gentleman, a man strongly attracted to markers of traditional Jewish culture, especially

Jewish food, rather than traditional observance or historical or textual knowledge. Gambling is the order of the day at the card party, and the author's narrating alter ego takes a bet of his own: that among the Chanukah party's fifty or so attending Jews there will be one who knows the holiday's origins and meaning. It turns out to be a hard bet to win. The story culminates with the appearance of a small boy—presumably this society's future—whose knowledge of all Jewish custom is best described as incoherent mishmash. And Purim, with its attendant commandment of memory (never to forget Amalek's attempts to destroy Israel; Haman is understood to be Amalek's descendant), becomes a natural moment to reflect on vanishing traditional and cultural memory: a celebrant ironically discovers that the time of merriment saddens him, in a 1900 feuilleton, because he remembers "the Purim of years gone by . . . [and sees] our old Jewish customs, which disappear little by little among the Jews and become defunct . . . especially among us in Yehupetz and in all the big cities." Though these may seem like very recent concerns, Sholem Aleichem wrote this at the very beginning of the twentieth century.

And he had reason to do so. His son-in-law noted that Sholem Aleichem's own children, raised in the Russified precincts of Kiev, didn't receive a traditional Jewish education—which certainly meant that they had, at best, a complicated relationship to the more allusive and esoteric references in their father's work. And, perhaps, not only the esoteric parts: even Yiddish, that most basic part of Sholem Aleichem's literary identity, was passing as well. Most of his letters to his children were written in Russian. But the anxieties in Sholem Aleichem's work offer their own solution. When "Purim"'s feuilletonist longs for his childhood *kheyder* days, with his grager and the taste of hamantashen, with Purim players and gifts given and received, he was replacing ritual and observance with ritualized acts of memory writing and observation; casting the old days and the old country as passing if not past, setting the shtetl in a fine and folksy utopian world, he was offering the recollection of that world as its own substitute. Reading holiday stories was, in its own way, holiday observance; celebrating past tradition was becoming its own means of traditional ritual, in a world more and more divorced from the daily flows of Jewish time and space.

Of course, Sholem Aleichem was too honest an artist to present the old world as anything simple, simplistic, or pure; in much the same way, his portraits of childhood were hardly simon-pure, but rather characterized it as a complex combination of churning and often dangerous emotions. This hadn't changed much since "The Penknife" had appeared over a decade before, and 1900's "The Flag" treads similar territory; both stories feature children's strong yearnings for the title object and end with powerful displays of loss, guilt, or both. "The Flag"'s flag, though, befitting Sholem Aleichem's new, more communal interests, is an object of ritual and cultural importance, not precisely a national standard, but not unrelated, either. Waving it during the holiday of Simchat Torah, complete with apple and candle stuck into the flagpole, is a sheer delight—until one of the other children whose flag is inferior jealously touches his candle to the narrator's flag, and that's that. Petty jealousy that leads to internal strife and self-destructiveness: an apt description of Sholem Aleichem's Jewish politics, best expressed in another of his greatest creations—one that serves up another vision of a vanishing world in the author's inimitable fashion.

Abramovitch, Sholem Aleichem's literary mentor, had often favored allegory to make his political points: his 1873 novel *The Nag* satirized the contemporary Jewish political position—both the downtrodden Jewish populace and the failure of the liberal right-thinkers of the Haskala—by creating a broken-down horse that had formerly been a Jewish prince and the student-turned-madman who hears his story. Sholem Aleichem tried a few animal allegories of his own, but "Rabchik: A Jewish Dog" and "Methuselah: A Jewish Horse"—each stressing the point that as bad as things are out there among strangers, it's worse among one's own—are deeply unsubtle failures. His weakness in working with pure allegory makes sense, contrasting as it did with his long-standing desire for the literary and political effect derived from grounding his stories in recognizable reality. At the same time, though, his developing creative sensibility was transcending the straightforwardly satiric approach of his youth: works like "The Intercepted Letters" and *Sketches from Berdichev Street* were *too* specific and familiar, largely limited to lampooning specific individual archetypes rather than taking on the community more generally.

Now he was ready to change that, and the title of the series of sketches he began to publish in 1901—"Berdichev *Entire*"—bespoke this broader view. Berdichev, of course, was a real city. But Sholem Aleichem's developing literary sensibility—along with at least one angry letter from a Berdichev citizen who didn't want his town picked on—made limiting his points to a specific, recognizable place problematic, and the stories' setting was changed from Berdichev to Kasrilevke, an unforgettable locale of Sholem Aleichem's invention that would help fashion the shtetl's image for generations of readers.

Fools' towns were old business in Jewish, Yiddish, and Russian folklore and literature: think, for example, of the citizens of Chelm, who tried to catch moonlight in a barrel; or of Abramovitch's Glupsk, or Foolstown, which harnessed conventional folly to maskilic critique. Paupervilles and Hypocrisyvilles made regular appearances in early Haskala Hebrew and Yiddish literature. Kasrilevke had features of all of these—its name, based on the Hebrew for "God is my crown" or "God surrounds and supports me," was modeled on another town of Abramovitch's invention, Kabtsiel (something like "God reduces me to poverty"). But Kasrilevke differed from these earlier creations. Perhaps it was its grounded origins: Berdichev, mixed with, on the evidence of his memoir, his boyhood home of Voronkov. But maybe it was because the stories—which he felt "encompass[ed] our provincial Jewish life so widely, from all sorts of revealing viewpoints"—took a broader, and more empathetic, view.

Even his explanation of the name took the sting out of Abramovitch's approach. There were many words for paupers and failures, Sholem Aleichem wrote, but a *kasril* or *kasrilik* is "not just an ordinary pauper, a failure in life. On the contrary, he is a man who has not allowed poverty to degrade him. He laughs at it. He is poor, but cheerful." The previous year, he'd praised the protagonists of Warshawsky's folk songs as "happy paupers" and for the most part "great men of faith, [who] lovingly accept all of their travails, both from above and from man"; similarly, the Kasrilevkans never give up, writes their creator, and they live so much in the halls of tradition and hallowed memory that their cemeteries are the objects of particular pride. Given Sholem Aleichem's attempt to cast himself as the people's artist, it's hardly surprising that he soon nominated himself as an honorary representative of *Homo kasrilevkus*, writing that "my muse . . . is, like all the folk of Kasrilevke, a merry soul, poor but merry" and asserting a year later that "I myself am a Kasrilevkite[, b]orn and bred" until he "set [his] little ship adrift in the great and tempestuous sea of life."

Adrift: despite being *from* Kasrilevke, Sholem Aleichem's narrator isn't *of* it, whatever its attractions may be. Though he's unafraid to wallow in luxuriant, sepia-toned description—an Anatevka *avant la lettre*, "stuck away in a corner of the world . . . remote from the noise and bustle, the confusion and tumult and greed, which men have created about them and have dignified with high-sounding names like progress, culture, civilization"—like with the holiday stories, the Kasrilevke tales themselves prove how false that characterization is. The town, it turns out, is a perfect venue to reflect the jarring transpositions of old and new, traditional and modern—and to make some points about Jewish politics and the art of Jewish comedy on the way.

The town's geography should warn anyone. The streets, built without any plan, "twist and turn uphill and downhill and suddenly end up in a house or a cellar or just a hole in the ground . . . If you are a stranger, never go out alone at night without a lantern." Kasrilevke is twisty, very twisty; unexpected surprises lurk around corners. For one thing, the town is full of criminals. Kasrilevke sausage occasionally boasts a nail or two thrown in to cheat customers on the weight; a house on fire is automatically assumed to have been burned down for the insurance money; a visiting "Sholem Aleichem" encounters thieves who casually engage him in a business conversation as they threaten him with a kitchen knife. But Kasrilevke's greatest danger, to itself more than to others, lies not in its criminals but in its talk.

Mockery is the Kasrilevkans' default mode of communication, at which they're "the most roguish practitioners on earth . . . a Kasrilevkite would walk ten miles, lose a day's work, and practically risk life and limb—all for the sake of one good jibe." But such smart talk, in the end, such a Jewish satiric, skeptical sensibility, is too clever by half. It's hardly a program for progress, and indeed imperils the Jewish future: Kasrilevkans "scorn the cleverest inventions of the day," making sport of scientists', scholars', and thinkers' efforts to improve the lot of the people, "and not in subdued tones or in secret either." But the Kasrilevkan mockery goes even further, to take on that warm view of the Jewish past, of the shtetl itself. One of Sholem Aleichem's masterpieces tells the tale.

"The Search" (1902) concerns a wealthy stranger who joins a Kasrilevkan congregation for Yom Kippur prayer. As the fast ends, he shouts, alarmed: knowing no one in town, he has safeguarded his funds by slipping them into his prayer stand—and now all 1,800 rubles are gone. A search commences. Everyone, even the sainted Reb Yosifl, turns out their pockets: the only holdout is the local rich man's son-in-law, who has a sour reputation for brilliance in Kasrilevke. He's finally searched by force to reveal, not the missing money, but moist plum pits and chicken bones, clear evidence he has eaten on the holy fast day. Though Reb Yosifl, a recurring character in the Kasrilevke stories and the closest thing the town has to a conservative moral conscience, turns away in shame, "the rest of us, hungry as we were, we could not stop talking about it all the way home. We rolled with laughter in the streets." The story's last line informs us that the money has disappeared without a trace; but what's truly forever vanished is the myth of intellectual and moral perfection the son-in-law represented—and robbed of this treasure, tragicomically, Kasrilevke only mocks.

And yet, this destructive power of Kasrilevkans gives them another power: to shrug off, not to say ignore, history. This can, in Sholem Aleichem's darker moods, be played to illustrate the pathology of Jewish self-destructiveness. After a fire burns down Kasrilevke, its citizens, after much talk, decide to go begging; though their journey leads to their imprisonment, and their eventual release stems in no small part from their pathetic natures (following the pattern of the Abramovitch masterwork "The Travels of Benjamin III"), they retell the disaster in their own imaginations as a heroic adventure story. For the Kasrilevkans, in short, loud, raucous talking, in which you create the truth you believe as it leaves your lips, has the power to outwit history.

And it was a time when history needed some outwitting. Sholem Aleichem's sense of modern times was profoundly tempered by the continuation of old, ugly anti-Semitic trends: and like many other Zionists, most notably Theodor Herzl, he had been deeply affected by one particular example, the Dreyfus affair. The case of the French officer whose arrest, conviction for treason, imprisonment on Devil's Island, retrial, reconviction, and subsequent exoneration over the course of twelve years sparked a public furor and opened fault lines about anti-Semitism throughout Western European society was, to put it mildly, a subject of some discussion among Yiddish-speaking Jews. "Who of you all hasn't read about that amazing trial?" Sholem Aleichem wrote in one of his Zionist pamphlets. "Who among you has been indifferent to the injustice committed before our eyes now at the end of the nineteenth century?" To opine on the Dreyfus affair was to present one's view of Jewish politics and Jewish history. Writers like Chaim Dov Hurwitz and Yankev Dinezon, writing in *Der Yid*, issued thundering proclamations calling for "common Jewish action against anti-Semitism" or asserting that "all the limbs on the Jewish body politic remain vitally interconnected, flowing with blood and energy in spite of all the abuse the body had endured." Sholem Aleichem would take a different, more nuanced tack.

As in "Zelig Mechanic," he was particularly interested in the gap between high affairs of state and their transmogrification in the eyes of the general Jewish public. Once again he was following in Abramovitch's footsteps: the older writer had flayed Jews who sat around the bathhouse stove fighting their own Boer War, moving armies and navies around while displaying ignorance and passivity when it came to their own actual circumstances. But Abramovitch's approach was more straightforwardly satiric: Sholem Aleichem's balance between criticism and empathy led to something far greater. Though he had previously used Dreyfus as a throwaway joke in earlier work, by 1902, the rapidly maturing writer used his thinking about Kasrilevke—and the dangers and opportunities their power of talk represented—to take on the big topic directly.

In "It Cannot Be!," better known by its later title of "Dreyfus in Kasrilevke," Kasrilevkans' hunger for Dreyfus news—and their intensive commentary when they get it—demonstrates the truth of the *Der Yid* writers' claim of the intense connection between these small-town Jews and the French captain half a world away. But the story's kicker comes at its end, when the newspaper reader reports that Dreyfus has been found guilty again:

> "It cannot be!" Kasrilevke shouted with one voice. "Such a verdict is impossible! Heaven and earth swore that the truth must prevail. What kinds of lies are you telling us!"
>
> "Fools!" shouted Zeidel, and thrust the paper into their faces. "Look! See what the paper says!"
>
> "Paper! Paper!" shouted Kasrilevke. "And if you stood with one foot in heaven and the other on earth, would we believe you?"
>
> "Such a thing must not be. It must never be! Never! Never!"
>
> And—who was right?

A typical Kasrilevkan reaction, to attack their own messenger, not the message. But still: what mattered was not that Kasrilevke was right on the facts (though they couldn't possibly have known that at the time); what mattered is that somehow their assertions made it so in the Yiddish landscape Sholem Aleichem was creating. Kasrilevke, balanced between reality and imagination, was becoming a homeland where Jewish talking was Jewish power—and Sholem Aleichem himself was both skeptically ironic about, and idealistically enchanted with, his creation.

But the Kasrilevkans weren't Sholem Aleichem's only talkers of the period. His contemplation of the relationship between power and talking marked a third major creative development in his writing during this same, critical period: his mastery of an unusual form, the monologue.

He'd always championed the swoops and idiosyncracies of the individual voice, first as a sign of plausible, realistic characters—he had attacked Shomer for the incomprehensible and unlikely half-German Yiddish his characters spoke. But his increased interest in folk culture and expression made the monologue form even more compelling; and in a literary world where talk is power, the monologue is a powerful weapon.

How so? First, Sholem Aleichem's monologues, almost by definition, are actually one-sided dialogues: they exist in relationship to someone else, a listener, and their continuation depends on ensuring that that listener doesn't get a word in edgewise. Even Tevye's like this, buttonholing "Sholem Aleichem" whenever he runs into him. Of course, Sholem Aleichem gets his revenge at having his ear talked off by printing Tevye's stories, despite Tevye's repeated requests that he not do so. On the other hand, if Tevye were really so upset about it, you'd think he'd stop talking to Sholem Aleichem. On still another hand, maybe he doesn't read the journals or newspapers the stories are published in . . . The multiplying hands testify to the narrative complexity Sholem Aleichem reveled in.

The monologue's an aggressive genre, in other words: the speaker satisfying his or her own needs at the expense of the listener, who lies helpless beneath the constant, punishing pressure, physical and psychological, of their breathless, unceasing delivery. Think of the classic language of stand-up comedy, that monologic art par excellence: I killed 'em. I slayed 'em. Unsurprising, then, that monologue and comedy—with Sholem Aleichem as exhibit A—have often been claimed as the Jewish counterattack to history's depredations; this is how Jews fight back, with, you know, a really vicious one-liner. More vociferous forms of opposition may be impossible, but you can talk at the problem, around it, suffocate it or minimize it or redefine it in a torrent of words.

The difference between talking at and talking around, it should be said, is the crucial thing that sets Sholem Aleichem's monologues apart from most stand-up. A Chris Rock or a Lenny Bruce generally gets his point across by simply making it. That's a satirist's approach, and Sholem Aleichem, no mean satirist himself in his early years, did much the same, but even then there were hints of things to come. Speaking with "Sholem

Aleichem" in *Sketches from Berdichev Street*, one character says: "I talk and I *talk* and I talk and I talk and talk fit to burst, but, damn it, I forget to mention precisely the main point!" When asked what that point was, he replies, "I'll tell you and I won't tell you." Yes, he's trying to be delicate (there's a local rumor that Sholem Aleichem has converted), but that coachman's approach would blossom in the mature monologues: talking around, underneath, and over the point can simultaneously obscure—and reveal—painful truths about politics, history, and life to the discerning reader.

Take the female narrator of 1902's "Geese," a goose seller who continually rehearses the rabbinic saying that "a woman was made with nine measures of talk." But Sholem Aleichem refuses to let us dismiss what she has to say as merely the stereotypical honking and gabbling of dismissible womankind. Superficially, the monologue is dedicated to sharing the merchant's not insubstantial professional knowledge; but what clearly emerges in the subtext is the narrator's searing critique of her gender's subordinate social position to weak, unproductive men—and her inchoate mindfulness of her own guilt in perpetuating the system. "So I sit and pluck," she says, toward her monologue's end. "I have a little help, too. Girls aren't boys, you know. Boys go to school. But what do girls do? Girls are like a bunch of geese; they sit at home, eat, and wait to grow up." And then, of course, comes the slaughter.

"Geese" is a sober reminder that, as with Kasrilevke, Sholem Aleichem had learned that the lethality of Jewish talking was all too often aimed inward, at Jews themselves. His first great monologue, 1901's "The Pot," was dedicated to the lesson. He had found precisely the right occasion to plausibly report an older, traditional woman's long speech: the rabbinic consultation, where authoritative legal decision is sought on a question of Jewish life and law—here, whether or not the titular pot is kosher. The answer, naturally, depends on the circumstances, and in the woman's attempt to explicate them, she provides a freewheeling tour of her grievances and sorrows, and her pugnacious stance against her situation. The fragile pot, in its teetering state—if found non-kosher, it may need to be shattered—clearly emerges for the reader, as the monologue unspools, as a stand-in for her sickly, fragile son, a yeshiva student who embodies the manifold concerns about Jewish manhood, power, and the Jewish condition writ large. Is it usable, productive? Or will it shatter? Faced with these grand stakes—to say nothing of their maker's overwhelming moral and existential claims concerning her long-deceased husband, precarious financial circumstances, unpleasant boarders, and hard childhood—it's no wonder it's the *listener*, the reader's stand-in, who runs out of breath and succumbs, swooning to the floor. The narrator, at least, has the therapeutic defense of talking; the audience has no such comfort.

Sholem Aleichem wasn't the only Jew at the time who was thinking about a talking cure; whether or not he was familiar with Freud's work directly, he was increasingly drawing on similar concepts. "A White Bird," for example, written in a week in the late summer of 1904, is a masterpiece of sublimation, where the monologist, discussing her hankering for a white hen to perform the *kapores* ceremony before Yom Kippur, unconsciously reveals the bird to be a symbol of the halcyon, romantic days of her own romance, now vanished. But if Freud offered the prospect of powerful speech—that talk would actually cure human conditions— Sholem Aleichem's own natural skepticism, about his chosen profession and its capacity to effect change, expressed itself through doubting such procedures and, ultimately, his own efforts.

Three years after "A White Bird," psychology's claims of power would meet their match in another masterpiece, "Three Widows." The monologist—"an old bachelor, an irascible man"—puts the field on notice from his earliest words: "You're sadly mistaken, my dear sir . . . You think because you're sitting here in this room, cigar in mouth and book in hand, you know it all; you've probed deep into the soul and you've got all the answers. Especially since, with the good Lord's help, you've hit upon the right word—psychology." The monologue provides a double joke. The first is the monologist's narrative itself, a family situation so tortuously constructed it would torment the most hair-splitting Talmudists, to say nothing of orthodox Freudians—since in it, the most basic stuff of Freudian psychology is laid right out on the page. (A full plot summary would take too long: suffice it to say that the old bachelor in question, over a series of sessions, tells the story of his romantically charged relationships with a widow, the widow's daughter, *and* the widow's granddaughter.) But the second, more important one is the grouchy bachelor's mastery of the monologue form, and, with it, the situation. The listener—a modern gentleman, maybe a doctor himself—is apparently skeptical at first, annoyed with both the bachelor's seeming digressions and his unwillingness to put things in clinical terms. But, as the sessions continue, the power transfers to the bachelor: "Why'd I let you wait so long? Because I wanted to. When I tell a story, I tell it when *I* want to tell it, not when *you* want to hear it. It's obvious you want to hear it pretty badly." And in the end, the bachelor walks out on the listener as the three widows call him to lunch, asking, "Well, what have you got to say now? Where's your psychology?" Stories beat explanations, every time, and have a lonely power that is no more or less than their own selves.

But if that's so—and this must have truly haunted Sholem Aleichem—then what kind of power do they have, after all? As he does with so many similarly bitter speculations, he turns the joke on himself. In "A Bit of Advice," "Sholem Aleichem" is confronted by a persistent visitor, an alternate version of himself—another young man who's married a rich man's daughter (though here family troubles have replaced financial ones: she's making eyes at a visiting doctor). Cowed by his visitor's stream of verbiage, "Sholem Aleichem" finally snaps: "I lunged for the odd creature's throat, pressed him to the wall, and screamed in an unearthly voice: 'Divorce her, you hear, you bastard! Divorce her, divorce . . .' . . . I spotted my cadaverous face in the mirror and hardly recognized myself." Though superficially testament to the power of the monologue—it drives the listener to practically homicidal action—in the end, the joke is more subtle: Sholem Aleichem, facing "Sholem Aleichem" facing the mirror, has essentially cut us out of the picture: as it turns out, he's just talking to himself.

And so the question of whether, or how, artful literature could have political effect would continue to preoccupy Sholem Aleichem, even as the modern Jewish politics of the tsarist regime were taking a fatal turn.

CHAPTER 15

In Which Our Hero Confronts
Pogroms and Politics

1900–1905

No one expected so many murders.

The vicious articles in the *Bessarabian*, the local newspaper, accusing Jews of a variety of crimes, certainly boded ill; and no one had forgotten the waves of violence decades earlier. But when a murdered child turned up in the months before Passover, even though it soon became clear a relative had done the deed, the press seized the opportunity to exhume the old blood libel and insinuate the murder had been committed by Jews to use the victim's blood in their matzah. (One of the editors, Pavolachi Krushevan, would later be instrumental in disseminating the *Protocols of the Elders of Zion*.) But it was Jewish blood that flowed in the streets of the Bessarabian capital of Kishinev on April 6 and 7, 1903, forty-nine Jews dead and hundreds wounded, along with massive property damage. Small numbers viewed through the prism of the blood-stained decades to come; but at the time they sent shock waves through Jewish and non-Jewish communities alike. This time, unlike in 1881, Russian writers denounced the pogrom, writers like Tolstoy and Gorky; and Sholem Aleichem, looking for an opportunity to help the pogrom victims, decided to involve Russian writers in a Yiddish project.

This wasn't as unlikely as it might seem at first glance: Gorky and

Sholem Aleichem had attempted to collaborate previously. The noted socialist had demonstrated his commitment to progressive causes throughout his career, earning even greater left-wing credibility when Tsar Nicholas II, dismayed at his constant criticism of the regime, had annulled his election to the Academy of Literature, sparking a furor among the Russian intelligentsia. He linked his philo-Semitism to this love for social justice, going so far as to write in 1900 that the Jews "may proudly claim to have been the first ferment that, working through the words of their prophets, forcefully and successfully awakened the idea of social justice" and that the "wisdom of Hillel has been a great comfort to me all my life." Maybe that was why, in a historical moment marked by increasing ethnocentrism, he had moved in the other direction, proposing to Sholem Aleichem in 1901 that they put together an anthology of Yiddish literature in Russian translation. The Yiddish writer had jumped at the chance, offering to assist with the Russian translations and drawing up lists of possible selections (including his own Kasrilevke stories). He'd been working on the project for years—translating, providing assistance with individual writers' biographical details, envisioning the illustrations by the famous Berlin Jewish artist Ephraim Moshe Lilien, who'd even traveled to Russia to visit Gorky and discuss the project—when the pogrom broke out in Kishinev.

The idea was simple, but powerful: Sholem Aleichem would edit a second anthology, for the *Folksbildung*, with proceeds going to support Kishinev victims (along with those of Homel, where pogromists had struck in September of that year). Getting the Russian writers on board was both a financial and an ideological necessity, and by early summer he had reached out to Tolstoy, Chekhov, and V. G. Korolenko, asking for either original contributions or previously published works he would translate into Yiddish himself. He also solicited their written responses to those "most despicable acts, incited by evil men like Krushevan and his ilk, which were perpetrated at the time of the 'resplendent' holy day in the capital city of Kishinev."

Korolenko offered a story, "At Night," for translation. Chekhov confessed he was writing "nothing at all, or very little," due to illness (in fact, he would die the next year), but granted permission to translate some older materials; for whatever reason, nothing appeared in the final version. But the most positive response came from Tolstoy, who'd already written a widely circulated open letter damning the church and the government bureaucracy for inflaming the hatred that had catalyzed the pogroms. He wrote Sholem Aleichem that the "terrible abomination which has occurred in Kishinev has sickened and shocked me. . . . I will be very happy to contribute to your anthology and will strive to write something fitting to the circumstances." He came through with a publishing bonanza: three original "Oriental" stories, which were set to appear simultaneously in Russian, Yiddish, German, and English. Sholem Aleichem's gratitude to Tolstoy would be everlasting: after the Russian author's death, he wrote that unlike so many of his compatriots, Tolstoy had not only spoken out against "the greatest injustice, the terrifying cruelty, that has been committed in his country with several million unfortunate creatures of my unfortunate brethren," but that he understood Jews, unlike "our Russian geniuses, like Gogol, Turgenev, Dostoevsky and others [about whom] I do not speak," who "knew Jews, I'm afraid to say, the way I know Martians."

Production of *Help: An Anthology for Literature and Art* didn't run smoothly; there were problems with the censors, and concerns that Tolstoy's stories would appear without authorization before the anthology's publication. (Sholem Aleichem went into fits when one of the stories appeared in Russian, and, what's worse, not in Tolstoy's original Russian but in a back-translation from a leaked French version.) But the anthology eventually appeared toward the end of the year, complete with Tolstoy's and Korolenko's stories, along with a who's who of Hebrew and Yiddish literature: Abramovitch, Frishman, Ravnitski, Spektor, Lilienblum, Ben-Ami, Berdichevsky, Yehoyesh, Reyzen—most if not all Sholem Aleichem's friends, acquaintances, or collaborators. His own contribution, "One Hundred and One," took its title from the number of towns barred to Jewish settlement under the May Laws, permitted once again by the tsar after Kishinev; the story's plot, though—in which a former resident of one town, after years of effort to return, goes mad when his hard-fought legal victory is rendered insignificant by virtue of the restoration—reminded the reader that the maliciously capricious nature of life under the tsarist regime was, at best, a mug's game.

But what were the other options? Yes, Sholem Aleichem on occasion descended into understandable pathos. A child narrator in a story written that year mused, "Does not our teacher himself tell us that all creatures are dear to the Lord? . . . then why do the people slaughter cows and calves and sheep and fowl every day of the week? And not only cows and other animals and fowls, but do not men slaughter one another? At the time when we had the pogrom, did not men throw down little children from the tops of houses? Did they not kill our neighbors' little girl?" The children's story was a particularly useful vehicle to suggest Jewish impotence in the face of anti-Semitic depredation. In a story written just after Kishinev, a young protagonist succumbs to his violent impulses while out gathering greens for the Shavuot holiday, and begins violently attacking the plants. " 'Vengeance,' I shouted without ceasing, 'vengeance.' I will have my revenge of you for all the Jewish blood that was spilled . . . for the Jews who fell in the past, and those who are falling today." The child's violence is both comic and tragically futile, and the critique was only sharpened in the fanciful allegory "Kapores" from that same year. There, the eponymous birds go on strike, refusing to submit to the degradations of being violently whirled over Jews' heads for purposes of atonement. Their comic attempts to parley with the townspeople, though, sidestep the main issue: that the human community kills and eats them with impunity. Impotence is bad enough, but willed impotence is worse.

And what makes things even worse than *that* is the seductive power of the Jewish imagination, something Sholem Aleichem had been gnawing at since his earliest writing. The *kheyder* students in 1887's "Lag Ba'omer" attempt to escape their terrifying teacher by heading to the hills and fields on the holiday, armed only with stories of Jewish strength and fantastic imaginations, in which, as he wrote in a letter, "trees were people, girls were princesses, rich men princes; grass, armies; and thorns and nettles turned into Philistines, Edom and Moab." Imaginative power is hardly identical to real power, though, and the difference leads to disaster: picturing the local villagers as Philistines, the young boys go soldiering off to fight them—only to be overwhelmingly assaulted by peasants and village children. Putting imagination in the dock was pretty close to saying that literature didn't offer any clues to a solution, Sholem Aleichem's anthological efforts notwithstanding. But his more considered response to the pogroms, authored two years later, tackled the question with the complexity that characterized his finest works.

In "Two Anti-Semites," Max Berlliant (who, as his name implies, is not quite brilliant), a traveling salesman and willfully assimilating Jew, has been assigned the Kishinev region, Bessarabia. Though he's tried to keep as much distance as possible between himself and other Jews, Kishinev has greatly affected Max, and he knows that in traveling the region, "he was bound to meet people in these parts eager to talk about the pogroms . . . to listen to the wails and groans of those who had lost their near and dear, and . . . to endure the righteous exhortations and malicious remarks of the Gentiles." He hits on a plan: to hide behind the pages of the *Bessarabian*, the anti-Semitic newspaper that had fanned Kishinev's flames, figuring the sight will drive away both Jews (out of disgust) and non-Jews (out of boredom). The plan works like a charm—until another Jew enters, twigs immediately to what's happening, and gets his *own* copy of the *Bessarabian*. Max awakens from uneasy dreams to discover the man opposite him: "Our Max is amazed and bewildered. It seems to him that it's he himself who is stretched out on the seat opposite, and he can't understand the logic of how he, Max, can possibly be lying there. How can a man see his reflection without a mirror?" Eventually, they identify each other: when the other man begins whistling Warshawsky's "Ofn Pripetshik," Max joins in, and then they both sing together.

The story—a version of Avrom Goldfaden's famous Yiddish play *The Two Kuni-Lemls*, whose culminating scene has a Hasid confront a maskil impersonating him who then convinces the (moronic) original that *he's* the ringer—thinks about the way in which, decades before Sartre, the anti-Semite reveals the Jew. But more important, it's a story about the power and impotence of literature—the *Bessarabian*, comically minimized from the inciter of mobs to a nuisance repellent—and the unpredictable nature of its success—working precisely the opposite of how it was intended, identifying fellow Jews, not anti-Semites. In the end, it's true, Berlliant reclaims his Jewishness, but by singing folk songs. The newspapers have been thrown aside. Shades of Sholem Aleichem's own experience: that original anthology with Gorky, the one he'd spent so much time on because, as he wrote after Kishinev, "one of the most useful and necessary things for Jews now is to make the nations acquainted with the Jews and their situation, which can be achieved only by translating our literary work in toto"—the anthology, in the end, never seems to have been released.

What about more active solutions? Kishinev led other writers to create wrathful, damning art questioning Jewish passivity and Jewish politics, most notably the Hebrew poet Hayyim Nachman Bialik's "In the City of Slaughter," which flayed Jews for their quietude during the pogrom and the Jewish way of life for creating that passivity. Sholem Aleichem, of course, shared Bialik's Zionist approach; but his explicitly Zionist writings over the previous few years had increasingly contained a touch of the Kasrilevke about them, betraying his concern that the business as usual of Jewish politics would vitiate a promising, and perhaps even increasingly necessary, approach to the problem. "Lunatics" (1900), a contribution to the official Zionist Organization paper *Di Velt*, and its sequel of sorts, "The Little Red Jews," applied his current preoccupations with folklore and small-town Jewish politics to his beloved movement. In the Jewish collective imagination (and, among many Jews then, belief), the "Red Jews," a subsection of the Ten Lost Tribes, live in a kingdom of their own beyond the impassable river Sambatyon—impassable because it vomits up rocks six days a week and, though it rests on the Sabbath, to ford it then would violate Jewish law—thus creating an equally impossible barrier.

Despite having their own kingdom, the Red Jews, surprisingly, become symbols of Diaspora Jewry. (Maybe because, unlike Kasrilevke, they provide an old satirist the opportunity to reflect reality through a fun-house mirror, rather than try to accommodate it to realism.) Their problems with Zionism are familiar ones to those observing the Eastern European landscape: it's not that they're anti-Zionist, just that their embrace of older customs means their visiting representative views the cosmopolitan, modernizing, and self-confident ways of European Zionists as the mark of the title's lunacy. The kingdom beyond the Sambatyon becomes a symbol of stasis, of tradition in the most hidebound sense: exactly like the Kasrilevkans when it comes to standing athwart progress, incapable of seeing the solution when it stands before their eyes. And if they do see it, logorrhea and argumentation preempt any actual progress. "Those Red Little Jews—as long as they keep quiet they're all right," writes Sholem Aleichem. "But when they start talking . . . [they] go on talking and talking till almost everybody gives up and goes home."

Occasionally, optimism reigned—in 1902's "Homesick," the Kasrilevkans eventually band together to purchase a share in "our own Jewish Bank" (though even its purchase proves difficult, and the share is delayed in its arrival)—but developments in the movement post-Kishinev must have provided confirmation for Sholem Aleichem's skeptical side. In the pogrom's wake, Herzl proposed accepting the British government's offer of territory in Uganda, causing uproar and dissension within the movement. Sholem Aleichem wryly parodied the chaos in two slight allegorical dramas: the first envisioned an ailing Israel "in bed, covered over with rags. Deathly pallor. Sunken cheeks," with professors and consultants named for Zionist leaders each providing their own suggestions for a cure. (A Russian "outside consultant," the anti-Semitic editor Suvorin, advises bloodletting: "I know it's an old remedy. Old fashioned. But it works!") The second portrayed the Territorialist movement—committed to finding a Jewish homeland, but not necessarily committed to that homeland being Israel—as a matchmaker seeking a match between Zionism, Madame Palestine's son, and Miss Uganda, described in the dramatis personae as "rich orphan girl, comely black beauty." Both end badly, with the cast dissolving into collapse and argument. And a scathing feuilleton ridiculed Baron Maurice de Hirsch's Jewish Colonization Association as a group of ninnies concentrating on lunch plans and pretty ladies and spending enormous sums on ridiculous projects (including, believe it or not, the original bridge to nowhere) while abrogating their core responsibility to care for the emigrating masses of Russian Jewry.

With Herzl's death in July 1904, one of Sholem Aleichem's most cherished links to the Zionist dream—the attraction to the individual great man—would come to an end. He would write an elegiac pamphlet in Herzl's honor, but for the moment his enthusiasms for change in the fortunes of Russia's Jewry would come from elsewhere—from movements that far transcended the Jewish community.

CHAPTER 16

In Which Our Hero Gets Caught Up in Someone Else's Solution

1902–1905

The first years of the century saw the Russian government under pressure. Socialist and anarchist currents of the left, despite regime censorship and persecution, had grown increasingly vocal, and spoke for a growing silent majority—particularly after the country's entrance into the disastrous Russo-Japanese War in 1904, when the government seemed weaker and weaker. Sholem Aleichem, as we've seen, had been a pretty severe critic of capitalism in his day, but much like current critics of the American financial system, mostly on its own terms: his concern was with the natural tendencies toward gambling and ignorant speculation, and the rampant optimism and bull-mindedness which he believed created bubbles that would create general ruin when they eventually popped. Booms and busts. Sholem Aleichem didn't abandon this theme entirely at this point; but as the political situation changed, his enthusiasm for new ideas—along with their growing purchase among the population—perhaps naturally resulted in greater sympathy with the increasingly active leftist Russian circles. He grew his hair longer, replaced the pictures of Gogol in his study with ones of the liberal activist Gorky, and even began wearing the black "Gorky shirt" that identified him as a sympathizer with the goals of the left. (The fact that he simultaneously wore the lacquered shoes of the upper-class gentleman was just another sign of the swirling contradictions that composed his life.)

Sholem Aleichem had always been sympathetic to the working class, and an early feuilleton of his, 1889's "A Few Words About Our Working Man," champions a kind of capitalism with a socialist face: cooperative groups or companies of, for example, tailors, each of whom would benefit from specializing in a single part of the business cycle, like marketing and sales, rather than trying to master all of it—and who would pool funds for insurance or family welfare. As more radical schemes became more politically compelling (and it may be uncharitable, but necessary, to recall that in the interim he had also lost his own fortune), Sholem Aleichem's own rising enthusiasm became matched by his own rhetoric.

By 1902, a Kasrilevke schoolteacher, dreaming of what he'd do were he a wealthy man, begins, as in a later, much-altered iteration, by musing that he wouldn't have to work hard. But unlike Tevye, he quickly begins thinking politically: of global charity, where "everything would be run with a view to the common welfare"; then eliminating war by buying off the warring governments; and then, ultimately, insisting that "I might do away with money altogether. For let us not deceive ourselves, what is money anyway? It is nothing but a delusion, a made-up thing . . . one of the greatest lusts. But if there were no more money in the world there would be no more temptation, no more lust." You can see why *Fiddler on the Roof*'s writers omitted this part; in 1960s America, this would have smelled a lot like communist talk to them—and they probably wouldn't have been too far off.

If the schoolteacher's musings are still in the realm of gentle dreams, Sholem Aleichem's stories on the theme got angrier with each passing year, increasingly critical of the intolerable gap between rich and poor. The protagonist of 1903's "An Easy Fast" starves himself to death to ensure his family has enough to eat: he begins to eagerly await the fast days that dot the Jewish calendar, when he needs no excuse to hide his actions. His death occurs on Tisha B'av, the classic day of Jewish mourning: the story, though, mourns not desolate Jerusalem, but a world with "people who found it necessary to exploit others and suck their blood." In that same year's "The Convoy," three arrested men from very different social classes forced to travel together begin a conversation impossible under any other circumstances: the poor man, addressing the magnate, confesses that as a child "I still could not understand why a rich man's child could step on the toes of a poor man's child, and the poor man's child could do nothing about it. So I asked my grandfather . . . and he explained it to me this way: that a rich man is not a poor man and a poor man is not a rich man. In short, the rich were rich and the poor were poor . . . [and] there is nothing I can do about it. Ever since that time I have had nothing but scorn for the rich." Even when, after their journey, the rich man regrets his former, haughtier actions, he has no idea how to make amends. In the current system, everyone is stuck, frozen.

Was revolution the answer? Some stories began featuring the revenge of the oppressed, and the repressed, framed in his increasingly prevalent folklike idiom. In 1903's "Simchat Torah," a year-round milquetoast transforms for that one holiday night into a shouter and a screamer; the next year, a similar story's protagonist shushes any talker in synagogue, no matter how rich or powerful, "because in a place of holiness all Jews are equal." A feuilleton in which a young woman, Rassel, gives birth after an illness ends by asking the reader the child's name. A good guess would have been "Constitution": at least that's what the censor thought, who (quite rightly) saw it as an allegory for the current political situation—the young Rassel being Russia, her busybody aunts Anzi and Franzi England and France, and so on—and who never let it see the light of day. Nevertheless, Sholem Aleichem was salient, as always, about what would prevail in the matchup between the realities of human nature and the utopian ideals of communist ideology: in "The First Commune," written for Passover in 1904, he suggested that "those old comforting tales about how one day we will all live together as brothers, share one communal purse . . . never to slander or be spiteful but to live in Utopia—that will only happen when the Messiah comes."

All those contradictory feelings poured into his first return to Tevye in five years. "Hodl," written in the summer of 1904, firmly establishes the daughters as the stories' central theme, living symbols for specific contemporary trials and tribulations; and Hodl's romance with Pertchik (Peppercorn), matched in its own way with Tevye's own infatuation with the fiery intellectual, are both clear stand-ins for Sholem Aleichem's attraction to the movement Pertchik represents. Because make no mistake, Pertchik is no friend of the tsar, nor does he keep that opinion of his to himself. The story's unhappy ending—and over the next decade, the stories of Tevye's daughters would end increasingly unhappily—is quite clear, if not explicit, about Pertchik's unhappy fate: he has been exiled, presumably to Siberia or somewhere similar, for his activity, and Hodl, following her love, will go with him. "God knows when we'll see each other again" are the last words of Hodl's Tevye gruffly confides to Sholem Aleichem, and this waiting for a reunion that may never come has grim echoes of both the Jew's long wait for messianic redemption and the particular tensions of the repressive tsarist regime. Sholem Aleichem and his readers, though, would not have to wait as long for the latter as the Jews had for the former.

The government, steadily weakening due to military reversal, pinwheeled between the willingness to placate hostile sentiment with liberal reform and the concern such reforms might lead to more unrest rather than less. Things were beginning to spiral, perhaps out of control. On January 9, 1905, "Bloody Sunday," Father Gapon led Petersburg workers to the Winter Palace with their families and their grievances and received bullets in return, 70 killed and 240 injured; in March, responding to growing unrest, the tsar decreed he would convene a parliament, cancel some peasant debt, allow the Poles to use their own language, and give "some vague relief to the Jews"; but this was very little, and too late to stop the momentum.

Sholem Aleichem had dedicated some of his travel and public readings in those first few months of 1905 to assist the quasi-legal left-wing organization the Bund. "Hodl," published as a stand-alone pamphlet, could have been seen as expressing revolutionary sympathies. And most powerfully (and seditiously), he wrote the mock lullaby "Sleep, Alexei," a satiric song about Nicholas II and his heir, along the lines of a poem by Lermontov, and allowed it to secretly circulate among Bund members. Some stanzas read:

> Sleep, Alexei, my fine heir
> My delightful little boy
> Sleep, my only son, my kaddish,
> Sleep, oh, sleep, don't cry.

> . . . You'll have policemen, and some Cossacks
> Guards to watch the door
> People who can smash and bash
> And beat up, forever more.

> Have no fear of that Japan
> Don't be such a fool
> Moscow still lives, so does Ivan
> A Tsar still needs to rule.

> You will pay some reparations
> Sha! Don't say a word!
> Just promise them a Constitution
> And then flip them the bird.

But with the revolution's failure to arrive imminently, he had to consider the prospect of making a living. The year 1904 had seen him expend a great deal of time and effort on a failed scheme to establish a newspaper in Vilna—the great white whale of Yiddish publishing, with hundreds of thousands of Jewish potential subscribers in Lithuania, White Russia, and southern Russian provinces. (The one bright spot was that while he was moldering in St. Petersburg trying to get permission from the Russian Interior Ministry, he finally met "the idol of our times, the master of ideas, Maxim Gorky" in person, who amazed him with his knowledge of Jewish history and his ability to quote Spinoza by heart.) But the spring of 1905 offered an incredible new prospect: a new kind of creative business that was to shape the rest of his life and his literary reputation up to today.

Ever since he was a child, Sholem Aleichem had been enchanted by the Yiddish theater. He'd seen it in its various incarnations: amateur Purim players dramatizing the book of Esther—*A Midsummer Night's Dream* in the shtetl, the grand narrative juxtaposed with the rude mechanicals who play the parts—and, as the institution began to encounter modernity, traveling Yiddish troupes performing the work of Avrom Goldfaden, the first great Yiddish dramatist. Though he'd employed the dramatic form from early in his career—probably in part, as one of his early cosmpolitan characters opines, because its ability to serve as "a mirror of our lives" fit in with his realist aesthetic—composing two one-act plays within five years of his literary debut, tsarist restrictions on Yiddish dramatic performance had limited the establishment of theaters, and so "The Divorce" and "A Doctor for a Bridegroom" were probably designed to be read rather than performed. When he thought about having *Yaknehoz* staged in 1894, he looked to a freer New York, not to Russia.

Almost a decade later, looking for other sources of income, he returned to his own dramatic efforts—but, bearing in mind the state of Yiddish theater, composed his full-length play, *Mayer Chalante*, in Russian, hoping it would play theatrically and then appear in the Yiddish press in translation. Published in the Yiddish press in 1903, the play finally appeared on stage in Warsaw in late April 1905, in Polish, under the new title *Scattered and Dispersed*. Sholem Aleichem, by this time in dire financial straits, didn't have the money for travel expenses from Kiev to attend the play's premiere; "another bitter drop in the great sea of sorrows for a Yiddish writer," he wrote. How was this possible, considering how much he was publishing in the expanding Yiddish press? Simple: a parallel explosion of Yiddish writers and writing meant the papers still weren't paying much—and Sholem Aleichem was unwilling to give up supporting his family according to the lifestyle to which they'd become accustomed. (His family would always say he had no idea of the worth of money, and would buy all sorts of fancy things, especially nice clothes or writing-related gadgets.) This meant constant cash crises, occasional recourse to friends, and, at least at times, taking out loans, interest payments on some of which followed him for years.

Aside from finances, author's nerves were probably involved: he asked his friend David Frishman to go to the Elysium himself to gauge public reaction. He needn't have worried. The director and translator, Marek Arnshteyn, paid out of his own pocket for the playwright to rush to Warsaw to attend the second performance. Though Sholem Aleichem had received warm receptions in his travels before, he wrote that "even in his writer's fantasies" he'd never imagined the kind of reception he got at the theater that night. He was deluged with flowers after the first act, and called out for applause after each subsequent one; the police held him in a closed loge for half an hour after the production ended, for fear of the crowd. (He was eventually smuggled out through the back door.)

What was this unbelievable work? Like the Tevye stories, it was a family setting; and, like them, the children's characters represent differing roads taken or not taken in the emerging modern Jewish story. But everything else is different. Mayer Chalante, the original titular character, has changed the family name from the homey, traditional "Tcholent," an image of integration where the cooked whole is greater than the sum of its parts. Fittingly, that move away from cohesion echoes in his children's behavior—four sons and two daughters, all contemptuous of their father's lack of education and cringing behavior toward the non-Jewish magnate. Mayer's eldest daughter and son, Flora and Matvey, are respectively indolent and dandified, robbed of tradition with nothing to replace it but card playing. His second son is a Zionist, disgusted with the rest of the family; Volodya is a revolutionary; and Sashka is spoiled rotten. The one possible exception, the closest to one of Tevye's daughters, is Mayer's second daughter, Khane, whose short hair and constant reading mark her as an emancipated type: rejecting the suitor her parents have chosen for her, she chooses to marry nobody at all, going instead to Bern to study. "I think no person has the right to tell any other what to do," she tells her parents. Her reason: "I've already told you: it's every man for himself." Sholem Aleichem may have been dramatizing personal anxieties: his oldest daughter, Ernestina, who'd been earning her own money tutoring, had moved to Mohilev-Podolsk over her father's objections to become an administrator in a girls' school. (Sholem Aleichem insisted he should support her until she married; she, knowing the family's economic situation, felt otherwise.) But Khane is different from Ernestina, Tsaytl, and Hodl; she rebels not to reestablish a familial connection on her own more modern terms, but because there is no center, nothing left she feels she can connect to.

A telegram congratulating Sholem Aleichem on the premiere insisted he had "masterfully portrayed the situation of the modern Jewish family." This may have simply been first-night exuberance. The playwright himself would later write that though "the audience gave the play and its author a rousing acclamation, and the balcony clapped bravo . . . [he felt] the play lacked much more than it had to offer." Suggesting it was "a feuilleton rather than a play," he speculated that "I was perhaps the only one in the theater who booed the author." But though Sholem Aleichem is right on the literary merits—even in its revised form, the play feels like a schematic essay with actors—his concerns about the center holding must have spoken deeply to an audience who felt themselves in the eye of revolutionary events, with the most basic footing of society and family slipping from their grasp. Whether the audience applauded out of literary appreciation or ideological sympathy, though, the cash-strapped Sholem Aleichem saw his financial future in them. "My God!" he wrote his daughter Ernestina. "What might have happened if it could have been possible to perform it in Yiddish? My fate and your future (I turn to my descendants) is tied up with the Yiddish theater."

But his other dramatic piece that year hinted at less buoyant prospects. The choice to put a new Menakhem-Mendl adventure in theatrical form might itself have been sparked by a recognition that the theater business wasn't all applause and flowers. Two years earlier, a bill had announced the forthcoming appearance, in Lodz, of a Menakhem-Mendl comedy that not only got Menakhem-Mendl's wife's name wrong—it called her Sore-Sheyndl—but also apparently featured a brother of Menachem-Mendl's named Jack, along with "Fishke the lame," the title character of a famous Abramovitch novel. (Sholem Aleichem was incensed not only by the false implication that he was involved but by the fact that the playwright didn't seem to have bothered to read his work.) But Sholem Aleichem's own Menakhem-Mendl drama, "Agents," also suggests a darker tone in a character famously noted for optimism. Set entirely in a third-class train compartment, Menakhem-Mendl, an insurance agent in the making, feels out a prospective client—who turns out to be another insurance agent, trying to sell to *him*. Then a third man comes into the compartment, and a fourth—both of whom turn out to be agents. At the play's end, Menakhem-Mendl growls: "Let's be honest. Business is lousy and we're all in one hell of a fix."

Previous stories, which, unlike "Agents," would appear in Sholem Aleichem's "canonized" version of the Menakhem-Mendl stories, had prepared the reader for this turn. Four years previously, a similarly structured story—Menakhem-Mendl the matchmaker manqué tries to arrange a match with another matchmaker, but each one, unbeknownst to the other, is trying to set up a girl—had the character seemingly acting not merely ignorantly, but unethically. Trading on inside information by picking up someone else's leads, he later even commits fraud, passing himself off as a longtime matchmaker from a matchmaking family when of course nothing of the sort is the case. And in the next installment, Menakhem-Mendl, selling a life insurance policy to someone under a false name and a cloud of suspicion he was attempting to defraud the company, lights out for the territories—his letter ends with the news that he's heading off to America, leaving home behind completely. You'd think Sheyne-Sheyndl would be on his case, trying to keep him grounded; but she's disappeared, her voice absent from these later works. There are logistical reasons for this, to be sure—Menakhem-Mendl is traveling and it would be impossible for her letters to find him—but logistics had always been less important to the stories than thematic balance. And now, in an increasingly scattered age, balance was more and more difficult to attain.

CHAPTER 17

In Which Our Hero Suffers a Revolution and Makes a Decision

1905

Sholem Aleichem's theatrical ambitions had blossomed, and, that summer, he attempted to give them material form, considering co-founding "a kind of Yiddish-literary art theater" in Odessa that would exclusively produce his plays, with him serving as creative director. (Thinking big, as usual, he saw it as the foundation of a national cultural movement: "Our task is to create a repertoire, a tiny repertoire, a young one, maybe not a ripe one, but at least some repertoire," he wrote. "Let's give something to the theater of our people!") As was often the case, nothing came of it: here, politics intervened—the Russian government apparently got wind (probably via a potential competitor) that the operation might possess a "revolutionary character" and put a stop to the process. But still full of what he believed to be lucrative ideas for plays, he once again began considering the attractions of shopping them to New York, with its booming Yiddish-speaking population and with no governmental intervention. Maybe he'd even bring along his own theatrical talents and energies.

But there was no immediate rush, that summer of 1905, and other pressing commitments intervened. Most pressing were the travels to give public readings around the Baltics. Sholem Aleichem loved walking in the streets and narrow alleys of the Jewish areas, seeing new sights and hearing new stories; the readings were lucrative, too, but they were exhausting, and somewhat embarrassing. Not the act of public reading in itself—if his longtime literary idol Charles Dickens had done it, there was nothing to be embarrassed about—but taking money for it. Not only was it a painful reminder of his financial reverses, but it seemed an uncomfortable fit with the genteel literary perspective Sholem Aleichem, for all his populist sentiments, had always wanted to embody ever since his *Folksbibliotek* days. Gallingly, in recent years some of that energy had concentrated in Warsaw, and around Peretz.

Yiddish writers from the Polish part of the empire flocked to the big city, and to Peretz's apartment, to seek the elder author's tutelage and advice, and the latter was happy to oblige, creating the most influential literary salon in the history of Yiddish. There, late in 1904, Peretz had pronounced the opinion that Sholem Aleichem's writing, his tales of the little people, failed to measure up to the definition of a great writer's work, which must deal with great figures and ideas; that his popularity might be a sign of his lack of merit rather than the opposite; and that it was hard to know where his characters ended and he began. Though Sholem Aleichem never wanted disciples—when asked, he responded, "No! I'm no Hasidic rebbe . . . I'll leave that for Peretz"—Peretz's dicta, whether that Sholem Aleichem's writing lacked merit or that real writers didn't take money for readings, had influence. In addition, one of the "disciples," H. D. Nomberg, had written a negative review of *Scattered and Dispersed* that, Sholem Aleichem muttered, had probably been dictated by Peretz himself—who hadn't even bothered to host Sholem Aleichem when he arrived, the way he usually did with visiting Yiddish writers.

But if Peretz was standoffish, Sholem Aleichem's audiences weren't—especially as revolutionary sentiment was at its height that summer of 1905, spreading even to more bourgeois households, and Sholem Aleichem, whose enthusiasm grew as the prospect of a constitutional monarchy looked increasingly possible, became more identified with the cause. He would often appear as a literary guest at public meetings arranged by revolutionary parties, to supportive crowds. Whether or not they knew he was now writing some of his letters on red postcards, they would have heard "Sleep, Alexei," or read his stories mocking Russia's fortunes in the war—maybe the one about the bully so pugnacious and self-destructive that he ends up fighting himself, or the one where complacent older students are walloped by the smaller, younger schoolchildren. And the most recent stories had been even more radical, more outspoken: a children's story published this year featured a group of children rising up against a corrupt, violently oppressive beadle, bonding together via a poem transformed into a universally spread song (think "Sleep, Alexei"). The story ended with "ordinary working men" selected by the people themselves ruling over a revitalized synagogue, the beadle a wrinkled, faded, figure in the corner. It was hard to imagine something more revolutionary—except, of course, for his recently published pamphlet "Uncle Pinny and Aunt Reyze," a transparent allegory for the tsar's failures in the Russo-Japanese war. Describing how the big, fleshy Aunt Reyze (Russia) got licked by the tiny Uncle Pinny (Japan), it sold tens of thousands of copies.

Sholem Aleichem provides a picture of someone not dissimilar to himself in one of his finest monologues, written that summer and appearing in a new Warsaw Yiddish daily almost precisely when the Treaty of Portsmouth ended the Russo-Japanese War. The monologist of "Joseph" disparages revolutionary types, elaborating that they're the "sort that likes letting their hair grow and favors those vulgar long black peasant blouses. You know, with the high collar which buttons at the side and the shirttails hanging out and that silly cord knotted round the middle? Just the sort of getup I hate . . . Oh. Meaning no offense! Though I see where you, too, seem to like wearing your hair long and have got the same kind of black blouse on." The listener's depicted as a sympathizer with the cause—he's wearing that Gorky shirt—but not exactly of it; which might explain the narrator's confiding in him. And Sholem Aleichem? Shirt notwithstanding, he's the listener, standing off to the side, evaluating. All his writing wasn't the same as being on the front lines of the revolution. But those front lines would come to him soon enough.

If the Russo-Japanese War had come to an end, the same was hardly true for the tensions within Russia itself. Quite the contrary. Strikes were breaking out all over the empire, including the army and navy; a general railroad strike caught Ernestina's future husband on the train on his way to visit her. Facing the real prospect of ongoing chaos or worse, the tsar issued the October Manifesto on the 17th, providing for a constitutional government that granted basic civil liberties and allowed the formation of political parties. Sholem Aleichem was so delighted he spent that evening going from one Kiev friend to the next, knocking on doors and spreading the news about the constitution, even sending his daughter a congratulatory telegram. He also joined the next day's mass demonstrations; waving red flags and singing revolutionary songs, crowds headed toward the city Duma to hear speeches.

The military broke up the demonstrations by firing into the crowd.

In a story Sholem Aleichem had written three years before, a father asked his son: "Do you mean to tell me I've ruined myself just for you to start a revolution? God help us all! I only hope they don't pin it on us Jews, because we're always the first to take the rap." Perhaps the author was remembering that story when he had what he'd later call the "prophetic sentiment" that the Jews would somehow be scapegoated for all this. Running home, he moved his household from their apartment building to safer quarters in the nearby Hotel Imperial. It was the right call. Conservative backlash to the constitution included a wave of pogroms headed by the Black Hundreds—whose slogan was "Kill Jews and Save Russia"—with local gangs and goons joining in. Pogroms broke out in 660 Jewish communities, and Kiev was no exception: they raged in the streets from the 18th to the 21st, with aftershocks continuing for several days. Huddled in the Imperial with other Jewish families seeking refuge, Sholem Aleichem watched the pogroms from the windows. Writing a friend from the hotel as the events were unfolding, he described the "cry that Jews should be attacked—and so it began, from all sides." Soldiers arrived, "and we were relieved: certainly they would help us. And indeed they helped, but not us; they helped to assault, rob, steal, attack. Before our eyes and the eyes of the world they helped to shatter windows, doors, locks, and line their pockets. Before the eyes of our children they beat Jews to death, wives and children, and cried: money! Give up your money!"

The family itself, thankfully, emerged unscathed, though Ernestina—who had lived through a pogrom herself in Mohilev-Podolsk—was briefly terrified by a confusing telegram from her father reading "Zdorov, Papa" (Healthy, Papa), not "Zdorovi, Papa," (We are healthy, Papa), possibly implying other family members had been injured or killed. It had just been a slip of the pen. It even turned out, as they'd discover days later, that the family house had remained untouched: their non-Jewish cook had convinced the pogromists it belonged to Gentiles by liberally displaying crosses and icons. This, however, seemed to have been the exception. Sholem Aleichem wrote his daughter ironically that "the Brodskys had tried to hide with good Christians, and a number of others had attempted the same approach; but the good Christians, with very rare exceptions, had refused the hospitality, expressing their full readiness, after everything had returned to normal, to come to the Jewish magnates' balls and dance the mazurka with their daughters." Converts, he noted, were hiding in Jewish cellars; tens of thousands of Jews feared for their lives.

Physically, yes, they had come through unscathed; but Sholem Aleichem was so deeply shaken by the pogroms and what they represented—the harshest rebuttal to his decades of optimistic hopes for a transformed Russian society—that for the next week his family was concerned he would fall ill. And just think, he wrote his daughter, after seeing the pogrom as the "ruination of Russian Judaism": "This is an optimist speaking to you. Can you imagine what the skeptics say?" Thoughts of mortality haunted him: and during this brief period, which he called the "dark days," he wrote a draft of Yiddish verses to be engraved on his tombstone. A rough translation reads:

> There was a simple Jew,
> Who wrote "Judeo-German" for women,
> And for the simple folk—
> Here lies a journalist, a writer.

He laughed off the whole of life,
And took the whole world on
The whole world did well for itself
Himself—oy vey!—tremendous troubles.

And precisely when the whole world
Laughed, kvelled, and used to rejoice,
He would cry—this God only knows—
Secretly, so no one should see.

But by a week after the pogroms, he was back to making plans: if Russia would be a graveyard both politically and financially—it seemed unlikely if not impossible to foresee a flourishing Yiddish press and theater at a time of conservative repression—then he'd have to support his family somewhere else. On October 24, he wrote that if he "had the means, I'd leave with my family to America and sit out the terrible time" there; two days later, he asked his daughter to join them in Kiev, writing, "If we die, it will all be together; if we leave Russia, it will all be together."

The popular lullaby Sholem Aleichem had written over a decade before, "Sleep, My Child," purported to be a mother's comforting words to her child, and herself, about their missing father and husband: he has gone to America, it turns out, to make enough for the family to join him. "America is for all, / They say, quite a joy, / And for Jews, an Eden," the lullaby attests, and a decade into the mass wave of Eastern European Jewish emigration to America, the situation had become so archetypal it could serve as the goodnight song of Eastern European Jewry. Escape from persecution, and, even more, from poverty—there, in the lullaby's words, they ate challah every weekday, not just on the Sabbath. Other works, though, put the starry-eyed optimism in (personal) perspective. Two feuilletons he wrote in 1894, while praising America for its egalitarianism, attacked it for its ravening capitalism and, particularly, for its

Jewish community's inability to support a Yiddish writer. The American Yiddish papers often behaved dishonorably—listing his name on their prospectuses without his approval, offering lowball prices, asking for work without clear payment plans, and, worst of all, habitually reprinting his works from their appearances in Russian newspapers and magazines without his knowledge, permission, or remuneration. (In doing so, they also choppily edited, retitled, and reworked them so substantially he sometimes couldn't recognize them by name.) To add chutzpah to injury, when he expressed interest in writing for them directly, some demurred on the grounds they could simply continue getting the material for free. "Columbus, you should be ashamed of yourself!" one sketch ended.

His knowledge of the American press was admittedly sketchy; Russian censors generally refused to let American Yiddish newspapers through. That also meant he lacked connections there—at least until the early fall of 1905, when he met Maurice Fishberg in Warsaw. Fishberg, a clinical professor of medicine at New York University who'd done groundbreaking work on tuberculosis and chaired the New York Academy of Science's anthropology and psychology department, cherished Jewish literature and culture, and began talking up Sholem Aleichem's plays to the New York Yiddish theaters. A regular correspondence developed; Sholem Aleichem even trusted him enough to write him about the growing revolutionary sentiment in mid-September, avoiding the censor's scrutiny by replacing political characters and groups with synagogue roles ("The main thing—we don't want the cantor [tsar] . . . the beadles [ministers] in the meantime are acting themselves: they're hiring sextons [Cossacks] . . . the head beadle is sitting at home, afraid to go out: bastards throwing potatoes [bombs].")

So after the pogroms, when America began looking like an immediate option, the author naturally turned to Fishberg for assistance in negotiating with the press and theaters to support his family's travel to the United States. He had already sent Fishberg two plays, a new reworking of *Scattered and Dispersed* and a theatrical version of *Stempenyu* (which he also called *The Jewish Paganini*). Never one for second best, he asked

Fishberg to approach both of the American Yiddish theater's leading actor-managers: Boris Thomashevsky at the People's Theater, Yiddish theater's first sex symbol (he danced around bare-chested onstage, and, it was rumored, made love to a different woman between each act of every show), and Jacob Adler, the Grand Theater's "great eagle," who had recently scored a Broadway triumph, playing a Yiddish-speaking Shylock while all around him spoke Shakespeare's English. At the Hotel Imperial, Sholem Aleichem was already adapting artistic principles in the face of exigent circumstances: he sent Fishberg a revision to *Stempenyu*'s final act, including a new ending where the heroine poisons herself for love. Yes, it was implausible, he wrote; but "what should one do, if America wants it?"

To generate additional excitement, and ready cash for moving expenses, he also sent a new play ripped from the headlines—"The Final Sacrifice (Based on the Events of the Revolution and the Pogroms in Russia)" no longer exists, though its title speaks volumes—and proposed a series of "Pogrom Sketches" drawing on his own and others' experiences along with the Russian papers' accounts for publication in the American Yiddish press. Fishberg had no luck with any of the plays, but found a buyer for the sketches. Kasriel Sarasohn's *Yiddishes Tageblat*, New York's first Yiddish daily, had 70,000 readers in 1900; under pressure from an up-and-coming paper, the *Morgen-Zhurnal*, which was eating into its Orthodox immigrant audience, Sarasohn saw Sholem Aleichem as a circulation booster and a jab at the competition. Forty-two brutal letters would appear between November 1905 and January 1906, along the lines of his letters to friends and family and with a constant emphasis on reportage: the times, he wrote, called "God forbid, not [for] fantasy [but] only facts, facts, and more facts." The fact was that the *Tageblat* would only cable Sholem Aleichem 300 rubles, half what they publicly promised him, insufficient for the whole family to make the trip to America; but events made it clear they had to move. Strikes were breaking out again; and though official post and telegraph strikes were quickly broken, word was spreading in the Russian press of a forty-day general strike, which, at least in the terrified minds of the Kiev citizens, meant the strong possibility of a second pogrom. In the course of two days, Sholem Aleichem sold off all his household items at a huge loss (donating his library to the Zionist reading room in Podol) and borrowed money from friends in preparation for departure.

On the second night of Chanukah, Ernestina married I. D. Berkowitz, in a wedding providing ample illustration of Sholem Aleichem's character and the intersection of life and literature. Berkowitz, trying to retain some measure of independence, objected to turning his wedding into a Kiev spectacle and to going to America on his father-in-law's dime; he hoped to get married in Mohilev-Podolsk, then work in Vilna to earn money for the couple's passage. Sholem Aleichem hated both ideas; he wrote Berkowitz that this "reminds me unwillingly of Tevye's daughter" (meaning Hodl), and informed his own daughter that Berkowitz, entering the family, had to understand how things worked: that they did everything together. (Though Sholem Aleichem and his wife eventually relented on the wedding, legal complications required the couple to marry in Kiev after all.)

On that Chanukah night, the officiating crown rabbi's sermon spoke of the eternally wandering Israel and the divine presence that accompanies it on its travels. Once the celebration ended, the household, now numbering nine, boarded a line of droshkies and left for the train station.

ACT IV

The Wanderer

CHAPTER 18

In Which Our Hero Takes Longer
Than He Thought

1905–1906

Sholem Aleichem clearly expected his travels to be as temporary as he hoped the Russian unrest would be; in late November, waiting for a tooth extraction, he wrote his daughter that he planned to return to Russia after a brief American stay to "benefit from the true freedom for a few decades." Things would not go according to plan.

The family arrived at the border town of Radziwill on the second day after they left Kiev. Berkowitz lacked official permission to cross the border to Brody, in Galician Austria-Hungary, and it took two days to figure out how to smuggle him across; they ended up enlisting a local woman experienced in such matters, who arranged for Berkowitz to "steal the border" by carrying a "half-pass" used by locals to travel back and forth across the border by train. Despite the chaos and concern—they lost their baggage in the confusion and weren't sure what to do with the featherbeds they'd brought along, believing exaggerated and false rumors that they'd gotten out on the last train from Kiev before revolutionaries attacked the railroads—Sholem Aleichem, fascinated by the ins and outs of the smuggling process, busily gathered material for future stories.

Brody was a boomtown, doing land-office business from the steadily increasing stream of frightened Russian emigrants. Sholem Aleichem marveled at the lack of anti-Semitic legislation and reveled in his reception: a public reading was so rapturously received that, at its end, "the students rushed onto the stage in a surging mass" and carried him on their shoulders through the hall and into a carriage—whose horses they unharnessed so they could pull it to the hotel themselves. Perhaps buoyed by the strength of his Galician welcome, he decided to move his family from the relative backwoods of Brody to Lemberg, Galicia's biggest city. (The fact that the remaining money owed him by the *Tageblat* had yet to arrive—with no word forthcoming—factored in, too: Lemberg had not only a congenial community of Jewish intellectuals, but its own Yiddish paper.)

It was an auspicious arrival: his hotel was flooded with visitors at all hours of the day, trying to get a glimpse of the author and his family. The community's standing-room-only welcome reception and celebratory banquet—largely organized by local Zionists complete with (fake) sword-wielding Jewish students dressed in blue and white—was an intriguing testament to the diversity of Sholem Aleichem's readership, and of their readings of his work. One after-dinner speech by the head of the Galician Zionist movement enlisted Kasrilevke as proof that Diasporic Jewish follies pointed clearly to Zion, and others drew precisely the opposite conclusion, insisting the author's work obviously suggested a call for Jewish political empowerment right there in Galicia. The stories' author gently calmed the crowd by telling the audience a different story, not his own: the midrash of Jacob's flight from Esau. Each of Beth-El's rocks, related the rabbinic legend, claimed the privilege of serving as the patriarch's pillow; God settled the quarrel by merging them all into one large stone. Insisting he was no Jacob, Sholem Aleichem noted he was fleeing nonetheless, and at this place where he rested his head, they should unify, not quarrel, and sing "folk songs and joyful Hasidic melodies." And so they did; perhaps proving that it wasn't Jacob's role Sholem Aleichem was taking, but God's, creating a body of work to bring together the rapidly diverging forces of modern Jewish life.

All this warmth certainly rendered Sholem Aleichem bullish on Galicia: and since he lacked the money to fund the remainder of his American trip, even when the *Tageblat* coughed up the rest of what they owed (probably in response to bad press), settling in Galicia, at least for the winter, seemed an obvious solution. (Bizarrely, the apartment they rented in Lemberg from one of Sholem Aleichem's readers belonged to a member of the city's secret police—the fan's father.) It was a relatively pleasant and profitable stay: the winter was filled with triumphant public readings throughout Galicia and Bukovina, and, later, Vienna and various cities in Rumania. Numerous places sent delegations to Lemberg to importune him to attend, because *everyone* wanted to get him first; the story went that in one small town so many ardent fans and followers turned out to meet him, ask him to touch their babies, and the like that the local Hasidic rebbe was upset at the competition. Not surprising that by mid-February, he wrote Fishberg he had postponed his travels to America until the summer; and, inspired by a rapturous reception based on his earlier work, pooh-poohed the suggestion that he should quickly capitalize on his pogrom experiences and writings. He would only, he wrote, read "small skits and stories about Kasrilevke, Mazapevke, Berdichev, and the like, from which the world dies laughing, often lets loose a tear, and that is the essence. In the readings all of the aspects of Jewish life in the bloody land are reflected, including the constitution, the pogroms, etc. . . . Art, my dear friend, never loses its worth, pogrom or no pogrom, Europe or America." Circumstances had certainly changed from the time, a few short months ago, when he'd been willing to change his play's ending for steamship tickets.

These months—the winter and early spring of 1906—were filled with the rigors of travel and touring, and so Sholem Aleichem's artistic output had slowed accordingly; some reworked Kasrilevke material, a lovely piece of fictional character assassination called "It's a Lie" set in a town, Kolomyja, right down the railroad line from Lemberg. A newly established newspaper from the other side of the border, Vilna's *Time*, got two holiday stories out of him (before he broke with them for not paying for his work). "The Purim Feast" is probably most notable for having been written in a coffeehouse in Vienna, where Sholem Aleichem had been giving a reading, in response to an emergency telegram from the paper for Purim material. But his Passover story was something else again, and, along with another work published just a month or so later, spoke volumes about his perspective on home: its past, its recent upheavals, and his hopes for its future. The titular guest of "The Guest" regales the child narrator's family Seder with marvelous stories of his home in the Holy Land, transporting the child "to that fortunate Jewish land . . . where the dishes are made of gold and precious stones lie scattered about on the streets." Skeptical readers, both current and contemporary, are less surprised to discover (spoiler alert!) that the guest in question, of course invited to stay the night, absconds with the family silver in cooperation with the housemaid. The child's loss of innocence—both in the dream of an uncomplicated, miraculous Zion and in human nature—also seems to express Sholem Aleichem's anxieties about the illusions of safe harbor anywhere: in the Zion of his dreams, the Russia of his past hopes, and even, perhaps, the America of his current travels whose streets were legendarily paved with gold.

If "The Guest" might obliquely allude to the quashing of Sholem Aleichem's idealistic sentiments about Russia, the second great story of that spring—perhaps the most important story he ever wrote—has a much clearer connection to recent events. "Chava," the heart of the Tevye cycle, was published in a Zionist weekly in late May, and, written in the teeth of revolution and anti-Semitic backlash, did nothing less than weigh the attractions of utopian idealism against the limits of what it means to be Jewish. Though "Chava" opens with Tevye's account of his long-standing (if good-natured) theological argument with the smiling village priest, that centuries-old argument has very little truck with Tevye; the rest of the tale, though, poses a more subtle, modern challenge, emerging from the heart of his own household and his author's own conscience. Chava—whose namesake, Eve, is the universal mother—has found her love outside the faith, in Chvedka Galagan, the village scribe. The stakes are extremely high: there was no such thing as "intermarriage" in the empire; the Jewish partner would have to convert to Christianity.

Chava, challenging the traditional, verse-quoting Tevye, asks him for a verse "that explains why human beings have to be divided into Jews and Christians, masters and slaves, beggars and millionaires," fusing religion and class in her universalist challenge; Tevye's response, a quotation of course, encapsulates his persona in its entirety. "You know," he says, "we Jews have an old custom that when a hen begins to crow like a rooster, off to the slaughterer she goes. That's why we say in the morning prayer, *hanoseyn lasekhvi bino*—not only did God give us brains, He gave some of us more of them than others." Tevye's Yiddish commentary on the Hebrew phrase—not an esoteric Talmudic source, but from the first prayer of the Jewish morning service, the basis of the basis, so to speak—is a Yiddish folk saying to the effect that women shouldn't rise above their place. The prayer begins by thanking God who *noseyn lasekhvi bino*, gives the rooster intelligence to distinguish between day and night (without which the rooster would crow not only at dawn but constantly, both removing his value as an alarm and making him deeply annoying), then continues with a series of blessings that thank God, without explanation, for His role in perpetuating a long series of Chava's sort of distinctions, including not only those between men and women, but also between Jew and non-Jew. Tevye's pithy response suggests, then, that limits and divisions are immutable, those between Jew and non-Jew as much so as those between day and night, man and woman. After the pogroms of 1905, this must have been a tempting answer: to reassert the existence of inherent limits, backed by tradition's authority. But Chava's question, which will haunt Tevye, shifts not to whether those limits *exist*—certainly recent events have brought their existence home with a vengeance—but whether they *matter*.

Tevye himself—whose constant refrain, "Tevye is not a woman," might suggest he's concerned some divisions aren't as immutable as he'd like to claim—complicates his position on the subject over the story's three subsequent "endings." (Talk about a story without an end.) Discovering Chava's conversion—no wonder, he says to Sholem Aleichem, the priest was always smiling—his actions are, and are firmly, those of a traditional Jew: he cuts her off completely, considers her dead, sits shiva. But this is only the story's first ending. Later traveling in the forest, that traditional symbolic location of doubt and despair, Tevye has a crisis of faith. "I tell you," he confesses to Sholem Aleichem, "I had even weirder thoughts . . . in the forest. What did being a Jew or not a Jew matter? Why did God have to create both? And if He did, why put such walls between them?" Almost supernaturally, the "ghost" of the daughter Tevye has declared dead arises before him (whether real or psychological projection is left for the reader to decide), beseeching him for acceptance and embrace. But Tevye resists—at what cost we can only imagine— and drives away, grieving "that I wasn't a more learned man, because surely there were answers to be found in the holy books." Another kind of return to tradition; while acknowledging, if only in the realm of thought, the possibility of alternatives.

But it's the story's last paragraph, its final ending, that renders the story a masterpiece and should remove any doubt that its author is a worthy heir to Gogol. Tevye makes a seemingly extraneous, narratively bizarre confession: "Once, for example . . . but do you promise not to laugh at me? . . . Because I'm afraid you'll laugh . . . Well, once I put on my best clothes and went to the station in order to take the train there—I mean, to where he and she live. I stepped up to the window and asked for a ticket. 'Where to?' says the ticket seller. 'To Yehupetz,' I say. 'Yehupetz?' he says. 'We don't have any such city,' he said to me. 'Well, it's no fault of mine if you haven't,' I say—and I turn right around, walk home again, take off my best clothes, and go back to work." Remember, Yehupetz isn't a real place—it's the name for Kiev in Sholem Aleichem's fictional universe. Tevye is, of course, a creature of fiction, a member of that same universe—so he should be able to get there, right? But he can't—because reality intrudes into fiction in this most important of moments. Only in Yehupetz, a land of fiction, can the intermarried Chava and Chvedka live together (as the couple could in Kiev, off-limits to most Jews), with Tevye actually going there to meet them. Only there can he be both the traditional Tevye and the man who loves and supports his intermarried couple, the Jew of faith and acceptance who can struggle with the newest intellectual challenges, the truly harmonized—not blended—figure. But alas: as the dour ticket seller tells us, you can't get there from here. Not in the real world, anyway.

As late as April, Sholem Aleichem still planned to travel to America with his family at summer's end; but plans were made to be changed, and after another reading tour of Rumania and Galicia, along with side trips to Paris and London, the summer saw the family arriving in Geneva. Sholem Aleichem had previously scouted it out and mused about settling there more permanently; Switzerland was a good place for the children to get an education—and could be a good home base for quick and hopefully lucrative trips to the States. Plus, old friends had landed there—first among them Abramovitch, who'd fled there after the pogroms in Odessa. If Geneva didn't work out, America was still a possibility.

So was England. It had the audience; if not quite America's numbers, there were still plenty—between 1881 and 1914, 120,000 to 150,000 Eastern European Jews settled permanently in Great Britain, particularly in the London districts of Whitechapel, St. Giles, and Southwark. In April Sholem Aleichem had written the British journalist Israel Cohen from Lemberg about the possibility of a trip, asking "what sort of a public" he would have there; eventually, toward the end of May, he arrived in London and was warmly received with a dinner at an East End restaurant. He stayed for more than two months, despite finding the city unappealing, its association with his idol Dickens notwithstanding. "Colossal, grandiose, oppressive, destructive, cold, damp, grey, smoky, toiling, free, limitless, cultural, wild, foggy, strange, frightening—that's London for you," he wrote. A character in a later novel would be even less restrained: "From the minute he set foot on English soil, the entire country revolted him, until his nose sniffed the familiar fragrance of Whitechapel squalor."

The familiarities went beyond fragrance. A personal visit to a Whitechapel Yiddish newspaper that had been publishing his stories without paying him yielded a single pound note, reluctantly extracted by the editor from his wallet; and his sojourn in a bedbug-infested Whitechapel room—and the house owners' insouciant reaction to his complaints— could have occurred anywhere in Yiddishland. He wrote his children: "I eagerly gave a feel in my pants pockets, to see if there were bedbugs there. Of course, what else? I found a few. And in your mother's corset, I swear on my honor, we caught a fellow comrade . . . Now put yourself, I beg of you, in our situation. Night. The capital of Great Britain. The English Constitution. Cromwell. Disraeli. A billion bedbugs." The householders' response, after Sholem Aleichem responded to their denials by pointing out a bedbug on their own pillow? "Bedbugs? Maybe one bedbug." He also suggests he and Olga might leave the writing and dentistry business to go into pest control.

In a postscript, Sholem Aleichem asks his children to copy the letter and send it to friends in Paris and Russia with literary connections; another letter several weeks later describing a disastrous trip to Leeds— where they were so ardently, ceremoniously, and lengthily received by their Zionist hosts that they couldn't get anything to eat (and when they do it's terrible)—was preceded by the warning that "everything that you read here is pure truth, i.e., this is not a feuilleton, but a true occurrence." Constantly aware of his own literary performance—even needing to issue warnings to his own family—and yet making sure everything's properly preserved for future publication speaks volumes about the odd dividing line between reported truth and created fiction for Sholem Aleichem, how he's more and more aware of himself as character, not person.

Part of this was undoubtedly his recognition that his celebrity had followed his readership westward and across the Channel, a good sign for his American prospects. London's Yiddish and English-Jewish press greeted him warmly; he gave readings in London, Leeds, and Manchester (one presided over by Chaim Weizmann, future president of Israel); and he met the great Anglo-Jewish writer Israel Zangwill, whose welcoming reception at his summer villa and warm introduction at a public reading must have both awkwardly reminded Sholem Aleichem of his own past

financial glories and suggested the possibilities of succeeding in translation, in a language with a wider circulation. The Manchester reading may
have served as a sober reminder: a man introducing him suggested that
"whatever might be the opinions as to the value of Jargon, the fact that
five millions of our people made it their language rendered it deserving of
their sympathy." Talk about faint praise.

For the time being, though, Sholem Aleichem's own contacts—and,
of course, his inability to write in English—meant continuing with his
plan of conquering the immigrant masses flocking to New York's Yiddish
theaters. A mid-August meeting with Jacob Adler was strongly encouraging: the great actor-manager had made the Atlantic crossing not merely
to perform at London's Pavilion Theater, but to find a new house playwright. The previous one, Jacob Gordin, had done invaluable work in
moving Yiddish theater away from its operetta and music-hall beginnings
toward more serious, topical fare, but he'd also insisted his material be
performed according to his own exacting specifications—and there was
no room for two bosses in Adler's outfit. Sholem Aleichem was no fan of
Gordin's work, either—he found the latter's Jewish characters entirely
unrealistic—and so was excited to take on a kind of second battle against
Shomerism, driving the impostor from the theater with an example of just
how it should be done. (Getting Gordin's kind of money—he had gotten
$5,000 the previous year for two original plays and two adaptations—
wouldn't hurt, either.) The meeting took place at the Three Nuns Hotel
in Aldgate Street: Sholem Aleichem read Adler the draft of the play he
was working on, and Adler felt it had potential. He advanced Sholem
Aleichem some money, cautioning him to make sure to write him a juicy
role, and sent him off to Geneva for a few weeks to write and spend time
with his family before finally setting off to America.

Sholem Aleichem tried to burn every copy of the results of his efforts.
(One survived without his knowledge.) Like much of his recent work,
"David Son of David" was about the gap between ideals and practice:
the title character, an orphan whose gold miner father died before his
birth—thus his unlikely name—decides to give up his fortune for a cause

he believes in, the colonization of Palestine. When he tells his community about the plan, though, they think he's gone mad, and his former guardian—an uncle who wants David to marry his daughter in order to keep the fortune in the family—piles on. The play ends with poor David roaming the streets, mocked by children. While echoing Sholem Aleichem's earlier concerns about Zionism, the play also showed the fingerprints of Ibsen's *Enemy of the People*, a subplot in *Oliver Twist*, and, most especially, the work of Jacob Gordin, whose play *The Madman* also featured a hero declared insane by the populace. Sensible, perhaps, given the need to please Adler, who'd been employing Gordin for years; but the strain showed. After all, the play itself is all about a dreamer's idea and its cruel rejection by others, Sholem Aleichem's current preoccupation.

A second source of stress emerged early that fall, after Sholem Aleichem traveled to London with Olga and their younger son Numa to embark on their New York voyage. Always trying to alleviate the family's financial situation, he arranged for the London *Jewish Chronicle* to buy "Cucumbers," son-in-law I. D. Berkowitz's first Yiddish work, for a princely sum. The editors, no fools they, asked if Sholem Aleichem would provide an introduction, and he agreed. In it, Sholem Aleichem, as in his *Folksbibliotek* days, tilted at conventional wisdom: but no longer as the young radical. This time, he was the defender, and a stalwart defender, of the status quo. Jewish literature—in Hebrew and in Yiddish—had exploded over the previous decade; new writers, new movements, new criticisms and critiques were coming into being on the pages of the newspapers, in the literary salons, and in the little magazines and journals beginning to crop up inside and outside Eastern Europe. Sholem Aleichem's introduction took on one such new movement: a growing, loosely affiliated group of young Hebrew and Yiddish writers (in Hebrew, literally called "The Young Ones"), who, unlike his son-in-law, focused their writings on mood. "Do you want to know what this mood is?" he wrote caustically. "Mood is: words, just words, high, puffed up, round, pointed, frightening words, with a lot of dots and dashes. . . . there's no story, no hint of psychology, no trace of description, types, characters—as long as the words sound good (and they don't always sound good), as long as it's difficult to understand the content—and more, the harder it is to understand, the less content, the more mood."

The introduction remained unpublished, at his son-in-law's request. Berkowitz may have disagreed with Sholem Aleichem's literary philosophy. He may have felt that his father-in-law's praise was the equivalent of mommy coming to save him from the bullies. He may have felt that the introduction would overshadow the story. Regardless of whether Sholem Aleichem was right or not (and I tend to think that in the main he had a point: there are an awful lot of dots and dashes in some of those stories, and less plot or character than there probably should be), he ends up sounding a bit like an old crank telling those young kids with their rock and roll to keep it down.

This, then, was the second concern: on the cusp of becoming an old fogy, he was set to encounter the New World.

CHAPTER 19

In Which Our Hero Enters, and Exits, a New Stage

1906–1907

Those who know America and know me," Sholem Aleichem wrote his niece, "predict a brilliant success." At the same time, he admitted that "the feeling of parting with Russia, with our Kiev and with you . . . evokes an tremendous longing. . . . I would have said tears, but I'm afraid that I will seem cowardly, like a woman." Sholem Aleichem's ambivalence couldn't have been helped by the fact that their ship, the *St. Louis*, departed London on October 13—a number the superstitious author disliked intensely.

Sholem Aleichem, Olga, and Numa all traveled second-class—not quite where the swells lived, befitting their reduced circumstances, but a far cry from the packed steerage where the majority of his readers would make the grand crossing. There didn't seem to be many of them on Sholem Aleichem's ship, which disappointed him: "Jews," he wrote in a letter to his family that took the form of a ship's diary, "have a peculiar nature: when there are a lot of them around, it's hard to bear them; when they're not—you long for them." Perhaps to assuage that longing, he visited third class; the crowding shocked him, but, he wrote, it was still better than first class; at least there were *some* Jews there. Getting their chance to see the author—steerage passengers didn't have full run of the boat and were limited to their own areas—his readers crowded around him excitedly. Later in the trip, he would wistfully hear the sounds of their singing coming from below.

The crossing would last eight days, the first half racked by tremendous bouts of seasickness on the Atlantic's stormy waters. All they could consume were oranges, water, and Madeira, and Numa cried for his beloved Geneva. By Tuesday, things were looking up a bit: they could now keep down soup and ice cream, and by the evening father and son could attend meals, bringing back herring and potatoes to the still bed-bound Olga. (Plain as it seemed, Sholem Aleichem wrote, it was a delight compared to English cuisine, which "was fit for the wicked in Gehenna.") With the waters calmer, Sholem Aleichem and Numa marveled at the sight of the ocean and at the wide range of passengers on the ship: card-playing Americans, beer-drinking Germans, balalaika-playing Russians—it was, as he wrote, "a small mobile colony . . . a little Bohuslav," 3,500 souls all told, even complete with a variety of streets and stores.

With so much time on their hands, minor naughtinesses were bound to occur. Sholem Aleichem and Numa snuck apples and oranges to eat later ("In general," he wrote, "the commandment of 'Thou Shalt Not Steal' is not honored on the ocean") and smuggled a fan up from steerage for a visit. (The man so loved Sholem Aleichem's work that, when no other tickets were available, he had agreed to travel third-class—despite being wealthier than the author—just to get on the ship.) Later that day, the ship's officers sent for Sholem Aleichem: some fellow Jews, jealous of the passenger's good fortune, had reported him for "smuggling"—the kind of behavior Sholem Aleichem might have chronicled in Kasrilevke stories. Fortunately, the passenger had already returned to his compartment, so there were no graver repercussions.

Land was sighted around noon on the 20th; the ship entered New York harbor several hours later. Sholem Aleichem saw the people massed on the docks, heard the loud hurrahs, watched the hats tossed into the air; and hearing the (doubly appropriate) words "Sholem Aleichem!" he realized many of them—along with members of the Yiddish and English-language press and representatives of Zionist and other organizations, the boldest of bold-faced names—were waiting to greet *him*. The welcoming committee, assembled by Dr. Fishberg and Sholem Aleichem's old friend Avrom Eliyahu Lubarski, "the picturesque representative in America of the famed Russian tea firm, Wissotsky and Company," included among others the communal leader Judah Magnes; Richard Gottheil, the head of Columbia University's Department of Semitics; the editors of the four daily Yiddish papers; and the leading lights of the Yiddish theater, Adler, Thomashevsky, and Goldfaden. The press and dignitaries approached the boat (still in quarantine) by special cutter; then boarded the *St. Louis* and joined him for the final lap to port. When Sholem Aleichem arrived, joyful chaos reigned; he was hoisted into the air; cameras flashed; "endless delegations" were presented, along with a bouquet of flowers, by Stella Adler; but the most welcome sight was his brother Bernard, who brought news via telegram that he was now a grandfather—Ernestina had had a baby girl. Thanks to modern technology, the news had beaten Sholem Aleichem across the Atlantic.

Chaos and energy were the watchwords of this new world in which Sholem Aleichem now found himself. Over 2 million Jews came to America between 1881 and 1924, and between 1899 and 1910, 86 percent of them came through New York; lots of them stayed there. The Lower East Side, at the time, had almost the highest population density on earth (beat only by Bombay and Calcutta); it was not quite, at the time of Sholem Aleichem's arrival, at its peak of 542,000 Jews, but it was close. And they were reading Yiddish, of course, lots of them: the combined circulation of the Yiddish newspapers practically doubled, to 120,000, in 1902, and would climb drastically from there over the next two decades, sparking a vitality and a creativity—not to mention a back-stabbing competitive ethos—that helped to make the city one of the major centers in the history of Yiddish.

That same Yiddish press, though, achieved unanimity in falling over themselves to praise the new arrival. They called him "The Great Jewish Humorist," "The Greatest Jewish Humorist," and "The King of Jewish Humor." One newspaper, the *Morgen-Zhurnal*, ran a huge photo of "The Jewish Mark Twain," crowned with a wreath, on the front page; and another, the *Tageblat*, even suggested that within five years Sholem Aleichem could be granted citizenship "like the rest of us; and if he retains the people's love which he now enjoys on his arrival, he could become a candidate for political office like those at present monopolizing the enthusiasm of the people." The packed reception and welcome benefit at Adler's Grand Theater on October 31 included choral selections from the Yiddish theater, a presentation of flower bouquets from the Actors', Composers', and Choral unions, and readings by Sholem Aleichem himself (breathlessly referred to in the run-up to the event as "one of the most famous lecturers in the world"). The speaking lineup, which included both the religious Zionist orator Zvi Hersh Masliansky and the labor leader Joseph Barondess, the "King of the Cloakmakers," testified to the breadth of Sholem Aleichem's ideological and popular appeal; the speeches—and the applause that greeted them—ran long, so long that Sholem Aleichem didn't give his own readings (including "If I Were Rothschild") until more than three hours had passed, after 11:30. And then there was the banquet for three hundred that lasted till four a.m. at Clinton Hall; a correspondent filing his report at three in the morning wrote there was no sign of it stopping.

There was a second reception, too; as the New York Jewish community at the time was divided between "uptown Jews" (the more established, wealthier German-Jewish community) and "downtown Jews" (poorer Eastern European immigrants), the former had to have their turn as well. At that reception, Sholem Aleichem was greeted by the luminaries of early-twentieth-century Jewish America: Jacob Schiff, the banker who had backed the Japanese against Russia in the recent war; Felix Warburg, Schiff's son-in-law, whose Fifth Avenue mansion now houses the Jewish Museum; Nathan Straus, who co-owned Macy's; and the New York Supreme Court justice Samuel Greenbaum—who, according to Sholem Aleichem's daughter, would introduce her father to Mark Twain. When he introduced Sholem Aleichem as "the 'Jewish Mark Twain,'" she would write, Twain "graciously replied, 'Please tell him that I am the American Sholem Aleichem.'"

The receptions helped spread Sholem Aleichem's reputation to the English-language press; and the sobriquet "the Jewish Mark Twain" helped put a handle on him. People loved that his name was a common expression—shades of that Missouri author—and his life story as rendered in the press, how the equivalent of a Russian "Wall Street broker" became "the voice of his people." For Sholem Aleichem's part, he was no less encouraged by the financials: that first evening brought him no less than $1,000 (over $23,000 in 2010 prices), a good sign for his American future—though needing to track down the evening's treasurer to pick up the check in person did put a bit of a pall on things.

He stayed at his brother Bernard's home in the Bronx for the first two weeks, fielding a madhouse of visitors and well-wishers—the papers had helpfully printed Bernard's address—and weighing a plethora of offers and options. Should he write for the Yiddish press? If so, which paper? What about the English-language press? Was that a possibility? Both the *Tageblat* and the *Morgen-Zhurnal* were strong possibilities, but the most intriguing proposal came from the *Yiddish American*, a newly established paper born of peculiar circumstance: William Randolph Hearst was running for governor that fall as an independent against Charles Evans Hughes, and as one of the original self-funded candidates, he put some of his significant resources into reaching Yiddish-speaking voters by creating a newspaper targeted at them. Landing the world's most popular Yiddish writer as a contributor would surely be a draw.

The wooing had begun even before the author set foot on American shores: the paper cabled him while he was still on board ship and offered him a healthy fee to write about the Russian situation and his visit's significance. Sholem Aleichem demurred, citing seasickness, but he'd been impressed by the commitment represented by the sheer cost of sending a ship-to-shore telegram just for his opinion. He was even more impressed when he got their real offer: $5,000 a year (almost $120,000 in 2010 dollars). An unofficial kitchen cabinet of ex-greenhorns helped him mull it over. Accepting the *Yiddish American*'s offer meant offending every other Yiddish newspaper, hardly the prescription for lasting American success—especially since, some argued, the *American* might not last very long if Hearst's candidacy failed. While deliberating, Sholem Aleichem published an open letter begging forgiveness, in the ancient penitential formula of the Day of Atonement, for his sin of having believed there was no future for Jewish life—and Yiddish writing—in America, that it was a nation of Jewish peddlers who cared only for business. On the contrary, he said, playing on the old biblical phrase—*ki meamerike tetsei torah udevar hashem minew york*—"From America would come forth Torah, and the word of the Lord from New York."

It was all amazing news, the boomiest of the booms. And Sholem Aleichem, as always, allowed himself to be carried away by it all, writing his daughter the day after his arrival that "mountains of gold are being promised from every side . . . a new era is coming on our horizon, full of success, happiness, and joy," and confiding to friends several weeks later that "hopefully, here lies the end of my exile." The material comforts didn't hurt, either. Renting an apartment near Bernard in the Bronx, at 921 East 156th Street—a little farther from the city since "we are still very green and don't know the language"—Sholem Aleichem raved to his children about the New World's amenities: easier garbage disposal, hot water in the kitchen any hour of the day or night, and the beauty of the furnishings, particularly the writing tables and chairs. If they could see these things, he wrote, they'd come in a flash. He was so enthusiastic about identifying with America that it decisively affected one of the most crucial decisions he had to make at the time: what he and Olga would be called as grandparents. No Bubbe and Zeyde for them, Sholem Aleichem wrote the children; they'd rather be known as "American Papa" and "American Mama."

Receiving Sholem Aleichem's glad tidings, the saturnine Abramovitch worried about America's fickleness, and, unfortunately, he turned out to be right. New arrivals from Europe pushed Sholem Aleichem off the front pages; Hearst's loss in the gubernatorial elections did lead to the *Yiddish*

American's closing, as had been darkly predicted; and now none of the other newspapers seemed primed to make a firm offer. In part, this might have been a reaction to Sholem Aleichem's somewhat condescending European attitude toward the contemporary American Yiddish press, his open letter notwithstanding. But some of it was simply local newspaper politics: if Orthodox newspapers like the *Tageblat* and the *Morgen-Zhurnal* were for him, seeing his stories as links to the old, traditional world that would resonate with their readership, then their more socialist or progressive rivals would have to be against him. Sholem Aleichem's own strategies hadn't helped, either. His refusal to affiliate with any one of the more established Yiddish papers had also stemmed from the hope that as a result none of them would oppose him in his real goal: to make money in the Yiddish theater. Newspaper reviews were essential in driving the audiences to the theater in sufficient numbers to make his plays profitable. But failing to side with anyone also meant no one felt as committed to supporting him. Sholem Aleichem's characteristic facility of being all things to all people failed him in the hyper-partisan environment of the press.

The best he got was a joint offer from the two Orthodox papers: $40 a week (about $50,000 a year in 2010 dollars) to write exclusively for the *Tageblat* and for the *Morgen-Zhurnal*'s weekly supplement, the *Amerikaner*. It wasn't enough to support the family; and taking the deal meant alienating all the other newspapers—with consequences that could make or break his theatrical career. The public readings that had supplemented his income over the last year weren't taking off in America: as in Europe, he had relied on Zionist organizations to arrange them, and the movement hadn't yet gained much of a foothold in the New World. In addition, outside New York the audiences were, in his daughter's words, "less sophisticated, mostly shopkeepers, and with overlong business hours"; their attendance at readings was hardly assured, and Sholem Aleichem wasn't quite a household name among that constituency. (At one reading, the speaker introduced him as "Sholem Asch Aleichem Abramovitch.") At best, the readings paid for some living expenses, but couldn't touch the debts he'd incurred to support the family over the last year. By mid-December, referencing the well-known Talmudic principle that a biblical passage beginning with *Vayehi* ("And it came to pass") introduces an unfortunate or tragic episode, he asserted: "Vayehi, And it was, that I arrived in America. Where a 'Vayehi' is a tragedy, and where an 'author' is a shlimazl!"

The press situation was paralyzing, the readings were ineffective: the only option left was the one he'd been thinking of all along, the Yiddish theater. And so he returned to playwriting in earnest by mid-January, settling into an intensive writing schedule: up at eight, a few minutes for coffee, working until twelve or one, a quick break to read the papers, back to work again, and mostly writing until as late as two or three in the morning. Success—especially if the plays crossed over onto the English stage—would solve all his problems. While a Yiddish play might net an author a thousand dollars (about $24,000 in 2010 dollars) over an entire lifetime—Sholem Aleichem's deal with Adler was potentially slightly better, though the money would depend on how long the show ran—a popular play on the English-language stage could yield its author as much as $10,000 to $20,000 (that is, up to half a million 2010 dollars) *a year*.

Adler wasn't the only one waiting: Boris Thomashevsky, the other great actor-manager Sholem Aleichem had mentioned to Fishberg back in Russia, wanted a play, too. Sholem Aleichem preferred Adler's more artistic sensibilities. On the other hand, Thomashevsky advanced him the thousand dollars up front, and he needed the money. So he had to write plays for both at the same time. Topping that, he was writing them for *simultaneous premieres*—the result of a game of chicken by the two actor-managers, neither of whom wanted their potentially hot property to fall behind. Adler's Grand Theater would premiere Sholem Aleichem's *The Scoundrel, or Shmuel Pasternak* at exactly the same time as *Stempenyu, or, Jewish Daughters* would be opening at Boris Thomashevsky's People's Theater, on February 8. Maybe it was the time crunch. Maybe it was his concern about the new medium. Or maybe it was the natural predilection of the artist. But Sholem Aleichem went with what had worked in the past: *Pasternak* was a significant revision of his old stock exchange drama *Yaknehoz*, and *Stempenyu* dramatized his "greatest masterwork . . . which has astonished the entire world and has been translated into every language . . .[as] a true original Jewish Hasidic play of real life"—at least according to the ad the People's Theater ran.

Opening against yourself, as any movie executive will tell you, is a deadly proposition, especially when the brand's the same. To make matters worse, Sholem Aleichem, wearing his literary critic's hat when he should have stuck with the playwright's, broke with established theatrical custom and used his podium on the stage of Adler's Grand Theater to seriously criticize Gordin's approach to depicting Jewish life. Perhaps not the most politic of decisions at a time when the regnant arbiter of Yiddish theatrical quality enjoyed significant critical support from some of the leading newspapers. Imagine if Jonathan Franzen had alienated both Oprah and the *Times Literary Supplement* simultaneously, and you get the idea.

Sholem Aleichem didn't seem to have grasped the evolving dimensions of this failure right away. Writing his children the following day, he informed them he had passed the test brilliantly, despite a lot of running back and forth between theaters: plenty of ovations and calls for the author. *Stempenyu* was poetically successful; *Pasternak* kept them laughing—an easy task, as the "humor of the local, popular dramatists is of such low quality" (there's that condescension again). One hint he may be putting on an intentionally sunny tone, though, comes from a small concern he lets slip about the press: the Yiddish press, he writes, is "partisan, and I expect nothing good from it . . . but the main thing is the public, the great audience."

That may not have been as true as he had hoped. The *Tageblat* and the *Morgen-Zhurnal* came through, writing that he had "open[ed] a new world for the theater public" and that "the hopes placed upon Sholem Aleichem, that he would bring a new spirit into America's Yiddish theater, have been fulfilled." But they were Sholem Aleichem's natural constituency. Other papers were less kind. The progressive *Varheit*, a strong supporter of Gordin's, was so incensed they titled their review of *Paster-*

nak "Monstrosity"; Louis Miller, the paper's editor, had left in the middle. Joel Entin, writing in the left-wing *Yidisher Kemfer*, called it "a still-born monster . . . a weak piece of furniture without legs 'master-minded' by a consumptive apprentice to a carpenter"; and Abraham Cahan, the editor of the powerful *Jewish Daily Forward* and a fearsome cultural critic, landed what may have been an even harsher blow to the ego of the man who had sought, once, to revolutionize Yiddish literature. Claiming the play was unrealistic, implausible, he wrote, "Years ago, Sholem Aleichem had pronounced a judgment on Shomer; and now one must pronounce a new one on Sholem Aleichem. Once Sholem Aleichem played a major role in Yiddish literature, but now, in 1907, when we have such talents as Sholem Asch, Sholem Aleichem's place in Yiddish literature is not as great or important."

It might have been the sulfurous reviews, or the market saturation. Or maybe it was the star-managers' changing the scripts, weakening their power at the expense of their own stage time—a common practice in the Yiddish theater. It might have been that the staging, the "cheap theatrical effects," inevitably altered the dramas' tone and, as the composer Joseph Rumshinsky suggested, dissipated all the charm with which Sholem Aleichem had suffused them. Whatever combination it may have been, neither play ran longer than two weeks—which, to put it mildly, minimized Sholem Aleichem's chances of writing for the theater, not to mention his desire to do so.

Sholem Aleichem bounced back, as he always did; by Passover time, his letters to his children were once more full of optimistic plans. He signed a contract with the same *Varheit* that had just eviscerated his play, and which stood an ideological league apart from the traditional, middle-class *Tageblat*. Sholem Aleichem noted in an autobiographical sketch that he didn't necessarily share Miller's left-wing politics; after what he had been through in Russia, it was easy to understand why. His project for Miller—a serialized literary novel published through the spring of 1906—illustrated the lessons of his experience; *The Deluge* (later published in a highly revised form as *In the Storm*) is probably his fullest statement on the subject of 1905, filtering various authorial preoccupations through the events immediately surrounding the constitution and its aftermath. He had preferred not to write a novel; but the stories and sketches that had been his stock in trade over the last few years paid badly, and a serial novel was a natural source of lucrative daily copy. (Well, semi-lucrative: Olga would later complain that Sholem Aleichem made as little as $30 a week on the deal.)

After *Scattered and Dispersed*—to say nothing of "Hodl" and "Chava"—Sholem Aleichem had become a master at using *tsuris fun kinder*, trouble with children, to stand in for the changes and stresses of the modern period. *In the Storm*'s parents are also mostly oblivious at first to their children's activity, their increasing, and increasingly dangerous, political radicalism. The plot centers on three children from various families; arrests, imprisonments, escapes, suicides, and madness all follow. The novel's strength lies neither in its contorted plot nor in its thin characters, but in the way it expertly captures the growing, churning activity preceding the storm of revolution to come—the gatherings, in serious, over-serious, and silly forms, the spying and counterspying—and the storm itself. The pathos-filled descriptions of Bloody Sunday and the terrors of the pogrom on the streets are as frightening and as fine-grained and as realistic as anything he had ever written. And—above all that—Sholem Aleichem masterfully used the events to level his own separate political and cultural indictment of the Russian Jewish community, suggesting that his major concern was less the bourgeois parents paying insufficient attention to their children's political activism but rather the abandonment, by parents and children alike, of Jewish culture. One of the children, learning of the work of Bialik and his post-Kishinev poem "The City of Slaughter," ponders her father's dismissal of their national poet as a "ditty writer": "It was unimaginable that even an uneducated Russian peasant would not know who Pushkin was. . . . [She concluded] that either Bialik wasn't a poet or we weren't a people, and if we weren't a people, what were we then?"

The failures of 1905, in Sholem Aleichem's novelistic imagination, reinforced his insistence on creating national solutions to the Jewish questions—solutions that can be most powerfully and profoundly found in the world of culture. Some of the characters do go to Palestine at the novel's end, but, fittingly, this seems more an unquestionably *Jewish* political solution rather than *the* essential political solution—it is, in its way, the fulfillment of a Jewish cultural imperative. The novel's end occurs at a train station, with talk of America and the essentially wandering nature of Jews: and suggests that the only grand solution possible is the literature that encapsulates the search for and struggle with grand solutions.

The contract for *The Deluge* notwithstanding, Sholem Aleichem was suffering in America. He needed his family ("his republic," as he called them), and determined to return to Geneva for the summer, perhaps temporarily, perhaps not. Writing like a demon that spring, he produced five hundred pages in two months, trying to finish so he could sail. His disastrous American experience weighed heavily on him, and he worked it out in the most unlikely venue: a new Tevye story. Tevye was his resilience, his persistence in the face of adversity. He wrote Spektor, his editor: "God is a great God; Sholem Aleichem lives and Tevye is not dead . . . the circumstances have changed, the years have taken their toll, but Tevye himself has remained the same Tevye." Another story of a daughter's disastrous match, "Shprintze" provides intriguing echoes of Sholem Aleichem's American disillusionment.

"God wanted to do us Jews a favor and so He sent us a new catastrophe, a Constantution," Tevye tells Sholem Aleichem; ironically, though, the post-pogrom flight from the cities has swelled the population where Tevye works, creating a potential boom for him—just as the constitution's backlash had led to Sholem Aleichem's consideration of the lucrative American market. Naturally, a bust follows—and what a bust it is. Tevye serves a rich widow, befriends her son Ahrontchik, Ahrontchik falls in love with Shprintze, and, though Tevye understands the facts of life—that Ahrontchik's family will never allow the match—he nonetheless briefly indulges the fantasy that Shprintze is meant to be his "reward for all [his] hardship and [his] heartache." But it's as ephemeral as Sholem

Aleichem's dreams of theatrical success: Ahrontchik drops out of sight, a business associate of the family's attempts to buy off Tevye, intimating that the whole relationship has been nothing but a honey trap, and Shprintze, understanding everything, drowns herself in the river. The story has little to do with the question of suicide per se. Tevye's final plaint illuminates: "My problem wasn't God, though—with Him I had somehow made my peace. My problem was men. Why did they have to ruin their own and other people's lives instead of being happy with what they had?" Looking at an American expedition ruined not by grand, universal forces, but by the grubby interaction of local newspaper politics and personal grievances, Sholem Aleichem would have had to agree.

CHAPTER 20

In Which Our Hero Has Joyous Meetings and Tragic Partings, and Seeks a Buried Treasure

1907–1908

Immediately after Shavuot, on June 7, Sholem Aleichem, Olga, and Numa sailed on the *Newark* for Europe (having borrowed money for the fare). Invigorated and inspired by a joyful family reunion, including finally meeting his new granddaughter, Sholem Aleichem got down to work in Geneva, indulging his predilections for writing out of doors. Visitors to the municipal gardens near the university during the summer of 1907 would have seen a Russian gentleman walking along the paths, accompanied by his children (and a baby carriage). He would sometimes stop, raising his head to the sky, and look searchingly into it, peeking over his half glasses, and then write earnestly in a silver-backed notebook with a fountain pen (a memento of his New York welcome ceremony). At times, he might sit down, legs crossed, hold the pen to his ear, and move his lips soundlessly, trying out the rhythms of sentences and of dialogue. Everything would have looked idyllic, though the viewer might have wondered why the gentleman was wearing gloves. The fact that the writer had to do so to prevent him from biting his nails bloody suggests the currents of Sholem Aleichem's state of mind were never that smooth.

He had taken pains, departing New York, to give the impression to editors and potential employers that his return to Geneva was simply a summer visit to see his family, and that he planned to return to the States by early the next winter. This wasn't exactly so, as his decision to rent a fourth-floor walk-up in a house on Plein Palais in Geneva for three years indicated. (The family was occasionally noisy, and their downstairs neighbor took them to court, threatening eviction; they retained a lawyer named Dreyfuss and called the matter "The Second Dreyfuss Case.") Missing his family, his Russia (despite its behavior to his people in recent years), and his audience, smarting from his treatment in America, he would prefer to make it in Europe if he could. But that was a big "if," and so it was politic to leave an open door behind him. This would later prove to have been a fortunate choice.

But the financial picture was hardly rosy: as the children grew, so did the family's expenses. (Misha, for example, was now studying in a Kiev *gymnasium*, and needed to be supported there.) The American publishers paid badly, the *Fraynd* was failing, but at least he was working steadily. He had contracts to write for the *Tageblat* and the *Amerikaner* while in Europe, and *The Deluge* was still running in the *Varheit*. The *Tageblat* would get individual stories. The *Amerikaner* got the rights to a new series: the adventures of a young boy named Motl, a cantor's son who would become one of the best known, most beloved characters in all of Yiddish literature. It almost never happened: the *Amerikaner*'s editor didn't like the first installment, neither did his editorial board, and they considered rejecting it. For all his critical independence and creative stubbornness, Sholem Aleichem was quite responsive to others' opinion. Had he gotten a rejection slip, he might well have quashed the story entirely and never returned to it, as had happened, for example, with his first theatrical attempt for Adler. Fortunately for posterity, the editor was a personal friend and didn't want to spoil Sholem Aleichem's upcoming Shavuot holiday. So he took it, chiding the author for giving the *Tageblat* good material while he got stuck with this new Motl.

It's probably a worthwhile coincidence that the Motl stories first appeared in the *Amerikaner*. Motl, the cantor's son, who makes mischief in the shtetl and then immigrates with his family to America, is Sholem Aleichem's living stratagem for contemplating arguably the biggest historical trend of his staggeringly eventful time: the mass Eastern European Jewish immigration to America and the immigrants' life on the Lower East Side. In his ship's diary of his own voyage to America, Sholem Aleichem had noted in passing that "all the passengers on the ocean are children"; and a child seemed to be the appropriate bundle of energy, optimism, and newness that resonated with the dream of America. As with Tevye, Sholem Aleichem takes his time about getting to Motl's grand adventure, his travels, but in making him a "happy orphan," he moves fairly quickly to another of his grand themes: how to turn trauma into joy, studied joy. ("Hurray—I'm an orphan!" Motl famously shouts.) In some way, this would be, thanks to its child narrator, an opportunity to rewrite his own misery-laden travels and American exposure; using a child allowed him to play with the gap between the child's perception and the mature reader's ironic recognition of what is actually happening. It's assisted by an almost imperceptible partial shift in register by the narrator—not all the phrases Motl uses are within a nine-year-old's lexicon.

Motl's joy, that joy that renders him an object of sympathy and even envy—what adult wouldn't want that emotional resilience?—is juxtaposed with his capacity for reinvention. His mother, a constantly weeping figure clinging to the memory of her husband and the Old World writ large—she's always, through the travails of emigration, going on about her pillows—is incapable of change. (The Kasrilevkans do the same thing when they travel. "No matter where they go to," Sholem Aleichem writes, "they take along their home—for which God's name be praised—yes, their 'ghetto' and their 'galut.'") Even his older brother Elye, modeled on Sholem Aleichem's own brother, changes, but grimly, almost mechanically, and oh so responsibly, moving forward in measured steps. By contrast, Motl reinvents himself spontaneously, energetically; his status as orphan is quickly replaced by that of entrepreneur (or, technically, entrepreneur's assistant), which in turn is replaced by that of emigrant. This doesn't make him callous or flighty, of course; it makes him a child, who values adventure and excitement over many other things. Motl's grand gestures and promises to protect little girls over the course of the novel are evidence enough that he acts from impulse, not malice, and the imagination to see himself as a providing hero. Energy, romance, reinvention, rebirth—signs of change not only through America, but from America: Sholem Aleichem's new optimistic mood, deepening as he returned to the home of his family, moving beyond Tevye's resilience to a different kind of progress.

The character's originality only developed as the installments progressed. Sholem Aleichem changed his plans for Motl's future: though the original emphasis on his beautiful voice bespoke the intention to make him a cantor or opera singer in America, it was neither sufficiently American nor sufficiently original, covering ground he'd treated back in *Yosele Solovey*. On board ship back to Europe, inspired by a talented young artist traveling to Europe to deepen his craft, Sholem Aleichem decided Motl would become a cartoonist for the rich English-language papers, a career path other Jews were then adopting. (It undoubtedly was also influenced by the example of his brother Abba, the family artist who had often spoken of his desire to immigrate to North America before his untimely death in 1882: Abba's pencil sketches of local rural types still exist, and are quite accomplished.)

But, as Sholem Aleichem's own dream of American riches had been foiled, his eye toward his own economic anxieties—and those for European Jews more generally—pervade that first section of *Motl* he wrote in 1907 in a variety of ways. Many of Motl's shtetl adventures, packed with characters modeled on composites from Sholem Aleichem's own childhood, revolve around his and Elye's moneymaking attempts, most borrowed from a book of get-rich-quick schemes Elye sent away for. They work out as well as Sholem Aleichem's jackpot boom-and-bust schemes generally do: selling kvass, for example, which Elye waters down a little, but then Motl dilutes a lot; or making ink and getting rid of the excessive unsold amounts by "flooding the world" at night. But one of the most unusual—and thus most illustrative—episodes is Motl's failure in a job of his very own: staying awake with a man who refuses to spend the night alone. Once everyone else but Motl has gone, the man becomes a monster out of fairy tale—"I'm going to eat you up!" he says—and his nightmarish claim is so powerful because overexpansiveness, be it overproduction or overconsumption, while simply comic when it comes to childhood failure, becomes ghoulish when transformed into an adult setting. Extremism is excusable in children; when it engulfs the adult world, it's a sign of monstrosity. Between the father's death, the mother's ghostly impotence, and the gentleman's extreme irrationality, it falls to the responsible "middle generation"—the practical-minded if not quite practical Elye and his nearsighted, argumentative, idealistic friend Pini—to decide that the family should leave and for Motl's adventures to truly begin. As we'll see, though, those adventures would be delayed for some time.

If it would be a while until Motl reached the New World, Sholem Aleichem was taking on America right now, and right away, in his *Tageblat* stories, in a "satire, a sort of political creature," about American politics and Jewish power. "The First Jewish Republic" features thirteen Jews of widely different backgrounds who bond aboard ship through heated arguments about Jewish politics; a symbolically corresponding storm capsizes the boat, and the group washes up on Edenic dry land, in a New World. The castaways include our writer-narrator, an American atheist, a millionaire, a female passenger, a belowdecks workman, an Orthodox Jew, a Zionist, an assimilationist, a territorialist, a socialist, and a nationalist; though we may now think of *Gilligan's Island*, Sholem Aleichem's model—as the second chapter suggests—was clearly *Robinson Crusoe*, that love of his youth.

Despite the island's natural bounty, unity proves impossible, and the thirteen withdraw to their own caves; whenever they do get together, arguments break out, clearly an allegory for the Jewish political community's divisiveness and confusion. They eventually name their area "Thirteen Island," chosen for its similarity to the United States' thirteen original colonies, and, as the possibility of rescue seems remote, decide "to set up a government, a state, a kingdom, a constitution, or perhaps a republic . . . the first Jewish republic on earth." They eventually decide on a loose confederation, "The First Jewish Republic of the Thirteen United States"—which of course means presidential elections, for which everyone runs, and so: thirteen presidents. Each president wants his or her own constitution; the writer-narrator agrees to make a "tutti-frutti" of all the respective constitutions; a debate breaks out about what language to write the constitution in; a wide range of suggestions are unsurprisingly advanced; the writer eventually suggests Yiddish, and though his suggestion is eventually adopted, the question emerges as to what *dialect* of Yiddish; until we discover that while all this arguing was going on forces from the other side of the island have snuck up and captured them.

Some of the politics are familiar, like the skepticism about the realistic possibility of Zionist, or indeed any political, success, given the Jews' factional and fractious nature. But it's also a powerful examination of the American political model as both unusually congruent with and problematic for the Jewish way of life. Robust and freewheeling American democracy perfectly suits beloved Jewish methods of jawboning, and a live-and-let-live philosophy deeply attractive to those who had suffered from coercive anti-Semitic legislation: but it simultaneously creates easy possibilities for gridlock when it comes to necessary concerted action— and there are always enemies waiting, on the other side of the hill.

Sholem Aleichem could hardly have been dissuaded from his opinion that August, attending the Eighth Zionist Congress in the Hague as an American delegate. (He may not have been the most ardent Zionist activist America had to offer, but he had the inestimable advantage of being able to pay his own expenses.) "Impressions from the Zionist Congress," recorded for the *Tageblat*, included a chaotic information bureau, where "all these girls with blue sashes and all these nice young men with Magen Davids keep getting in each other's way"; the scrambling for chairs in the buffet—"If you haven't a chair, you must get one, grab hold of one from somebody else. If he won't let you, take it by force"; and waiters who speak "some queer language similar to our Yiddish" and who won't let the bottles of Carmel wine out of their grasp until you pay in advance. "The whole place was in such a muddle," in short, "that a wedding in Mazapevka would have looked like a quiet, well-behaved, orderly gathering in comparison."

Which is not to say he didn't enjoy himself. He basked in his celebrity there, constantly being asked for his autograph as part of the new craze of sending signed postcards from the congress (another breaking trend: taking group photographs). Conventioneers behaved the same way then that they do now: one man, pressing him while he was eating, "pushed one card after the other in front of me, till I had to take the fork in my left hand and let the young man hold my right hand and do with it whatever he wanted." (One wonders what he got for them.) Most excitingly for Sholem Aleichem, he finally got the chance to meet Hayyim Nachman Bialik in person for the first time, after years of warm and humorous correspondence. They "fell on each other's neck and kissed," Sholem Aleichem wrote, "a long lingering kiss, like a newly betrothed couple, who really love each other."

Easy to see this—the encounter between Hebrew literature's presiding genius and Yiddish's increasingly central voice, at a Zionist conference—as a watershed in the war of languages, a recognition of the necessity of cultural unity and synthesis. Moments aren't just symbolic, though, and the story's more complicated. As we've seen, Sholem Aleichem had loved Hebrew and Hebrew literature since childhood, and had read everything Bialik had ever written: he'd even recite his fellow Ukrainian's poetry in some of his own public readings. At the same time, though, he was happiest when Bialik wrote in Yiddish. Four years earlier, Bialik had published a Yiddish poem in the *Fraynd*, and Sholem Aleichem wrote him that "I was truly in Paradise when I read [it]. My daughter even laughed at me because I was kvelling so much . . . Let them see, those [Hebrew] dogs, that we, the Yiddish writers, also have a Bialik." We, the Yiddish writers: when it came down to it, as capacious as Sholem Aleichem could be, there were still sides to come down on. Yiddish was still finding its place, and its voice.

While at the congress, Sholem Aleichem received word from Geneva that an operation on his mother-in-law, who was dying of carcinoma, had been unsuccessful and that she'd taken a turn for the worse. Rokhl Loyeff had lived with Sholem Aleichem's family for twenty-two years, and Sholem Aleichem had acted the respectful, dutiful son—certainly ever since she had rescued him from his creditors and lost her life savings through his speculations. This isn't to say they were affectionate: she never forgave him the loss of the family money and the concomitant blow to her status; they almost never spoke to each other, "and avoided even formal greetings." And yet, Sholem Aleichem's daughter reported, "my father treated her with utmost respect, yielding to her the seat at the head of the table and primacy in family affairs in other matters," even keeping a kosher home at her insistence, though he himself was no longer traditionally observant. When Loyeff asked to see him on her deathbed (though she wrote "she didn't want to bother him" and take him from his work—talk about a Jewish mother), Sholem Aleichem dropped everything—including his series of "Impressions"—and rushed to Geneva. He arrived just in time for her burial. Abramovitch recited the "El Malei Rachamim"; Sholem Aleichem said the kaddish, at Loyeff's request, and would continue to do so throughout the thirty-day mourning period after the burial. He also refused all invitations to public appearances, another sign of respect for the departed.

The family's gloom would lift a bit early that fall, when Bialik came to stay with them and spend time with Abramovitch and fellow writer and Zionist Ben-Ami (the pseudonym of Mark Rabinovich). The leading lights of Jewish literature joked and laughed like anyone else: there were drinking sessions filled with Carmel wine, with Sholem Aleichem, quoting one of his characters, repeating the phrase "A Jew is never sober" over and over again. And there were the practical jokes: Bialik arrived on Rosh Hashanah, and Sholem Aleichem sneaked him into synagogue to meet the observant Ben-Ami—who wasn't too happy that the national poet had traveled on the holiday; Bialik forgot his slippers, and Sholem Aleichem promised to send them back one at a time—sending a photograph of them spending the interim period on Sholem Aleichem's feet. But there was gravity, too; walks in the Alps and discussions of "literature, Talmud, history, politics, poetry, and revolution," which Sholem Aleichem described (blended with his own imaginative re-creation) in a series of sketches he began publishing in the *Tageblat* that fall, then called "My Vacation" but later better known under the title "Once There Were Four."

Appropriately paradoxical for a memory piece, all four tell personal tales about forgetting (they've forgotten the name of the mountain they are climbing). The authors are presented as living stories as well as storytellers: symbols of the literature at whose summit they stood—symbolized by the mountain they're climbing in the feuilletons—with iconic personalities and styles. Sholem Aleichem sets his story in his pre-constitution touring days; invited to three neighboring cities by three rival movements, he mixes up all the dates. Arriving at the wrong town on the wrong day, he first claims the townspeople have the day wrong, and then cables his wife: WHERE AM I TODAY? TELEGRAPH REPLY. The problems cascade: his wife is confused (though not *that* confused: he's done this sort of thing before on several occasions), the organizations suspect foul play, and so on. Presenting himself as the hero of a "Sholem Aleichem story," the absent-minded celebrity whose adventures lead to both comedy and trauma in shared measure, Sholem Aleichem continued to craft his own myth, the writer as culture hero, but with feet of Kasrilevke mud.

Abramovitch tells a story of his own in "Once There Were Four." A young woman, preparing to nurse her child, finds a poisonous snake suckling at her breast. The press picks up the story; thousands buy the newspapers to see what happens. What happens, of course, is that the story remains inconclusive, and people keep buying papers: poisonous snakes, sucking away at their readers' marrow for eternal sustenance. To say nothing, one might add, of the *author's* symbiotic, if not parasitic, relationship with readers and with trauma. There's no story without the snake, after all; what is Sholem Aleichem's dark laughter without the traumas of Jewish history?

Sholem Aleichem probably envied the snake's success. The *Tageblat* never published "Once There Were Four" in full, over arguments between author and publisher about whether he was to be paid three or four cents a line. (Sholem Aleichem's annoyance that the publisher habitually hijacked the manuscript for personal reading for unspecified periods of time couldn't have helped.) Even worse, the *Amerikaner* was giving him problems with the Motl stories: Sapirstein, the publisher, complained it was dragging. Why couldn't he put in more plot, not this Russian psychology business? Pouring salt on the wound, Sholem Aleichem's reading tours in Holland and Belgium that fall led to irregular submissions, and when Sapirstein found a specious loophole to get out of his contract—he claimed Sholem Aleichem's agreement about republishing the stories in Europe didn't cover their appearance in the Yiddish supplement of the *London Jewish World*, on the grounds that London wasn't part of Europe—that was all the excuse he needed. He stopped publishing it three chapters shy of the end of the first section, and Sholem Aleichem wouldn't return to Motl's adventures for another eight years, until half a year before he died. The reading tours hadn't brought in that much money, either, and Sholem Aleichem's finances got so dire that in order to save money he asked his children not to go to the theater any longer.

It got worse. In January, he discovered the editors of the Warsaw Yiddish paper that had serialized *The Flood, Undzer Lebn*, had cheated him outrageously: while paying him only 150 rubles for the newspaper rights, they'd been selling tens of thousands of copies of the novel in book form in violation of their contract. Thundering that "they never did such a thing in Sodom," Sholem Aleichem threatened "to raise a storm in the press" unless they immediately desisted and turned over the plates and any remaining copies. The paper refused, counterclaiming that they weren't selling the novel, just giving it as a free gift to new subscribers. Sholem Aleichem was in such financial trouble that not only did the paper prevail, but he even agreed to provide them with additional copy at an astonishingly low price in return for a cash advance, and to sell rights to some of his works to another Warsaw publisher, Lidski—who, anticipating this, had been the ones who spilled the beans on *Undzer Lebn* in the first place.

And they weren't the only ones taking advantage. Two new New York publishing houses decided to make their debuts with unauthorized selections from Sholem Aleichem's Kasrilevke stories. Another Warsaw publisher, M. Krinski, refused to provide him with account statements to clarify his appropriate royalties. Sholem Aleichem would moan that over the last decade "others have earned tens of thousands, yes, tens of thousands of rubles from my works. And I've received from them the poor sum of around several hundred rubles!!!" When a generally complimentary article that February suggested that Sholem Aleichem could occasionally act childishly naïve in his personal life (it appeared in *Undzer Lebn*, of all places), Sholem Aleichem wrote the author that the latter had erred in thinking the naïveté "might be a 'joke' [i.e., a pose]; the true source of it is foolishness—plain and simple!" Sholem Aleichem was entering his twenty-fifth year as a published Yiddish writer—his jubilee year, which would be celebrated in October—and it looked to be an annus horribilis. How could someone of his talents—and more, his justly recognized talents, his celebrity—be in such a state?

Hardly surprising, then, that in that dark winter of 1908 he once again entertained hopes of a jackpot on the American Yiddish stage, his previous disappointments notwithstanding. (It was an auspicious time for Yiddish drama: Sholem Asch had just premiered his play *God of Vengeance*, which had combined success and scandal in equal proportion.) After a few false starts and minor efforts—like the apparently destroyed "The New Life," about emigrants turned American farmers—he made a first full attempt in Berlin, where he spent several months that winter. In the company of Berlin's expatriate intellectuals—the Yiddish refugees and activists, Zionists and literary figures who used to congregate around the Monopol coffeehouse (Martin Buber was one of the people who showed him around)—Sholem Aleichem came up with an "idea piece." "Whither?," like "David Son of David," was another story of a young

Zionist type who met a tragic end misunderstood by his fellow townspeople. Sholem Aleichem had his son-in-law read it to Adler, thinking he'd gravitate to the intellectual material. Adler was visibly uninterested, but perked up when he heard the author was working on a comedy as well: he asserted he'd pay $5,000 cash on the spot for a Sholem Aleichem comedy. Having suffered the additional indignity of an extremely lukewarm response to a reading of "Whither?" in Germany, Sholem Aleichem burned it and returned to work on the meaningfully titled *The Treasure*.

The Treasure's protagonist, Benny, is an American immigrant who's returned to the shtetl as a successful adult. By contrast, the shtetl has stagnated economically, nourishing itself on the legend of a buried treasure: Napoleon was said to have buried thirteen barrels of gold in the old cemetery. The play also boasts a second treasure: Esther, whom Benny hopes to marry. Like the hero of an old Haskala drama, Benny uses the town's Old World superstitions against them. (Unlike those old heroes, Benny is an American ignoramus—Sholem Aleichem's satiric side never lets anyone emerge unscathed.) Sholem Aleichem traced the play's history back almost two decades, claiming its origin in a story from *A Bouquet of Flowers*. (It actually appeared in *Hamelitz* in 1889, but, relying on memory rather than files, Sholem Aleichem often made such understandable little mistakes.) There, it was predicted that the buried treasure's discovery would bring the town peace and prosperity; but the constant arguments about it, alas, merely drive it deeper and deeper into the ground. What was in its original version an allegory for political factionalism or perhaps aesthetic fractiousness becomes a meditation on the differences between Old World and New World desires and flaws, and arguably a struggle over the nature of theatrical gold—at this point, Sholem Aleichem's own most urgent desire.

In short, a lot depended on *The Treasure*. On February 21, several days after returning to Geneva, Sholem Aleichem read the play to an audience of Russian-Jewish émigrés in the city's Handwerksaal, the same hall in which Lenin would occasionally lecture about the Russian revolutionary movement. The reception seemed very positive: an audience member sent a warm review to *Undzer Lebn*, and some audience members even suggested it was a Yiddish equivalent to Gogol's great Russian comedy *The Inspector General*. Sholem Aleichem preened—in a letter the next day, he refers to himself only half-facetiously as "The Jewish Mark Twain, the Yehupetz Gogol"—and sent *The Treasure* to New York's Yiddish actor-managers in early March. Of course, he had particular hopes for Adler: he insisted his son-in-law read him the play personally—not over the telephone!—and mindful of Adler's previous claims, instructed him to ask for $2,000, $1,500 if the reception was more negative.

Adler played hardball. Despite responding positively and enthusiastically throughout the reading, "the Great Eagle" only offered $1,000—and even that wouldn't be entirely cash up front. Sholem Aleichem still owed him money from the previous advance for *Pasternak*, which had closed so precipitately. (It might also have had something to do with the fact that the best role in the play, Adler's natural role, ends up converting to Christianity, which would have hardly endeared him to his audience.) Negotiations ended inconclusively. The play fared even worse elsewhere: maybe it was Sholem Aleichem's toxic theatrical reputation, or the recent failures of more literary Yiddish material on the stage. Thomashevsky was only doing operettas that season; another great Yiddish actor, David Kessler, grudgingly offered $300—but only if the author would rewrite the whole play, optimally as a burlesque. Adler asked for another reading, then left in the middle. Sholem Aleichem, climbing the walls back in Europe, took the news as a personal injustice, testament to the debased state of the American Yiddish theater.

Sholem Aleichem thought he could at least get some money for *publishing* the play; but when he proposed placing a revised version in *Literarishe Monatshriftn*, a new highbrow literary journal, one of the editors commented in his hearing that though they'd make room for him, he didn't belong—he was old guard, not their generation. Despite—or because of—seeing the journal as a natural sequel to his *Folksbibliotek*, Sholem Aleichem passed on what he saw as a gesture of pity. And as far as more middlebrow venues went, the *Fraynd* had just published another play called *The Treasure*, by the Yiddish playwright Dovid Pinski. So not only was selling there not an option, but he had to change the title to *The Gold-*

Diggers—"notwithstanding," as he snippily wrote, "that [the] comedy is already somewhat well-known under the title 'The Treasure' (having been read by me in Geneva, Paris, Bern and other cities), notwithstanding that a review of my comedy has already been published under that name." He would soon abandon the play; it would remain unpublished until a decade after his death.

Sholem Aleichem got back a little at American philistinism in "Five Letters. The Shortest Novel in the World, Written in Three Parts with an Epilogue and a Riddle in the American Fashion, Special for the Lodz Tageblat," a 1908 feuilleton in which the deeply enamored protagonist visits his beloved's father, his own rich Uncle Sam (get it?), on Fifth Avenue. When Uncle Sam, in his cups, refuses his suit for her affections, our hero murders him. If "Five Letters" was a blunt allegory for Sholem Aleichem's homicidal feelings toward the boorish Americans, drunk and indifferent to true value, who prevent him from achieving his heart's desire and the wealth that comes with it, a story he published in New York was a subtler knife. In "An Early Passover," German Jews mock their Eastern European brethren, particularly one calendar seller, for their backward ways. But their own ignorance, combined with their affection for basic Jewish traditions—their desire to observe Passover, bar mitzvahs, and yahrzeits on their proper dates—allow the calendar seller his revenge. He passes off expired calendars as next year's by making a tiny change in the date—the equivalent of bisecting 1980's last digit so it looks like 1988—and the purchasers therefore celebrate Passover on Purim, a month earlier, as they've failed to add the appropriate "leap month." Farcical happenings ensue. An allegory of the American community (with its noted split between German and Eastern European Jews), Sholem Aleichem outlines his revenge: the seller of repackaged tradition that, accurate or no, has power to disrupt and cause chaos in its new settings, thanks to the consumer's ignorance and philistinism. If the American readers didn't see the joke on themselves—or, for that matter, on Sholem Aleichem—well, that just proved his point.

But a set of satires was no substitution for money in the bank.

CHAPTER 21

In Which Our Hero Falls Ill

1908

The Treasure's American failure—in no small part, Sholem Aleichem believed, the result of American philistinism—led to a fateful decision: to return to Russia, where he and his literature were actually appreciated. "The land of Ivan," he wrote, "may his name be blotted out, is drawing me in all year. Not Ivan, that is, but Yiddish literature, Yiddish theater, Yiddish society. It's calling me there, winking to me from afar: 'Come, come, my dear boy, we'll do this and that for you, you'll soon have a bar mitzvah—we'll make you a jubilee, come to us, etc., etc.'" America was "Dollar-Land," he wrote his son-in-law that April, and perhaps it was "a decree from Heaven" that he would not find his salvation there; in Russia, despite its being a "bloody land," the place of pogroms, there were "good signs." It was precisely there his kind of Yiddish theater would develop, "and we, we will be the rulers of our world." Yes, he was ambivalent about returning, but "to remain here is impossible, and if I am lost, I am lost," he wrote in mid-May, using biblical and liturgical registers to allusively accentuate his sorrow.

His stories from the time seethed with the uncertainty, the impossibility or futility, of action. In "Elijah the Prophet," a young boy is told before the Seder that Elijah will carry him away in his sack if he falls asleep; when he does so (after imbibing too much kiddush wine), he's accordingly accosted by Elijah, who intones, "Either say good-bye to your parents and come with me, or remain here fast asleep forever. For all eternity." Elijah gives him a minute to think it over—and that's where the story ends. It's a story about the agonies of impossible choice: Elijah, the harbinger of messianic—and thus political and personal—transformation, forcing the child to choose between clinging to quiescence and tradition or unknown and possibly dangerous or fatal action. Especially since Sholem Aleichem was under no illusions about Russia's dangers. Another contemporary story, "Beareleh," about a childless village couple who take in a bear cub and raise it as their own, is dedicated to the notion that a bear, even when cared for and loved, remains a bear, and will eventually rampage and murder. The story is a hardly subtle dig at both the Russian bear and those who expect it to change its nature; not surprising that Sholem Aleichem, surveying the devastation the bear wreaks, employs the word "pogrom"—not an entirely unusual Yiddish locution, but its placement here speaks volumes.

But an invitation to Warsaw to give readings and to see his old friends Spektor and Dinezon tipped the scales (though he needed to raise money for travel expenses first). He arrived the day before Shavuot, and his first reading took place at the Elysium the next day. It was a small venue, and hundreds of Jews spilled out onto the street. The rumor mill had it—in marked contrast to the author's actual financial condition—that Sholem Aleichem was wearing "diamond lockets, that his fingers were covered with emerald rings and that the rims of his eyeglasses were made of pure gold"; it was Peretz, though, who showed up in the luxurious carriage— his attendance there, and at the welcoming reception, the beginning of a thaw between the two, and another proof that writers were becoming Yiddish celebrities. Sholem Aleichem read from the Motl stories, among other work, in his pleasant tenor and recited Bialik for an encore; he was rapturously received. After a quick side trip to Lodz, Sholem Aleichem returned to Warsaw for more readings, this time in the much larger Mura-nov theater, an enormous converted shed, which allowed more affordably priced tickets—always a concern for an author mindful of his public.

Further travels followed; the next weeks and months saw Sholem

Sholem Aleichem received a rapturous reception on his first trip to America in 1906, including this welcome banquet at Clinton Hall. (*From the archives of the YIVO Institute for Jewish Research, New York*)

His second visit, in 1914, was far less dramatic, even as the audience for his works had swelled along with the immigrant population. The caption to this cartoon, which appeared in the satiric weekly newspaper *Der Groyser Kundes* in December 1914, reads, "Where am I? My sense of logic tells me it's New York, but my sense of smell says Kasrilevke." (*YIVO Institute*)

Whether Mark Twain should shine Sholem Aleichem's shoes or vice versa (or the author should just shine his own shoes), everyone agreed that comparing the Yiddish writer to the American one made good copy. This appeared in *Der Groyser Kundes* in 1915. (*YIVO Institute*)

American newspaper editors would often fight over the chance to print Sholem Aleichem's works. In this cartoon, which appeared in *Der Groyser Kundes* in January 1915, he is triumphantly carried off by the editor and the publisher of *Der Tog*. (*YIVO Institute*)

אַסעריקאַנער יודענטהום: פֿאַני שלום־עליכם,
סילא וועגען פּרנסה לאַמיר איצט בֿט רעדזאַ,
אַבער כבֿוד־די גרעסטע פּאַרצע האַבּ אֿיך
בעהאַלטען פֿיר אֿייך !

But paying him properly for his work was another matter entirely. As the man at the window of the "Respect Department for Jewish Big Shots" advises him, "Mr. Sholem Aleichem, don't even talk about making a living. But respect—I've saved the biggest piece for you!" This appeared in *Der Groyser Kundes* in December 1914. (*YIVO Institute*)

A poster advertising one of the two dueling Sholem Aleichem premieres during his first American trip. *The Scoundrel, or Shmuel Pasternak* was being performed at Jacob Adler's Grand Theatre, on the Lower East Side, with Adler, the "great eagle" of the Yiddish theater, in the leading role.

Sholem Aleichem's funeral took place in New York City on May 15, 1916. It was one of the largest funerals in the history of the city, with crowd estimates ranging from between 150,000 and 250,000 people. Here the procession has stopped at Ohab Zedek, a synagogue then located on 116th Street between Lenox and Fifth avenues. Note the police presence. (*YIVO Institute*)

The working writer's desk, at his home on Kelly Street in the Bronx, was kept neat and ordered, if often covered with gadgets. On the top shelf, at the extreme right, is the iconic photograph with Abramovitch, Bialik, and Ben-Ami. (*YIVO Institute*)

Sholem Aleichem's headstone, in the Workmen's Circle section of Brooklyn's Mount Carmel Cemetery, displays the famous verse epitaph he had written several years earlier. (*YIVO Institute*)

The set of the Moscow State Yiddish Theater's 1923 production of Sholem Aleichem's play *The Jackpot* (there titled *200,000*) spoke volumes about harnessing avant-garde aesthetic sensibilities to new Soviet ideologies.

In 1939, on the other side of the Atlantic, on a potato farm in Jericho, Long Island, Maurice Schwartz was creating an indelible portrait of the iconic Eastern European Jew in the Yiddish film *Tevye der milkhiker*, as Hitler's shadow fell across Europe. (*YIVO Institute*)

Even critics of *Fiddler on the Roof*—those who found it cloyingly sentimental and untrue to the historical life of the shtetl or to the nuance and complexity of the author's stories—agreed on the incandescence of Zero Mostel's performance. (*Photo by Friedman-Abeles © The New York Public Library for the Performing Arts*)

Those critics, of course, were in the minority, as the play's impact—aided inestimably, no doubt, by its talented team's success in highlighting the universal themes in the work—spread throughout the world. Here, Tevye (seated, far left) and other Anatevkans prepare to leave their home in the original Tokyo production.

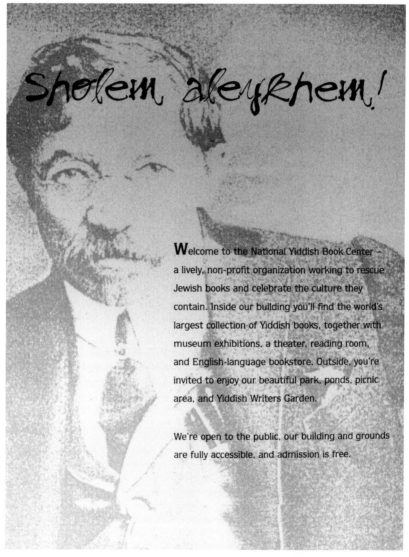

Sholem aleykhem!

Welcome to the National Yiddish Book Center – a lively, non-profit organization working to rescue Jewish books and celebrate the culture they contain. Inside our building you'll find the world's largest collection of Yiddish books, together with museum exhibitions, a theater, reading room, and English-language bookstore. Outside, you're invited to enjoy our beautiful park, ponds, picnic area, and Yiddish Writers Garden.

We're open to the public, our building and grounds are fully accessible, and admission is free.

A welcoming presence at the Yiddish Book Center in Amherst, Massachusetts. One of America's leading Jewish cultural institutions, the center is taking Yiddish and Jewish literature—including works by Sholem Aleichem and many others—into the twenty-first century via download, podcast, and old-fashioned reading and discussion. (*Courtesy Yiddish Book Center*)

Aleichem in dozens of cities in Poland and the Baltics. Touring the provinces, he stopped at major towns and transit centers like Slonim and Baranovitch ("Pinsk went mad," he wrote Spektor; "all of Pinsk escorted me
home from the theater, like a groom, with ovations") and felt much better
about his decision to leave America, which he referred to as "the land of
cultural servitude and senseless humiliation." One particular event, early
in his trip, served as a particular symbol of Russia's promise: an Odessa
"Evening of Yiddish Writers" to support the family of Yehuda Steinberg,
the deceased writer and former Vilna censor. Sholem Aleichem had been
mindful of this issue since the beginning of his career, writing an 1889 letter to *Hamelitz* calling older writers' poor financial condition "the shame
of our entire people"; that same year, he sent a writer's widow 300 rubles
out of his own pocket. In the *Hamelitz* letter, he insisted it was a communal obligation to celebrate writers on their anniversaries; two decades
later, comparatively impoverished, celebrating his own anniversary, he
must have ruminated on how his own wheel had turned, that the benefac-
tor must become the recipient.

But the evening itself showed how much everything else had changed
from those days, the days of the lonely *Folksbibliotek*, and how successful
he'd been in every other aspiration. That an "Evening of Yiddish Writers" could even exist—with a collection of highbrow talent like Sholem
Aleichem, Abramovitch, Frug, Bialik, Asch, and Peretz Hirschbein
assembled on the stage, novelists, poets, playwrights—illustrated Yiddish's advancements and achievements as an acknowledged, valued literature, part of modern Jewish culture on every level. That the evening
was the first of its kind to be granted permission in Odessa meant there
had been some change in the political weather, no matter how slow. The
fact that it sold 2,000 rubles' worth of tickets (almost $24,000 in 2010
dollars) and netted 1,500 after expenses—some of the audience members
paid three rubles for standing room—meant Sholem Aleichem's kind
of elevated literature could be a moneymaking proposition. And by no
means least of all, Sholem Aleichem had been "afraid of murders in the
theater. I'm serious. They had to provide police. Jews didn't want to know

from tickets-shmickets—they wanted to see all six writers, period!" This meant that the cult of literary celebrity was alive and well, arguably with Sholem Aleichem in the lead. One man clamoring for tickets claimed he was leaving the country for a potentially fatal operation, and just wanted the chance to see Sholem Aleichem before he died.

Olga came east with some of the children for a brief reunion in Warsaw, and then he was off on another trip. The travel schedule was grueling, and it took its toll; to make all his appearances, he had to take night trains, and he began to catch cold and develop a severe cough. Toward the very beginning of August, he gave a successful reading in Baranovitch, an important railway junction where the Warsaw–Moscow and St. Petersburg–Lviv lines crossed. About half its population was Jewish, and many of them showed up—twice as many as the hall could accommodate—and they wouldn't let him off the stage. Tired and pale as he was, he gave encore after encore. At the hotel, he coughed up blood while preparing for bed, and hemorrhaged during the night. Specialists arriving from Vilna and Minsk the next day diagnosed acute pulmonary tuberculosis; he spent the next seven weeks in Baranovitch in critical condition.

The next year, Sholem Aleichem would end a story with the phrase "Baranovitch station, why don't you burn to the ground!" But this may have been a bit of an in-joke: the Baranovitch citizenry, as a matter of civic pride, did all they could to care for him. They organized volunteers to serve as round-the-clock nurses and helpers and even scattered straw on the stone pavement in front of his hotel so he would sleep undisturbed. (The solicitousness paid off: he advised his daughters to stay there when they returned to Russia.) Prayers and psalms were recited for his health in synagogues and at gravesides throughout the Pale, and he received a personal blessing from none other than the great Talmudic scholar Reb Chaim Brisker, who wrote him he must recuperate; he was needed by the Jews.

Sholem Aleichem would get out of bed for the first time right before Rosh Hashanah. Immediately after the holiday, he wrote Spektor that he'd had "one foot in the other world, [and had been] tearing myself away from the angel of death, begging for a little time" to finish writing "the something like a few hundred subjects wandering around in my mind," and revise his previous works, and "after that, when I'll be finished with all that, then, all right, after you, Sir Angel of Death!" He was ready to get to work, but the doctors wouldn't let him: "And, by the way, I've no strength. The feet won't move (bastards!). The hands also won't follow orders (stubborn asses!). And the head spins (a failure of a head!)." Especially frustrating was that his illness had sidelined him from one of the great moments in the language wars: the first international conference supporting the Yiddish language, at Czernowitz (now Ukraine's Chernivtsi) in late August and early September. The conference had begun with an agenda of language planning—Yiddish schools, support for Yiddish art and literature, translating canonical works into Yiddish—but became quickly and vitriolically embroiled in charged debates over whether Yiddish was the, or a, national language of the Jewish people. Though lying in Baranovitch, Sholem Aleichem wrote, his soul was in Czernowitz; regardless of the debate's outcome ("a" national language, by the way), a strong cultural movement forcefully speaking for *Yiddish* culture had spoken, and would only gather momentum for what would transpire to be the last three great decades of European Yiddish life.

Sholem Aleichem was slowly recovering, but his newly diagnosed condition was an expensive one. To fully heal, he wrote Dinezon, you needed "light, sun, and good eating, and for these three things you need money, money, and money." These three things, the doctors suggested, were best found on the Italian Riviera, and an appropriate seaside place cost approximately 1,500–1,800 francs a season (about $30,000 in 2010 dollars). Any less and you'd be in a pension without sun—"which is no good, Dinezon. One needs sun; sun is what's needed." Word had begun to spread among his friends and correspondents of his dire circumstances, and one friend, Moshe Weizmann, had an idea. Weizmann, whose older brother Chaim would become Israel's future first president, was a good family friend; in fact, after receiving word from Olga, he'd been the one to break the news about Sholem Aleichem's illness to most of the family. He proposed using the author's twenty-fifth jubilee—arriving imminently, in October—to raise money from a public presumably unaware of the author's financial distress. After all, they just saw him selling thousands and thousands of copies of his works; they'd have no idea of his disastrous contractual arrangements.

In August, Weizmann published an open letter in the Yiddish press detailing Sholem Aleichem's financial woes; Frug, the noted Yiddish poet, bemoaned in his own notice that the man who had created Jewish laughter now had a "red laughter" all his own—the blood he was coughing up. Some Warsaw supporters, probably at Dinezon's suggestion, decided to go a step further: they'd actually buy back his copyrights from the exploitative publishers and return them to the author, a jubilee gift that would keep on giving. Notices placed in Hebrew and Yiddish newspapers and weeklies reminded readers that "Sholem Aleichem is practically the only Jewish author of our time who has pleased everyone . . . no matter his allegiance or party" and asked his audience to rescue him, as he had saved them before in so many ways. Not, however, by "crying 'Hurrah' and sending telegrams . . . that will not suffice. Sholem Aleichem is ill, and your love for him must be displayed in an entirely different, non-platonic manner. Were Sholem Aleichem not a Yiddish writer, one would certainly speak of diamonds, estates, villas by the sea, and so forth. He is a Yiddish author, though, and so, unfortunately, one must deal with the minimum," i.e., buying back his works and allowing him to spend a year or two in a temperate climate without worrying about making a living. Private donors were solicited; an account was opened in Sholem Aleichem's name at the Bachrach Brothers' bank in Warsaw to store the donations; a committee to negotiate with the publishers was formed. Meanwhile, Sholem Aleichem left Russia on doctor's orders before the winter arrived, and traveled to Nervi, on the Italian Riviera, meeting his family in Basel on the way.

Judging from the satires of the medical profession he'd written since the late 1880s—the mandates, often playing on pampered women's hypochondria, that sent large swaths of the upscale Jewish population to spa towns like Marienbad for the water and to "reduce," and the pushing of nostrums, special diets, and pills healthier for the doctor's bottom line than the patient's—one might have expected Sholem Aleichem to be a recalcitrant patient. (He did, in a story from the period, define the Riviera as "a spot in Italy dreamed up by the doctors in order to wring the public dry.") But he took his medications at the precise time suggested and ate and drank precisely as ordered; he even gave up smoking. Olga and Numa watched sternly to prevent any potential infractions. The tragic irony is that a little less listening might have helped. In his daughter's words, "as medicine was to learn only many years later, exposure to sun was just what tubercular people should not have . . . The cure, which was to be in the sun, aggravated his condition and only the special care and food prevented deterioriation. The nights in Nervi were agonizing, for he could not sleep for coughing," and he needed observation by a family member, usually one of his daughters. They often read him Chekhov.

The questionable medical benefits notwithstanding, the setting was hard to beat. The Villa Briand "was situated on the top of a cliff jutting into the sea"; Sholem Aleichem's bedroom directly overlooked the water, so that he could hear the lulling waves, and he had a separate veranda for a writing table. From there he watched the ships go by, musing how they could sail directly to Israel. Awakened by the sunlight entering the room, after a seawater rubdown and a full breakfast he'd write from nine to twelve at a spot he found on the marina, a kind of amphitheater-like semicircle he called "the little oven." Then back home, where the table was set for lunch—fish, soup, meat, fresh vegetables, and ripe fruit—then to the balcony to lie out for about two hours, protected from the sun by an umbrella and drinking a great deal of sterilized milk. Teatime around four, then a stroll around the marina; take in the sunset; dinner at six, then a card game, a large snack at eight, and to bed at ten. It sounds like a dream, he wrote, but it's all true.

Unsurprisingly, despite some minor health setbacks, he fell in love with Nervi immediately, writing his daughter a flowery "Italian" letter incorporating all the phrases he had learned so far. Equally unsurprisingly,

given his regimen, he regained much of the weight he'd lost in Baranovitch: by early December he could write his Odessa friends that he'd put
on almost ten pounds during his few weeks at Nervi, joking that if he
continued at that rate, he'd be better off as a carnival attraction than as
a writer. He even crafted the handbill: "Wonders of the World! Come!
See! Come one, come all! And be amazed! The GREATEST humorist in
the world! Weighing 330 pounds!—Sholem Aleichem—Entrance one dol-
lar. Don't pass it by! Tell your friends!" The only medical instruction he
chafed against was the injunction to write as little as possible. He wrote
more slowly, and for more limited periods of time, but he kept writing,
scribbling secretly on his walks, and turned to a lead pencil, scrawling big
letters on small, light pages.

He dedicated the little booklet that resulted to "all of my dear little
people from Kasrilevke," and sent it to the many jubilee committees in
cities worldwide working hard on his behalf. Its tongue-in-cheek introduction explained that the doctors "had sternly forbidden him three
things: talking, reading, and writing. Whoever understands what it's like
for an alcoholic not to drink, a liar not to talk and a woman not to look
in the mirror—that person correctly apprehends my situation." Nonetheless, succumbing to the "papery Evil Inclination" and the "Devil of
Ink and Paper," he'd produced "Shmuel Shmelkes and His Jubilee." In its
introduction, Sholem Aleichem compares writing to looking in a mirror,
and "Shmuel Shmelkes" offers a fun-house-mirror version of his own biography, distorted by the anxieties of financial pressures remaining after
a quarter century of writing for a Jewish community that is and isn't
Kasrilevke.

Young Shmuel Shmelkes, who attempts to navigate his way through
the Kasrilevkan mud while holding high the newspaper with his first publication, who marries a wealthy man's daughter, suffers at his father-in-
law's hands, inherits when he dies, and loses all the money—and who, at
every turn, is mocked by the Kasrilevkan Greek chorus: all this is Sholem
Aleichem's story, recast for an audience who were supposed to chuckle
at the difference between the small-time shtetl Jew and the big-time

writer—but simultaneously feel the kinship between them. Particularly when the narrative skips ahead a quarter century to Shmuel Shmelkes's jubilee: when the humble writer, having toiled steadily, "faithfully and lovingly," for his community all this time, writing his Kasrilevke stories and never thinking of reward or critical attention, now dreams of his townspeople praising him to the skies, outdoing each other to reward him with business, money, estates. And he returns home to find a gathering of people, just as he had dreamed—but, alas, they're only there to gawk at his wife and children put out on the street, subject to his landlord's eviction proceedings. Quite a contrast to Leo Tolstoy, celebrating his fiftieth jubilee to universal acclaim at the same time.

Several years earlier, in his pamphlet mourning Theodor Herzl's death, Sholem Aleichem had excoriated the Jewish community "for not having sufficiently prized him, looked after him enough . . . he did not get from us what he expected from us. Here lies the real tragedy. The Jewish people were not destined to produce a true hero and know him as such. If they do have a hero sometimes . . . they don't know what he is, and they don't want to know. They become aware of him only later, when he is on the way out. And he leaves behind a glorious legend." Sholem Aleichem probably wasn't thinking only of Herzl then; he certainly wasn't thinking only of Shmuel Shmelkes now. Though any fair reading of his own history would hardly have blamed the audience for his troubles—publishers, yes; legal obstacles to the press and theater, absolutely; critics and politics, fair enough; and his own business decisions, certainly; but the audience, especially in recent years, had been more than good to him, in terms of allegiance both financial and personal. But fairness, when you're ill and facing medical bills and family expenses, isn't necessarily uppermost on your mind; and self-pity—played off as ostensibly ironic, maybe, but still self-pity—suffuses "Shmuel Shmelkes." Dinezon, reading it, had to assure Sholem Aleichem that he would not share his fictional counterpart's fate.

And indeed he did not. The jubilee (marking the twenty-fifth anniversary of the publication not of his first story but of "The Intercepted Letters") was celebrated on October 25, 1908, and the festivities were appropriate to his station as Yiddish literature's most popular and, indeed, most representative writer—the one who epitomized, more than anyone, Yiddish's rapidly expanding empire. Readings and performances of his work took place in dozens of cities around the world, including Paris, New York, Buenos Aires, London, and Moscow. Peretz spoke at Warsaw's celebratory banquet, which featured a song with the refrain "Long live Sholem Aleichem"; asked about his participation, given the two writers' complicated history, he simply responded: "Sholem Aleichem is still Sholem Aleichem." Hundreds of congratulatory telegrams flew into Nervi from all ends of the earth, tying up the telegraph operator there for days. (The operator didn't necessarily know all the telegrams' languages, so identifying their authors became something of a guessing game.) The Nervi postman, shocked by the sudden massive change in his mailbag's weight, took to leaving the whole bag at Sholem Aleichem's door and asking the family to pick out all the mail that *didn't* belong to them.

The honoree, for his part, was maudlin, morose about missing all the celebrations—Nervi not being, to put it mildly, a major Jewish center. A tear-stained letter to Spektor lamented that "at the moment when there, in our dear home, Jews celebrate my jubilee, I am here, alone, ill . . . and I cry. . . . I can write no more"; he wrote a journalist that hardest of all was not being in Kiev for the celebrations. He loved three things in life, he wrote, newspapers, dairy food, and Jews—newspapers he received from everywhere and read voraciously, as was his practice, and dairy products were plentiful, but he missed his Jews. He even worried whether if he died in Nervi he'd be buried in Jewish ground. He tried to busy himself by answering all his well-wishers, as was also his practice, even the cranks and the nudniks, ignoring his doctors' orders entirely; and as the fall went on and more and more of the celebrations' profits rolled in—300 rubles from London; 500 from New York; 500 from St. Louis; 400 from Alexandria, Egypt; 200 from Montreal; and 450 from Johannesburg—he was markedly more upbeat. By late November, he even wrote the Warsaw committee that they didn't need to send him any more money; he had enough.

But his good mood didn't last; his condition had turned slightly worse by November's end, and, suffering from insomnia, he asked a doctor friend to prescribe him something to help him sleep. Olga thought much of the trouble stemmed from the lack of progress in getting his rights back from the publishers. When the author had heard about the jubilee gift, he'd written Dinezon ecstatically that "by saving my spiritual children—you are saving me!" But salvation was more easily promised than attained: ironically, because the jubilee had deepened reader interest in Sholem Aleichem's books, their publishers were even less willing to part with their increasingly lucrative rights. One even had the nerve to announce a special "Jubilee Edition" of Sholem Aleichem's works. And, despite the jubilee events' successes, Sholem Aleichem wasn't sure they had enough money in the fund to rescue his works from "such poor, small, grubby hands": as of early December, he figured they had a little over 2,500 rubles (about $30,000 in 2010 dollars) for the purpose, and he estimated they'd need twice that.

The new year brought some progress. They settled with a major publisher, Lidski, in January, buying out the contract for 2,813 rubles, 39 kopecks; Sholem Aleichem wrote Dinezon that it had "simply put, revived the dead, brought my soul back. And at precisely a moment of the greatest despair." The subsequent settlements looked trickier, though: Tushiya would only settle if Krinski did, and in the meantime Sholem Aleichem's sales were slowing as readers became confused or discouraged by press reports critical of all the legal wrangling. The logjam was finally broken when the committee decided to bring in the big guns, asking Olga to come to Warsaw to help twist the publishers' arms; she arrived during Passover, and her efforts over the next several weeks—along with the publishers' increasing desire to avoid scandal in the press—helped close the deal with almost everyone. The family then issued a new, authorized jubilee edition of their own, which allowed them, through a clause in Sholem Aleichem's final contract, to finish the job. The new edition's distributors—Lidski, the first of the publishers to have sold back their rights—guaranteed the family 200 rubles a month with the promise of increases as additional volumes appeared, along with regular sales reports.

The editions were soon a great success, and by the late spring and summer of 1909 Sholem Aleichem began to feel a sense of financial security once more. Olga returned triumphantly to Nervi, bearing expensive writing paper and Wissotsky's tea, and Sholem Aleichem, in a warm letter to a member of the Warsaw committee, described himself "in shining Italy, with all possible comforts, surrounded with the great love of close family and strangers, with good hopes for the morrow . . . and, especially, with a free, ransomed soul!" With improved spirits came a renewed attention to writing. Aside from "Shmuel Shmelkes," the months after his illness were spent attempting an autobiography: though he'd toyed with writing his life story as early as 1895, he hadn't acted on the impulse until after his brush with death. Perhaps the pseudo-autobiographical "Shmuel Shmelkes," with its vision of the unloved, unrespected, forgotten writer, drove home the sense that he might have to arrange for his own posterity— and the controlling, precise writer would certainly want to be in the position to shape his own legacy. But he put it aside after writing six or seven chapters: perhaps associating autobiography with mortality, health improving and bursting with new energy and financial prospects, he was perfectly willing to put it off.

The illness did change his writing habits a bit: as the doctors had discouraged him from writing by hand, one jubilee gift from his New York colleagues—a Remington Yiddish typewriter—was extremely timely. (In a coincidence worthy of a Sholem Aleichem story, the local typewriter repairman turned out to be a deeply assimilated Jew, who nonetheless traveled from Genoa to see a Yiddish typewriter and to marvel at the Hebrew letters he faintly recognized.) Though initially enthusiastic about the Remington, as he often was about new gadgets, he ultimately returned to writing by hand, adopting the habit of writing in bed with a pencil on a desk of his own design, a habit that would continue off and on for the rest of his life. He sloughed off the typing and retyping of drafts to his son-in-law, who also took over some of his Hebrew correspondence.

But his illness also strongly affected something else: his newest Tevye story. Ever since the word had spread that Sholem Aleichem needed warmth and sunlight, his Zionist supporters had debated purchasing him a villa in Palestine, perhaps in Jaffa, near the newly established city of Tel Aviv. He could become one of the thirty-five thousand Jewish immigrants to Palestine between 1904 and 1914, a member of what would become known as the Second Aliyah. The author himself certainly wasn't averse, writing a friend in January that he hoped to go that summer, settling in a garden villa by the sea. An idea naturally suggested itself: if this was the plan, what better company could he have than Tevye? The dairyman could be sent ahead, as it were, to report on conditions, and provide his own perspective on the development of the Zionist dream. The dream would be dashed within two months as friends with medical expertise advised against it—despite Palestine's welcoming climate, there was no sufficiently developed sanatorium or recuperative facility there, so he would have to remain in Western or Southern Europe. (He wrote Ben-Ami that he was jealous of Bialik, "that he merited to go to the land of Israel, and I do not. And God knows if I will able to be there, because I depend now not on myself and not on circumstances but on doctors!") Sholem Aleichem was always a dutiful patient (except when it came to the writing), and there's no reason to think he would go against doctor's orders here. Perhaps he believed he'd be cleared to travel there at some later point. Regardless, he had already written Tevye's story by the time he learned the disappointing news.

Sholem Aleichem's own brush with mortality pervades "Tevye Leaves for the Land of Israel"; for one thing, Tevye is surprised to hear that his listener, "Sholem Aleichem," is still alive, a playful nod to all the readers who'd followed the news of the real Sholem Aleichem's health. But an even more surprising intimation of mortality is the news of the death of Golde, Tevye's wife. (Readers weren't the only ones surprised. Sholem Aleichem had the habit, after finishing a story, of reading it aloud to the family in the evening. The proceeding eventually took on the tone of a literary premiere; were it a new story about a favorite character like Tevye, Sholem Aleichem would even dress for the occasion. When he got to the news of the death, Olga involuntarily gasped.) Golde's death may have resulted from the accumulated weight of the family's many tragedies; but it may also be, as the story suggests, that we're reaching the end of her—and their—narrative purpose: Sholem Aleichem informs us that we have reached Tevye's final daughter. And the story's final death, perhaps its most crushing, is the death of Tevye's dreams: for as the beautiful, virtuous Beilke "sells herself down the river so that I could live out the rest of my life in the Land of Israel," he learns the crushing unhappiness of discovering what you thought you wanted isn't what you wanted at all, because the price is simply too high.

Again, Sholem Aleichem filters his speculations through a marriage plot; though Beilke's intended, Podhotzur, is described by the matchmaker as "a steal, a catch, a rare find, a colossus, a prince among men, a millionaire, a second Brodsky," the name's similarity to the Yiddish word for penis is probably intentional. Podhotzur is indeed as rich as advertised, but he's unquestionably a shmuck; Beilke marries him only out of a sense of obligation to her father, and when Tevye confronts her with her sisters' example—by now, he's a full-fledged champion of romantic love—Beilke reminds him that there's no place, in this modern world, for optimism and idealism. "Don't go comparing me to Hodl," she says. "In Hodl's day the world was on the brink. There was going to be a revolution and everyone cared about everyone. Now the world is its own self again and it's everyone for his own self again, too."

But this isn't entirely accurate: Beilke is looking out for Tevye, after all, and if this makes Tevye uncomfortable ("Tevye is no charity case," he insists), Sholem Aleichem's own experiences over the last few months were similarly discomfiting. Goals, plans, ideals, self-pride—all of these had taken a beating in the last six months, and perhaps that's why there's another death in the tale. For Tevye symbolically dies in this story as much as Beilke: when a dairyman father-in-law proves too much of an embarrassment to Podhotzur, he's shuffled off to Palestine, "where all the old Jews like you go to die." Sholem Aleichem even has Tevye question his very raison d'être, his relationship with his daughters: he thinks,

"What's the point, Tevye, of butting in between these children? A lot it helped for you to think your other daughters' marriages were your business!" Though Tevye reasserts his faith, he adds, in the same breath, "I only wish I had a ruble for every dirty trick He's played on us." These last months had been a period of questioning the most basic assumptions of Sholem Aleichem's life; and Tevye, as always, was one way for him to work through them.

As 1909 progressed, with improving health and news, Sholem Aleichem's creative juices began flowing more and more easily. (He told one editor he had so many topics for stories that the editor should be sure to remind him about a particular one right before Passover; otherwise, he'd probably forget about it and fail to send it in.) Earlier preoccupations persisted— many of the first tales he produced at Nervi were variations on earlier themes. Another farce of arranged marriage, another Kasrilevke tale (the ominously titled "Two Dead Men"; even though they were simply dead drunk and dead broke, mortality prevails). And another variation, "The Pair," Sholem Aleichem's best animal story, is the most philosophical statement of his deep pessimism, even if it's farcically rendered: it's told from the shortsighted perspective of a pair of turkeys that are fattened up and eventually slaughtered for the holiday, while falling in love and discovering themselves in the meantime. Though the story could theoretically be read as a vegetarian manifesto, Sholem Aleichem was hardly committed to the cause; instead, it's a combination of money anxieties (the poor literally get it in the neck, exploited by the more powerful for their own purposes) and of existential speculation. Are we nothing more than blind animals, subject to forces beyond our control, and the only liberation we can find is death? What value love in the face of that?

These reflections on love, death, and the literary imagination found their fullest treatment in a work he began that summer: "Pages from the Song of Songs" appeared in installments (since "my health does not permit me to write it all at once") between 1909 and 1911. He had considered using the archetypal biblical love song as a literary model as far back as 1899, musing about a two-part novel, "The Song of Love," but this version would, he wrote, "crown everything I have written in the course of 25 years." That's debatable, but "Pages," which followed the star-crossed romance of the narrator Shimek and his beloved Buzi from childhood into young adulthood, was dedicated to advancing precisely the opposite proposition of the biblical motto that had so attracted him in his youth: "Many waters cannot quench love, neither can the floods drown it." Attempting to evoke the story's national resonances, he wove "the high moments of the romance" together with the Jewish holidays, which contain "the source of the inspiration of the Jewish soul"; the four installments that appeared—more were planned, on different holidays—were set on Passover and Shavuot, two each.

Sorrow and mortality lie across the romance from the outset. Buzi, modeled on Sholem Aleichem's wife's niece Natasha, is technically Shimek's niece, though she's about two years older; after her father, Shimek's older brother, drowned, she was raised in Shimek's house. A verse in the Song of Songs, traditionally read on Passover, reads "my sister, my spouse," hinting at the love story's complications; the same book contains the verse "love is strong as death," though, and the question of whether history, or biography, will triumph over ideals and imagination is the essential one animating the story. Buzi constantly reminds Shimek of the Song of Songs, he tells us: primarily because both are capable, in the narrator/author's imagination, of transmogrifying the surrounding landscape into mythical and magical space, Jerusalem of old. Shimek, the romantic side of Sholem Aleichem's personality who says that "everything, everything is from the 'Song of Songs,'" childishly boasts of his kabbalistic powers, and turns those boasts into stories of mythical journeys and magic lands in language repurposed in *From the Fair* just a few years later. The older, wiser, sadder Buzi, touched by loss, understands limits. "You need not fly so far. Take my advice, you need not," she says, taking his hand. But he doesn't listen: and later installments show how, called away by the lures of modernity (he becomes a student), he has lost her and the transformative, imaginative capacity his love for her represented.

Hardly surprising, then, that the narrator, in his lonely ending "bewailing and bemoaning my unforgettable Shulamite," falls back on the comfortable pleasures of the first flights of imagination, the pure magic of the beginnings of things, whether they be ideas, lives, or stories. "Don't press me to tell you the end of my romance [the Yiddish word can also mean "novel," remember]. An ending, even the very best, always contains a note of sadness. But a beginning, even the very worst, is better than the finest ending. Therefore, it is much easier and far more pleasant to tell you the story from the beginning, once and twice and even one hundred times." And so he does. In a period of recuperation, Sholem Aleichem's own sense of possibility isn't what it used to be; imagination is less a catalyst for moving forward than an aid to cushioning escapism.

CHAPTER 22

In Which Our Hero Rides the Rails, and Returns to the Stage

1909

That spring of 1909, as the money from the jubilees began to wane and before the money for the copyrights began to flow, Sholem Aleichem wrote "The Goldspinners," the tale of a Kasrilevke family who, despite their extraordinary capacity to make money on Purim (thus their enviously bestowed nickname), only ever managed "just enough for shoes for themselves, jackets and dresses for the children, matzos for Passover, goose fat, a crock of borscht, and a sack of potatoes." The author confessed in March that despite the jubilee money, he was going into debt in Italy ("an expensive country"), and though he could stay there through May, he planned to summer elsewhere. A resurgence of his hemorrhaging was a sober reminder that he'd need to dedicate the summer to his health, and after consulting with his doctors, the decision was made to spend a month in Switzerland, in the mountains around Montreux.

Sholem Aleichem left Nervi for Switzerland in mid-May; but by month's end, it was clear the move had worsened rather than improved his condition. After more consultations, he decamped for the famous Sanatorium St. Blasien in the hills of Schwarzwald, Germany, which specialized in treating lung illnesses. The cloudy, rainy St. Blasien was no Nervi, and though the sanatorium was luxurious, he hated the monotony. "The whole art of healing as far as the Germans are concerned," he wrote, "is just about lying around. From the morning until late at night the sick lie out in the air, in the woods, under God's heaven. One may only stand to eat and to go for walks . . . I, thank God, am in such favor with the doctors that already I can walk for two hours in the day and lie around for eight hours (not counting the ten hours one must sleep)." And the lying around was "among the half-dead, coughing and listening to others cough, which is even worse, because at least with my own coughs I'm in charge."

And at least he could spend some of that lying-down time writing, using the technique he'd learned in Nervi of writing in bed with a pencil. It was a good time to be feeling productive: his stock was at a new high after the jubilee had proven his appeal, and a new Warsaw daily co-edited by Spektor was willing to pay him 3,000 rubles a year (about $36,000 a year in 2010 dollars) for weekly copy, when the average Yiddish writer was lucky to make 40 percent of that. The paper would have great difficulties coming up with its name. (Sholem Aleichem, in a satiric feuilleton he published there, claimed it was such a difficult task—as all the good names had been taken and used again and again—it had caused the "nervous breakdown" that had sent him to the sanatorium. Telling readers with good suggestions to send them to him c/o "Sanatorium St. Blasien, Schwarzwald," he combined his actual and imagined maladies.) Eventually, *The New World*—*The World* was already taken—appeared, and before the year was out, Sholem Aleichem published a central series of works there: works that in no small way helped to combat his sense that everything was falling apart by making the detached, far-flung, modern sense of uprootedness a home for Jewish life and Jewish storytelling.

That is, he was going to write about the railroads.

He had done it before: from early in the century, he had seemingly intimated that the railroad was a place for entertainment and adventure in its own right, not just a means of getting to the adventures and entertainments, producing stories illustrating the business discussions, general *potzing*, and opportunities for financial chicanery and scamming that could occur on and around the rails. His 1902 tour to raise money for the *Folkstsaytung* not only inspired him directly, with a "whole gang of road images . . . [that] surrounded me and beg to be put on paper"—but created a new possibility, at the precise period Sholem Aleichem was seeking solutions for a coherent national Jewish identity, of a portable Jewish homeland in the Diaspora. That year's "Third Class" extols the joys of traveling in that particular section of the train: in first class, the narrator explains, no one's Jewish, and in second, no one will admit to it. But in their own noisy, freeing element, Jewish history and creative possibility combine. "Before long," the narrator writes, "each of us not only knows all about the other's troubles, he knows about every trial and tribulation that ever befell a Jew anywhere."

Sure, nobody knows you on a train, and so no statement can be taken at face value—and sometimes Sholem Aleichem played that for straight comedy, like in 1903's "Burnt Out" (where the complaining monologist claims it's just a coincidence that the store he'd insured for 10,000 rubles just a few weeks before burned down, and we don't quite believe him). But sometimes the railroad served as a symbol of how hard it was to get a foothold on anything—a symbol of difficulty, rather than of mischievous, playful liberation. Maybe it was a simple shift of interest that led him to put away his gang of road images; but, on some level, it may have been that his underlying goals of coherence, of identity building, at the beginning of the century weren't quite in tune with what the railroad theme could do for them. Six years later—after years of hard touring; after months away from that touring, and the Jewish voices that had cheered him; after the realization that, given health concerns, a permanent return to his home would lie in the distant future, if it would ever occur; and after a period of disillusionment, through age, illness, and revolution, with grand, coherent solutions—the railroad began to look quite different. Its diffuse and far-flung possibilities, its blurring and shifting venues, its capacity to host different identities, made it as all-encompassing of seemingly insurmountable Jewish and Yiddish diversity as, well, as the figure of Sholem Aleichem himself. And it almost allowed him, the wanderer, to be as rooted in his material as anyone else: since the rails were almost a no-place, not a Warsaw or a Kiev or even a shtetl.

Still, he was concerned about being out of touch: and asked friends traveling around Russia for impressions and discoveries he could use as raw material. "Types, encounters, stories, histories, misfortunes, good fortunes, events, love affairs, marriages, divorces, fatal dreams, bankruptcies, *simkhes*, funerals God forbid—in a word, everything you see and hear, or that you have seen or heard, and will hear on the way," he wrote a reporter friend. "Only one thing to remember: *no made up things, just facts and facts!* Life is rich with facts, full of curiosities, many misfortunes, a sea of tears, which, as they will pass through my prism, will already become by themselves comic, beloved delights." He also buttonholed visitors, sternly giving them the same advice when they tried to exaggerate to make things more "Sholem-Aleichem-like": their facts, his fancy.

The newer railroad stories still played the same games with unreliability. A 1911 collection features an introduction from the perspective of a "commercial traveler" who insists he just "bought himself a notebook and began jotting down everything I saw and heard on my trips." The artfulness of the claim of artlessness would have been self-evident; but there are other types of unreliability in "The Railroad Stories," as this series of tales would become known, and they show where the author's fancy was taking him—artistically and even politically—now that his illness had rendered his own homeland, his beloved Russia, off-limits. In 1909's "Baranovitch Station," for example, its location linked infamously to his own biography via his collapse the previous year, a gaggle of passengers, seeking a sufficiently diverting story, are finally enticed by a bystander's story about a blackmailer. Blackmailers, of course, gain power by the potency of the stories they tell, and don't tell; and our storyteller, using the story to get a seat in the crowded compartment, spins it out, abruptly ending his performance to run off as the train reaches Baranovitch station.

"The Railroad Stories" are aesthetic blackmail, the flexing of the power storytellers have over their listeners at a time of their author's own personal weakness: sudden endings that refuse to give the audience the craved satisfaction of narrative closure, or twist endings that force the reader to review everything that's been said so far with new, skeptical eyes. (In "Competitors," for example, the two peddlers selling identical merchandise for the same price who compete "solely [by] seeing who can make you feel sorrier for whom" end up being married to each other.) It even seems kind of predatory, this power the storyteller has; and Sholem Aleichem gives a sly portrait of the relationship in one of the best of the tales, the oily, sneaky "The Man from Buenos Aires." Its narrator strikes up a conversation with a talkative, well-dressed fellow passenger, who flashes a wad of cash, wines and dines the narrator, and alternates between telling a sob story of a life of poverty, hunger, and abuse and boasting of his success: he claims he's en route to his hometown, a returning hero, to marry a nice local Jewish girl.

Whether any of this is true is for us to judge, especially since he's cagy about his profession. "I'm kind of a middleman," he says. "That is, I provide a commodity that everyone knows about but no one ever talks about." Readers would have known early on what that commodity was— since at the time mention of Buenos Aires, then a center of the white slave trade, only meant one thing. (The year of Sholem Aleichem's story, 51 percent of the licensed brothels in Buenos Aires were supervised by Jews, and 49 percent of the authorized prostitutes were Jewish.) The narrator, though, lags behind, and finally puts the question at the story's end. The man's reply, "Not in etrogs, my friend, I don't deal in etrogs," is a nasty sexual pun, suggesting the reason he came home to marry: once the etrog's stem is broken, it's no longer usable for the Sukkot holiday. But unreliability abounds: Is marriage what the gentleman really has in mind? False matrimonial offers were one way to lure unsuspecting shtetl girls away, after all. And the man's behavior—telling his story, keeping the narrator on the hook—is a classic seducer's; but, on the other hand, maybe it's the narrator who ends up having the power after all, since he gets a story, that most precious of Sholem Aleichem's commodities, without having to provide anything in return. Maybe *he's* the con man.

Another story of con men and a train, published two years later, uses

its own twist ending to remind us of the railroad's other symbolic significance: as a hard-charging, intrusive symbol of the modern world, and the
disruptions that come with it. More of an honorary railroad story—the
train only appears in its final moments—"Cnards" is a delicious little
tale about card sharks posing as holy men so unworldly they don't know
the proper noun for those pasteboard articles, and shaking down the liberalizing, modernizing townspeople who think they're teaching these
suddenly lucky "saints" a lesson by slipping non-kosher meat into their
meals. (This actually provides perfect cover for the "horrified" con men
to make their escape.) Most card games, like life, depend on understanding the person sitting across the table. And the man who purports to
be the Ba'al Shem Tov's grandson understands his marks well enough to
know that the reason they don't immediately twig to charlatanry is that
deep down they're still folklike enough to believe on some level in the
power of a Hasidic miracle, or in the supernatural currents that are the
gambler's currency. Their disillusionment takes place at the train station, where the con men, now clean-shaven and in modern dress, reveal
themselves to the townspeople. (As the train pulls away, they give their
victims the finger.) Losing their winnings is nothing compared to losing
the ideals they thought, wrongly, they'd rid themselves of: in this new
world, even the comforting possibilities of a center left behind are no longer available.

That sense of failure is brought out most clearly in the set of stories that
are *about* a train, not merely transpiring on one: the machine Hillel Halkin
has masterfully termed "the Slowpoke Express." The Express, born in the
speculative frenzy of "railroad fever," another typical Sholem Aleichem
bubble where everyone tries to get into the business and loses his shirt in
the process, isn't just an ode to economic failure. The train's adventures
serve as a perfect commentary on the failure of idealistic, reform-minded
politics and the doubtful possibility of Jewish and non-Jewish coexistence. Take, for example, the tale of a post-constitution pogrom where
the pogromists are arriving by rail (a historically accurate possibility),
since there are too few locals to put a real assault together. Fortunately,

they're riding the Slowpoke, which gives the Jews time to arrange reinforcements; unfortunately, the Slowpoke—for once—makes good time, and salvation only stems from the discovery that the pogromists-to-be were so drunk they forgot to hitch the passenger cars to the engine. Thus the story's title: "The Wedding That Came Without Its Band."

The Slowpoke Express, it turns out, is such a remarkable failure that it even fails at failing—and so, too, the stories of the railroad. Though they succeed in creating a diverse gallery of Jewish life and character, a portable homeland on tracks, they're ultimately, as filtered through Sholem Aleichem's current sensibility, drenched with the specter of impossibility, not possibility. For a symbol of the future, they seemed, in the end, to lead nowhere.

Sholem Aleichem's dyspepsia couldn't have been helped by the fact that, despite being paid punctually by *The New World*—an unheard-of experience for him—he was having difficulty contacting the editorial staff. He worried that this boded badly, and he was right. That early fall of 1909, the paper was getting shellacked by its competition, who'd discovered a surefire way to their readers' hearts: serialized potboiler novels, the kind that might have made even Shomer shudder. The *Haynt* in particular was having a runaway success with a particularly juicy example called *In the Nest of Sin*, whose heroine, Bertha, had to navigate the perils of white slavery, the criminal underworld, and a sultan's harem (don't ask). Spektor and his co-editors figured a novel of their own by their regular contributor, Yiddish literature's most popular writer, would give them a shot in the circulation wars. After all, *The Deluge* had been a huge success.

Sholem Aleichem, who had returned from Germany to Switzerland as the summer ended, wasn't crazy about stopping his series of railroad stories before he'd finished with them. But he saw the rise of these serial novels as another instance of Shomerism, the movement he'd been fighting all his life—and he knew the Americans, with their coarse tastes, would just make matters worse. Producing a literary version of this newly popular phenomenon would be just the thing, and would also allow him, as he wrote *The New World* editors, to fulfill an old promise "to end my trilogy with a third novel, after 'Stempenyu' and 'Yosele Solovey.'" But not to worry: while this third artist novel would be "an epoch-making one in our literature, from one side," with a wide range of characters and scenes reflecting both American and Russian Jewish life, it would also be enormously popular—though he was coy about providing a title or outline.

It was probably inevitable, and, given his own recent experiences, certainly unsurprising, that he picked the theater as the setting for the final artist novel. Its basic idea, Jewish youths running away to join the theater, had appealed to him since before *Stempenyu*: he'd written about it in a Hebrew short story as early as 1889. But his more recent experiences—including meeting a group of theatrical personages while in Galicia in 1906—helped bring it into focus. Though "focus" may not be precisely the right word: *Wandering Stars* itself is a bit of a muddle. It begins promisingly, with the spectacle of a young boy and girl, Leibel and Reizel, leaving their sleepy town to join the theatrical world—deeply attracted to each other, to the theater, and to the prospect of something larger than themselves. "Both would go into exile, but they would find salvation in that exile," as the novel puts it: a romance made in, and of, the Yiddish theater. Of course, like Sholem Aleichem's own romance with the theater, things don't turn out the way they're supposed to: they both end up, in the words of a fortune-teller, "traveling, always traveling . . . want[ing] more than anything to rush toward each other, but you wander, you are always wandering . . . like stars in the sky."

Separated soon after they leave their town, the two take separate paths to success: Leibel becomes the actor Leo Rafalesco, justly famed for his earnest, natural acting manner; Reizel becomes Rosa Spivak, a noted singer. Romantic complications ensue. Despite still loving Leibel/ Leo, Reizel/Rosa develops strong feelings for a brilliant violinist, Grisha Stelmach; Leo, for his part, has not only entered into a largely loveless engagement with a fellow actress, but has left behind and, unbeknownst to him, impregnated Zlatkeh, the sister of his friend, partner, and mentor

Hotzmakh. (He sends Rosa a letter expressing his true feelings, but—shades of Sholem Aleichem's biography and fiction—the letter is intercepted, and Rosa reads it too late.)

The action moves to America, and the wandering stars' paths begin to converge. Grisha and Rosa announce their engagement in New York, literally making beautiful music together as they do so, and celebrate by attending the Yiddish theater—where Leo is making his local debut. Discovering Rosa has both attended and left the theater before any possible reunion, Leo entirely loses his composure, and his ability to perform. Like Sholem Aleichem's experiences in the New York theater, one night's disaster can be enough; but the experience allows Leo to come to terms with his moral failings, his obligations to his child, his fiancée, and his feelings. The first, American version of the novel, befitting the author's feelings about that audience's sensibilities, ended melodramatically: Leo reunites with Rosa and dedicates his life to reforming Yiddish theater. Sholem Aleichem, who would have suppressed the American version if he could, took a different tack for the Russian publication, providing only a brief rendezvous between the lovers at the Zoological Gardens (now better known as the Bronx Zoo).

"Never, never when we meet someone we have long awaited, do we find what we expected," writes Sholem Aleichem. For "someone," read "the novel's ending"; but its emotional disappointment notwithstanding, something feels right about it. There's been too much wandering, and in the end romance must give way to obligation: Leo marries Zlatkeh, and Rosa Grisha. In the novel's final moments, Rosa writes that "apparently there is no happiness here on earth. There is only the striving toward happiness . . . There is no love, just an image of it, an ideal that we ourselves create in our fantasies." It may be that a wearied Sholem Aleichem, tempered by experience and history, wants to give up on idealistic love; but the novel's existence, which is the catalog of those strivings and fantasies, proves his inability to succumb to the full temptations of such skepticism. In fact, *Wandering Stars* meets, in its own way, the challenge posed by "The Railroad Stories," finding an amenable homeland for Sholem Aleichem in the world of Jewish and Yiddish culture.

The novel's most revelatory aspect, though, is its almost granular look at the business of the early Yiddish theater. Sholem Aleichem captures how business and family ties knotted together and were ripped apart as theatrical troupes are created, form, break, and re-form; and the novel provided him with the opportunity to settle some old scores with the American theater industry that had treated him so badly. He takes on the American Yiddish theater critics, who arrive at Leo's debut "with already-written reviews"; fillets the bluff and nonsense in the American Yiddish press, with its columns "filled mostly with short notices, bits of news items, innocent lies circulating backstage, and outrageous gossip"; and excoriates the American Yiddish repertory, "old pieces brought across the ocean . . . expertly adopted to the American style, designed to suit current Jewish tastes, so their true origins were indiscernible. In a word, they were now 'all right.'" Even the audiences aren't spared: "the same pregnant women with the same nursing babies disturbing the theater with their crying, the same boys and girls throwing orange peels at each other, talking and laughing so loudly, and making themselves so at home that the Pavilion Theater looked more like a small-town synagogue courtyard on a warm holiday morning when the Torah service was going on inside . . . the symbol of naïveté, coarseness, and vulgarity."

But none of this detracts from the novel's—and its author's—almost magnetic attraction to the theater. Given Sholem Aleichem's own variety of personal and biographical transformations, it's unsurprising that its main appeal is its capacity for personal reinvention, which happens again and again to the novel's characters, both on- and offstage. Leibel is amazed by "a world where people literally re-created themselves." Reizel, after essentially being kidnapped, is given new clothes to wear, and when she looks in the mirror, she "didn't recognize myself. Where had the tears gone? My appetite returned, and I had the urge to sing! And I began singing like a nightingale, as if I didn't have a care in the world." As Rosa and Leo become increasingly famous, more and more outrageous backstories are invented for them: though Sholem Aleichem's (that is to say, Rabinovich's) own backstory was sufficiently outrageous in real life to need no significant reinvention, enough aspects were smoothed, heightened, or blurred in "Sholem Aleichem"'s public presentation to make this resonant territory.

Of course, Sholem Aleichem is present in, and entirely separate from, all the characters and situations; and to see him in any one is to court reductionism. But two characters in particular stand out as providing insight, either into Sholem Aleichem himself or into the persona he was cultivating, characters who form a team for a good part of the novel. The first is Leo, the actor whose aesthetic ambition is to make fiction feel like a realistic life portrait; his great role, the soulful rebel Uriel Acosta, is the success of a "hard-won fruit of a war he waged heroically not against another but within himself." Leo's personal war is waged, in part, against his own desires, both for erotic satisfaction and to allow other events and people to passively control him—both of which get him into trouble. If these aspects seem less present in Sholem Aleichem's life (though his romance with Olga and his submissiveness in contractual matters suggest they're not entirely absent, either), his partner and friend Hotzmakh's struggles are also indicative.

Hotzmakh, a jester character—his name was already becoming archetypal in Yiddish theatrical history—was, like the young Sholem, an excellent mimic. But, far important, he also felt miscast in life, a "jolly clown" who, though "no one suffered as much, no one was as hungry, no one coughed as much or received as many blows and shoves from whoever felt so inclined," always seemed "cheerful and ready to laugh." Laughing on the outside while suffering on the inside, Hotzmakh attempts, on occasion, to play the romantic lead: the truth was, says the novel, that he was a natural-born comic, and so he eventually accustomed himself to the role that nature—and audience response—gave him. One imagines, given the other self-presentations "Sholem Aleichem" had provided over the years, the readers saw the author in the character. Whether the author himself did, of course, is a different story.

CHAPTER 23

In Which Our Hero Looks Backward

1909–1911

B y late fall, back in Nervi, Sholem Aleichem was thirty pounds heavier than he'd been immediately after his illness the previous year; but health concerns remained. He was sufficiently ill that he didn't travel to attend his second daughter Liali's wedding on November 26; instead, he mounted his own celebration, marking the day with a special "concert" where he, his son, and some friends sang songs and gave dramatic readings. Olga represented the parents at the wedding; these days, the couple were often separated, as Sholem Aleichem recuperated in Italy and Olga alternated between visiting the married children and spending long periods in Warsaw attending to her husband's publishing business. Sholem Aleichem wrote her regularly, loving letters with sentences like "Once more, I wait and I yearn, just as in Lugano, if you remember. . . ." If the precise circumstances are obscure, the sentiment is not.

But despite his separation from his full "republic," he was happy in Nervi. The town had even rectified its one flaw, from his perspective: more Jews were there this season, drawn, in no small part, by Sholem Aleichem's presence. His lodgings became a hub of social activity: Jews of all different backgrounds and ideologies would drop by and heatedly argue the pressing questions of the day. Their host would sit back, taking it all in: who knew what might be the germ of another story? His sense of mischief and whimsy returned in full force. He wrote letters parodying the fancy menus at the hotels he ate at, "Yiddishizing" the courses ("Salad—one of a kind salad! From Salad-Land!"), and tweaked his family: hearing his son-in-law and daughter had sought an apartment rental in a Warsaw Yiddish paper, he wrote the editorial staff suggesting he had rooms to supply—in Nervi, if only the couple would come.

As always, good spirits made for good writing conditions: he wrote Liali that "I write a great deal and publish almost everywhere." Unfortunately, his prolific output wasn't translating directly into material success. Despite Spektor's hopes, *Wandering Stars* never caught on with Warsaw readers or with a wider Polish audience (though it met a better reception among Ukrainian Jews, Sholem Aleichem's landsmen). The staff's diagnosis: It wasn't lascivious enough, certainly not compared to the *Haynt's* new serial novel *The Bloody Wife*. But being lascivious had its own challenges. Sholem Aleichem had received a letter from a man who refused to let his daughter read *Wandering Stars* because inappropriate material kept appearing in other parts of *The New World*. And what's more, the *Haynt* was introducing other reader-pleasing features, like a lottery sending twelve winning readers to Palestine. *The New World* considered countering, proposing giveaways of twelve dowries to indigent women, or new sewing machines: both Spektor and Sholem Aleichem detested the ideas, thinking they smacked of gimmickry. Sholem Aleichem satirized the whole process in a feuilleton, "A Mighty Uproar," suggesting the whole system of "can you top this" would lead to madness on the part of newspapers and their readers alike.

Sholem Aleichem had put his finger on something. Nearly a decade after the empire had begun relaxing its publication restrictions, a generation of mass readership was developing, with more and more readers coming from provincial backgrounds and, increasingly, growing up in modern, urbanized households. In 1906, there were five Yiddish dailies and three weeklies with total circulation of over 120,000 in Warsaw alone, serving a Jewish population of 5 million; by 1911, two leading newspapers would have over 100,000 subscribers *each*. The audience was becoming as diverse in interest and capacity as audiences in mass culture are, and cultural institutions were diversifying to match—and the ones that were attentive to profit, which is to say almost all of them, had to take note of audience taste in the marketplace. Material that could cross boundaries, play in multiple quadrants, appeal to high and low, sacred and secular (since traditional Jews could read secular papers, too, of course, and "traditional" was itself an umbrella term describing a diverse set of constituencies), was, as it perennially is, in demand. Often the result is a race to the bottom; and attempts by Sholem Aleichem and others to provide literary material with popular flair—the promised formula of *Wandering Stars*, remember—often struggled in the process.

Fiscal realities began to take their toll. The paper soon stopped paying Sholem Aleichem his promised rate; in return, he began threatening to withhold further installments of *Wandering Stars*; and several months later, in the late spring of 1910, he severed his connection entirely with *The New World*, leaving the novel unfinished (only a quarter of it had appeared). But some intriguing business opportunities were starting to arrive from an entirely different direction.

Sholem Aleichem had always been interested in reaching non-Jewish audiences. Russian ones in particular—some individual works had appeared in Russian—but others, too: he'd pitched the German publisher of the *Help* anthology on publishing his stories in translation. The Russian press, he wrote, trying to sell the idea, is "*very* interested in plays about the life in the Jewish ghetto; I would think the Germans would not be opposed to becoming acquainted with a way of life and characters new to them." Over a half decade later, that Russian interest came to fruition with the founding of a new press, Sovremnye Problemy, dedicated to making modern European writers like Strindberg available to the Russian reading public. Unsurprisingly, the press's founders were Jewish, a pair of brothers who were also interested in introducing Russian readers to Yiddish writers—Sholem Aleichem first among them.

Sholem Aleichem began working with the press in 1909, and by winter 1910 it had been decided he would make his Sovremnye Problemy debut with a collection of his children's stories—which, he wrote a potential translator, will be, "in any case, original, even if not highly meaningful. You know well that the life of children is generally more interesting than every other part of life, and the life of Jewish children—certainly so. You also well know that none of my fellow writers have dedicated as much attention to this world, the world of Jewish children, as I." Weighing titles like *Children of the Pale*, *Children of the Jewish Quarter*, *Children of a Forgotten Quarter*, and *Children of the Ghetto*—though they recognized Zangwill had gotten to that one first—they settled on *Children of the Pale*, and two volumes of children's stories, including a generous selection from *Motl*, were released that year.

They were, to put it mildly, well received. Maxim Gorky wrote him: "Your book was received, read through, laughed with and cried over—a wonderful book! . . . It sparkles throughout with such good, fine and wise love of the folk; such a sort of sentiment is truly rare these days." Alexander Amphiteatrov, a Russian writer and critic with whom Sholem Aleichem had become acquainted in Nervi, confirmed his earlier opinion that he "heard the breath of Dickens" in his talent, and insisted to "Russian elders" who wished their children to have the "sentiments of righteousness, love to their near ones and human equality" that they familiarize them with Sholem Aleichem. "Sholem Aleichem," he wrote, "is an artist in the full sense of the word and a nationalist in the deepest and best sense of the word. He is national as Maupassant, Dickens, and Chekhov are national. We can consider his Jewish types no differently than Maupassant's Frenchmen, Dickens's Englishmen, and Chekhov's Russians." As those first volumes were published, and increased in popularity and critical attention through 1910, a new meme began to develop. If Jewish critics had often seen Sholem Aleichem as mixing satire and affection, taking on the vicissitudes of Jewish life and comforting its members by, as David Roskies has wonderfully put it, "laughing off the trauma of history," Russian critics, with the distance and perhaps the unfamiliarity their position offered, instead tended to view Sholem Aleichem as an artist of joy and simplicity, in comfortable coexistence with his folk and his people. Sholem Aleichem—to the outside world—

was beginning to become the archetypal Jewish writer. It was a trend that would only deepen over the decades.

Other volumes featuring the Kasrilevkans, Tevye, Stempenyu, and Yosele Solovey, among others, would follow over the years. By the outbreak of the First World War, a dozen volumes of Sholem Aleichem's work would be available in Russian; in some years, they provided royalties almost equal to his Yiddish work. But despite his Russian success, he still couldn't find an appropriate European home for *Wandering Stars. Undzer Lebn* was interested, but Sholem Aleichem, remembering his shabby treatment at their hands, demurred. It was a rare case of having the opportunity to do so: with close to two hundred thousand of his small volumes published in a single year in runs of "booklets" that numbered up to five thousand, profits flowing to him through an authorized dealer, along with the increasing success in Russian translation, he had enough money to make sure he did things the way he wanted them.

His health, though, remained unsteady. He got sick in the spring of 1910; it was serious enough he couldn't even write Gorky personally to thank him for his warm comments on *Children of the Pale*—his daughter had to do it on his behalf. (She told Gorky her father had said the words were worth more than all the distinguished medical professors in the world.) Visits to Swiss doctors had revealed some heart weakness, and, after recuperating for several weeks in Lugano, he was sent to Badenweiler, a German town known for its mineral waters and where visitors regularly came to take the cure. He arrived there in June for the summer, writing an old friend around then: "If I am to believe the doctors, I suffer from different maladies, and drag myself all over foreign countries, Italy, now Switzerland, soon Germany, etc., with no end, that is, with an end that will come in a large black frame: Yiddish Writer Dead."

When it came to Badenweiler, Sholem Aleichem's superstitious nature probably didn't help his fatalism. He knew Anton Chekhov had spent the last month of his life there several years before; he might have heard that Stephen Crane had visited to treat *his* tuberculosis and died there as well. He certainly didn't enjoy the intimations of mortality he got from seeing the large statue of his beloved Chekhov in the city park; his point of view was like that of Woody Allen (a kind of comic *eynikl* of Sholem Aleichem), who once remarked he would rather achieve his immortality through not dying. Mortality of major writers notwithstanding, the place was lovely; and soon he was sending for his family to join him, including—at last—his older son, Misha, who had just finished *gymnasium* in Kiev with honors and a silver medal.

Sholem Aleichem's complex relationship with Misha, as with many of his growing and grown children, was full of opposing impulses. In a series of letters, his paternalism mixes with his tendencies to autocracy, both as a writer and more generally. He chides Misha to attend to his studies, worrying he wasn't keeping up his grades; he questions his literary tastes, his indulgence in the new strains of decadent literature; and he asks him to run errands related to his literary business in Kiev. Both encouraging of Misha's desires to translate his father's work into Russian (so long as it didn't interfere with his studies) and mindful that such translation was necessary for his growing audience not only of Russian non-Jews but of Russian Jews—even his own children were far more comfortable in Russian than in Yiddish—Sholem Aleichem well understood that the common dynamic of adult children flying far from their parents' original orbit was tied up with every change that had taken place in the Eastern European Jewish world—and his own personal circumstances—since he was young.

But he simultaneously understood that their relationship to the world of their fathers was as diverse and complex as that new world itself, complete with narratives of cultural return and involvement on their own terms, not just those of their parents. Sholem Aleichem's one-act holiday plays "The King of Spades" and "Shraga" give another portrait of the friction that exists both between and within generations, a theme already evident in the portraits of Tamara and Sasha in *The Deluge*. The former satirizes the upper-class, assimilated Kiev speculators who barely remember Chanukah (the guests, for example, believe they're coming for "blini"). But it doesn't spare the children, either: while the host's daughter Bertha insists on being known as "Batya, daughter of Yisroel," on celebrating the Maccabee "heroes" and "our national holiday," and on speaking Yiddish rather than Russian to the guests, her fiancé, Grisha, is far less committed, more interested in card playing than in Hebrew. And in the sequel, "Shraga," a Hebrew instructor who insists on speaking Hebrew regardless of the context—"What do I care if people understand me or don't understand me? This is my language! . . . I speak Hebrew in every place and with everyone. Even when I'm on the train, I say to the conductor: *ten li kartis!*"—is satirized for his narrow-minded ideological inflexibility. As we'll see when we get to Numa's bar mitzvah, raising children in this revolutionary world—in both senses of that term—was a struggle for Sholem Aleichem to work through, in life and literature both.

By all evidence, though, Sholem Aleichem was genuinely, wholly, uncomplicatedly delighted whenever he could have as much of his family with him as possible; and was delighted to pass the Badenweiler summer days with them. He indulged a vogue for geometrical puzzles, and worked on *Wandering Stars*. That hot summer, a series of fires had broken out in various Jewish communities; following a familiar pattern, Sholem Aleichem proposed producing an anthology, *The Book of Fire*, with profits going to those rendered homeless. Though his suggestion, which ran in all the papers, garnered a number of preliminary positive responses, the project eventually fell apart. Peretz might have been partially responsible: he claimed it would benefit neither the victims nor Yiddish literature— and, adding insult to injury, he argued that Sholem Aleichem was doing this in an attempt to maintain his ostensibly dwindling Yiddish popularity. The message was clear to Sholem Aleichem: he needed to return to Russia—and certainly required a regular presence there in the Yiddish press, hopefully with *Wandering Stars*. As the summer ended, though, he'd begun coughing again; his Swiss doctors still found traces of disease, and insisted he return to Nervi. A visit to Russia would be impossible until at least the summer of 1911.

But perhaps a regular home in the press would come more quickly. That fall, Sholem Aleichem was invited to become a regular contributor to the newly established Warsaw Yiddish paper *Moment*, Warsaw's fifth Yiddish paper, which would immediately become *Haynt*'s major competitor. The terms were less generous than Sholem Aleichem had hoped, 2,000 rubles a year (about $23,000 in 2010 dollars) rather than 3,000; but they agreed to take *Wandering Stars* rather than the short stories they preferred, though they did insist on some holiday short stories, that Sholem Aleichem specialty. In an illustration of how Yiddish culture was spreading, Sholem Aleichem's handwritten drafts from Nervi would go to Vilna for his son-in-law to type up and send on for publication in New York and Warsaw. Talk about wandering. In a by now familiar routine, though, Sholem Aleichem quickly grew upset with his new employers, who were, to his mind, insufficiently responsive to his many letters containing edits, changes, and corrections. The editors, for their part, were increasingly interested in chasing the rapidly growing market of religious Polish Jews beginning to read newspapers—who, early evidence indicated, were more interested in reading about people like them, and thus presumably less attracted to stories about Yiddish actors of assumed dubious character. Sholem Aleichem, increasingly offended and dismayed, considered breaking his contract with the newspaper.

He would become even more determined over the winter of 1910–1911; after returning to Nervi as the weather changed and renting the Villa Rosengarten, his health worsened once more (probably, again, because Nervi's climate was actually harmful, rather than the reverse). Signs of age and death were all about him. The year 1910 marked Abramovitch's seventy-fifth birthday, and the fifty-two-year-old Sholem Aleichem celebrated by writing two essays about his *zeyde*. The first is a sweet confection about Abramovitch's love for and inspiration by nature; "Auto-da-Fe," on the other hand, recalls the writer's more astringent side, and the inspiration he'd provided to his younger colleague. Two decades ago, Sholem Aleichem wrote, he had been staying in a dacha near Odessa, working on an allegorical novel à la Abramovitch. He invited the master to the dacha, hoping for the opportunity to show him the work. Abramovitch, an excellent guest, finally asked if he was working on anything; Sholem Aleichem presented the manuscript, and eagerly waited the next morning for his response. Abramovitch merely asked if breakfast was being cooked in the kitchen. "Breakfast? Certainly. Are you hungry, perhaps? I'll tell them to get you something." "Hungry? God forbid! I just wanted to know if they had heated up the oven." "Naturally they heated up the oven." "If it's hot, then go and throw in, you should pardon me, the entire manuscript and burn it up, because it's not your genre. It is—it is—feh!"

Sholem Aleichem ended the memoir with what seems a genuine confession of gratitude to Abramovitch for his uncompromising stance, which he credited with preventing him from releasing inferior work. As we've seen, Sholem Aleichem resorted to his own auto-da-fés on a variety of occasions, and the master's insistence on editing and polishing—the hard work of writing—had caused the tyro to learn a lesson he'd take so deeply to heart that the man who once by his own admission sent things out without looking them over was now considering giving up a well-paying job because they didn't let him edit *enough*. But such valedictions were clearly suggestive of the fact that Abramovitch's literary career was nearing its end (though, as it would transpire, he'd outlive Sholem Aleichem), which was certainly pause for reflection on the part of the man who'd created a direct chain of familial and literary influence between them.

"It's good you've reminded me about death. I myself also think at times about it, sometimes at night, when I can't sleep. And sometimes also during the day," Sholem Aleichem wrote a friend. He was referring explicitly to the death of another good friend, the Hebrew writer A. L. Levinski; but mortality would have been strongly on his mind that winter for other reasons—he had discovered that his oldest son, Misha, had contracted tuberculosis, like his father. Olga discovered the terrible diagnosis while visiting him in Kiev, where he was attempting to matriculate at Kiev University, and took him back with her to Nervi. It's impossible to know for sure how all this affected his dealings with *Moment*; he did become sufficiently angry with them, though, that he decided to publish his Passover holiday story—the third installment of "Pages from the Song of Songs"—as a separate booklet rather than giving it to the paper. *Moment* seized this as an opportunity to break their contract, and after some fruitless negotiations, Sholem Aleichem left the paper for good, meaning that, frustratingly for author and European readers alike, *Wandering Stars* would stop appearing in June—for the second time.

With the panoply of newspapers now publishing, though, there always seemed to be another option, and Sholem Aleichem had the opportunity for sweet revenge. Shmuel Yatzkan, the editor of the *Haynt*—*Moment*'s biggest rival—came calling in Badenweiler, where the family had returned for the summer. Sholem Aleichem had his objections to the paper, with its sensationalism and its prize giveaways, but Yatzkan convinced him it was becoming slightly more upscale—and Sholem Aleichem certainly wanted the kind of exposure that one of the biggest Yiddish papers could give, along with a forum that could keep up with his productivity. In addition, with Misha's illness, a whole new set of medical expenses burdened the family finances. Yatzkan still wasn't interested in *Wandering Stars*, and the deal was a little less rich than the previous one, but it was worth it nonetheless.

The newspaper switch was covered extensively in the Yiddish press; then, as now, the media were quite concerned with reporting on themselves as well as the news. Sholem Aleichem had stoked the fire with an open letter in the *Fraynd* insulting his previous employer for its own engagement with prize giveaways. The resulting war of broadsides only stopped thanks to Olga. As Madame Sholem Aleichem, she could often project the image of floating genteelly over debate and controversy involving her husband, using a combination of business savvy, intelligence, upper-class upbringing, and the mores of a society that aimed for European norms of delicacy toward women; and her open letter explaining all the facts seems to have tamped down the controversy. The *Haynt*, of course, was gleeful about sticking it to its rival, and gave Sholem Aleichem a tremendous debut, dedicating its entire front page to him. And he in turn stepped up to the challenge, producing "Gitl Purishkevitch," one of his finest monologues, for the occasion.

Gitl Purishkevitch, an agent for Wissotsky's tea who, as she repeatedly asserts throughout the monologue, "owes everything she is to God and then Wissotsky," is distraught beyond measure over her only son, her future source of support in her old age, having been inappropriately taken for the draft when a local rich man's three grandsons have all been mysteriously rejected. Working her way up the bureaucratic ladder—armed only with her tea to deliver, her demand for justice, and her gratitude to God and Wissotsky—she manages to wangle an invitation to attend the proceedings of the Duma, the Russian parliament, in St. Petersburg. Finding no supporters there, she claims she needs a Jewish Purishkevitch—a genuine populist, his vicious anti-Semitism notwithstanding. But she ends up being her own Purishkevitch. When the idea is floated on the floor that the Jews enrich the imperial coffers by being granted permission to buy their way out of the draft—another way for the rich to evade their obligation at the poor's expense—and the real Purishkevitch takes advantage of the opportunity to press his claim that no Jews were in the service, she uses her own voice, screaming, "What about Moi-i-i-she!" from the gallery.

As is so often the case in Sholem Aleichem's stories, victory comes hand in hand with defeat. True, Gitl gets the justice she wants: Moishe, who shouldn't have been drafted in the first place, is released, and the local draft board is indicted for taking bribes. But she's unjustly mocked by her community—the common fate of Sholem Aleichem's diffident heroes and status quo breakers—nicknamed Purishkevitch by the town; and she continues being exploited, at her own hands, insisting to "Sholem Aleichem" that he should "write [the town] up so that the whole world will know about them. Write it all down so that not a single one of them will escape being written up." Superficially, the story's an expression of populist rage—certainly one reason the work was so popular, deepening the impression Sholem Aleichem was on the people's side, expressing the people's sentiment. (Gitl Purishkevitch became a household name, and readers regularly asked him what Wissotsky had paid him for product placement—the answer was nothing, though it was a huge payday for the company.) But Gitl Purishkevitch's final assertion—that it's the Jewish community, not the anti-Semitic system or its parliamentary representatives, who deserve the writer's assaulting attentions—allows those other forces to flourish unimpeded, making our monologist and Purishkevitch analogues. The real Purishkevitch's appearance in Sholem Aleichem's work was a sober reminder that the post-1905 world for Russian Jews was a dangerous one—and the events occurring that spring of 1911, events we'll discuss in the next chapter, made the specter of anti-Semitism more and more sobering.

But there were other matters to think of that summer as well. Sholem Aleichem was trying to finish *Wandering Stars* for its American serialization, for one. There was a new grandchild to play with, Liali's first, a daughter named Bela, who would eventually garner literary fame in her own right as the author of *Up the Down Staircase*. And there was the regular commitment for the *Haynt*, which was the subject of some disagreement: Yatzkan, *Haynt*'s editor, pushed for a return to the Menakhem-Mendl stories, an idea which Sholem Aleichem rejected along with several others. They finally came to terms on a series chronicling the summer lives of wealthy Jews at the European spas—which would certainly alleviate any of Sholem Aleichem's anxieties about being alienated from his material. Known as *Marienbad* when released in book form the following year, it appeared, thanks to the newspaper's insistence on a Warsaw-centric emphasis, under the title "From Nalewskis to Marienbad," after the largely Jewish street in Warsaw.

Marienbad is a tribute to relaxing into and accepting one's fogydom. An epistolary novel combining characteristic themes like intercepted letters (or at least letters read by unintended recipients), the concerns of the nouveaux riches with living à la mode, the bunk of doctors, and a young wife whose virtue is threatened by sleazy types, it suggests that the "bitter taste of a hell called Marienbad" brings out the most cosmopolitan (read: hedonistic, louche, amoral) in everyone there. A character writing her husband from Marienbad that "it's a new world today, Shlomo, a world that is open-minded and liberal," receives the response that while maybe he's "as you say, a man of the old school and [doesn't] know what's what," his disgust with the environment isn't about the relaxation of traditional law but the boorish, rude, and inappropriate behavior on display. And, by novel's end, we may sympathize with him.

That summer provided Sholem Aleichem with yet another occasion to feel out of joint. The previous winter, he had re-encountered his inseparable childhood companion Elye Barkhash—Elye Dodi's in *From the Fair*—after a thirty-five-year interval. (Barkhash hadn't had an inkling, over the decades, that the famous writer was actually his old friend.) Sholem Aleichem had written him a sweet letter in January 1910, musing on how much time had changed them; but now, a year and a half later, their actual reunion showed the changes were deeper than he had supposed—Barkhash's refusal to accompany him to the Tenth Zionist Conference in nearby Basel amply illustrated how their interests and beliefs had diverged. He enjoyed the conference nonetheless, holding court at the coffee tables and conversing with all sorts of delegates, many of whom were afraid to approach the great and forbidding cultural Zionist Ahad Ha'am, also present. The congress, noted for the conciliatory tone it struck between the various Zionist camps and approaches, was in a celebratory mood: and Sholem Aleichem returned home with a notable gift from Wissotsky, a pocket watch with Hebrew letters instead of numbers engraved on the dial. He loved it, especially the loud, chiming noise it made.

With summer ending, the family had to leave Badenweiler, but no one wanted to return to Nervi for a fourth year: its hospital-like atmosphere was no place for children, and the family didn't want Numa, approaching school age, to be raised there. And if he ever wanted to return to Russia, Sholem Aleichem would have to start weaning himself off the mild Italian winters. Eventually, the family decided to winter in Montreux, in French Switzerland, which was mostly a location for American and English patients to take the cure. While there, he would begin another major attempt to turn bloody Jewish history into gripping literature.

CHAPTER 24

In Which Our Hero Fights Back Against Libels of a Frivolous and Tragic Nature, and Encounters His Alternate Selves

1911–1913

The problems kept piling up that fall. Sholem Aleichem was battling a case of influenza. He was missing his two older daughters, who were with their spouses in, respectively, Vilna and Berlin. And that October he discovered that an Odessan had begun to publish a newspaper titled *Sholem Aleichem*, naturally giving the erroneous impression that he was personally involved. It made him so upset and nervous, he wrote Abramovitch, that he couldn't even write, "which is, for me, a remarkable occurrence, like for a goy—you should excuse the comparison—to not even look at a drink." The offending publisher claimed somewhat implausibly that he had first decided on naming the newspaper *Sholem Aleichem* and only subsequently remembered the existence of a writer by that name. Abramovitch, a fellow Odessan, finally intervened at Sholem Aleichem's request, Solomonically persuading the offending publisher to cut his title in half and just call it *Sholem*.

His biggest newspaper problems, though, were with the *Haynt. Moment*, the *Haynt*'s lead competitor, had leapt ahead in the circulation wars: they'd cracked the traditional Polish audience question with a series of immensely popular sketches featuring a group of Hasidim humorously reviewing the week's events while preparing for the Sabbath. An editor at the *Haynt*—his old friend David Frishman—argued in staff meetings that the feuilletonist was just doing what Sholem Aleichem used to do himself in works like "The Intercepted Letters"; the *Haynt* should simply get the master himself to do it better; and only a popular character like Menakhem-Mendl would do as a central focus. Yatzkan, who had wanted more Menakhem-Mendl stories all along, loved the idea, and as Sholem Aleichem's annual contract negotiation approached, increasingly pressured the author to do it. Sholem Aleichem was still opposed to the idea, and the resulting standoff lasted for several months.

His increasingly elegiac mood was apparent in the first two entries in a planned series, "Sketches of Disappearing Types," he published that fall in honor of Yom Kippur and Simchat Torah. Introducing the first sketch, he wrote, "Among the different types that the Jewish life produces, there are found those who are standing on the edge of extinction, that are moribund. Depicting living people is a pleasure; describing the types that are passing on is a mitzvah. They plead: 'Depict us, describe us; let us not be forgotten by the coming generation.' . . . Such types I give an entire sheaf, a serial." This concern with chronicling a vanished world—decades before the Holocaust—was a theme gaining more and more momentum as the years passed, personally felt as friends departed and children grew. But his concerns weren't only about modernization and acculturation. "Times have changed," he writes in the second sketch, "and the mayor and constables have changed with the times. Now we are thankful if they permit us Jews to get drunk once a year and go freely from house to house singing holiday songs. For in some towns, they tell us, even this is forbidden." Reaction and anti-Semitism had hardly vanished since the 1905 pogroms, which hadn't been so long ago, anyway. And the year's events had only made the Russian Jewish community more concerned about how things would develop.

On March 20, 1911, the mutilated body of twelve-year-old Andrei Yushchinsky, who had disappeared eight days before, was discovered on the outskirts of Kiev. The nature of his wounds led the anti-Semitic press to suggest he was murdered in order to use his blood to bake matzah: the ugly, medieval blood libel rearing its head in the twentieth century.

At the child's burial, leaflets were already being distributed calling for vengeance against the Jewish murderers; a criminal investigator who'd traced the murder to a local gang was dismissed. Pressure from the top—the minister of justice—led to the Kiev district attorney's pressing for a Jewish connection. A witness testified that on the day of the victim's disappearance he was playing in a Jewish-owned brick factory's yard and was kidnapped by an employee; the factory's manager, Mendel Beilis, was arrested on July 21, 1911, and would remain in prison for two years. During the trial, in September and October of 1913, the witness would admit to being coached; eventually, a jury of Ukrainian peasants found Beilis not guilty.

By May of 1911, Sholem Aleichem was already begging Alexander Amphiteatrov and his Russian colleagues to mount a collective protest against the trumped-up accusations, writing that if indeed "there are ritual murders in the world, it is not by those who are the victims of pogroms, but by those who perpetrate them. What else can one call the fine deeds of the Kishinev and other pogromists if not ritual murders?" He claimed that those pushing the ritual murder—and increasingly, in his and others' opinion, that clearly meant the regime, not simply the anti-Semitic press—had only one aim in mind: "to bring back the unforgettable year of 1905, that is, put plain and simple: a Russian-wide pogrom against Jews!" In the end, Amphiteatrov would only be able to publish the protest in his own name; and, if that was of course disappointing, Sholem Aleichem resorted to his usual consolation. He wrote Frishman that, reading a satire on the blood libel the latter had published in *Haynt*, "I was holding my sides, plain and simple. I simply don't remember when I have just so strongly and plainly laughed . . . until now I have cried about the blood libel, actually cried . . . but now I laugh, and for that I thank you. That still is our own bit of comfort, that we can, if among ourselves, scoff at our enemies really well . . . I had the true vengeance, the pure satisfaction, the finest equivalent." Always aware that literature was not the world, he was never unmindful of its influence on people's capacity to live in that world. The concept would inform his next novel.

The fall brought an increased wave of governmental repression, crackdowns, arrests, and censorship after the assassination of the Russian prime minister, Pyotr Stolypin, by Dmitri Bogrov, who came from a family of Jewish converts, in the Kiev Opera House directly in front of Tsar Nicholas II. Censorship became so severe that work could now be confiscated retroactively, even after it was published: *The Deluge*, for example, with its fair share of anti-governmental sentiment in its treatment of the 1905 revolution and reaction, was confiscated in Warsaw. But this made speaking out more, not less, important—and reaching the Russian public, who in the last two years had become more familiar with his voice, imperative. It was, as it turned out, a perfect time to be in contract negotiation with your newspaper. *Haynt*, knowing how dangerous it would be to lose Sholem Aleichem entirely at this competitive point, agreed to renew his contract in January 1912 with a novel rather than the feuilletons they would have preferred. Their condition, that the novel be topical, ripped from the headlines, was music to Sholem Aleichem's ears: topical, those days, meant only one thing—the Beilis trial and the blood libel. And his interest in eventually reaching a Russian audience with it suggested doing something almost unheard of in his previous work: incorporating a significant non-Jewish character.

He decided as a result to combine a story of blood libel with an idea he'd been contemplating for a decade, inspired by Mark Twain's *The Prince and the Pauper*, about the respective fates of a Jew and a Christian who decide to switch passports. Writing an up-to-the-moment story about Jewish-Christian relations in Russia could pose some difficulties for an author who'd been out of the country for some time; but making the protagonists university students could not only take on youth culture and thus provide melodramatic love plots, but also allow Misha to help with the factual background. Before contracting tuberculosis, Misha had been encountering legislative difficulties matriculating at Kiev University: despite his honors and silver medal for academic achievement, which would have normally made admission clear-cut, new regulations had decreed that only a gold medal would be sufficient for Jews. His experiences would be invaluable in sketching out the difficulties the newly Jewish character would encounter; Sholem Aleichem even named the character Rabinovich for his son (at least mostly). Sholem Aleichem was partial to calling the novel *The Great Hoax* or *The Kiev Tragicomedy*, but, perhaps remembering the success of the old serialized *Haynt* novels, the editor changed the title to *The Bloody Hoax*. It began running in 1912.

Unlike *Wandering Stars*, the plot of *The Bloody Hoax*, though occasionally convoluted, keeps thrumming smoothly and suspensefully throughout—a particularly noteworthy achievement given its length, which was substantially greater than almost everything else Sholem Aleichem had ever written. (His brutal pace on the novel probably helped its coherence: he wrote almost a chapter a day.) A necessarily radically condensed summary, omitting numerous plot points: Grisha Popov, a Gentile, had been friends with Hershke Rabinovich ever since he saved him from the schoolboy hazing ritual of having his lips smeared with lard. He nonetheless insists that reports of Christian anti-Semitism are overblown, as is the Jews' sense of their own suffering; to test the proposition, the two agree to switch diplomas, names, and passports for a year's time. When they do, Grisha, now Hershke, finds himself unable to get into university, victim—despite "his" sterling grades—of the quota system.

Though there are constant flirtations with discovery—it's hard for anyone to believe that this Jew speaks no Yiddish, and he seems unfamiliar with basic tenets of Jewish religion and culture—much is explained away by his ostensible assimilated background, and more is excused by his wealth. Shocked by the Jewish situation and by anti-Semitic discrimination, he also finds love with his landlord's daughter, Bertha (Betty) Shapiro, but his (still hidden) Christianity comes between them. Meanwhile, a Gentile boy, Volodka, turns up murdered, stabbed multiple times; Grisha, who knew the boy, assumes the stepfather, who beat the child regularly, is the culprit, but the anti-Semitic journals are beginning a drumbeat of blood libel. Through circumstances too long to explain, Grisha is arrested and accused of the murder and blood libel; though he could stop the process at any time by revealing his identity, he refuses, finding it impossible to believe that "they could build a case against him on the basis of such laughable, flimsy evidence"—a potentially fatal miscalculation.

Grisha's arrest also means the fragile system of communication set up between the two hoaxers grinds to a halt: after hundreds of pages, the novel now switches to Hershke's perspective. He's had far more success posing as Grisha, and is haunted by the fact that he will soon have to return to his old life, which will be "a thousand times more difficult and unbearable than before." Like Sholem Aleichem at the Loyeffs', he imagines himself in royal surroundings, and the princess duly arrives in the form of Sasha, the older sister of his new tutees. Falling in love with her, he discovers her family dispassionately believes the blood libel to be true, and, heartbreakingly, discovers that Sasha is afraid of Jews herself. As the hoax begins to unravel from both ends, Grisha begins to believe it was "no mere accident" that he had undertaken this experiment, instead convinced "it was fated that he, the Gentile Popov, should become a martyr, a Christian atonement for the suffering the Jewish people had endured as a universal scapegoat." He becomes even more convinced when he does reveal his identity—and no one believes him.

The trial is mobbed. Grisha, brought into the courtroom, anticipates "the end of the tragicomedy . . . the historic moment, when it would finally be proved, not only that he was innocent of this blood-ritual murder, but above all that such a crime had never been committed anywhere by Jews." But Grisha's father, alerted by Hershke, arrives before the trial begins, and everything simply . . . fades away. (Sholem Aleichem always did like resisting closure, particularly when it came to the ambiguities of the Jewish historical future.) We do learn some personal details. Betty rejects Grisha "out of love for her people, because of whom and for whom she had been persecuted and was prepared to be persecuted in the future." Though Grisha considers suicide, he rejects it, considering his pain just punishment for his hoax; and the novel's final lines strongly suggest Hershke *has* committed suicide, or, at least, has retreated from reality.

The main characters' different fates do suggest, as does the entire novel, the essential, unbridgeable difference between Jew and non-Jew—albeit a culturally determined, not natural, one. If Grisha (read: Sholem Aleichem's Russian audience) can grow to understand the "sad, tragic story of a spirit which from childhood had been seared on the slow flame of poverty, loneliness, and want, tormented by needless racism, every kind of humiliation and insult, venomous and poisonous," he's nonetheless incapable of ever acting like a Jew—he's never really afraid, never feels himself truly endangered by the plot's or history's depredations. The novel's Jews, on the other hand, alternate between an extreme pragmatism that looks pusillanimous to the external, Christian eye and a pure idealism that is often dismissed as unattainable. At the train station where the Jews are gathering to flee from the expected pogrom, Grisha encounters Hurvitch, Betty's eventual mate, who says that "they won't triumph over me! Do you know why? Because I am not a nation, not a government, not a people. I am a thought, I am an idea, nothing more than an idea!"

But the blood libel is also an idea, and so was the liberal dream of a Russian-Jewish reconciliation based on mutual understanding and reason. Ideas battle one another in the court of public opinion, and the best ones don't always prevail. *The Bloody Hoax*'s partial censorship was testament to that: Sholem Aleichem was informed, after Passover of 1912, that an issue of the *Haynt* in which a character in the novel claims the Russians are the bloodthirsty ones, not the Jews, was confiscated according to paragraph 149 of the law codex of the tsarist government. There was even talk of putting the editor on trial. (It didn't stop him from publishing his hit novel, though.) *The Bloody Hoax*, it emerges, is a strong candidate for the antithetical pole to Tevye in Sholem Aleichem's works: it offers few grounds for hope.

G rand narratives of politics and melodrama were one thing; but Sholem Aleichem's best work brought the questions down to personal size—and often brought him or his persona along for the ride. After one adventure in 1912, when Sholem Aleichem decided on a whim to visit a frenzied fan who had promised him and Olga a restful villa to indulge in—and arrived to find an impoverished chamber of horrors—he wrote his children, "There are so many Yiddish writers—why does nothing happen to them of the sort that happens to me?" Why? Because he puts himself into the story, turns the jokes of Jewish history into personal comedy with characters he dares his audience to take as stand-ins for himself and themselves. And, of course, they are and they aren't.

To explain, a quick look at a Beilis-era story of politics, and identity, and aesthetics, and narrative play, and, well, everything Sholem Aleichem ever did: arguably his finest story, 1913's "On Account of a Hat." Sholem Shachnah "Rattlebrain," a Kasrilevkan, has broken his regular streak of business failures by catching the crumbs of a deal. Flush with his "success," he telegraphs his wife he'll be arriving home for Passover "without fail." Now travel, as we've seen, is no easy feat, and guaranteeing an on-time arrival is hubris in the extreme. But Sholem Shachnah's nemesis takes a particularly intriguing form. Arriving at the station on time, he settles down on a bench next to an official for a nap, asking the porter to awaken him in time for the train's departure. After an uneasy dream, he wakes in a rush—grabbing his hat, which has fallen off, he scrambles onto the train.

He meets with a surprising reception: the non-Jewish conductor ushers him to a first-class seat with repeated cries of "Your Excellency." Sholem is understandably confused—until he catches sight of himself in a mirror, and discovers he's wearing the official's hat instead of his own. His response? To blame the porter: "Twenty times I tell him to wake me and I even give him a tip, and what does he do, that dumb ox, may he catch cholera in his face, but wake the official instead! And me he leaves asleep on the bench!" And he runs off the train to wake himself up—thus missing both his train and Passover at home. When he finally does arrive, the Kasrilevkans mock him—not, as we might have assumed, for his almost inconceivable stupidity, but rather because of what they take to be his inconceivable hubris in dress and behavior: " 'How does it feel,

Reb Sholem Shachnah, to wear a cap with a red band and a visor? And tell us,' said others, 'what's it like to travel first class?' . . . 'Your excellency! Your excellency! Your most excellent excellency!' "

"On Account of a Hat" is written in honor of Passover, and Sholem Aleichem's Passover stories, like "In Haste" and "Home for Passover," are all about getting home; they're goal-oriented. In that way, they're political. For Sholem Aleichem, Passover was a return to the central Jewish essence—a traditional holiday he celebrated traditionally, even after leaving traditional observance behind. That celebration, and indeed that essence, could be expressed through clothes. Sholem Aleichem, immersed in the stories of Jewish culture, would certainly have known the midrash that a central reason Jews in Egypt retained a sense of political and national identity was their refusal to change their clothing: and simultaneously, as a snappy modern dresser, he was a man who insisted in 1906 that both he and his son-in-law get new hats for Passover. And five years before *that*, a young protagonist in one of his stories suffers a childish breakdown at the Seder because of the stress of preparing his old-fashioned clothing for Passover when he wants it to fit another way: a clear allegory for the difficulties of balancing tradition and modernity's individual liberation. Almost like a newfangled train that's speeding right back toward the shtetl.

Sholem Aleichem himself had had, as we've seen, his share of train mishaps; when traveling alone he'd often arrive late to his own public readings. "The more I study the Travel Advisor [the train guide]," he confessed to his daughter, "the less I understand it." At least one of those mishaps, in March of 1905, involved oversleeping. (He missed his station entirely, and had to wait eight hours at the next one.) But he understood one thing about them: their politics. After the 1905 pogroms, trying to convince his daughter and future son-in-law to join them in Kiev, he suggests that the latter buy an official's hat, with buttons, so as to travel undisturbed in second class. That last seems to be the most direct moment of biographical inspiration to the story—which, in its essence, is based on an old Jewish joke.

In the 1892 prospectus for the *Folksbibliotek*'s unpublished third volume, Sholem Aleichem had asked readers to send him "*true* Jewish jokes, parables, and tales" for publication. But as the years went on, in tales like 1902's "Reb Yosifl and the Contractor," whose plot (Reb Yosifl's request for charity results in a slap by the contractor; he responds that that was for him, but asks what's for the poor) was told, in shorter form, about the nineteenth-century Lithuanian rabbi Reb Nochem Grodner, or 1904's "The Squire's h'Omelette" (poor man sees rich man having an omelette, wonders what it's like; wife makes omelette but for financial reasons must replace all the ingredients with poorer-tasting ones; poor man, tasting, can't see what all the fuss is about), he had taken it to the next stage, using old jokes or folktales as the skeleton for his own creative imagination.

Here, the jokey outline is perfectly straightforward, but hides much under its surface. Its essence is that inconceivable stupidity: who can't recognize themselves in a mirror? Babies, victims of brain injury—humans who lack the most basic moorings of their own identity. If the story's about progress and its discontents, no wonder its action involves changing hats; switching clothing was, after all, an essential strategy of modernity. But Sholem Aleichem's horrific, nervous genius here isn't about the strategy's failure at non-Jewish hands, even in those days of blood libel. After all, when Sholem (and note that name!) wears his new hat, the officials attend to the clothing, not its wearer; as far as they were concerned, Sholem could have arrived home not only on time, but riding first class to boot. The fault is not theirs: they're fulfilling modernity's promise, to treat all wearers equally. The joke is clearly on Sholem Shachnah, on his own incapacity to accept the possibility of success. So impossible is it for him to believe such an outcome that he'd rather accept that he's not he. And the pathology's communal: the Kasrilevkites—behaving typically for them—react identically, mocking the *idea* of wearing such an outfit, rather than the foolish behavior of the man who wears it.

But the joke goes further, turning on the author himself, via his regular kind of stand-in. The story isn't as straightforward as it's related above: it appears in a series of nested narratorial boxes—Sholem Shachnah's story is told by a "Kasrilevkan paper merchant" to an unnamed narrator, who, for his part, confesses to the reader "that this true story, which he related to me, does indeed sound like a concocted one, and for a long time I couldn't make up my mind whether or not I should pass it on to you. But I thought it over and decided that if a respectable merchant and dignitary of Kasrilevke, who deals in stationery and is certainly no litterateur—if he vouches for a story, it must be true. What would he be doing with fiction?" The narrator, despite his elitist tendencies, becomes part of the community as he himself is hoodwinked by his own prejudices into passing off an obvious joke (or a less obvious allegory) as a true story. What goes for the narrator is hardly true for the author, well aware of the story's provenance and artifice; but is this his own way of acknowledging a tendency to be too clever by half, of perpetuating confusion between life and story? Or are we the ones who are the butt of the joke for judging Sholem Aleichem that way, mistaking his persona for himself, and his reported personal activities for anything other than a life lived in public performance?

All, and therefore also none, of the above, I suspect, which is the basis of willed comic confusion; and it seems significant that as Sholem Aleichem reports the story of his and Olga's horrific experience with his admirer— which promises to be first-class all the way, a true "Your Excellency" experience, and ends up being a damp room above the chicken coop; as they starve, as their hosts are boring, inappropriate, quarrelsome, and *never want to leave them alone*, Olga and Sholem laugh; laugh so hard that, at the end, they begin to cry.

A quick, recuperative trip to Nervi after that horrific experience turned into a month's stay; Sholem Aleichem spent from mid-February to mid-March at the Eden Hotel, Verdi's temporary home three decades before. *The Bloody Hoax* was improving, and gaining admirers, with each installment; though Yatzkan and the *Haynt* editorial staff grumbled at first, sending stern missives insisting on more plot and fewer character sketches, the serial's growing success quieted them down soon enough. It was the product of hard work: responding to a critic's claim (who hadn't actually been reading it) that the serial was simply ripping off material wholesale from the Beilis trial to make easy money, Sholem Aleichem asserted he rewrote each chapter six to ten times. In addition, he noted, not only did he never write for money—an assertion we may, at various points in his life, take with more than a grain of skepticism—he didn't need the money right now, as his books were selling tens of thousands of copies. (Another source estimates he was making 15,000 rubles a year from books and newspapers at this point—well over $165,000 in 2010 dollars, though this includes his *Haynt* contract.)

Though the novel was a sensation—the author figured that since the *Haynt* had a circulation of 100,000, and each copy was read multiple times, he probably had half a million readers—and thanks to his copyrights and newspaper sales his finances were in good order, there were other family troubles. Olga became ill in the late spring of 1912; she was confined to bed for weeks. Phlebitis was diagnosed, requiring an operation, and so the family spent the summer in the village of Clarens, slightly north of Montreux, near a well-known doctor in neighboring Lausanne; they eventually moved to Lausanne proper in the fall. By sheer coincidence, their Lausanne villa, the Rosemont, 14 Avenue Tissot, was where Charles Dickens had lived in 1846, sixty-six years before. Sholem Aleichem mused on the similarities he and others had noted between the two authors, particularly the panoramic breadth they shared in their settings and characters. Though to be honest, he believed, Jewish Warsaw might provide an even wider range for literary exploration than Dickens's London.

He must have also noted the similarity in their relationships with their warm and supportive fan base: the throngs who flocked to their readings, who pooled their money to buy installments or pamphlets or serials they could read aloud to each other. Not surprising, perhaps, that, in contrast to his earlier satiric scorn, he now wrote them a mutual love letter, a sweet little feuilleton called "Purchased Eternal Life." In it, Sholem Aleichem is giving a reading in Bobruisk; making his way to the hall through the snowy, muddy streets, he meets a young woman who, not recognizing him, offers him paradise if he'll help her get in; she doesn't have the money. Doing so, he subsequently sees her shining, happy face during the reading, and afterward, as he stands alone preparing to depart, arms emerge from the darkness to embrace him, and he receives a sweet, friendly kiss. Unlike the protagonist of "Eternal Life," that horrific, snowy "story about a corpse" almost a decade before, Sholem Aleichem is assured he has received paradise, and doesn't disagree. He knows he's done something eternal; not, of course, in providing the free pass, but in creating the work that survives him, that turns him into an icon that allows young servant girls to have the possibility of aesthetic rapture. They create him, but, in return, he creates them as well. It's this prospect—that Sholem Aleichem created a Jewish world not in fiction but in some sort of ethereal fact—that will be contemplated in the years and decades to come.

Montreux, warm in the summer, wasn't the greatest place for lung patients, but Sholem Aleichem's health had improved to such an extent his doctors were even intimating he could return to his beloved Russia for a visit. To prepare his lungs for the cold, and to accompany Misha, who required a sanatorium in proximity to a university, the two tuberculotics headed inland and fifteen hundred meters up into the Swiss mountains for the winter, to Leysin's Hotel Anglais. The rest of the family stayed behind in Lausanne, but husband and wife could now easily communicate via the new technology of the telephone. Soaking up the sun, experiencing "the pleasures of paradise," he worked on *The Bloody Hoax*, which was coming to a close along with 1912. Finishing the novel put Sholem Aleichem in good spirits; he held a contest among close friends and family, offering a prize for correctly guessing Betty's final romantic fate, and wrote his daughter and son-in-law he planned to continue writing at the rate of a story a week. Not to write, he told a friend, would almost drive him mad.

But things changed quickly. The very next week, in mid-January, Sholem Aleichem developed a different illness; later describing it as "hypertrophy of the prostate," an inability to pass urine, he wrote his son-in-law that "the pain and the trouble that I feel is indescribable. . . .

all the torments of Gehenna are nothing in comparison to what I'm going through." Hiding the news from most of the family, he visited a specialist at Bern's Lindenhof Clinic, mordantly suggesting that if he died there, at least he'd have a nicer funeral than in Lausanne, where there were no Jews. The specialist, diagnosing stones in the bladder, suggested operating. Sholem Aleichem, fatalistic, wrote that he wasn't upset about dying, "since I've lived long enough, had a little honor in life, and even left a bit of an inheritance for my people"; he was only troubled he had no one to whom he could dictate his will. "A man is a fool," he wrote, "who puts off writing his will from day to day." He was alarmed about the operation, though, and could only sleep with medicinal aid; but by February's end, he felt better enough to get a second opinion, and once more postponed writing his will, calling it "foolishness."

The second opinion was in Vienna; Professor Otto Zuckerkandl, head physician at the Rothschild-Spital, would literally (co-)write the book on this sort of thing (1922's *Studien zur Anatomie und Klinik der Prostatahypertrophie*). Zuckerkandl, diagnosing a "sphincter spasm" resulting from nerves and strain, told him an operation was unnecessary, but recommended he go somewhere for several months, rest, and not write. The news naturally cheered him—along with his reception by Vienna's Jews; not only did they stage a production of one of his works in his honor, but they celebratorily escorted him and Olga to the train. A bit like a funeral procession, Sholem Aleichem wrote, but so heartwarming "it was almost worth getting sick for." They returned to their old haunts at the Eden Hotel in Nervi via Venice, "the most beautiful city in the world," and he began relaxing and calming his nerves; he spent the first few weeks back in "absolute rest," not writing, trying to regain the eight pounds he had lost during his most recent illness. By mid-March, he could report his illness was "gone as if it had never been," and that he felt like "a hooked fish that has been thrown back into the sea." By three weeks after his arrival, he could tell his granddaughter, who was writing her own little stories, that he was writing, too, and was able to rejoin his family in Lausanne by the spring.

He didn't tell his granddaughter, who would have been too young to care, but he was working on his autobiography, at that point tentatively titled *Step by Step*. As when he'd been previously ill, Sholem Aleichem turned to the autobiographical upon feeling intimations of mortality; since his death seemed not to be imminent, he wrote at the end of January, he'd continue working on the memoir he'd begun during his first battle with tuberculosis, and hoped to finish it despite the great pain he was in. His addressee, Yekhezkel Kotik, had just sent a copy of his own just-published memoir about life in small-town Eastern Europe to Sholem Aleichem (among others; in an amusing mix-up, the copy he sent him had been autographed for someone else, who had, in turn, received a copy autographed for a third person). The book enchanted Sholem Aleichem; he wrote Kotik that it wasn't "a book—it's a treasure, a garden, a paradise full of flowers and of birdsong. It reminded me of my youth, my family, my cheder, my holidays, my dreams, my types." Aside from Kotik's inspirational influence, he was well aware that as his own fame had grown and grown, others had begun telling his story. An earlier article that had purported to characterize his youth was, in his words, *gornisht*, nothing, but the careful if playful control over his own image that he had curated for decades was necessarily slipping; its very playfulness, known to author and audience alike, stoked the demand for the "real" story, and if he didn't control his image, others would do it for him.

But, besides his usual inclination to stop working on memoiristic matters after his health and mood improved, there was another, perhaps more important, impediment: he wasn't sure where to place it. After negotiations failed with one venue, the autobiography might have been dead were it not for a unique character's reentry into his life: a wealthy naphtha merchant (naphtha: a kind of petroleum product), Sh. Shriro. Their friendship had had an unlikely beginning: around the author's jubilee, Shriro had written the author, in "a Sholem Aleichem–like style," asking for Menakhem-Mendl's address and advice on what kind of political approach or ideology to embrace. He also included 200 francs, calling it "a loan." Sholem Aleichem, bemused by the millionaire's literary ambitions, nonplussed by the loan, considered sending back the money but saw an opportunity.

"Menakhem-Mendl" responded, ostensibly from America, suggesting Shriro venture into philanthropy: that he become the first Jewish Maecenas, a patron of the arts, and in particular that he should support the Warsaw fund to buy back his copyrights. He also cheekily suggested, in the conventional Menakhem-Mendl postscript, that there must have been a mistake in the gift—the number seemed to be missing a zero. Shriro didn't bite, but a friendship developed, and he had visited Sholem Aleichem in Montreux. Now, hearing of the author's interest in writing his autobiography, Shriro came up with an interesting proposition: he'd give Sholem Aleichem a monthly advance of 300 rubles to write the book, and would personally take on the task of finding a buyer for it.

Sholem Aleichem was naturally enthusiastic. To him, this wasn't just his personal story, "a novel of an original Menakhem-Mendl, who has experienced a world [where he's grown from] small to large, then from large to larger, and then fallen, then grown large once again, only in another world with other interests." It was the story of Jewish society writ large: "The hero of my autobiography has encountered all sorts of types, merchants, large and small and very large, millionaires, actually—and has gotten to known them very, very well." It was the story of Jewish literature: "A whole literature has grown before my eyes (and along with me), our Yiddish literature. A whole generation of writers; great and small, young and old, of all different stripes and of different talents—they're all my good acquaintances, and in most cases my good friends. 'Your biography is the history of our literature,' one critic of our new literature wrote me." It was the story of Jewish politics: "A whole chain of movements and our communal life and communal activists: Hasidim, mitnagdim, assimilationists, nationalists, Chovevei Zion, Zionists, Territorialists, Socialists—everything that I myself have lived through. Not invented, but living people."

In short, he wrote, "this is not *my* biography, but the biography of our Yiddish world and by necessity my figure, as a person and a writer, will shine through." Sholem Aleichem understood how his own life had it all—and, more precisely, could be made to stand in for it all, that the persona he'd invented for himself could finish the act of representation his remarkable life had begun. His insight explained the two additional aesthetic decisions he shared with Shriro. The first was to write the memoir in the third person, calling it a "biography" and not an "autobiography"; it was, in many ways, his persona's story, the representative man's, as much if not more than his; and since that was so, he needed the entire range of experience—and so decided to begin from childhood, rather than, say, the beginning of his writing career.

Despite his—and Shriro's—enthusiasm, the author was skeptical about the publication prospects. The work as planned would be too long for the daily papers (publishing it in that form would take years, he estimated); there were no appropriate substantial monthly journals; the finances didn't work to bring it out with his own publisher; there were non-compete clauses in Warsaw. But Shriro pooh-poohed Sholem Aleichem's concerns and told him he would handle the business side; the author should be the first to admit his lack of financial ability. Sholem Aleichem couldn't share another concern with Shriro: that the merchant would fail to make his payments regularly. But he certainly wanted to write it, and given his, Olga's, and Misha's recent medical expenses, the money would come in handy. (He'd already had to ask Shriro for a temporary loan.) He suggested sending Shriro the material chapter by chapter, hoping to finish the project in a year, and over the next few months he reworked the chapters he'd written five years before and wrote a substantial section of the book. Unfortunately, the easily distracted Shriro didn't always send the money regularly—by July, the frustrated author was writing him to mention his payment hadn't arrived—and with his bills mounting, the autobiography was abandoned once more.

Needing cash, Sholem Aleichem reluctantly embraced the idea he'd turned down just a year or so earlier: to write additional, topical Menakhem-Mendl stories for the *Haynt*. The peripatetic businessman explained his employment at the Warsaw newspaper (and his return from America, for that matter) by telling readers that he'd briefly worked as a writer for the American Yiddish press, but decided to return home after a strike broke out—home, where, oddly, everyone has heard of him and his letters, and he was deferentially invited by an editor "to write about whatever your heart desires: about politics, about wars, about decrees, about troubles, about business, about the world, about people, whatever you hear or see, what you read and what you know." (We see Sheyne-Sheyndl's responses, despite the editor's agreement not to print them.)

The same deferential treatment pervades the stories, and not to their advantage: Sholem Aleichem, two decades after originating the character and a world away in reputation and popularity from the author who created him, presented a Menakhem-Mendl whose opinions on politics, mostly the Balkan conflicts preceding and presaging World War I, were supposed to be attended to. When *Haynt*'s editor objected that the letters were insufficiently serious, the author angrily responded that "if you were clear about my Menakhem Mendl and his Sheyne Sheyndl, you would know there's no plain babbling there. Within lies a mixture of foolishness and wisdom, moral instruction and joking." Many have agreed with Menakhem-Mendl's overarching, central insight in the letters, that geopolitics can learn a lot from the way financial markets work; and it's hard to imagine Menakhem-Mendl's wife ever writing him previously that "what you write me about your immigration plan . . . would be a marvel and the arrangement you're suggesting in your letter is also not a bad deal." It's true she supposes "it'll just be talk and more talk and that's how it'll end. All Jewish undertakings are like that," but the idea of Menakhem-Mendl as even something of an authoritative voice—even, or most of all, to his own wife—cuts pretty deeply against the very essence of what it is to be Menakhem-Mendl.

At one letter's conclusion, Menakhem-Mendl asks his wife, offended, "Do you think I am writing simply for money?" Sholem Aleichem's friends thought it a reasonable question to ask his creator, who they thought was making a big mistake. Abramovitch worried he would ruin the character. Menakhem-Mendl was finished, he said; he shouldn't be disturbed anymore. Sholem Aleichem, for his part, strenuously denied he was doing it for the money, replying to Dinezon's suggestion to that effect that "*You*, Dinezon, *our* Dinezon . . . should know Sholem Aleichem enough to know all the Yatzkans in the world don't have enough money to have an influence on Sholem Aleichem's creation. Sholem Aleichem, when he writes, no questions of money exist for him . . . Sholem Aleichem has never sold his pen for money. He *always* writes for writing's sake." We may believe that the writer, in financial straits, protests too much, but the circumstances of the series' end seem related to another sort of literary integrity.

As the series continued, the letters increasingly featured the Beilis case; in a neat symbolic linkage, Sholem Aleichem reveals Menakhem-Mendl is a distant relation of his (as he is to Tevye), and the businessman's head "is brewing with schemes and schemes and more schemes," including becoming Beilis's manager upon his acquittal, taking him to America, and securing their mutual fortune. Apparently there was more; but Yatzkan refused to print it, and Sholem Aleichem quit the series as a result. Was this a way to get him back to America for more adventures, the way he'd sent Tevye off to Israel? Would the (presumably inevitable) failure of such schemes have symbolic resonance with the crushing blow Beilis represented to Sholem Aleichem's dreams of comfortable Russian Jewish coexistence?

Sholem Aleichem never published another Menakhem-Mendl story, so we'll never know.

CHAPTER 25

In Which Our Hero Adapts

1913–1914

By the summer of 1913, Sholem Aleichem was in the best health he'd been in since his collapse in Baranovitch five years before; the doctors gave him a clean bill of health and told him he could travel anywhere. The natural destination was Russia, from which he'd been separated for so long; but he was concerned about climate both political (the Beilis trial) and meteorological (good health notwithstanding, a Russian winter was still something to take seriously). He considered spending time in Berlin and Paris, and, while making up his mind, traveled to Bad Soden, a German town known for its waters (and maybe, to Sholem Aleichem, from its appearance in *Anna Karenina*), and then, when the atmosphere there was too stultifying, to Wiesbaden, staying at the hotel pension and traveling around the area.

Much of the summer was spent revising earlier works for collection and republication; as was frequently the case, that meant drastic changes—*Children's Game* was cut almost in half, *The Deluge* renamed *In the Storm*. Hard at work, he hung a Hebrew sign on the wall reading "You've come to a busy man. Finish your conversation and—get out!" You could see why people dawdled, distracted not only by the writer but by his surroundings. Sholem Aleichem loved gadgets and gewgaws of all sorts; on his desk, at various points, he had, along with ordered stacks of paper and prepared pens, "many objects . . . pencils, clips, inkwells, glue, scissors, as well as a few odd playthings, one of which was a perfect miniature bicycle with rubber tires and a bell that rang at the slightest pressure," none of which anyone else was allowed to touch—part of his general insistence on order and neatness.

He spent part of the fall in Lausanne, then returned to Berlin; in part to visit his daughter and son-in-law, and in part to revisit its thriving émigré Jewish community, which had increased to 70,000 Eastern European Jews by 1910 and, since 1905, had become Zionism's world headquarters. Personal and national milestones marked his visit. He held his first public reading since his collapse in Baranovitch; more momentously, he was there when he, along with the rest of the world, received the news of Beilis's acquittal. Weeping with joy, Sholem Aleichem celebrated with Sholem Asch and many others at the émigré hangout Cafe des Westens, and sent Beilis a set of his works, expressing the hope that the books would help him forget his troubles. Though he had considered traveling to Russia to give readings, everything he would read had to be first submitted to the censor, and the delays stretched out; so he decided to finish out the winter in Nervi—the last time he would be there.

But first, readings in Switzerland, Belgium, and Paris. "The sensation created by his coming was so great," the great Yiddish writer Avrom Reyzen recalled, "that it seemed during those days Paris was almost a Jewish city." One Parisian event drew 800, the other 3,000; posters advertising the latter were "displayed in all Jewish clubs, societies, reading rooms, book stores, Jewish restaurants, food stores, and even beauty salons." The event was December 29. On New Year's Eve proper, the author dined with Misha and Reyzen at a fancy restaurant; after Sholem Aleichem turned in for the evening, the two younger men went to both the Bundists' Ball and the Anarchists' Ball. But though Sholem Aleichem may have been the toast of Jewish Paris, it was in Berlin that he'd been working on what he hoped would be his new jackpot.

Sheyne-Sheyndl had written to Menakhem-Mendl that year of how the movies came to Kasrilevke. "There are, they say, in Yehupetz, 'illusions,' a kind of theater where they show guests live people on the wall, as well as animals, birds, horses, dogs, cats, whatever you want. The people on the wall move as if they were living and the horses gallop. It is really lively, a party! And all to cheat some money out of people." Kasrilevke was only a little late to the party. The first Russian movie houses appeared around 1904, and soon businessmen would be going town to town setting up projectors and screening travelogues and dramas; by March of 1911, the year that *A Brivele der mamen* (A Little Letter to Mama) premiered at the Modern Electric Theater in Minsk, a columnist was predicting that "soon, in Volhynia, you won't be able to find a single more or less decent-sized shtetl with a population of five to seven thousand where, during the evenings, there will not flicker the alluring lights of illusion." Sholem Aleichem was a quick convert to the medium. As early as October 1910, he apologized to his son-in-law for cutting a letter short because his granddaughter was dragging him to the "cinematograph"; and he wrote that same granddaughter that winter that a Parisian theater "shows such comic pictures you'd split your sides for laughing." A few years later, in 1914, Charlie Chaplin would make his film debut, and Sholem Aleichem would become a particular fan: not only mentioning him in the final Motl stories, but even helping a few unaccompanied minors get into one of Chaplin's latest pictures.

Generally forward-looking when it came to new media, Sholem Aleichem firmly believed silent pictures would overtake live theater and even literature. The writing was literally on the wall: that past summer, Adler's former theater had been showing Yiddish photoplays along with vaudeville acts, and of the 123 movie theaters in Manhattan, nearly a quarter were found right around the Lower East Side tenements. And if these first Yiddish films were making money using Gordin's material, which Sholem Aleichem had always considered second-rate, how much more could be made if they drew on well-known works of his like Tevye or *The Bloody Hoax*, with their built-in fan base. You didn't even need to stop at Yiddish audiences—since it was a silent medium, simply swap out the intertitles and presto, it wasn't even a "foreign film." He had set to work that summer creating scenarios. Aside from the two mentioned above, he adapted his story "The Enchanted Tailor" and wrote a "cinema-fantasia in honor of Chanukah," "The World Goes Backwards."

The latter doesn't strike new conceptual ground—various tableaux from the holiday, stretching generations and tracking a path from tradition to acculturation to cultural return—but the word pictures he paints on the page display an excellent visual imagination, oddly one far better suited for the screen than his stage directions are for their medium. Perhaps the dreamlike, stylized aspect of some of his finest works were, or could be, more effectively transmitted through the film lens than represented on the comparatively unmediated stage.

While in Berlin, he'd suggested to the famous stage actor Rudolph Schildkraut, then just making his film debut in *The Shylock of Krakow*, that he play the lead in a film version of *The Bloody Hoax*. Nothing ever materialized; no Russian censor at the time would pass such sensitive material, and removing that huge potential market clouded the film's prospects, the appearance of Beilis films in America notwithstanding. Toward the end of 1913, Sholem Aleichem corresponded regularly with the Riga Jewish Dramatic Society's director about filming *The Bloody Hoax*; he also sent him two Tevye dramatizations, "Tevye the Eternal Optimist" (based on "Tevye Strikes It Rich") and "Chava—Tevye's Daughter." Both Russian scripts contain original scenes, and display ample comfort with the new form and its capacity to represent dreams and fantasies.

Sequences in "Tevye the Eternal Optimist" present Tevye's daydreams as filmic reality. In one, he discovers a bag in the middle of the road; unloading it bit by bit, he pulls out challah, a roasted duck, winter and summer dresses, and children's wear, and loads up his wagon. In another, he dreams of becoming wealthy: meeting Rothschild, he hands him a card with just the word "Tevye" on it; we see him become a mill owner, then a shop owner, then a banker—until the illusion is spoiled through another illusion, this one of the women turning into witches with gnarled hands, who place him on a big broom. "Chava" employs flashbacks, a number of them, to present her childhood and youth. But it also includes a major plot change: Chava commits suicide at the scenario's end, throwing herself into her father's well.

The altered ending, problematic and shocking as it was, emerged from sensible dramatic calculations: the Tevye stories, in whatever medium, needed a real ending, not just Tevye shuffling off to Israel. Sholem Aleichem was a canny enough writer to know that. He also understood that the shifting of Tevye's emphasis over the years to focus on his daughters meant its conclusion had to do the same, which really meant dealing with Chava, the daughter stories' central, dramatic crux. But how to handle it? As the film prospects languished—apparently, a potential backer didn't materialize—he explored the solution in other media. By January of 1914, he'd prepared a four-act stage version with the name "Tevye's Daughters," telling Jacob Adler he was perfect for Tevye: "Only such an artist as yourself," he wrote him, "will be able to portray him in his proper and living image, because only you can *feel* his soul." Knowing his audience, he suggested Chava be played by Mrs. Adler, who would "carry off the part brilliantly," and the other daughters be played by Adler's own girls—"In short, this is *your* family play." And the play itself? Well, he wrote, it had none of the special effects that provided New York audiences with their cheap thrills, no tearful, melodramatic scenes; nor did it have patriotic songs "that aren't worth a nickel but are dragged out to a quarter." Just "a Jew, a father of five daughters—a common man, but a full one, an honest one, a kosher one, a suffering one." He never sent the letter, though; he heard Adler, who had had mixed experiences at best with Sholem Aleichem's plays, didn't think much of Tevye's theatrical possibilities, and it's hard to imagine a businessman would have jumped at a letter explaining how the play was precisely the opposite of all the plays that made money in New York.

While reworking the play and thinking of other dramatic venues, Sholem Aleichem shifted Tevye to prose and wrote "Lekh-Lekho (Get Thee Out)," the last full-fledged Tevye story. The story was designed to align the Tevye-in-stories with his theatrical (or, perhaps eventually, filmed) counterpart: both, Sholem Aleichem decided, should end by acknowledging his growing sense of the impossibility of Russian Jewish existence—but with a form of solace that reflected a combination of personal psychological necessity, Tevye's evolving character, audience desires, and affiliation to traditional Jewish faith. What better way of accomplishing that—and solving the daughter question—than with the return of Chava? There was a small logistical difficulty—readers had last seen Tevye on his way to the land of Israel—but it was an easy, if dramatic, fix: Sholem Aleichem would kill off Motl, Tsaytl's husband, at the beginning of the story, ensuring Tevye's return to care for his daughter and grandchildren, and he'd bankrupt Beilke's husband Podhotzur, the man who would have sent him into forced retirement, sending him to live in poverty in America.

But how to precisely handle the balance between disillusionment and faith was trickier, though paradoxically aided by the worsening political situation, the blood libels, the trials, the recent anti-Semitic legislation expelling Jews from the villages. *The Bloody Hoax*, with its message of the distance between Jew and non-Jew, had been largely set in the cities, but the last few years had seen Sholem Aleichem focus that same perspective on the countryside, the shtetls and villages in stories like "A Country Passover." "Lekh-Lekho" begins with a flashback to an encounter between Tevye and his neighboring villagers in the charged, violence-filled period immediately after the constitution and the events of 1905. Tevye, who's always lived in the village among Gentiles in peace and tranquility, is faced with the specter of a pogrom against him—not particularly out of animus, but because of the infernal logic of bureaucracy: "A pogrom is a pogrom, and if the village council has voted to have one, then that's what must be."

Tevye, the talker, finds a solution through conversation, appealing to universalism: "I just hope you realize, though, that there is a higher power than your village council in this world . . . I'm talking about the God of us all." Maybe this worked in 1905, when universalism still had some possible appeal, when its representative, Chava, still had power in her challenge; but almost a decade later, particularism was having its day. Right now the relevant higher power was not God with his universalist judgments but the bigoted tsarist government that had ordered the Jews expelled from the villages; utopian messianic days, ushered in by an arrival on a white donkey, are parodied by an official's arrival on a white horse mandating that Tevye sell his house.

So how to address the Chava problem? Chava, who at this point is neither precisely Jew nor non-Jew? Given both Sholem Aleichem's current political sensibilities and the current demands of his audience, only one kind of solution suggested itself: a story of return, which is cast in the language of (re)conversion. As Tevye bids farewell to his house and cat, Tsaytl informs him that "the minute [Chava] heard we had to leave, [she] made up her mind to come with us. Whatever happens to us, she said to me, will happen to her too—if we're homeless, so will she be." Chava's language, consciously adopting that of the biblical Ruth, the ur-convert, unambiguously links her realization of Russian anti-Semitism to her decision to once more embrace the Jewish shared fate: it confirms the failure of the universal project she had championed earlier, drawing a bright line between us and them. The conflict of the story, then, becomes once more less about history—over which Tevye has no control—than about his own character: will he accept her return?

In the printed story, we don't know for an absolute certainty: Sholem Aleichem provides one of his trademark open endings. Here's what Tevye tells the listening "Sholem Aleichem," after describing Chava's appearance in his house, holding out her arms: "What do you say, Pani Sholem Aleichem? You're a Jew who writes books and gives the whole world advice—what should Tevye have done? Taken her in his arms, hugged her and kissed her, and told her, as we say on Yom Kippur, *solakhti kidvorekho*—come to me, you're my own flesh and blood? Or turned a deaf ear as I did once before and said *lekh-lekho*—get lost and stay lost! Put yourself in Tevye's place and tell me honestly, in plain language, what you would have done . . . Well, if you can't answer that right off the bat, you're welcome to think about it, but meanwhile I have to be off, because my grandchildren are getting impatient." The ellipses is in the original text: Tevye, who began the story cycle by importuning his listener with the words "*I am not worthy!* So I must say using the words our forefather Jacob said . . . If this is not quite right, I beg you, Mr. Sholem Aleichem, not to hold it against me. You, of course, know more than I do—that goes without saying," now waits for Sholem Aleichem, who's at a loss for words—then dismissively moves on. Tevye, who's been submitting his stories, his life, to Sholem Aleichem for judgment all along, has now decided to trust his own compass. Whatever Tevye's decision is, he'll be the one to make it. That power—and "Sholem Aleichem"'s concomitant weakness—may come from the fact that Chava's return has given Tevye an optimism that for Sholem Aleichem is necessarily incomplete: one that comes from a triumphant restoration of traditional faith.

It's not coincidence that Chava echoes Ruth, whose conversion embraces a family, a people, and a God all at once: Tevye's transformed situation, politically and familially, allows him to take leaps of faith that embrace his ultimate roles simultaneously, as a father with deep love for his children overmastering all and as a Jew with a deep love for his God overmastering all. Early on in "Lekh-Lekho" Tevye informs Sholem Aleichem that though communally and conventionally the Jewish world may be reading the weekly portion of *Vayikra*, he himself is reading "Lekh-Lekho"—that is, "Get Thee Out." On a superficial level, of course, this refers to his expulsion from the village. But, more deeply, it refers to the Abrahamic leap of faith that God levied on his first Jewish servant—to go off into the unknown, cherished only by his household and the promise of divine love and care. As the Tevye cycle ends, Sholem Aleichem can't help but provide an open narrative ending while at the same time enacting the possibility for optimism in faith, family, and even the Jewish people—as Abraham's journey is the beginning of the Jewish story as distinguished from any other.

Emboldened by these changes, Sholem Aleichem's reworking of his dramatic version, on which he tinkered almost until his death, would focus on Chava more and more. Roughly speaking, though he produced multiple versions in the last years of his life (and the play was revised posthumously by his son-in-law to boot), in the best-known version all the other daughters except Tsaytl essentially disappear, with little evidence they ever existed. The plot focuses entirely on Chava. Numerous scenes with no analogues in the stories exist (a family dinner, for example, where Chava faints dramatically after Tevye says he'd prefer a daughter of his dead rather than a convert), and melodrama pervades the play, a marked switch from the understated ironies of Tevye's monologues. I'll take one example from a long scene in act 2, original to the play, an encounter between Chava and Fedya, as he's now known:

> CHAVA: You don't know my father, Fedya! He's a man with a character! He would rather see me dead than forgive such a step! Never!
>
> FEDYA: Because of you the whole world is a paradise to me, and to me, you are the queen of the paradise, and I will be your faithful slave!
>
> CHAVA: Oy! Fedya! Fedya! You make me ill! You make me crazy! I will take leave of my senses—that's how much I love you!

And so on.

There are more understated moments, true, such as a third-act scene with Tevye and Golde at Fedya's house begging to see their daughter; she emerges after they leave empty-handed, and we're treated to the remarkable spectacle of a non-Jewish wedding where, in a coup de théâtre, the singing and dancing slowly shifts into a minor key and the stage darkens and darkens until it goes to black. But the play's conclusion, set several years later, returns to high drama: Tsaytl explicitly blaming Golde's death on Chava—seeing the pain her conversion had caused Tevye, "slaughtering him without a knife," was too much for Golde to bear; Chava's assertion to Tsaytl that she has known about the expulsions for a while, and when reproached by her sister, she responds, "Don't talk about what you don't know anything about! I didn't come here to get a sermon from you"; her revelation that she never converted in her soul (she claims she's been visiting her mother's grave and fasting on Yom Kippur); her hiding as Tevye bids farewell to the walls of his house ("I would kiss the walls! . . . Because I was born here, I was raised here, here I had troubles, here I had joys—true, more troubles than joys, but that's how God made it . . ."); and the curtain falling with her in his arms.

Melodramatic as it may have been, it was a definitive ending. Tevye's story was coming to a close. It would not see a stage, though, until after its author's death.

ACT V

The Old Man

CHAPTER 26

In Which Our Hero Sees War and Warsaw

1914

With Sholem Aleichem's mounting medical bills, the ending of his *Haynt* contract, and the acrimonious dissolution of his Russian publishing company, a Russian tour was becoming a financial necessity (even if, as was his wont, he was overoptimistic in his estimation of its potential revenue). But the logistics were difficult: in the aftermath of the Beilis trial, it was virtually impossible to get police permission for public readings, for fear he would stir up revolutionary sentiment. The permissions finally came through, and Sholem Aleichem would head to Warsaw after the first days of Passover. But before he departed, a family celebration: Numa was bar-mitzvahed in Lausanne on April 4, 1914, service at eight thirty and an afternoon tea at the Pension Helios at four.

At the time of Numa's bris, Sholem Aleichem had given his mohel a bottle of "Ein-Gedi" Carmel wine to hold, saying he would toast with it at the bar mitzvah. Now the mohel wrote him asking if he would need the wine—in other words, whether or not he'd be celebrating his son's bar mitzvah. Put another way, one might ask: Is he Chava, or Tevye? Sholem Aleichem's answer, of course, revealed he was his own complex, all-encompassing, idiosyncratic self: taking great offense at even the suggestion, he expatiated at great length not only about his personal

commitment to Jewish holidays, but also to his son's Jewish identity—
Numa went to a *gymnasium*, he wrote, but received private Yiddish and
Hebrew lessons from the Lausanne rabbi. Yes, he wryly commented, his
son wouldn't deliver his bar mitzvah sermon in his father's Yiddish, but
"what can you do—one is in *golus*, Heaven have mercy!" One is in exile,
but not from Zion; from Yiddishland, from the traditional landscape of
Jewish society. In this changed world, you have to celebrate what you can,
however you can.

In honor of the occasion, like many a Jewish patriarch after him,
Sholem Aleichem implored his married daughters and sons-in-law to
come together in Lausanne for Passover to celebrate the bar mitzvah
boy, using a family celebration as an excuse for a family reunion. Sholem
Aleichem, loving his family and wanting them around him however possible, was unafraid to play the ultimate trump card, writing his two sons-
in-law in Berlin: "Who knows how many Passovers are left for us to *all* be
together?" (Indeed his final letter to family members, two years later, is
about the importance of getting everyone together for the Seder.) They'll
take a family picture, he writes, the caterer is booked, there's plenty of
room—a conversation one could easily hear in its precise details a century later.

Throwing that complex negotiation between tenderness and autocracy into his own work, he crafted a Passover story that, like that first
effort, "Two Stones," audaciously rewrote his own story; only this time,
as with Tevye, he could see it from the other side. "Afikomen" is another
story about a firm-willed man and his equally stubborn daughter, another
romance between the rich man's daughter and her tutor. The battle
between father and daughter is conducted via the afikomen matzah, traditionally bartered back to the paterfamilias at the Seder by the child in
return for a gift. (This allows the Seder to continue, which is impossible
without consuming the afikomen.) This year, instead of requesting her
normal jewelry or gifts, the daughter extracts, after a negotiation mediated by the tutor, a promise that the father will grant a request to be
made later. Of course the request is to marry the tutor; but the infuri-

ated father has the last laugh, insisting his son-in-law essentially enter the business rather than continue his studies, perpetuating his own values and position at the expense of the son's future plans. The tutor, the real afikomen here, is consumed by the autocratic father, warping the future around his own wishes. How much did Sholem Aleichem see himself in this, insisting on his own republic's presence and obedience on Passover and off, as he increasingly employed his sons-in-law in the business of himself and his operations?

Sholem Aleichem's love for his family, expressed in his insistence that he could and would provide for their financial needs, meant leaving for Warsaw soon after the two Seder nights had passed; though to avoid chaos his arrival had not been announced in the papers, a mob awaited him at the Vienna train station anyway when his express arrived from Berlin. Before that evening's sold-out reading, hundreds of ticketless people lined the streets to at least catch a glimpse of the writer; Sholem Aleichem read "Lekh-Lekho," and Peretz whispered into a memoirist's ear, "The illness has done him good: he has become more popular, and he reads better." But that first day's warmth and unity—Peretz had even accompanied the other Yiddish writers to meet him at the train station!—didn't last long: Sholem Aleichem's visit became embroiled in the latest scrap in the language wars, which had hardly abated since Czernowitz.

In 1911, three years before, Sholem Aleichem had forcefully articulated his position to a Yiddish newspaper in Jerusalem that had attacked him for his "approbation" of Yiddish—not so surprising if you consider the confluence of the ideology of those who moved to Jerusalem and the realistic linguistic circumstances in which they lived. The writer told them their premise was simply absurd: "A language that a people has used for centuries and that already possesses its own literature needs no 'approbation,' even when it 'smuggles itself in' to the land of Israel from the Diaspora." Ultimately, he wrote, "It's past time for our 'right-wing' chauvinists to begin to understand that their 'struggle' against 'jargon' is a mockery in itself and a crime against the people, who need comprehensible material in the language that they speak and think. Our 'left-wing' chauvinists, who have called out a child's game-war against the old 'Hebrew,' are also risible . . . speak to the people in Hebrew, Yiddish, Turkish—as long as they understand it." But common sense and a widely encompassing love of Jewish writing and Jewish language was not necessarily the order of the day—as events would prove in Warsaw.

The question came down to banquets. More specifically, who would have the honor of providing Sholem Aleichem with the first one. The Yiddishists of "Hazamir" had issued the author his official invitation, and so would seem to have the edge over the "Lovers of the Hebrew Tongue"; but, complicating matters, they met in a cramped, low-ceilinged hall that would create medical difficulties for him. In addition, Peretz was insisting on the Yiddishists' prerogative; Sholem Aleichem hated the arbitrary divisions between the two languages, disliked ideological attacks, detested being threatened, and wasn't always fond of Peretz. He attended the Hebrew banquet, infuriating his fellow Yiddish author; when he attempted to extend an olive branch by going to his house the next day, Peretz went out in protest, sending word he was not at home to Sholem Aleichem. The two were reconciled several days later when Sholem Aleichem attended a Hazamir literary evening and, at least in his remarks there, cast himself as a citizen of Yiddishland: "Six years ago," he said, "I had the honor of coming close to acquainting myself with the angel of death, and in the end he drove me in exile to Italy, under a bright sky. But from that land with a blue sky I always yearned for my Kasrilevke; my body was in Italy, but the heart, the soul—was here with you."

Sholem Aleichem was so popular in Warsaw he couldn't walk down the street without being mobbed. (One Sabbath he was in the Saxon Gardens, the city's magnificent public park, and attracted such an enormous crowd, thousands of people, that he was forced to hide in a restaurant until it was dark—only then, once the Sabbath ended, would he be able to make his escape in a carriage.) He was just as rapturously received, if not more so, in the two dozen cities he visited throughout Poland, Lithuania, and Courland on his tour that summer, including, as he wrote, "Warsaw, Lodz, Brisk, Bialystok, Vilna, Petersburg, Riga, Minsk, Grodnow, and now again Vilna"; only health and time prevented him from seeing many more during that "Sholem Aleichem summer." Though he insisted his arrivals be secret, as in Warsaw the word always got out. In Dvinsk, he wrote, "the station was flooded with Jewish youth; besides the bouquets, magnificent bouquets, they drowned me in flowers, the entire way, from the train to the carriage, was bedecked with flowers. Flowers, flowers, flowers! They cried hurrahs, and hurrahs resounded. . . . Some [observers] thought a great rabbi had arrived. Others explained that it was the Jewish Chekhov, the Jewish Gorky." In Lodz, he wrote, the workers almost suffocated him trying to kiss his hand; in another town, they threw yarmulkes along with the flowers and money. Like last time, the rigors of touring had their effect; he grew ill and was forced to recuperate for several weeks in Vilna. What's more, the tour's expenses ate up almost all the income it generated. But it nonetheless offered an almost equally valuable exchange for Sholem Aleichem: a reminder of his audience's love for him. It would, as it turned out, be a valedictory experience. Sholem Aleichem, Yiddishland's greatest writer, would never again return to Eastern Europe.

Sholem Aleichem returned to Western Europe after ending his tour in the early summer; he arrived at Ahlbeck, a resort on the German coast of the Baltic Sea, hoping to spend an idyllic summer with his family at a villa they sublet for the season. He wrote outside, as was his habit, and the grandchildren built sand castles around him. They arrived there on July 22, 1914—the Ninth of Av, the saddest date in the Jewish calendar and a traditional moment of Jewish misfortune. It would hardly have sat well with the superstitious Sholem Aleichem.

And not incorrectly. Less than ten days later, the First World War began.

With the outbreak of hostilities, the ruble's value plunged, placing the family in increasing financial straits. Worse, Sholem Aleichem was beginning to suffer a new set of medical symptoms, an unquenchable, painful thirst. But even that wasn't the worst of his troubles. That would be that the family were Russian nationals in the middle of Germany. All "Russians" were required to leave the coast immediately. They attempted to settle accounts with their landlord, Herr Gruber; he insisted on the full rent for the season, and refused to take rubles. Sholem Aleichem was asked to part with his beloved Yiddish typewriter, but eventually the landlord took Russian money in gold bullion instead.

The train stations, first Ahlbeck, then Berlin's Stettin Station, were packed with refugees, many of them Russian Jews who'd come to take the cure in Germany; they were all trying to get to the same place: Scandinavia, especially Copenhagen, as all the other borders were closed. Staying in Berlin for any length of time, though, was not an option. The word was spreading that German police were moving from house to house, rounding up any Russian men of military age. Once war was declared, Russians "were, under international law, enemy aliens and subject to internment for the duration of the war. The men, particularly, were liable to be drafted for nonmilitary labor, according to the will of the state." This made it vital for Sholem Aleichem, Misha, and his sons-in-law to leave the capital immediately. Sholem Aleichem agonized: there weren't enough deutschmarks for the entire family to travel together, but the men were in far greater danger. Misha and Sholem Aleichem's son-in-law Michael Kaufman got on a train heading north; Sholem Aleichem himself managed to squeeze his way onto a train, but it was so crowded he wasn't fully inside the compartment, and was forced to jump off. Hotels didn't want to allow Russians in, so Sholem Aleichem had to go to the western neighborhood of Charlottenburg, where the Kaufmans lived.

Berkowitz arrived, delayed, from Ahlbeck, where he'd been guarding the wooden case that contained his father-in-law's archive; they finally managed to board a train, Sholem Aleichem still suffering from his terrible thirst. After a suspenseful trip, during which they were never sure if they'd be stopped and taken off as prisoners (or if, in fact, the train was actually heading directly for an internment camp), they managed to reach Sassnitz, a coastal town across the water from Malmö, a ferry ride from Copenhagen. The port itself was packed; unable to leave that day and with the port under curfew, they returned to Sassnitz proper for the night—only to find they'd left Sholem Aleichem's case with all his writings at the port. Berkowitz risked heading back to recover the irreplaceable collection. At their lodgings, they encountered an unexpected figure: Leon Casso, the tsarist minister of the enlightenment (and noted anti-Semite), who had in the past "ordered the local police in a number of places to refuse permits" for Sholem Aleichem's literary affairs; normally this would have been grist for Sholem Aleichem's creative mill, but he was too sick and weak to take much notice.

Returning to the port the next day, Sholem Aleichem was surrounded by enthusiastic supporters, which never failed to cheer him up. Thanks to the aid of a worshipful fan and the right (high) price, they managed to board a smaller, more private boat to transport them to Malmö and avoid the packed crowds—but not, it turned out, Casso himself, a fellow passenger on the boat. Unsurprisingly, the Jewish students on board were disgruntled at his appearance, and suggested a confrontation; Sholem Aleichem counseled reticence, reminding them of the verse "Rejoice not when your enemy falleth" (though he did note that the bedraggled Casso resembled Haman after his wife Zeresh, as the rabbinic legend had it, dumped a bucketful of slops on his head). Sholem Aleichem would get his own revenge, though. It was a rough and rainy crossing, but as the rain subsided a bit, both men ventured on deck. Casso, seeing a Russian-looking gentleman, asked to share his umbrella; Sholem Aleichem agreed. After a few short exchanges, the pair were distracted by a seasick Jewish woman; Casso, after assisting her, remarked to Sholem Aleichem that such situations make one merciful. Sholem Aleichem, staring at him, slowly and meaningfully replied that mercy never hurt in any situation. That essentially ended the conversation: that night, after landing and taking the train to Malmö, they ran into Casso once more on the way to the hotel—seeing Sholem Aleichem, he turned and headed off in the opposite direction.

From Malmö it was a short ride to Copenhagen, which was overrun with refugees. A desperate search for any available lodging yielded a hotel where the cattle dealers stayed when they came to town; though they weren't there currently, the smell had stuck around. Nevertheless, thanks in large part to a Russian-Jewish porter—who'd been elevated to managerial rank under the circumstances—the hotel quickly became a nerve center of the Copenhagen Russian-Jewish refugee community, home to various stranded journalists who, with communications to Russia cut off, were unable even to correspond with their papers, much less their families. Sholem Aleichem, of course, suffered the same communication problems: when added to the family's constant motion, it was impossible to get information about everyone's whereabouts. They haunted the train stations, which were packed with masses of refugees; Sholem Aleichem looked for familiar faces and extended sympathy and support where he could. Five days after they arrived in Copenhagen, the family was reunited. The men had apparently left just in time: the maid where they'd been staying, frightened by the foreign lettering on Berkowitz's Yiddish typewriter, had reported him to the authorities as a spy.

Copenhagen wasn't a terrible port in the storm, but it was hardly a long-term solution. The war disrupted any Russian income, and Sholem Aleichem's currency was worthless. His health was precarious; he didn't even have his luggage, which meant no appropriate clothing for the harsh Scandinavian winter. Olga fretted the climate would ruin his health. More immediately, he was growing thirstier and thirstier. He thought it was diabetes; the doctors diagnosed it as diabetes insipidus, "false diabetes"; all he knew was that he was thirsty. He felt so badly, so depressed, he stopped writing; that hadn't happened even when he'd been recovering from the first assaults of tuberculosis six years before. He saw the world around him being destroyed, he claimed; what was the point in writing? For Sholem Aleichem, even when he was angry, or skeptical, or disillusioned, even at the most dyspeptic or self-pitying, the essential constructive, creative act of writing had its own therapeutic value: for himself, and, he understood, for his readers and the community they created together. But now, he thought, his Jewish world was under the deadliest of assaults; the majority of Yiddishland lay precisely in the battleground between Russia and Germany. For the first time, as the world was descending into war, he seemed truly to have, at least momentarily, let loose his grip on hope.

Perhaps that defeated impulse played into the new plan of action to return to America. Sholem Aleichem was hardly enthusiastic about the possibility, to put it mildly—the response to his recent European tour had highlighted just how shabby his American treatment had been. Several years ago, he had written Kaufman that America, literarily speaking, was a "wasteland"; and though the following year, in 1912, he'd written that "I've traveled all over the world, and never felt as good as in America" and that "America is my second home," given the sentiment's location in an introduction to an American edition of his stories we may take it more as sound commercial strategy than as truth—he wrote the introduction in Montreux, with no real plans to return. But the specific nature of his praise might have resonated two years later. America's greatness as a home for Yiddish culture, he claimed, lay in its *heymishness*, or "hominess"—its ability, as a melting-pot country, to simultaneously transform its immigrants into ardent patriots by sharing its freedoms and allow them the opportunity to cherish the language and humor of their former lives and homes. In his earliest writings on America, he had suggested he could provide news of Eastern European life to an American audience; but now, as he suggested that reading his stories might provide an opportunity for people to gather together, laugh together, cry together, he was beginning to offer himself as the gateway to shtetl nostalgia—a role his life and work would certainly play for later generations.

Such thoughts might have loomed large now more than ever, as the war created greater distance from his home than illness ever had; and now, more than ever, the chronicler of a changing world began to think of himself as the elegist of a vanishing one.

While Sholem Aleichem was stranded in Copenhagen, his friends across the Atlantic were busy. A committee of prominent American Jews scrambled to ensure his passage to the United States and to welcome him upon his arrival; Jacob Marcus's bank lent the family money for their passage to New York (against the income from his first reading). Misha was too sick to make the ocean crossing, and the family decided to split up: one daughter and son-in-law returned to Russia; Misha would remain in a Danish sanatorium, accompanied by his sister Emma; and everyone else would sail to America. Before their departure, they attended a lavish farewell dinner thrown by the Copenhagen Jewish community; the dinner's host, the Danish Jewish professor and archaeologist David Simonsen, lectured warmly and at length about Sholem Aleichem and his work—a lecture no one in the family understood, delivered as it was in a Danish-inflected German. As the steamship *Frederick VIII* sailed away from the harbor on November 19, an assembled crowd chanted, in words adapted from *Motl, the Cantor's Son*, "Say, our Sholem Aleichem is off to America!" It wasn't the first—or last—time Sholem Aleichem had become woven into his own story.

The crossing was stormy, like the last time, but now there was an additional threat: the Germans had mined the North Sea, and their submarines were patrolling the waters. Because the family was traveling first class, in close proximity to the ship's officers, they could see the hectic and occasionally frantic activity as the ship slowly, excruciatingly slowly, navigated the narrow straits—which hardly improved their state of mind. Nonetheless, Sholem Aleichem was fairly upbeat; he was reunited with most of his family, after all, and the seasickness was much more manageable this time. He was especially excited when the ship stopped at Oslo, then called Christiania, because he wanted to see the city the Norwegian writer Knut Hamsun, whom he greatly admired for his acute psychological portraits and monologues, had described in such detail; he even caught a glimpse of the coffeehouse where Ibsen would write. (Sholem Aleichem's admiration notwithstanding, he was highly disparaging of Yiddish writers who tried to adopt Ibsen's or Hamsun's Scandinavian style too slavishly, calling them "Chroniclers of the Berdichev Fjords.")

Back on the ship, first class began to pall for Sholem Aleichem: there was no one to talk to, since, as before, all the Jews were traveling belowdecks.

So he visited third class, as he had on his last voyage, and found to his bemusement that though he was greeted warmly, attention was mostly focused on an African-American convert to Judaism, a woman returning from visiting her husband's family in the "old country." Speaking to the passengers and hearing their stories, Sholem Aleichem became inspired once more. Though he'd started writing again while still in Copenhagen, that had stemmed largely from financial necessity: another effort for the American Yiddish theater, another adaptation of his own work, one that showed the stresses of the circumstances of its composition. "Hard to Be a Jew," a substantially reworked and retitled version of *The Bloody Hoax*, is far slighter than its novelistic counterpart: Sholem Aleichem's decision to reunite the two hoaxers much earlier in the play transforms it into a set piece for comic confusion and a melodramatic love triangle. Its political dimensions recede; the blood libel's menace is reduced to a "stupid and ridiculous" story; and the panoramic novel is diminished to a slight, mildly topical farce. Sholem Aleichem's optimism about it—"If *this* doesn't make a furor on the Yiddish stage, it's the end of the world—and one has to entirely part from the Yiddish theater!" he said—seemed testament to how low he'd set his sights. But "One Thousand and One Nights," with its title's ancient and ambitious provenance, was another order of creative magnitude—and returned Sholem Aleichem to the fierce urgency of interpreting current events that characterized some of his finest work.

Like its predecessor, "One Thousand and One Nights" has a Scheherazade. Here, it's a Jew from Krushnik, traveling on Sholem Aleichem's boat from Copenhagen to New York, whose experiences in the months since war broke out have yielded "innumerable stories, and all of them fine, wondrous tales, truly Exodus from Egypt tales, how do you say: tales of a thousand and one nights!" He, like that earlier tale-teller, is also talking for his (psychic) life: threatened not by beheading but by the stark horror of the desolation and destruction the war has wrought on his family and his Eastern European town. His only power is the storyteller's: to create cliff-hangers, forcing "Sholem Aleichem," and his audience, to keep listening. And that he does. Starting, like "On Account of a Hat," with an old joke given flesh in the telling (here, the narrator's son Yekhiel, turned Russian rifleman, refuses to shoot at the advancing German soldiers because "there are people over there"), he develops a savage portrait of a town besieged by ravening war. The victorious Germans are suspicious of the welcoming Jews, assuming them to be Russian sympathizers; they first take Yekhiel hostage, then make him town burgomeister—setting him up for disaster if they retreat and the Russians return. When they do—incidentally interrupting a scene where the Germans have made townspeople dig their own graves in advance of being shot—they run riot in the town so badly that "Kishinev wasn't worthy of washing Krushnik's feet," hanging the old rabbi after dragging him through the marketplace, in a scene evoking Holocaust literature for the modern reader. Not only that, but they ask the narrator to hang his own son for treason. (He should be shot, the official explains, but shooting is too good for him, and a waste of bullets and powder in wartime.)

The narrator refuses; telling the official the tale of the Binding of Isaac, he insists that only God can give such a commandment, and asks only to be executed before his son, so the latter, as is the way of the world, can recite kaddish for his father. Once more playing Scheherazade, he tells the moved official of the experience of one of the Ten Martyrs, ancient rabbis murdered by Rome for practicing their faith. The rabbi mystically ascends to heaven to seek the reason for these heavenly decrees; when told it is a punishment for the sale of Joseph, he reasonably asks why the punishment was so long deferred. The answer? No generation sufficiently pure and innocent had existed until then. The narrator explains to the official he feels much the same way about his own time. Though Sholem Aleichem puts his regular twists in the tale—though the narrator's speech saves them both from the gallows, the Russians send Yekhiel to the front, where he is killed his first day, not even to be buried in a Jewish grave, and his second son's fate suggests this dark universe is not only hostile to gentle pacifists—the narrator's speech hangs in the air, elegiacally suggesting a generation of martyrs. After all, as he tells Sholem Aleichem, there are plenty of others with similar stories in third class.

CHAPTER 27

In Which Our Hero Makes His Farewells to His Vanished World, and Feels the Pain of Children

1914–1916

Sholem Aleichem's second arrival in New York, on December 2, 1914, was a far more subdued affair than its predecessor six years earlier. Though still welcomed by friends and reporters, there were no celebrities or notables, and, even worse, the crowd was substantially smaller; at the press conference, a Yiddish journalist appointed himself the interpreter, "not bothering overmuch to translate, but himself answering the majority of the questions directed to [Sholem Aleichem], for he assumed he knew in advance what the answer would be." When he did translate the questions and answers, "they bore only a slight resemblance to the original." It would serve as a useful allegory for Sholem Aleichem's posthumous career in New York.

New York's Jewish community had exploded while he'd been away, flush with some of the greatest years of Jewish immigration on record; Harlem had cemented its reputation as a Jewish neighborhood, and the family was briefly put up at the recently opened Hotel Theresa on the corner of Seventh Avenue and 125th Street. (At the time, it was white-only, but, decades later, would become *the* place for African-Americans to stay while in Manhattan.) The rooms were too small and the prices were too high; with the assistance of a young Columbia student named Ben Goldberg, who'd invited Sholem Aleichem to read at the university under the auspices of the Jewish Students' Lecture Committee, they managed to find an apartment of eight small rooms for under $75 a month at 110 Lenox Avenue at 116th Street. (The apartment building still exists, sandwiched between a bodega and a wholesale florist's.) Ben would later marry Sholem Aleichem's daughter Maroussia.

The Yiddish press had boomed along with its immigrant readership, ostensibly boding well for Sholem Aleichem's prospects. He made the rounds of the various newspapers' editorial boards, ill as he was; he was a supplicant in these dark days, and needed to pitch himself and his work. Depressed, exhausted, ill, and constantly thirsty—he asked for water everywhere he went—he met largely indifferent or negative responses.

He expected even less from the most important paper of them all— the *Forverts*, or *Jewish Daily Forward*. Its avowedly socialist origins had been obscured, if not entirely effaced, by its brilliant, domineering editor Abraham Cahan, who'd transformed the paper into the largest forum for Americanization in Jewish history, preaching to the public on everything from politics to politesse (as their wildly popular advice column, "A Bintel Brief," amply illustrated). Sholem Aleichem had heard terrible things about the cross-eyed martinet, though, including, falsely, the latter's low opinion of him. As a result, he was pleasantly surprised when Cahan treated him respectfully during his office visit.

For his part, the populist Cahan was shrewd enough never to look down on a talent with mass appeal; even if Sholem Aleichem's diminished American arrival had scared some of the others off, he'd hedge his bets. And events proved him right. On December 14, less than two weeks after his arrival, Sholem Aleichem held a reading at Cooper Union; though the organizer, worried about the writer's appeal, had actually rebooked a smaller hall there, seating only 1,400, his concerns were baseless—the hall was bursting, and hundreds who couldn't get seats filled the surrounding streets for blocks. The organizer got the message. Three weeks later, on January 9, Sholem Aleichem played the 7,000-person-capacity

Carnegie Hall. Income from the two nights paid off the costs of his trip to America, and now the newspapers came calling: he had read his "One Thousand and One Nights" to the crowds, and everyone wanted to publish it. The author weighed his options. Besides the *Forverts*, the most serious contender was the *Tog*, a new progressive, Zionist paper. The radical *Varheit* was pro-Allies and therefore pro-Russian, which took it out of the running; the *Tageblat* was too cheap; the *Morgen-Zhurnal* was rudderless, looking for new leadership. Though he preferred the *Forverts*—it had the widest reach by far, and he respected Cahan's literary sophistication (not to mention his kind treatment when few others had behaved similarly)—the *Tog* provided a better offer: $100 a week for two small pieces, guaranteed for a year (almost $112,000 a year in 2010 dollars). The *Forverts* wouldn't go above $75 a week—that was Cahan's salary, and no one could top that. Sholem Aleichem, desperately needing the money, took the *Tog*'s offer.

In the partisan, hyper-competitive environment of the flourishing Yiddish press, any commitment was bound to create enemies. Possibly the phenomenon reached its most absurd proportions early in 1915, when Sholem Aleichem gave another reading at the annual meeting of the Educational Alliance, an institution created by "uptown" Jews to assist the "downtown" immigrant population that had feted him during his previous American stay. While the rival Yiddish papers could hardly fail to cover a story like the noted magnate Jacob Schiff and his peers speaking on the Lower East Side, they didn't want to give their competitor free advertising. And so while the papers reported the illustrious German Jews' speeches in praise of their "guest," at least one paper left Sholem Aleichem's name out of the story entirely, leaving the reader to guess who that guest might have been. Unsurprising, then, that a major series he produced for the *Tog* after finishing "One Thousand and One Nights" took the newspaper wars as their main subject. And, in the process, would serve as a farewell to Kasrilevke.

In 1913, Sheyne-Sheyndl had written Menakhem-Mendl that Kasrilevke had changed a great deal since he last left—"In a million years you would not recognize it if you came here," she wrote. She was right; "Progress in Kasrilevke" painted a picture of a world where the old guard, including Reb Yosifl, has passed on, and many citizens have gone to America. Even the famed Kasrilevke mud has been paved over. But some things never change, particularly the townspeople's capacity for rivalry and internal dissension. But Sholem Aleichem's venue for exploring that venom—the competition between newspapers—feels as much American as European, if not more so: and it makes the reader wonder whether Kasrilevke had been superimposed upon the Hudson. The sensationalist strategies, fierce invective, and regular intellectual property theft of the *Skullcap* and the *Bowler Hat*, stand-ins for the papers appealing to traditional Orthodox and progressive elements respectively, must have elicited knowing smiles not only in Warsaw, but in New York. (When the *Bowler Hat* reported the birth of a two-headed baby, the *Skullcap*, not to be outdone, duly noted that of a three-headed child; and the competitors' serialized novels are respectively titled "The Stolen Bride's Forbidden Kiss" and "The Forbidden Bride's Stolen Kiss.") Kasrilevke's stubborn inability to change—its ongoing factionalism over culture, politics, the language question, even over supporting the families of deceased writers—illustrated the continuity of Sholem Aleichem's satirical impulse: comforting, somehow, to make the same kinds of points, keeping the world of "One Thousand and One Nights" at bay from invading Kasrilevke. But the suggestion of the American world, gleaming darkly underneath the image of the shtetl, suggested otherwise, as did the inspiration for the deceased writers scene: the word from Europe that Peretz had passed away.

The news hit Sholem Aleichem hard. People came to comfort him as if he'd lost a member of his own family: which, in many ways, he had. For all their conflicts and squabbles, Sholem Aleichem knew Peretz was also Yiddish literature: different strategies, different personalities, different styles, but a giant of the age when jargon became Yiddish, and his death, at a time when Yiddishland's future seemed perilous and uncertain, felt like the darkness was rising. He wrote of his intent to formally mourn him, and opened the memorial *shloshim* ceremonies held at Carnegie Hall.

On a more personal note, the death only deepened Sholem Aleichem's sense of his own mortality. After a fractious meeting was held about how to honor Peretz's memory—Sholem Aleichem's suggestion of a fund to support Yiddish writers and Yiddish literature sank beneath argument—the pale and shaken writer left the hall muttering, "I have to get out of America quickly and go die somewhere else." Writing his will a half year later, he specifically proscribed debates and discussions among his colleagues about how to remember him.

As always, his expenses outpaced his income; though working hard for the *Tog*, writing his Kasrilevke series and, as per the terms of his contract, publishing installments of his autobiography, he needed more work. After the success of his first two readings, he considered that might be a viable income source, but his chosen representative didn't understand how to connect with Yiddish audiences (he neither advertised in the Yiddish press nor connected with local Jewish organizations), and broke his contract with Sholem Aleichem following unsuccessful trips to Baltimore and Washington. His son-in-law arranged some trips that winter and spring of 1914–1915, to destinations including Toronto, Montreal, and Detroit. His visit to the Detroit Opera House as a guest of the Progressive Literary Dramatic Club on May 15, 1915, was fairly typical, not only in that there were hitches (Jacob Adler was arriving the same evening to put on a performance) but in many of its features. There was the reading of some short stories ("A Game of Sixty-Six," his American story "Berl-Ayzik," and the performance, by locals, of "Agents"); the participation of local Jewish organizations ("young ladies from Junior Hadassah were in white uniforms, red mogen david embroidered white kerchiefs on their heads. These walked through the aisles, with blue and white canisters, collecting funds for Hadassah"); the presence of children from the local Hebrew and Yiddish schools (who presented Sholem Aleichem with flowers); and a decent intake ($500, almost $11,000 in 2010 dollars) for the evening.

But there weren't enough of those evenings to send money to Misha for his medical support, and, as was the case whenever he toured, the strain of travel and performance played havoc with his health. That May, he sent what would be his final letter to Abramovitch. It read, in part, "Do you still live? Are you in good health? . . . That is truly the main thing of all things. Everything else is simple foolishness." In despair, Sholem Aleichem even considered borrowing money from a loan shark. Some of this extremity, it should be said, had to do with his personality, his own pride. His brother Berl Rabinovich—Bernard Roberts in America—was a successful luggage manufacturer in Newark. (He had lit out for America at sixteen along with his sister Sophia, after a particularly vicious session of abuse at his stepmother's hands.) He certainly could have helped out, had he known the full story. But Sholem Aleichem had always wanted to be the generous one, the one who gave with a broad hand, not one who extended it for a handout. More than that; maybe Sholem Aleichem had fallen victim to his own sense of the American dream. Berl had shown it was possible to succeed; how was it possible that Sholem Aleichem had failed to do the same, to emerge victorious in America's meritocratic crucible, the land where the right person can be a success?

That might have explained the tenor of some of his American prose. He had never appreciated certain aspects of the country—the habit of chewing gum, which he compared to cows chewing their cud; the hustle and bustle of the New York streets; the subways, which he claimed (in a belief shared by many generations of New Yorkers) were out to get him, departing the moment you arrived at the station—in fact, he described his first stay in America as living "in a train station, waiting on a train," where "everyone hurries, and we, too, hurry, not knowing where." But those were small grievances, of a man who really did know where he was hurrying: back to Europe, as soon as he possibly could. But now he was less a visitor, not even really an immigrant: now he was a refugee, from a world he saw disappearing, and America had failed him in its classic promise. No wonder his America-set stories of the period pulsed with a kind of anger and disappointment at the Golden Land.

Take the title character of 1915's "Berl-Ayzik," who, returning to the old country from America, is full of bluff and tall tales, of the skyscrapers so high that when he climbs to the top of one he feels the moon graze his left cheek. America's vaunted freedom, though, is no bluff: in the tale's twist, Berl-Ayzik tells his audience you can "swell from hunger, die in the street, and no one'll bother you, no one'll say a word." A small playlet from that same year, "Mister Boym in the Closet," explains the eponymous Mr. Boym's odd choice of location: he's hiding from his sister Shprintzl, whom he persuaded to emigrate—to her marked regret. Happy emigrants, by contrast, were just fools and suckers, greenhorns who didn't get it. In 1915's "Mister Green Has a Job," Green (changed from Greenberg) tells "Sholem Aleichem" about his American plan to go from rags to riches: he discovers a talent for hot air in the form of blowing the shofar—and takes every synagogue offer he can get his hands on, apparently unmindful that he can only minister at one congregation at a time. Applying Mister Green's American model of mass production to Jewish life will inevitably yield catastrophic results.

But his firmest statement about the dark side of the American experiment came the next year, in his monologue "A Story About a Greenhorn." Its monologist, longer resident in America, is furious at the titular greenhorn—fury stemming from sublimated lust for the greenhorn's nest egg, his beautiful wife, and, perhaps, his innocent faith in American possibility. Through a series of schemes and double-crosses, he plunders the first two and, by extension, destroys the third. Though the narrator is successful in America, his is no American success; it's achieved by understanding that to succeed here, one should behave just like the Eastern European con men Sholem Aleichem chronicled in so many other stories. You'd have to be a child to believe otherwise. And so Sholem Aleichem, who was always seduced by hope, returned to a child who believed otherwise. If it's true, as F. Scott Fitzgerald famously noted, that the test of a first-rate intelligence is the ability to hold two opposing ideas in mind at the same time and still retain the ability to function, then Sholem Aleichem's fine intelligence was well on display in this as in many other instances, simultaneously crafting his dyspeptic perspectives on America and continuing his finest love letter to the country.

After *Motl*'s ignominious halt, Sholem Aleichem had stopped publishing new installments for years; but its 1910 appearance in the Russian *Children of the Pale* volumes and its rapturous reception, had, he said, made his head spin; the completed work to date was published in book form the following year to positive response, and by 1913 he was telling a critic that *Motl* was his favorite. Motl haunted his dreams, he claimed the following winter, and would only exercise a greater and greater pull once he returned to America: but Motl's value as an American commentator could only commence when the character actually arrived. Which meant chronicling his travels.

Sholem Aleichem drew on his own memories for some details, and his standard method of constantly eliciting information from acquaintances for others. His careful investigation of the various ways to cross the Russian border illegally shaped the chaos of Motl's family's experiences; the woman who'd helped Berkowitz to cross, for example, would inspire a character. Like Sholem Aleichem, Motl and his family travel to Brod, and a local innkeeper with whom Sholem Aleichem stayed found his way into the novel; like Sholem Aleichem, Motl's family travels to Lemberg, where Motl, like his creator, wonders at the city's beauty and marvels at the Jews walking openly on the streets; the author's trips to Krakow and Vienna and London provided similar fodder for his descriptions of those cities.

Through his description of Motl's progress, Sholem Aleichem beautifully illustrates how emigration is not a smooth, forward motion but a constant push and pull of supporting and retarding forces; he sketches not only the various assortment of aid agencies and assistance providers who attempt, in their understaffed, overcommitted fashion, to deal with a monsoon of emigrants, but the impossible-to-solve problems of poverty, crime, and misery endemic to the group. Like his creator, Motl and his family are, comparatively speaking, extremely lucky: they make it across the border relatively unscathed, with most of their money and tickets (just not those pillows). The family's great worry, that Motl's mother's constant weeping will result in trachoma, the eye disease that would bar her from entrance to America, largely fails to materialize. Motl relates to us—in transit, on ship, and at Ellis Island—quite a number of stories of people *far* more unfortunate than they: a reminder, for Sholem Aleichem, that his own family's situation should also be seen in perspective.

Motl occupied Sholem Aleichem in various ways through the spring and summer of 1915; he worked extensively with Ben Goldberg on an English-language film scenario, playing every role in every scene, even narrating the intertitles. (Nothing came of the project.) When 116th Street proved too hot, in those pre-air-conditioning days, to spend the summer there—it was noisy, too, as two streetcar lines crossed there, and a loud dance hall was nearby—he left the city, like hordes of other New Yorkers, and headed to the Catskills, like Jews for two generations after him. He first stayed in a small boardinghouse in Pine Hill; the only good thing about the place—he couldn't walk the heavily sloped paths around the area, for one thing—was the friendship he struck up with the innkeeper's five-year-old daughter, a personal connection with Motl's future world. (His youngest, Numa, already a teenager, was now too old to serve in that capacity.) By late June, he'd found a place of repose in Fleischmanns, New York, which, he claimed, was like nowhere else he'd found in America, and spent time near the summer's end in Belmar, "a small, quiet, not yet commercialized resort in New Jersey on the Atlantic coast," writing and entertaining the leading American Yiddish writers. Just like in Yiddishland's European capitals, New York had begun to assemble and to grow a new generation of literary masters—who, though of the immigrant generation, were becoming Yiddish and American in style and sensibility much as Peretz had been Yiddish and Polish, or Abramovitch Yiddish and Russian. Sholem Aleichem enjoyed the work and company of the Yiddish poets Yehoyesh and Mani Leib, and had warm praise for the novelist Joseph Opatoshu, comparing his eye and ear for America to Dickens's and Thackeray's for their own milieu. "Write about American Judaism," he instructed Opatoshu. "Make pictures of the New York ghetto—this is your genre."

As the summer ended, he put his work on *Motl* on hold to pursue other more immediately potentially lucrative projects in other media. He began negotiations with Vitagraph about film work, and on September 7 he traveled to the Victor Studios in Manhattan to work with another new technology: the phonographic recording. (His reading of "If I Were Roth-schild" survives, along with the beginning of another never-completed work, "A Merry Wedding.") But his primary efforts, as always when it came to making money, were theatrically oriented; and they intertwined two of his new interests, film and America, with old concerns about money, getting and losing it.

A slight one-act farce, 1915's "Paradise," skewers a couple of allright-niks who, having made it in America, figure they'll just buy their way into heaven; everything, even metaphysics, is subsumed to the art of the deal. (They almost get hustled by a "sage" who's willing to sell.) But Sholem Aleichem needed a jackpot of a play, to hit the lottery and get out of financial distress once and for all. And so: *The Jackpot*, which Sholem Aleichem said was really about Americans in the guise of Kasrilevkans, wish fulfillment and an attack on the seductiveness of wish fulfillment simultaneously.

The play tells the story of a poor but proud tailor, Shimele Soroker, who wins 200,000 rubles in the lottery. (From an early age, Sholem Aleichem had seen the lottery agents make their way through the small towns of the Pale, writing in his memoir that almost all of Pereyaslav played.) Soro-ker immediately Russifies, hires an impudent maid and a haughty butler, and insists on changing all their friends and acquaintances. (In the pro-cess, he reads "a satire by some joker who makes fun of the whole world. His name is Sholem Aleichem . . . [about] some tailor who was a pauper among paupers and overnight became a rich man." The play's audience wouldn't only enjoy the suggestion of Soroker uncomprehendingly read-ing his own story; they'd probably get the autobiographical wink, too, given the widespread knowledge of Sholem Aleichem's own narrative.) Soroker's daughter insists they're no different than they were; they just think they are—and their susceptibility to illusions of transformation, that any jackpot will have permanent resonance, sets the stage, literally, for their undoing through the film business, that spectacle of light and sound with nothing behind it. (Had Sholem Aleichem had more success in the movies during his lifetime, perhaps he'd have chosen another medium.)

Soroker, who loves the movies, invests 15,000 rubles with two unscrupulous partners to buy up all the town's theaters; since he has not, indeed, changed, he's still insufficiently educated to write the check himself—so the partners do, and, adding a zero to the amount, clean him out. (Another old joke of Sholem Aleichem's; remember that first letter to Shriro, insisting his jubilee gift was missing a zero.) Returning to his original state, Soroker ends the play happy, not only at his daughter's decision to marry a tailor, one of their own, rather than the snobbish drip of an aristocrat he'd pushed on her in his puffed-up period, but at the wisdom he's gained of accepting his true identity: as a member of *amkho*, the general nation, who sing and dance together as ingenue marries apprentice at play's end. The play purports both to burst illusion and to perpetuate it—Sholem Aleichem casting himself as his usual scoundrel writer persona and as the first among *amkho* equals—a wonderful example of that most seductive of illusions, having it both ways.

He himself was victim to the identical temptation, writing a play about the impossibility, or at least the evanescence, of an American jackpot while firmly believing the play would be a major American success. He worked hard, writing and rewriting, hoping for a fall premiere; but it would not see a stage in his lifetime. Sholem Aleichem's American Yiddish theater, that grand first phase of a cultural institution, was coming to an end. Adler was getting old. Kessler was entirely in the operetta business. Thomashevsky had never been supportive. *The Jackpot* would be a huge success, but decades later, and in another country.

The summer was coming to a close. Sholem Aleichem, complaining about shoddy accommodations and family illnesses, impatiently waited for the war to end so he could return to Europe. Meanwhile, he eagerly awaited his reunion with Misha and Emma, still in Denmark. He had originally hoped they would come to America during the summer; perhaps, he mused, if his film or record ventures were succeeding, he and his son would travel to California together to benefit from its warm climate. But there was no money to bring them over, and the summer stretched out. Eventually, he borrowed fare for their passage from a friend against future earnings from the *Tog*; the children were expected to leave September 2.

No cable arrived confirming their departure on the *Frederick VIII*. A telegram went unreturned. Sholem Aleichem withdrew to his room; isolation was a common response of his to ill health or ill moods. The ship was scheduled to arrive in from Copenhagen on the 13th, at the Hoboken docks. Hopefully Misha would be on it, Misha, or someone with news of him. He went out to meet the ship with Ben Goldberg; they took the Ninth Avenue El as far as they could—there was no money for a taxi. They arrived at the docks; the ship was delayed; there was no choice but to wait. Sholem Aleichem sat on a barrel and wrote. Eventually the ship arrived, without Misha.

Misha had died on the 11th, of tuberculosis of the brain. He was twenty-four years old, still a student in his final year at Lausanne University. Sholem Aleichem would not find out for another eight days. In the interim, on the 15th, he wrote Misha and Emma a letter, knowing there was bad news, but not how bad the news was. He understands, he wrote, that moving Misha from Copenhagen is impossible, and Olga will come immediately after Yom Kippur to tend to him. He himself will follow in the summer as soon as health and circumstances permit. But if conditions change, he'll send money for them to come immediately. Their rooms are ready; there's even a writing table for Misha. And he dreams of California for them both.

The 17th was the night of Kol Nidre, ushering in Yom Kippur. Sholem Aleichem went to Congregation Ohev Tzedek, an Orthodox synagogue on 116th Street, so he could hear the prayer chanted by the famous cantor Yossele Rosenblatt. The admiration was mutual: Rosenblatt would occasionally sing particular tunes for him, and Sholem Aleichem, for his part, asserted Rosenblatt was precisely the kind of Yossele he'd intended when writing *Yossele Solovey* all those years before. The news arrived by telegram the morning after Yom Kippur ended. As Olga wept, Sholem Aleichem tried to console her: "What can one do, what can one do? He will not return to us, we will go to him soon enough." That night, he disappeared into his office for several hours; writing, tears dripping down his face and onto the paper, he finally composed his will.

It would begin with the sentences, "Today, the day after Yom Kippur [9/19/15], a new year has just begun, and a great misfortune has befallen my family. My oldest son, Misha (Michael) Rabinowitz, has died, and with him part of my life has gone down into the grave." Among its more personal provisions: to beg his children and their descendants to "guard their Jewish descent"—divorcing his feelings about their religious convictions, of which, he writes, they can have whatever they will, from their "cut[ting] themselves off from their race and want[ing] to join another faith." Those who did so "have thus erased themselves from my will, 'and they shall have no portion and inheritance among their brethren.'" (Though not explicitly mentioned in the will, the evidence of "Chava"— and the historical vicissitudes of early-twentieth-century Jewish life in Russia and even, at that point, largely in America—strongly suggest Sholem Aleichem imagined intermarriage as one powerfully motivating force for such actions.) Another personal provision: "If I am not able during my lifetime to place a stone over the grave of my recently deceased son, Michael (Misha) Rabinowitz, in Copenhagen, my heirs should do this with a generous hand." What it must have taken to write those sentences.

Sholem Aleichem sat shiva "according to the law," and a minyan came to his house twice a day. Though he would not insist his son recite the kaddish for him, he was a "Jew of the old traditions," and he would do so for his son. Nonetheless, he adds in a postscript to his daughter a kind of plea for her to do similarly: "If you want, that is, if you feel the necessity, you can sit shiva—for an hour." Misha's death aged Sholem Aleichem. He changed locale, moving from Harlem to the Bronx, to 968 Kelly Street. It would be the last place he would live. He would continue to say kaddish there, attending the Montefiore synagogue in the Bronx, the nearest one to his home.

A story, perhaps apocryphal, perhaps not, is told by a journalist friend of his who accompanied him one Friday night: as they walked to synagogue, Sholem Aleichem was almost knocked down by a young boy wearing roller skates. He asked the child why he wasn't going to shul with his father; in very Americanized Yiddish, the boy answered that his father was out of town, on the road. Sholem Aleichem didn't quite understand the boy; he had never quite gotten the hang of this new version of Yiddish. The journalist translated. Sholem Aleichem told the boy that if that was the case, he should feel free to skate away, just not to knock anyone down. "You're a funny man, mister!" the boy said as he skated away. The author didn't get this, either, and his friend was forced to translate once more. "Correct," Sholem Aleichem said, softly and sadly, as he climbed the steps to the synagogue.

Several years before, extremely close Odessa friends of his had lost a daughter. Sholem Aleichem wrote them, in a condolence letter, "Comfort? I should try to comfort you? Where is there comfort to be found in such a matter? Words? From where would they begin?" He then goes on to write many, asserting that to go on under such circumstances one must believe in some sort of continuation beyond the limited aspects of what we perceive of as life. The letter's most intriguing part comes at its end. There, he writes: "If you can, and want to, answer my letter, it will ease the great sorrow, a little, for you and for me. And if you do write, you should write everything: from what sort of illness did the dear unforgettable lovely Lyali die? And everything that you can and in whatever language you want, and everything separate, and of her last days, and of her last weeks and months—you should write *everything* . . ." As a friend, he would still, inevitably, remain a writer, looking for material, using grief as inspiration.

So, too, in his own circumstances. Several days after hearing of Misha's death, a long letter to his daughter and son-in-law began once more bewailing the insufficiency of language to express his grief: "it would come out faint, banal, even laughable. . . . I carry a coffin in my soul which I will take with me to the grave." He bemoaned the war that had scattered them across the globe, and desperately hoped for its end, which would allow him to return to Europe and beg forgiveness at his son's grave in Copenhagen. Writing again three weeks later, he reports his tears have not dried despite the passage of time; though Olga has physically recovered, she can hardly bring herself even to put pen to paper, so no letters should be expected of her. He then writes: "About my spiritual-creative life I cannot complain. I write as usual, as is my way, and publish two works simultaneously, aside from ancillary works. The enthusiasm to create does not abandon me even in the most difficult days. It may be that it gives me the strength to endure the blows of fate." For Sholem Aleichem, it would always be possible to find solace, at least partial solace, in writing.

He had been steadily producing installments of his autobiography for the *Tog*; when the editorial staff complained, asking for more American-oriented material, he composed many of his late American stories, including a novel of New York Jewish life called *The Mistake*. None seemed to please the staff, who, as the year came to a close, seemed uninterested in renewing his contract. Desperate, Sholem Aleichem took the unprecedented step of going directly to the editorial executive of the newspaper to plead for a renewal, but without success. The contract went unrenewed; he wrote the Kaufmans that as terrible as things were, "a small comfort was that in Europe they were much worse." Toward year's end, he contracted a mild case of influenza; his old friend Lubarski, who'd taken the author's fortunes in hand as a personal matter, brought the *Varheit*'s editor and publisher directly to Sholem Aleichem's sickbed, and a deal was struck right there for 1916. (They had also approached the *Forverts*, but Cahan, still steaming at being second fiddle to the *Tog*, refused to make a deal.) It was overall a slightly better arrangement than he had with the *Tog*: $90 a week (about $1,750 in 2010 dollars) for two pieces, and an additional $25 a week (about $500) for the book rights to *From the Fair*'s first two parts. Delighted at the paper's enthusiasm about his autobiography, Sholem Aleichem agreed, and chose to publish Motl's continuing adventures, now in America, in the paper as well.

Along with quite a few other papers, and in English translation to boot. Sholem Aleichem was on the verge of another kind of jackpot, after all: he had signed with *The New York World*, the paper made great by Joseph Pulitzer and at the time the largest newspaper in the city, for an illustrated version of *Motl* to appear every Sunday in the syndicate's over twenty papers, reaching almost 5 million readers. The words of the *World*'s copy department, sprinkled with hyperbole though they might be, provide a clue to the American paper's motives for adopting Sholem Aleichem—and adapting him, packaging him for a wider audience. An announcement in the *World*'s Sunday magazine on December 26, 1915, "Introducing Sholom Aleichem of New York," boasted that "he is one of the world's greatest writers. He is called the Jewish Mark Twain. *The World Magazine* will publish the first of his new series of humorous stories next Sunday."

The biographical sketch that followed is worth quoting at length, as it's one of the first steps, if not the first, in the story of Sholem Aleichem in the American world. "One of the world's greatest writers lives in New York. He is unknown to the larger community of Manhattan, though to his compatriots of the East Side he is a figure of light and learning. He is a humorist. He has been called the Jewish Mark Twain. His fame is international, for his stories and sketches and dramas are read and quoted and laughed and wept over in Russia, in Poland, in Austria and Germany. A genius of whom we know little or nothing and acclaimed one of the brilliant figures of the day. Impossible—you may well say. It is true nevertheless. Solomon Rabinowitz, called Sholom Aleichem, writes in Yiddish. . . . It is difficult adequately to translate his work into English[; but r]eaders of the *World* Magazine are now to have the opportunity of knowing Sholom Aleichem. Next Sunday we begin the publication of sketches 'Off for America,' in which he describes the exodus of a family of Russian Jews from their little home village to this land of prosperity and peace across the Atlantic . . . And while you are laughing at the foibles of Muttel, and Elihu and Pini and Brocha, you catch glimpses of their souls. From beneath their strange cloaks and prayer shawls their real selves struggle to the surface. You see the utter helplessness with which the Russian immigrant faces the gap between the life and thought of the Russian Pale and the Golden Land. You learn why the 'Children of the Ghetto' are really children, groping toward the light of freedom, dazzled after the darkness of oppression. Travel with Muttel and his family from the little Russian village to the gates of America. Sholom Aleichem will make you laugh—and love."

Recasting Sholem Aleichem's stories as American stories while managing to create a saintly, childlike community of oppressed Jews, who under their exotic outward trappings are just like you and me when their "real selves" emerge, the announcement sounds many of the themes—not to mention the sweetly saccharine and somewhat patronizing tone—that will characterize Sholem Aleichem's legacy in the century to come. Everyone, deep down, is alike, the announcement purrs, while real strangeness—even the strangeness of the Yiddish language—is sanded away as a foolish, comic, and unnecessary set of behaviors to be shed in order to eventually adopt the fine, perfect perspective of American conventional wisdom, where the outside will finally match the inside. This sense of the comic difference of the Jews—alien, but not, you know, really *too* alien—would reappear in appreciations of Jewish comedians for decades.

Sholem Aleichem reveled in the *World*'s mass advertising, appearing in all the city's elevated train stations: "Read Sholem Aleichem, the Yiddish Mark Twain, in the World Newspaper! Original! New! Comical! Read Sholem Aleichem!" He hoped this would mark the beginning of substantial inroads into the English-language market, and talked excitedly about the English translations of his other works—while simultaneously bemoaning the lack of appropriate translators. (He had no such complaints about illustrators; he loved Samuel Cahan's illustrations in the *World*, remarking that he'd captured exactly what Motl looked like.)

All this enthusiasm bled into the Motl adventures. Not everything is rose-colored there, by any means; Motl's American experiences begin with quarantine at Ellis Island—with no guarantee that any, or all, of his group will be granted permission to enter the country. For each of his friend Pini's speeches about America's full equality or boundless opportunity, a new character, a tailor, serves as his skeptical nemesis, throwing cold water on his effusions—and is invariably proved correct. People take bribes at Ellis Island. The noise is terrifying, the crowds are suffocating, and the machines are too fast. Pini's belief in the Horatio Alger version of the American story—that the jobs they will land will be a simple first step to unlimited success—are belied by their experience of unscrupulous shop foremen and strikebreakers. Motl's optimism, so appropriate in a child, has to be tempered in an adult: they shouldn't swallow everything they're given. (In a lovely symbol, Pini immediately takes to Sholem Aleichem's detested American chewing gum, but goes too far and swallows it.)

Still, the characters' comparison of their storm-tossed voyage, like Sholem Aleichem's, to crossing the Red Sea is not inapt; for Motl, the youngest, possessing a flexibility his older relatives and creator could never possess, the Exodus has led to a promised land. Like Sholem Aleichem, Motl is amazed by the country's material comforts, the apartments with so many rooms and the hot and cold running water; and, after some false starts, the family does seem to be climbing the upward ladder of American financial success—they buy a candy and newspaper stand, and, in the final chapter Sholem Aleichem wrote, are attempting to sell it to buy an entire store. This said, we don't know Sholem Aleichem's endgame, as he died before finishing the novel. And we've learned enough to be skeptical of permanent financial success: a mysterious stranger's presence may hint at a darker current ahead, perhaps along the lines of "A Story About a Greenhorn."

But one thing is clear: Motl himself, whatever mixed feelings his family may possess, has almost unalloyed joy in America. America is portrayed as deeply, utterly, for the children. Motl is struck by how the government here *forces* children, including Jewish children, to go to school, rather than try to keep them out—the opposite of his creator's history. Motl is *not* struck by his brother; the physical abuse encountered in Eastern Europe (perpetrated by, among others, Sholem Aleichem's stepmother) has been replaced, as some other children tell Motl's brother, by the ethic of picking on someone your own size. There are no linguistic problems: Motl takes to new language, English and Americanized Yiddish, like a duck to water. And the streets are paved, not with gold, but with games: "There are thousands of games: button games, hoop games, ball games, curb games . . . The noise the children make is deafening. The street belongs to them. No one would dare tell them to leave it. In fact, America is a land made for children. That's what I love about it."

But in Sholem Aleichem's vision, the lines between Old and New World are not as starkly drawn as might be supposed. "All Kasrilevke has moved to America," says Motl, and with the creation of a Kasrilevke synagogue—and the subsequent possibilities it creates for Motl's mother to find Elye and the family jobs—we see the Old World's reach into the New, and through it, Sholem Aleichem's search to see what power that world has in the form of memory, as history and circumstance render it less and less of an actuality.

CHAPTER 28

In Which Our Hero's Story Comes to an End, and a Beginning

1915–1916

The additional income the *World* syndication provided helped alleviate Sholem Aleichem's financial situation; it allowed him to winter in Lakewood, New Jersey, now perhaps best known as a center of Orthodox Jewry but at the time a noted winter resort (the Rockefellers had an estate there). Sholem Aleichem called it his American Nervi. He was often sick that winter, beginning to suffer from cardiac events; his kidneys began to be affected by his diabetic illness. So that his loved ones wouldn't see him at his worst, he retreated to his room frequently; but he tried to put on a good face for family and visiting company as much as possible. He was still writing, working hard on *From the Fair*, *Motl*, and the Tevye dramatization, relaxing from the stress by reading the papers voraciously and playing cards.

On March 4, he traveled to Philadelphia to read at the city's Metropolitan Opera House; it would be Sholem Aleichem's final public reading, and was, in miniature, a metaphor for his American experience. The pair of Jewish businessmen who arranged the evening promised the sick man significant income and that they would see to everything, including providing a doctor to attend him constantly. Sholem Aleichem, apprehensive when the doctor failed to appear, went anyway; though the reading was packed, over five thousand people, and took in over $2,000, not only did the businessmen write him a check for only $250, but it was made of genuine rubber to boot. Some Philadelphia friends eventually tracked the men down and forced them to pay up, but the damage was done: Sholem Aleichem suffered another cardiac event soon after, a severe one. He rallied, though, telling his attending physician, "I still have ten books to write, ten important books, and will not die before I write them."

He survived another seven weeks, working on *Motl* and his autobiography to the end, thinking about America and about his own posterity. He tossed off an American adaptation of his earlier "Four Questions," putting the questions he'd previously posed about maintaining Yiddish and Jewish cultural knowledge in the face of acculturation into an American context. His parents have insisted, asks the boy, that he pay attention in school to learn English and the dates of American holidays, but they pay no such attention to the work of Jewish writers. Will America, Sholem Aleichem wonders, be a marvelous home for Jews and not Jewishness? In creating a portrait of a child chastising his parents for irresponsible behavior, the author may have also been reflecting on his own case. His tremendous guilt over Misha aside, Sholem Aleichem's own (albeit sometimes suffocating) warmth toward his family—his desire to travel with them and arrange family reunions, his hundreds of letters to them (often chiding them for not answering quickly), his assignation to them of the role as first audience for his works and the great work of his personality, being "even more Sholem-Aleichemish [to them] than to the outside world," as his son-in-law wrote—did not mean that his choices and his circumstances had led to an outcome any different from the one he fretted about for his public. Assuredly Sholem Aleichem would not have inserted that clause about conversion in the will had he not worried, in some way, that it might be necessary.

In 1911, responding to an article charging that he spoke Russian in the home rather than Yiddish, he insisted that though it was true his children *had* addressed the article's author in Russian, that was simply because the journalist had talked to *them* in that language. In truth, he wrote, "many languages are spoken in our house: Yiddish, Russian, German, French, and Italian, as we are wanderers in all of the countries, summer and winter. Satisfied?" But perhaps the letter's defensiveness means we shouldn't be, quite. A note written four years previously, to his then twenty-year-old daughter Liali, chides her for not having finished learning Yiddish so she can translate his novel *The Deluge* into Russian properly. "What's the problem?" he writes. "Are you sixty years old? Begin with the alef-beys." The letter's context, along with the family ceremony of reading Sholem Aleichem's work aloud, suggests Liali was familiar with spoken Yiddish, and her inability was in reading and comprehending written Yiddish (particularly its Hebrew component); a letter to Misha the next year, suggesting he find a Yiddish speaker to run hard words by if he wishes to translate his father's stories, is similarly suggestive. It's not that Sholem Aleichem didn't try—numerous letters speak of Hebrew and Yiddish tutors, especially for Misha and Numa—but the world of Sholem Rabinovich, always different from that of Sholem Aleichem, differed from that of his children's in no small part in that most fundamental question of lived language, of Yiddish.

Sholem Aleichem's own elegiac and skeptical perspective about the future was also apparent in his last explicitly political stories, written against the backdrop of war and flight. Aside from "One Thousand and One Nights," the finest of them may be "From Passover to Sukkot": there, the political playing field, so to speak, is a chessboard, the metaphorical and actual game of kings. The narrator tells the story of his grandfather, whose reputation for having defeated the governor earns him an audience with the tsar—which means being dragged from his home at Passover and walked via convoy in the company of criminals over the entire summer (until Sukkot, as the title implies), to St. Petersburg for a brief audience. "They tell me that you are the foremost chess player in my kingdom," says the tsar; before he can think of any answer, he's summarily dismissed. "It's enough," the grandson ends, "that he got home alive." If the entire story is a chess game between Jew and non-Jew, it suggests that all victories on the board are temporary; unless the real victory is the Jew's survival, the king of chess—the weakest but most central figure on the board—managing to eke out an escape. Either way, the battle, at the cost of great effort, leads to nothing better than a draw.

Compare this to the deliciously weird "The Malicious Matza," undated but probably written toward the very end of his life. The satirical fable tells of an anti-Semitic king who swallows some matzah—after proposing to outlaw it across the land—and then, feeling ill, discovers the cause: a Jew singing in his belly. The Jew refuses to leave. "If you come out, you'll receive a fine present," says the examining specialist; "I'm quite familiar with the present you have in mind," the Jew responds, "twenty-four hours to pack up and leave town" (as Jews are prohibited from living in the capital). He refuses to leave until the king passes a new law allowing the Jews freedom to live where they want. The story, while a nice parable of Russian-Jewish history—the empire swallows the Jews, who promptly give them indigestion, and the more they attend to them the more indigestion they get—begs the question, to return to the chess metaphor, of the endgame. An entirely bizarre playlet that Sholem Aleichem revised the year of his death, "Haman and Mordechai: A True Story in Honor of Purim," may offer a hint.

In an Eastern European town, a fancy coach pulls up, and out comes Mordechai, a footman to Haman. These are not frauds, or crazy men, the story takes pains to make clear. These are the actual biblical Haman and Mordechai, wandering around the shtetl streets. This postmodern oddity, however, is largely lost on the town's inhabitants, who react to them as they would to any other visiting magnate: they try to make deals, to embroil them in their own little ideas and schemes. "Haman and Mordechai" is in part a satire of Jewish ignorance, of the kind critiqued in "Four Questions" and satirized in "What Is Chanukah?": the Jews don't know enough to recognize their biblical characters, even when explicitly identified as such. But, more deeply and disturbingly, it's about Jewish politics, internal and external, a cynical speculation on the eternity of Jewish suffering and the relentless sameness of Jewish behavior. Here, Mordechai is forced to play the eternal, wandering Jew, constantly in Diasporic subservience to his enemies, because the Jews play their own eternal role in responding to him; the story's epigraph, "Every Jew has his *poritz*, his local lord; every *poritz* has his Jew," is a weary, self-fulfilling prophecy.

Sholem Aleichem provides a trademark lack of closure to "Haman and Mordechai": "I see . . . that you want to know the end of the story—that's the main thing for you. If so, have a bit of patience, until . . . next Purim. It's not that long to wait. Just a year. What sort of weight does a year have in the face of eternity?" Readers would, of course, have waited in vain one way or another for an ending; but Sholem Aleichem didn't have a year to give them. On March 25, he made his last public appearance, attending a benefit organized by Judah Magnes in Grand Central Palace for orphans and victims of the war. The benefit marked the beginning of a weeklong "Yiddish bazaar," which auctioned off valuable items for the charity; Sholem Aleichem donated manuscripts, a letter from Tolstoy, and portraits of various Yiddish writers, and signed autographs at $10 a pop (about $200 in 2010 dollars)—another testament, were one needed, to his popularity.

Passover began three weeks later, on April 18; it was, as always, a time for family gatherings, and for remembering older, better times. The day before the holiday, he wrote his final letter to a family member: regretting that circumstances prevented them from attending the Seder, he wrote, "But what can I do with fate, which goes whither it will! . . . We must submit to the will of He who runs the world . . ." As in previous years, though, holiday preparations helped distract him and improve his mood; he particularly enjoyed affixing "strictly kosher for Pesach" to the seltzer bottles adorning the Seder table, and, as usual, he presided over the Seder. That Passover warmth, that warmth of memory, pervaded his final full work: an article on Bialik for a celebration of the latter's jubilee. It told of their meeting, their wonderful Geneva visit (not omitting the practical joke with the house slippers), and warmly praised their shared literary efforts—"until," Sholem Aleichem wrote, "the God of vengeance grew wrathful and sent a bloody deluge upon the sinful earth . . . the storm seized me and transported me here, to America." On the first day of May, several days after finishing the article, he complained of abdominal pains and took to his bed.

The doctors didn't think it was that serious at first, just a simple stomach illness. Soon, under the impression he was suffering from esophageal cancer, the illness his father had died of, and realizing he had reached the age of fifty-seven, the age at which both his father and his grandfather had died—given his superstitious nature, that loomed large—he began to lose the desire to fight, refusing to eat solid food and repeatedly asserting, "He was being summoned over there." His mood rallied briefly four days before his death: he asked about current events, and told family and friends to reassure the *Varheit* he wouldn't leave them in the lurch without material, that he was working on *Motl*. One of the benefits of his insomnia, he joked; his thoughts wouldn't let him rest until he got them down. The next day, Wednesday, May 10, his condition took an abrupt turn for the worse; two doctors were called out, and diagnosed blood poisoning and uremia. He asked his relatives and close friends for greetings to give those on the other side, and listened to Yehoyesh read him the daily papers for the last time.

From Thursday, May 11, on, he couldn't talk much; he just groaned a few words here and there about how it hurt, especially to Olga, clinging to her, feeling the touch of her hand. Desperately thirsty, he barely spoke, gesturing to his mouth when he wanted a drink of water. His family was at his bedside, accompanied by a nurse he had known for years, since that first illness in Baranovitch. He sat up for a while that afternoon, biting his nails as he would in the throes of literary creation; one observer, the Yiddish playwright Dovid Pinski, could not help but wonder what he was inventing, even then. The next night, Friday night, more members of the Yiddish literary community arrived to join the family, and the house filled with writers and friends; word had spread. A conference with the doctor indicated there was very little time left, especially, it seemed, as Sholem Aleichem was refusing to drink the water he needed—a sign he had stopped fighting once again. The final stage lasted well into the early hours of Saturday morning. Sholem Aleichem occasionally muttered, "I want to sit up, I want to sit up." He was still biting his nails. And he weakly gestured as if he were holding a pen, as if he were still writing.

Family, medical professionals, and Pinski gathered around the bed. Olga pleaded with her husband to open his eyes; Numa cried that he had promised, promised he would live. Sholem Aleichem was beyond response now; after an hour or two of long-drawn-out, rattling breaths, he passed away, his heart stopping, then after a few moments starting again, then continuing for another hour or two. The time of death: 7:29 a.m. on the Sabbath, the 10th of Iyar, May 13. The house was soon filled with mourners from all over the city. Judah Magnes read Sholem Aleichem's will to the assembled crowd; overcome with emotion, he couldn't finish the reading, and the Zionist leader Shemarya Levin had to finish for him.

EPILOGUE

An Afterlife in Ten Scenes

Scene 1

New York/Washington, 1916

Arrangements had to be made.

It would have to be a public funeral, there was no doubt of that; and the Lower East Side had seen its share of those. Both respected figures like the Yiddish newspaper publisher Kasriel Sarasohn and the Yiddish playwright Jacob Gordin and less respected ones like the Jewish gang leader Jack Zelig had been accompanied to their eternal rest by crowds and spectacle. (And at least once, during the funeral of the Orthodox rabbi Jacob Joseph in 1902, by a riot: an outbreak of violence that started when workers tossed bits of iron out of factory windows at procession members led to two hundred riot police "slashing this way and that with their sticks . . . shoving roughly against men and women alike.") But the question transcended simple logistics and security: How do you bury, in the words of one of his eulogists, "the Jewish people in microcosm"?

First, the family decided, you needed an arrangements committee, and they asked Judah Magnes, the head of the New York Kehillah, to head it up. Though the Kehillah didn't always succeed at its stated goal of unifying New York's Jewish communal affairs, Magnes was still probably one of the few individuals who could draw together the multitudinous constituencies bridged by Sholem Aleichem's appeal. Some backstage political struggles notwithstanding, Magnes and the rest of the committee—all friends or associates of Sholem Aleichem's, as well as committed Zionists—would produce a smashing success, a national pageant.

The committee's first decision was to invite over a hundred Yiddish writers to watch over the body in fourteen consecutive three-hour sessions as it lay in state for two days at 968 Kelly Street. Twenty-five thousand people, alerted by black-bordered extra editions of the Yiddish papers, stood in lines stretching for blocks waiting to pay their respects. That Monday, May 15, three Pereyaslav *landsmen,* Jews from his hometown, purified and prepared the body. Everything was done strictly according to tradition, though few if any of the writers were traditional—a fitting tribute to Sholem Aleichem, whose own behavior was less traditional than his sensibility.

At 9 a.m, ten prominent Yiddish writers bore the coffin to the hearse; as they exited the house, the cantor of the Reform Bronx Montefiore Congregation sang the "El malei rakhamim," the traditional funeral prayer. Other Yiddish writers headed a vast procession, twenty thousand strong; the writers were accompanied by over a hundred psalm-reciting children from the Orthodox Talmud Torah and the National Radical School, strange bedfellows united by the author's appeal. The procession's first stop was at Ohab Zedek, the Orthodox synagogue on Harlem's 116th Street. There, "El malei rakhamim" was chanted again, this time by the synagogue's world-famous cantor, and Sholem Aleichem's friend, Yossele Rosenblatt. Crossing the Harlem River, the procession lost some members, but gained them back and more as it traveled south down Fifth, then Madison Avenue. It stopped at the Kehillah's offices at the United Hebrew Charities Building, on Twenty-first Street and Second Avenue, where it was met by members of the Yiddish Writers and Newspaper Guild. They had assembled at the Forward Building (whose windows, like those of other offices of the Yiddish press, were draped in black) and had marched northward, four abreast, up Second Avenue to join the cortege.

Rosenblatt conducted a brief memorial service at the Charities building, and the procession continued south, to the heart of the Lower East Side. Six mounted policemen cleared the way, and two hundred officers managed the crowds: Inspector O'Brien had learned from the riot fourteen years ago to provide an adequate police presence. Opposite the headquarters of the Hebrew Actors' Union, a company of actors, led by Jacob Adler, joined the procession. (They had paid their respects more concretely Saturday night, when the Yiddish theaters had shuttered for the evening in the departed author's honor.) Then it stopped once again, at the Educational Alliance, where the main memorial service took place. Police struggled to hold back the crowds: only six hundred ticket holders were admitted into the building. The coffin was ushered into the auditorium, where the dignitaries waiting on the podium, from Jacob Schiff to Chaim Zhitlovski, made up a who's who of Jewish New York. Magnes read the crowd Sholem Aleichem's will, which the author had asked to be published on the day of his death.

After the service, the procession continued south, stopping for another brief service at the Hebrew Immigrant Aid Society, where Rosenblatt recited "El malei rakhamim" once more, then crossed the Williamsburg Bridge and wended through Brooklyn to Mount Neboh Cemetery in Glendale, Queens. Sholem Aleichem's surviving son, Numa, recited kaddish at the grave; the Yiddish writers Sholem Asch and Avrom Reyzen spoke, as did the socialist poet Morris Winchevsky and the Zionist leader Nachman Syrkin, among others. Thousands stood there, in the bad weather, listening patiently.

Those thousands at the cemetery were a small percentage of the throngs who lined the streets of the Bronx, Manhattan, and Brooklyn and watched from fire escapes and rooftops. Estimates for the total number of participants vary wildly, ranging from 30,000 to 250,000; the actual number was probably somewhere between 150,000 and 200,000. This out of a population of about 1.5 million Jews in New York City—and about 6 million New Yorkers overall. Sholem Aleichem's audience—like the details of his funeral, like his work, like himself—contained vastnesses.

And that audience, thanks in no small part to the circumstances of the funeral, was spreading fast, and perhaps more widely and to more unlikely precincts than Sholem Aleichem might have expected. The floor of the United States House of Representatives, for example, where, after a discussion of savings and loan discussions and agricultural banking bills, a member of the New York Republican delegation, William Stiles Bennett, spoke of "the greatest spontaneous gathering of the people in the history of our city," 120,000 people, "toilers, men and women alike, who could ill afford the loss, [who] sacrificed the day's wage to join in the tribute" to "a man whose very name is unfamiliar." Bennett credited his fellow representative Isaac Siegel, a New York lawyer who'd made his way up through the public schools to rise high in the Republican hierarchy, for alerting him to Sholem Aleichem's reputation. That reputation, according to Bennett, was not only for his "humorous stories with a kindly cast," but for the "trenchant pen . . . in behalf of those in public life whom he cared for."

Bennett's evaluation was certainly inspired, at least in part, by a document he asked to be read into the record: Sholem Aleichem's will, which the family had released to the public following the funeral service. Bennett had also entered into the record a *New York Times* editorial that breathlessly began with the thought that "in the whole great domain of testamentary literature, it would be hard to find a will better deserving to be viewed as a 'human document' in the full sense of that term" than "that of the man whose least apposite title was 'the Jewish Mark Twain.'" Both were probably struck—as was a news reporter who covered the will's public release for the *Times*—less by the details of the disposition of the estate than by the larger social and ethical questions the will posed.

The *Times* titled its story "Aleichem Begs to Lie with Poor: Will of Noted Writer Says His Ambition Is to Rest Among Plain Jewish Laborers," struck, apparently, by the will's first clause, which reads, in full: "Wherever I die I want to be placed not among aristocrats, or among the powerful, but among plain Jewish laborers, among the people itself, so that the gravestone that is to be placed upon my grave should illumine the simple graves about me, and these simple graves should adorn my gravestone, even as the plain, good people during my lifetime illumined their Folkschrieber." The editorial, by contrast, singled out the will's tenth and final clause for praise, in which Sholem Aleichem begged his children and successors "to protect mamma, to beautify her old age, to make her bitter life sweet, to heal her broken heart; not to weep after me, on the contrary, to think of me with joy; and the main thing—to live together in peace, to bear no hatred one for another, to help one another in bad times, to remember one another upon occasion in the family, to have pity on a poor man, and when circumstances permit, to pay my debts, should I have any. Children! Carry with honor my hard-earned Jewish name, and may God in heaven come to your help. Amen!"

In his remarks, Bennett told the story of the loss of a huge fortune and of an oldest son, but added that "no tinge of bitterness crept into his writings . . . [and the] shining radiance of his affection turned his falling tears into a rainbow of promise." At the time of Sholem Aleichem's death, very little of his work had appeared in English; and so for much of the American audience—certainly the English-speaking, non-Jewish audience—their first meeting with Sholem Aleichem was because of a funeral and through a will. It was an encounter with a ghost who claimed, in his testament, to be of the people and to be their own writer, and who asked to turn sadness into joy, almost, in so many words, to turn tears into laughter; and an introduction to the writer as family man, thinking of his children and expressing, from beyond the grave, his overwhelming husbandly love. Following the tone set by Jewish leaders and intellectuals, the non-Jewish world was crafting their image of Sholem Aleichem as, to use some other adjectives Bennett employed, hopeful, sincere, humble, and joyful.

Not all of this, as we now know, was an entirely accurate depiction of the facts.

Scene 2

New York/London, 1912–1922

C arnegie Hall was draped in black.

It was the thirtieth day after Sholem Aleichem's death—his *shloshim*, in traditional Jewish parlance—and twenty-five hundred people crowded into Carnegie Hall to pay tribute. The writer had stipulated in his will that a percentage of the family's income from the sale of his works be donated to a fund for needy Hebrew and Yiddish writers, and the Sholem Aleichem People's Fund would be the beneficiary of the memorial evening. (The cheaper seats went for a dime; eventually, demand dictated that the pricier ones be opened to the general public as well.) From the darkened stage, Sholem Aleichem's portrait looked out at the audience from behind a row of distinguished speakers.

"Let my name be mentioned by them with laughter rather than not be mentioned at all," the author dictated from beyond the grave, and the evening self-consciously attempted to emulate that sensibility of turning mourning into merriment. A lugubrious recitation of a mourner's prayer by Yossele Rosenblatt and his choir early on notwithstanding, the noted Yiddish writer Sholem Asch—famous throughout the Yiddish world for his scandalous play *God of Vengeance*, soon to become a best-selling English writer—chided the audience that "we are taking his death too sadly . . . he was an apostle of joy, and it was his wish that we be joyful. If all the world were like Sholem Aleichem, there would be no sadness." And as the great figures of modern Yiddish literature in America—Asch, the playwright Dovid Pinski, the humorist Moyshe Nadir, the poet Avrom Reyzen—read from Sholem Aleichem's work, laughter rolled through the cavernous hall.

In his opening remarks, Judah Magnes reminded the audience of the deceased author's testamentary wish that, as he wrote, "the best monument for me will be if my works are read and if there be found among the better-to-do classes of our people Maecenases who will publish and distribute my works in Yiddish"—or, as the will specified, "in other languages." Everyone knew the will also suggested that, in lieu of saying the mourners' kaddish if his family was unable or unwilling, absolution would be granted if "they all come . . . and read this my will, and also select one of my stories, one of the really joyous ones, and read it aloud in whatever language they understand best." Literature was the new generation's religion; and, looking to posterity, Sholem Aleichem took care to accommodate not only changes in faith but changes in language, as he saw his children, and grandchildren, moving away from the Yiddish his world was composed in and of.

He had lived to see his work published widely in Russian translation, among other languages. English, however, with some few exceptions, had seen little of Sholem Aleichem between hard covers. But the translations of those early years, like the early memorial service, continued the process of creating a very particular version of his persona, and of his legacy.

His first appearance in English came courtesy of an unusual Englishwoman.

Helena Frank was the granddaughter of the Marquis of Westminster; her father, a Christian convert, would open his house to Sholem Aleichem when he was visiting London. (Sholem Aleichem suggested that she embodied "the transmigrated soul of Mother Rachel," Hannah, or Queen Esther; "a noble tender Jewish soul in a Christian body.") Her 1912 anthology *Yiddish Tales* is a sampler of work by various authors; though Sholem Aleichem is only represented by five examples, Frank's introduction would help set the tone for reading Sholem Aleichem (along with Yiddish literature in general) in English. Describing the tales as each having "its special echo from that strangely fascinating world so often quoted, so little understood . . . a world in the passing, but whose more precious elements, shining, for all those who care to see them, through every page of these unpretending tales . . . will surely live on," she has them fall somewhere between symbolic keys and cultural curiosities rather than works of literature—presenting Eastern European Jewish life as a vanishing world decades before the outbreak of the Second World War.

And the trend would continue. Hannah Berman, a Dubliner who had received copies of Sholem Aleichem's newspaper serials straight from the source, had translated *Stempenyu* in 1913 in London; seven years later, she published a translation of Sholem Aleichem's stories with Knopf called *Jewish Children*. *The New York Times*, covering the book's publication, linked the stories directly to the author's posthumous celebrity: "Shalom Aleichem, the 'Jewish Mark Twain,' whose 'Jewish Children' has just been published by Alfred A. Knopf, is perhaps the best loved writer of his race. Thousands upon thousands of Jews mourned at his funeral, which was held in New York several years ago." Choosing children's stories certainly made sense: as we saw, Sholem Aleichem himself had chosen that segment of his oeuvre to present to a non-Jewish reading public. And Knopf tried to stir up crossover appeal by getting Dorothy Canfield Fisher, an early advocate of the Montessori movement in America and herself a prominent contemporary author of children's books, to write the introduction. And here's her argument for reading Sholem Aleichem:

"Like many Americans (probably the majority)," she wrote, "I had more notions, blurred and inaccurate though they might be, about life in Thibet [*sic*] than about life among Jews." She clarified, though, that she meant what in Woody Allen's famous locution were called "real Jews": "When I say 'Jews' I mean those who have not diluted the ancient traditions of their race and religion; not the East Side, partially Americanized Jew, nor the sophisticated, intensively cultivated cosmopolitans . . . But the people into whose hearts Sholom Aleichem bade me look were not only new to me, but richly dowered with an unbroken tradition complex and ancient beyond belief for an upstart Anglo-Saxon."

What was valuable about Sholem Aleichem's stories, particularly for non-Jewish readers? They showed non-Jews what real Jews were like. And what made an authentic Jew? Tradition.

Sholem Aleichem, whose genius came precisely from artfully delineating tradition's reaction to modernity's stress and strain, might have begged to differ.

Scene 3

The Soviet Union, 1921–1929

American Jews wouldn't be the only ones using Sholem Aleichem to help them tell their story. Newly created "Soviet Jews" had precisely the reverse problem from their New World counterparts, however: while America, its barriers and challenges to acculturation notwithstanding, was an established presence, Eastern European Jews were in a homeland in which the nation had changed on them overnight. At first, the signs seemed positive: Stalin had expressed interest in developing Soviet ethnic minority cultures that were, as he famously put it, "national in form, socialist in content," and—as Yiddish had been declared the official language of Soviet Jewry as early as 1919—the official policy of supporting cultural production in all Soviet languages meant a bonanza for Yiddish, with state-sponsored publishing houses and theaters, among many other institutions.

The Moscow State Yiddish Theater's first success, on New Year's Day of 1921, was an evening of Sholem Aleichem one-act plays. (The show would be performed over three hundred times; the fact that Russian-language synopses were sold to 60 to 80 percent of the audience each night spoke volumes about the changing nature of the audience, Jewish and non-Jewish alike.) A notable triumvirate lay behind the triumph. The show's director, Alexander Granovsky, had founded his Jewish Chamber Theater in the recently renamed Petrograd; he moved it to Moscow soon after. He insisted Yiddish theater should strive for aesthetic heights— and was willing, in the process, to use Sholem Aleichem's satires to highlight the ideological bankruptcy of the pre-revolution way of life, part of the bargain of Soviet cultural production. Turning his actors into living, farcical embodiments of Marxist historical determinism, Granovsky instructed them to adopt exaggerated, acrobatic gestures whose preciseness echoed industrial machinery. The effect was heightened by makeup and sets designed by none other than Marc Chagall (his paintings of a fiddler floating above a roof would later prove influential on another generation of theatricals), whose thick coats and broad, colorful strokes would provide additional grotesquerie to the mix. Making up the lead actor, the immensely talented Shloyme Mikhoels, for a performance, it's reported Chagall complained he could have done a really terrific job if he could only have dispensed with Mikhoels's right eye.

The productions were many things—provocative, arresting, polemical—but subtle they were not. Tableaux vivants with rich men facing each other in rows, a street cleaner's broom hanging over them—symbol of the coming revolution that would sweep away what was portrayed as Sholem Aleichem's world. Capitalists with gargantuan padded bellies. A pince-nez made of bagels. A character, receiving news of new wealth, is crowned with a hamantashen in lieu of a Napoleonic hat—a sign the new emperors of capital had no clothes. Rich men droop and shuffle along; garment industry workers, by contrast, stitch in upright, joyful chorus. A nonproductive type like a matchmaker, often dismissed in Yiddish as a *luftmensh* or "air man," was literally flown through the air through the magic of stagecraft.

Some members of the Soviet press didn't like that first theatrical evening, finding it overly artificial, untrue to Sholem Aleichem's profound connection to folk reality. But to suggest Sholem Aleichem was "really" a critic of capitalism or "really" a folk artist isn't the point: the reason he was so profoundly important to these Soviet artists, in the early days after the revolution, was that they could see in his work a set of themes and characters they could adapt to their own purposes. And they weren't the only ones: the same interpretive energy that drove the early productions of the Moscow State Yiddish Theater soon spread to the Soviet Yiddish literary establishment, where a generation of critics, struggling uneasily for footing between Marxist inspiration and Stalinist persecution, rose to the task of "invent[ing] a 'progressive' cultural heritage."

I'll just mention two. Max Erik practically invented the study of Old Yiddish literature and moved to the Soviet Union in 1929 because he fell in love with the Marxist dream—and was forced to give up his chosen, ideologically unpalatable, field as a result. The other, Mayer Viner, arrived in the Soviet Union in 1926 after stints in Paris and Berlin. The former hailed one of Sholem Aleichem's creations as his greatest because of its "rejection of the possibility that the petty bourgeoisie will succeed through capitalism; the satire of the bourgeois illusions of the lower middle class; the scathing, demolishing critique of the *luftmensh* and his so-called livelihoods." The latter, writing on Sholem Aleichem's humor, sees that same creation as particular proof that the source of his humor is "that the prevailing social conditions oppressed and crippled man until he became not only miserable but ridiculous." That creation: Menakhem-Mendl, the perfect foil—in the right light—for illustrating the flaws and failures of the capitalist system (and who had, as a result, featured prominently in the Moscow State Yiddish Theater performances as well).

It wasn't surprising that he was headed for bigger things. A gossipy squib in *The New York Times* on May 17, 1925, read: "Through the Russian Information Bureau, in Washington, we hear that motion pictures are gaining a huge clientele in Russia . . . . Plans are . . . underway to put on the screen 'Manakhem Mendel' [*sic*], by the late Sholem Aleichem." The *Times* was a little late to the party. Russian Jews had been going to the movies for over a decade, and Sholem Aleichem's work had been adapted as early as the summer of 1917, when Alexander Arkatov had shot a version of *The Bloody Hoax* during a period of revolutionary ferment. With the Soviets encouraging national minority cultures in the 1920s, though, Yiddish film prospects looked even brighter, and the mid to late twenties saw the first great cinematic adaptations of Sholem Aleichem's works, films that eloquently testified to the complexities of wrestling art through the confining demands of time, place, and ideology.

Four Soviet films based on Sholem Aleichem's works were produced between 1925 and 1928, their history in no small part the history of increasing Soviet repression and persecution of the creative industries. The 1927 adaptation of Sholem Aleichem's theatrical novel *Wandering Stars* was withdrawn from circulation for "idealiz[ing] the pathological and decadent mood of the decaying bourgeoisie and populariz[ing] covert prostitution and debauchery"; an adaptation of *The Deluge*, a novel about the 1905 Russian revolution, took three years to see the light, with two directors replaced for apparently ideological reasons and significant reshaping of the film to ensure a final product free of "petty bourgeois psychology." (Other production troubles suggested different dark currents in Russian society: locals, portraying pogromist Cossacks, got a little too immersed in their roles, refusing to stop beating the Jewish actors when the director cried cut.)

The 1928 *Laughter Through Tears* was a greater success, both as an artistic work and at mollifying Soviet authorities. Merging two of Sholem Aleichem's greatest works—the story "The Enchanted Tailor" and Motl's adventures—the film infuses each original narrative with ideologically appropriate content. The practical joke bewitching, or plaguing, the tailor in the story transmogrifies into a flashpoint of the inveterate hostility between rich and poor, leading ultimately to class war—the town's working class rises up and sets upon the joker, a rich innkeeper, with sticks. Motl becomes a symbol of the revolution, throwing mud in the innkeeper's eye. The ancien régime, for its part, is portrayed as gluttonous and violent, refusing mercy to the poor; one official literally turns his back on the poor tailor, who—as no good citizen goes unpunished— has been expelled from his hometown "for creating an uprising."

The film's undoubted aesthetic merits notwithstanding (its realistic capture of the chaos of daily shtetl life, the stellar performance of the child actor S. J. Silberman playing Motl), the Yiddish poet Itzik Fefer was right when he intuited, without being explicit about it, that the film was harmed by its accommodation of an unironic ideological sensibility. "We find here," he wrote, "none of the lyrical irony which is the essence of Sholem Aleichem's writings. Sholem Aleichem is not a sentimentalist. His works do not simply evoke 'tears,' he portrays a way of life which provokes laughter—laughter through tears. The screenwriters have consciously or unconsciously killed his humor." Fefer, though yet again trafficking in the common "laughter through tears" image, perceptively noted that the best understanding of Sholem Aleichem's work was to see it as the embodiment of forces struggling against each other, so it's unsurprising that the finest of the quartet of movies came from a trio of brilliant, creative individuals who would increasingly be forced to strain against Soviet repression.

In 1925, *Yidishe glikn* (Jewish Luck), focusing on Menakhem-Mendl's adventures, marked the collaboration of three immense talents. Granovsky, who'd studied film direction in Sweden before achieving fame as the Moscow State Yiddish Theater's presiding genius, directed; Mikhoels plays Menakhem-Mendl as an almost literal incarnation of the *luftmensh*, the air man—mincing, his belly thrust forward, he practically floats across the Berdichev streets; and explaining whatever moments were not thus rendered self-explanatory was the job of the great Russian-Jewish writer Isaac Babel, a literary celebrity after the publication of his *Red Cavalry* stories, who handled the silent film's intertitles (and who called Sholem Aleichem "the funniest writer in the world").

Though the original Menakhem-Mendl's painful testaments to the failures of commodity capitalism would seem a natural fit for filmmakers within the Soviet system, Granovsky and Babel went another way, mostly adapting their story from his later adventures as an insurance agent and, particularly, a matchmaker, prefaced by a slapstick failure as, believe it or not, a corset salesman. Maybe the focus on these jobs stemmed from the success of their theatrical version, which had featured the later Menakhem-Mendl; maybe they realized it would be much harder to portray those earlier episodes pungently on film. But there might have been another reason, too. Menakhem-Mendl, marked for failure from the beginning (literally—one of the film's earliest images is of a baby urinating on him) manages success of a sort, when his matchmaking mix-up, accidentally arranging for two brides to marry each other, results in his poor assistant marrying the rich man's daughter he loves. Presumably we're expected to take vicarious pleasure in the rich man's thwarted desire to hoard his capital, in money and daughters, out of the poor's reach. Not an unpleasing message for the Soviet censors.

But the film's genius, in my opinion, lies in yet another explanation for focusing on matchmaking. It's expressed in Menakhem-Mendl's particular paean to his new profession: "He travels here, there, gets people together, gets money for it, even dances at the wedding." The movie's big finish, a wedding ceremony, does just that, unifying peoples—but its best sequence, by far, suggests a far grander sort of union: a lavish dream sequence where Menakhem-Mendl fantasizes exporting Berdichev brides by the train-car load to America, even loading some onto a ship by winch. (The film had been proposed when an American theater tour was canceled, as a way to familiarize American audiences with the troupe's work.) Menakhem-Mendl is urged to "Save America!," and a superficial party hack might have mistaken this as exporting the new ideology to other lands, but Babel, in *Red Cavalry*, had already amply displayed his skepticism about exporting communism. The Old World stereotypes of treating women like good commodity stock—"Merchandise good enough for Rothschild," Menakhem-Mendl says, inspecting the brides in a military-type line-up—suggests a yearning for a kind of unified culture, a match between Old World and New World Jewish life with Menakhem-Mendl, and Sholem Aleichem, as the matchmaker. Granovsky and Co.—not to mention a judicious dose of Sholem Aleichem—could save American Jewish culture by forging a universal Jewish identity.

The Soviets would beg to disagree, generally speaking. Mikhoels and Babel would be eliminated by the regime; Granovsky defected; Erik was arrested and died in a prison camp; Viner was killed in action during the Second World War.

Scene 4

New York, 1917–1939

The Yiddish-speaking immigrants who had thronged New York's streets, who paid little attention to the doings of the House of Representatives or the Knopf publication lists, had had their own opportunities to remember Sholem Aleichem and enjoy his work. The gatherings and concert benefits continued: a year after his death, a standing room crowd filled Thirty-fourth Street's 3,500-seat Manhattan Opera House, which had not long before hosted a revival of *Ben-Hur*, to hear readings and incidental music; the wryly named Shnorrers' Association sponsored the next year's sold-out reading, which featured Yiddish actors and playwrights reading from Sholem Aleichem's works. But while Sholem Aleichem was being celebrated with laughter in midtown, a more complex posterity was coming into being just two miles southeast, right off Union Square.

The Yiddish theater, now in full flower as the waves of immigrants had swelled demand, had been going through its own cultural struggles. Much of the material on the boards was *shund*—a word Sholem Aleichem could easily have used to describe Shomer's material and might best be translated as "garbage." Hack melodramas, mishmash plots, actors mugging to a half-attentive audience—this was, at least according to its reform-minded critics, the state of Yiddish theater. Playwrights like Jacob Gordin and Sholem Aleichem had tried to do their part to bring high literary values to the theater, but they needed partners on the production side: actors, producers, directors. In the second decade of the twentieth century, they started getting them, from Vilna to Manhattan. None are as important to Sholem Aleichem's story as Maurice Schwartz.

Schwartz's own story could have come straight out of a *shund* melodrama. Born in Sudilkov, in the Ukraine, he set off to America with his family—but his mother mixed up their ship tickets in England, and they crossed the Atlantic without him. He remained alone in London at age eleven, sleeping in the gutter, collecting rags for spare change, and surviving as well as he could; he arrived in New York the following year, in 1902, helping his family in "a smelly and ill-lit rag shop in a cellar slightly larger than a clothes closet." He worked his way up in the theater business in America, acting and shifting scenery in Baltimore, buying a secondhand spotlight for a song in Cleveland, and (perhaps apocryphally) getting his big break on Second Avenue on a day's notice, filling in for a sick actor.

In 1918, Schwartz, ambitions hardly satisfied by merely acting, took over the Irving Place Theatre from a group of German actors and published an artistic manifesto in the *Forverts* under the title "Can a Better Yiddish Theater Survive in New York?" Schwartz, unsurprisingly, answered in the affirmative, insisting that "for a theater to be a financial success it must first be a moral success" and that "the theater must be a sort of holy place, where a festive and artistic atmosphere will always reign." With a troupe of like-minded professionals, he created the Yiddish Art Theatre Players and began staging more literary works at Irving Place. (Schwartz's sacred sensibility applied to the audience as well: he instructed ticket takers to sniff out theatergoers bringing lunch baskets with them, not an uncommon practice then; "such persons," as the *Times* put it, "were halted at the door and their food peremptorily snatched from their convulsive grasps.") His first three productions were flops. The fourth, Peretz Hirschbein's *Abandoned Nook*, ran for fifteen weeks, marked Hirschbein's breakthrough as a major dramatist in American Yiddish theater and put the lie to anyone who said that only melodramas make money.

The fall 1919 season opened with a production of *Tevye the Dairyman*, starring Schwartz, that confused some of its viewers. Not because of the production's radical telescoping of the Tevye story to focus largely on the story of Chava and her non-Jewish love and on Tevye's eviction; these would have strongly resonated with an immigrant generation trying to acculturate into non-Jewish society. No, the reason "the public couldn't make up its mind whether the play was a success or not, and of how they should relate to it . . . was the fact they did not expect a serious drama from Sholem Aleichem. Everybody knows Sholem Aleichem as the great Jewish humorist." Sholem Aleichem—and, particularly, Schwartz's vision of Sholem Aleichem as a serious, literary playwright—was central to the Yiddish Art Theatre's history as it grew in reputation and in stature over the next decade. When it moved into a specially built 1,265-seat theater in 1926, Olga Rabinovich laid the cornerstone; a speaker at the foundation ceremony, remarking that Yiddish dramatists had "stood through the ages for a Jewish soul and a Jewish spirit," could have been channeling the funeral speeches for Sholem Aleichem.

And throughout, there were productions of Sholem Aleichem plays. *Tevye* was revived in 1927, but there were others, one featuring a young man who would change his name to Paul Muni. But, again and again, Schwartz's efforts to present Sholem Aleichem as a Yiddish counterpart to Shaw, Gorky, or Ibsen were stymied by critics' and audience's attempts to fit what they saw into an emerging narrative about Sholem Aleichem and the world he increasingly was seen to represent. A warm 1922 appreciation of the Yiddish Art Theatre in the *Times* mentions the troupe's attempt to stage works by those three playwrights, and then damns with faint praise their productions of what the critic calls the "folk plays" by Hirschbein, Anski, and Sholem Aleichem: "Intelligently as [the non-Jewish plays] are done, it is no reproach to the Art Theatre to say that it is more vindicated in its presentation of the folk plays than in these others. For it is a folk theatre, rather than an art theatre in any sophisticated sense. It has reopened a whole tradition of culture that was in danger of being forgotten . . . These are spontaneous combustions of the imagination, authentic from being close to a remembered tradition of beauty."

Authentic, unsophisticated tradition, helping the folk remember what they are in danger of forgetting as they stand, immigrants in a new land, on the cusp of personal reinvention: this is, increasingly, seen as the wellspring of "real" Jewish artistic worth. Reviews of later productions, one of which even compliments the Art Theatre for turning "atavistic and parochial," are cases in point. The *Times* reviews often single out something amateurish about the productions, primarily their overblown running times and the performances' volume and enthusiasm—"art was forgotten and the play became a turmoil," reads one review; a "continuous racket," notes another. But these insults are (condescendingly) turned upside down, with the latter review noting that the result leads to actors so immersed in the proceedings "they seem to forget themselves at times and become so real as to be almost unreal," and that the play "again reveals Sholem Aleichem's insight into Jewish life." One might wonder at the picture of authentic Jewish life the critics were conjuring up, with its noisy, gabbling racket, its reality derived from unreality. An image of the Eastern European Jewish past, shaped by Sholem Aleichem's complex literary vision, was being reshaped on the stages of Yiddish Art Theatre and refined, for American audiences, through the critical eyes of the New York drama critics. This would have consequences.

Over the next decade, Maurice Schwartz kept busy. There were some failures: flush with ambition, he'd moved his theater uptown in 1931 and mounted an English-language production of Sholem Aleichem's play *Hard to Be a Jew* (the stage adaptation of *The Bloody Hoax*). Those muttering about his "betrayal" of the Yiddish theater or his "permanent loss" to the English-language stage were gleefully silenced by Brooks Atkinson's review of the production, now renamed: it began, "If for some inscrutable reason this department were required to give a straight answer to 'If I Were You,' which was acted at the Ambassador last evening, the answer would be in the negative," and got worse from there. The best he could muster, aside from some faint praise for the star, was a patronizing dismissal of the play as sentimental Lower East Side ghetto fodder of the sort the critics had been doling out for years: "It is festive. Like all simple-minded festivals, it is warm and hospitable. Written by a Jew for Jewish audiences, it has a family intimacy of spirit, and what you may think of it critically is quite beside the point."

It wasn't beside the point for the play's star. Licking his wounds, Schwartz returned to the Yiddish theater, scoring a great success the next season with an adaptation of a novel by I. J. Singer, Isaac Bashevis Singer's older brother. He also turned briefly to film, appearing in the 1933 adaptation of the Sholem Asch novel *Uncle Moses* and then spending eight months in Hollywood under contract to Metro. Schwartz had been involved in film since the midtwenties, when he had starred in a silent film while touring in Vienna. A 1926 film he had directed about life on the Lower East Side, *Broken Hearts*, had failed thanks to his "inexperience as a director"; now, years later, he had gained more film experience and explored the right moment to return to directing. In the meantime, he toured internationally with the Singer adaptation for two years, returning to New York's theater scene in September 1936 along with four tons of props.

While in Warsaw in 1936, Schwartz had begun considering making a Tevye film, but was dissuaded from shooting it in Poland given the rising tide of anti-Semitism there. And so he waited to make it in America, partnering with friends (including the co-owner of the largest kosher restaurant in the Times Square area) to create the Mayman Film Company, and started prepping to shoot in the summer of 1939. He knew the superficial problem—can you make America look like Tevye's Ukraine?—was easily solved. An earlier American version of Tevye, Charles Davenport's 1919 silent, had built a shtetl in Leonia, New Jersey; and Edgar G. Ulmer, who would go on to direct some of the greatest Yiddish-language films, had created a mock-Ukrainian village on a farm outside Flemington, New Jersey in 1936. Schwartz's own shtetl would rise in Jericho, Long Island, ninety minutes from Times Square, on the Underhills' 150-acre potato and wheat farm; the barn would serve as the Greek Orthodox priest's home, and Tevye would live in the cowshed.

Nor was he overly concerned about production problems. The cameraman, script girl, and technical crew didn't speak Yiddish? Not to worry; though the scripts would be in Yiddish, English dialogue transcriptions were provided. High production values a necessity? (As Schwartz said to an interviewer: "You can't hope to pass off a cheap, inferior picture, even if it's in Yiddish, on audiences today.") Rehearse the actors for weeks at the Yiddish Art Theatre before production starts, then work fast—besides, the summer heat meant you had to move quickly, or greasepaint dissolved and actors suffered from the sunlight reflected into their faces "from huge chromium-plated sheets of metal." (And the faster they moved, the lower the costs—important when the film was budgeted at $70,000—the equivalent of over a million in 2010 dollars—coming right out of the producers' pockets.)

Not everything went as smoothly as Schwartz would have liked; good as the Underhills' farm looked ("If you don't think Long Island can impersonate the Ukraine beautifully, you must see 'Tevya,'" wrote the *Times* reviewer), its proximity to Mitchell Airfield meant numerous shots were ruined by the sound of airplanes. The biggest problem, though, ended up being politics. An invasion of Poland seemed imminent; the Molotov–von Ribbentrop pact shook everyone, particularly the numerous communist supporters or sympathizers involved in the production. Many actors and crew members had family in Europe. Some who'd planned to return were stranded when the production's delays meant filming extended past the Nazi invasion of Poland.

Since *Tevye*, following Sholem Aleichem's earlier theatrical adaptation, focuses entirely on the story of Chava's marriage to a non-Jew, it wasn't unreasonable to see geopolitics peeping its head through. Unquestionably, the film's surface tension has everything to do with intermarriage: we noted earlier that Chava returns to Judaism using the language of Ruth, that first convert, and there's a plausible argument to offer that the film speaks to that increasing American phenomenon (the *Times* claimed it expressed "the 'Abie's Irish Rose' theme in a semi-serious vein, with the difference that in this case the orthodox point of view is triumphant"). But Schwartz's film also connects Chava's marriage to Tevye's expulsion from his village, two events unrelated in the original stories; some villagers, upset Fedya has married a Jew, not only discuss expelling Tevye in a council meeting (and then blaming the distant tsar), but gleefully take advantage of his forced emigration to buy up his belongings at fire-sale prices. "If the prices weren't low, we'd steal it all," one says; indeed, one villager actually does steal a dress of Tevye's wife's—the actual, immediate catalyst for Chava's return. Any resemblance to the Nazis' policies in the thirties of beggaring Jews who wanted to escape an increasingly impossible situation seems entirely intentional.

At least one Yiddish critic felt the subtext keenly, but drew what might be an unexpected conclusion: Nathaniel Buchwald, writing in the *Morgn Frayhayt*, insisted that the film boasted "scenes which are obscene, false, bungling, and insulting—not for goyim but rather for the dignity of a Yiddish film and of Jewish artists. We should leave the 'art' of slandering entire peoples to the Nazis." Of course, when the film opened at the Continental Theater on Seventh Avenue and Fifty-second Street, next to Roseland, running for five weeks in the winter of 1940—it premiered several days after *Gone With the Wind*—the war had only just begun.

Scene 5

Vilna, 1942

One small, tragicomic moment, to stand in for so many fully tragic ones.

The Nazi war against the Jews, so callous and inhumane to their persons, was of course no respecter of their property; and so along with the murder and torture came looting and pillaging—in the euphemistic name, of course, of cultural "rescue" and "recovery." In Vilna, in 1942, the great Yiddish poet Avrom Sutzkever encountered two such champions of culture: Johannes Pohl, a Hebraist who had served in the Frankfurt Municipal Library's Jewish division—his other credits involved advising on the Nuremberg Laws and contributing to *Der Stürmer*—and one Dr. Mueller of Berlin. The latter gathered an assemblage of Yiddish and Hebrew experts to perform, in Sutzkever's phrasing, a selection on Vilna's books similar to that now being imposed on Vilna's Jews. To the right meant back to Germany, to ensure, as Mueller solemnly asserted, that the furies of the war would not consume such treasures; to the left, to the paper mills at bulk prices—a fate which befell 80 percent of the 100,000 books taken from Vilna's Jewish libraries, houses of study, and institutions of learning.

One of those last was YIVO, the Jewish Social Science Institute, the crown of Jewish—and Yiddish—secular scholarship in prewar Europe. Sutzkever writes of papers and documents strewn on the floor of the cellar like trash, as a German ordered a locksmith to crack the organization's safe. Apparently, Sutzkever writes, he thought he'd find gold there; and he did, after a fashion. When the door was forced open, "Sholem Aleichem and Peretz's manuscripts mockingly observed him." His cultured response? "He hurled them from the safe out of anger and trampled them beneath his feet," like a child.

Scene 6

New York, 1943

By April 1943, the *Contemporary Jewish Record* was already reporting that only a third of Polish Jewry remained alive. That same month, *The New York Times* alerted the paper's readers, had they not already known, to Hitler's genocidal intentions. The venue? A review of a new book on Sholem Aleichem.

The reviewer of Maurice Samuel's *The World of Sholom Aleichem* began by picturing "a small, teeming world . . . whose people are infinitely poor but are sustained by a faith and a piety incredible in our time . . . The so-called Jewish Pale in Russia and Poland has never been a very happy world, and today what is left of it is being ruthlessly destroyed by Hitler's hordes." Samuel's book, the reviewer asserted, "is, to all intents and purposes, a memorial to that world . . . now in the process of extinction." The *Chicago Tribune*'s reviewer added a perverse, horror-movie uncanniness to his balance of nostalgia and elegy, praising the book for its depiction of the chronicler of "the ghetto" where "Jews led an old, peculiar and specially 'spicy' existence . . . a culture which has now been destroyed . . . Just as the embalmed mummy in a museum tells the tale of the civilization of ancient Egypt, so this book preserves the remains of an old and lovely culture." Generally, though, the reviewers weren't misreading Samuel's book, whose publication was a epochal moment in defining Sholem Aleichem—and the Eastern European Jewry he was increasingly identified with—for wartime and postwar American audiences.

The World of Sholom Aleichem mixed biography, cultural and historical background, and some retellings of Sholem Aleichem stories to create
a smooth, organic portrait of a writer Samuel presented as "the mirror
of Russian Jewry . . . Russian Jewry himself." Identifying him so firmly
with the folk meant, in turn, a concomitant emphasis on artlessness and
simplicity. "It is hard to think of him as a 'writer,' " Samuel wrote, a point
picked up on by the *Times*: "The fact is—Mr. Samuel stresses this point—
Sholom Aleichem was no professional writer," wrote the *Times* reviewer.
"He happened to write something, and it was liked." If, to Samuel, it
was hard to imagine Sholem Aleichem a writer, it was easy to see him as
a medium, seamlessly transmitting a now-vanishing world: he claimed
one "could write a *Middletown* of the Russian-Jewish Pale basing ourselves
solely on the novels and stories and sketches of Sholem Aleichem, and it
would be as reliable a scientific document as any 'actual' study; more so,
indeed, for we should get, in addition to the material of a straightforward
social inquiry, the intangible spirit which informs the material and gives
it its living significance." That "intangible spirit" not only replaces hard
work, craft, and talent with ineffable magic, but claims Sholem Aleichem
and his stories as a pure wellspring of authenticity, a channel to a vanished epoch.

Crucially for an American audience, that disappearance was framed as
a double dying: not only the result of Nazi depredation, but the simultaneous (if far less horrific) passing of the generation of Eastern European
immigrants, along with the growth of an American Jewish community
increasingly detached from their parents' and grandparents' culture.
Asserting that "some millions of American citizens" whose parents and
grandparents lived in Sholem Aleichem's world would find the subject of
his book "almost unknown," he remarks, "This is not simply a literary
loss; it is a break—a very recent and disastrous one—in the continuity of
a group history." The book, in many ways, thus marked a beginning of the
English-language Sholem Aleichem—and Yiddish—nostalgia industry:
it ends with Sholem Aleichem's massive funeral, imagining the throngs
mourning not the author, but the "part of their life which had been torn
away from them . . . saying the *Kaddish* in advance over their way of life,

for they knew that none would say it afterwards." Audaciously identifying those vanished immigrants with Sholem Aleichem's characters—"Tevyeh himself left his milk-cart at the corner of Intervale Avenue, and came with Goldie to say farewell to Sholom Aleichem"—Samuel began to create a Sholem Aleichem tethered to American concerns and anxieties, as our story of Sholem Aleichem's afterlife increasingly narrows to the United States.

Though the book achieved some attention, Sholem Aleichem was still a generally unknown quantity to the American literary industry; when the *Times* announced that "the first general selection of [Sholem Aleichem's] work to be published in English," *The Old Country*, would appear in 1946, they incorrectly noted that it was being timed by Crown to coincide with the author's 100th anniversary. The book's publication was delayed a month, and the reviewers in the major papers greeted it with relative indifference. Orville Prescott's *Times* review opened with the sentiment that "little [Yiddish literature] has been translated, and some of that little has proved of limited appeal," and, though presenting the author once again as a chronicler of old-country Jews who were "devout and honorable, simple in a timelessly provincial fashion and at the same time emotionally sophisticated," he ended by questioning the works' attractiveness for non-Yiddish readers. *The Washington Post* was similarly dismissive, calling the tales "interesting and colorful on a folk level, but scarcely the masterpieces they were thought to be by many of the author's contemporaries."

More positive reviewers had a reason, and, preemptively, offered a few excuses. In one startling review, the self-proclaimed Gentile William Barrett follows Samuel's line, praising Sholem Aleichem for his "direct relation between the writer and his audience," inaccurately noting that he was no "self-conscious writer, obsessed with the problems of his art or the tradition to which his works are to be inserted," and suggesting his true contribution was "what he reveals about a destiny that was to be played out outside the Pale." In addition to its value as memorial, he adds, is its worth as cautionary tale: "If this world has largely vanished, through slaughter or immigration, there is still on this side of the Atlantic an extraordinary persistence of some of the old patterns . . . For example, let me tell you, Mr. Sholom Aleichem, the story of the ten Jews on the *Harvard Law Review*." That's the reason: not art in itself, but useful in its own way.

The excuses are addressed in two essays, each remarkable in its own way, by two highly influential mid-twentieth-century Jewish writers: Ben Hecht, in the *Times*, and Isaac Rosenfeld, in *The New Republic*. Hecht also plays the elegiac card; "*The Old Country*," he writes, "is more than a book. It is the epitaph of a vanished world and an almost vanished people . . . massacred, six million strong, by the Germans." But despite his profound love for the book, he has his concerns about it: Sholem Aleichem's genius, he insists, "was the genius of idiom," and the book's necessary failure "is one which must befall anyone who touches the genius of Sholom Aleichem and tries to carry it into another tongue." (The translators, Julius and Frances Butwin, didn't disagree, discussing their extensive use of translators' license in the introduction.)

But it was more than just word choice. Rosenfeld, agreeing that "the quality of Sholom Aleichem's Yiddish . . . is well-nigh incommunicable," digs down for a deeper diagnosis. Brilliantly articulating a notion of translation that is, in its broadest sense, about allowing us to know another, he suggests that translating Sholem Aleichem is "a hard, hopeless, even tragic enterprise" because his "work is almost deliberately at cross purposes with English and with the history the language subsumes . . . The extraordinary poetic of Sholom Aleichem's Yiddish is its consciousness of what is peculiarly Jewish in existence . . . A turn of phrase, an additional syllable, and what would have been, as in any other language, a report of experience, becomes in Yiddish a comment on Jewish experience." If Sholem Aleichem's stories failed among English-language readers, Rosenfeld argued, it wasn't because of their limited nature, but because literature's greatest achievement, the opportunity to encounter a world deeply, was impossible to realize in any translation from Sholem Aleichem's Yiddish (and, perhaps, from Yiddish in general). How could what remained, elegy, or sepia-toned folk material, be enough?

Book-buying audiences didn't seem as concerned as the critics. They put *The Old Country* at number 8 on *The New York Times* best-seller list by mid-August; it stayed on the list for a month. Its success meant other translations would soon follow: a collection of Kasrilevke stories was published in 1948, and the following year Frances Butwin returned with a new, more focused volume of Sholem Aleichem tales. Though *The Old Country* had sampled a wide range of the author's output, incorporating holiday stories, children's stories, Kasrilevke tales, and others, Butwin had certainly noticed the reviewers' focus on one particular character. Prescott, the *Times* reviewer, had noted that Tevye was "a humorous triumph . . . his presence makes many of the other stories in 'The Old Country' seem insipid by comparison"; Rosenfeld had devoted much of his essay to portraying Tevye as a Sancho Panza to a kind of divine Don Quixote. Add to that the indifferent reviews to the Kasrilevke collection, and Crown's announcement toward the very end of 1948 that their new Sholem Aleichem collection would be called *Tevye's Daughters* seemed almost an inevitability. And the next chapter in Sholem Aleichem's story—the increasing focus on Tevye—would soon begin.

Scene 7

New York, 1949–1959

Frances Butwin, introducing *Tevye's Daughters*, characterized the collection's stories as "a part of the life, forever vanished, which Sholom Aleichem reproduced so faithfully, with tenderness, with humor and with sharp penetration, but never with malice or bitterness." Butwin's approach was by now becoming the received line for reading Sholem Aleichem—and, indeed, for considering the vanished world of Eastern European Jewry: the *Times*, tracing the tales' appeal to their warmth and wit, noted that they revealed, in the distance, "the movement and mutter of the outside world that was already stirring, not only to destroy this life, but also the people who lived it." Tevye—and Sholem Aleichem—were becoming seen as representatives of a national sensibility. "A folk-poet," Alexander Klein wrote in his *New Republic* review. "Sholom Aleichem forgoes complex individual characterization and explicitly tragic themes in favor of the spontaneous revelation and archetypal creation of folk-truth."

The precincts of folkdom, which are, almost by definition, vanished, halcyon, and simultaneously sacred and marginal, were increasingly seen as Sholem Aleichem's address. The year after *Tevye's Daughters* was published, the choreographer Sophie Maslow presented a work, "Festival," at the New York City Dance Theatre that, according to the *Times*, "captured the hearty and tender folk spirit of Sholom Aleichem's stories." The work, a part of a longer piece called *The Village I Knew*, would eventually include "a gentle and lyric Sabbath number" and "a closing 'Exodus' in which the community is uprooted by the authorities and driven from its home." Perhaps most interesting, looking back over sixty years later, is how those elements would be echoed in *Fiddler on the Roof*; but equally important was the insistence on Sholem Aleichem's work as folk material, inspiration for adaptive art—much as Maslow had done earlier with American folk material. This idea—Sholem Aleichem as Jewish folk drama, a suitable subject for music and dance—led once more to the prospect of integrating Tevye into this kind of material.

An English-language theatrical adaptation of *Tevye's Daughters* existed as early as October 1949; it had been done by the playwright Irving Elman, who had begun to package it—the actor Sam Jaffe had expressed interest, and Norman Bel Geddes was reportedly interested in producing. No contracts were signed, though, and by the end of the year even more exciting news emerged: Rodgers and Hammerstein had acquired an eleven-month option on Elman's script and hoped to do the show next fall. Rodgers and Hammerstein being Rodgers and Hammerstein, it would be a musical—set to folk music Elman had collected. Danny Kaye's name was bandied about for the lead; by the beginning of 1950, reports suggested that Menashe Skulnick would make his Broadway debut in *Tevye's Daughters*. "There's a likelihood," Rodgers told the press.

But the duo had taken on a number of projects, and though they had jokingly suggested that all their activity was "better than loafing in Miami—it's more fun," they couldn't get to everything at once, and as they left the country to attend the London premiere of *Carousel*, there was still no word as to whether *Tevye's Daughters* would be one of their projects for the next season. It wasn't. By July, the word came that Rodgers and Hammerstein would be putting their efforts into another musical for the 1950–1951 season—a musical adaptation of *Anna and the King of Siam* called *The King and I*—and they allowed their option to expire. It was duly purchased by Mike Todd (probably best known today as Elizabeth Taylor's third husband), who had raised the hundred thousand dollars to begin production within a month of picking up the option. The *Times* reported that he would simply finish a television special he was working on, then begin. He didn't. Tevye would not appear on a New York stage in English for another seven years, and then in prose. But Sholem Aleichem would be the talk of the English-language theater world well before that.

In April 1953, a notice informed *New York Times* readers that Howard Da Silva, who had committed three of Sholem Aleichem's stories to record three years before, would play the role of Mendele, "the fabled bookseller," in a "Sholem Aleichem work," for a three-week theatrical run. The few knowledgeable readers aware that Mendele was an entirely different author's creation were right to be skeptical of the work's precise identity. Of the three skits by Arnold Perl that composed the evening, only one was a straightforward Sholem Aleichem adaptation—"High School," the tale of a couple's extensive efforts to get their child admitted to a restricted school, and, following their success, his walkout from that school, impelled by revolutionary sentiment. A second, though clearly based on Sholem Aleichem's "The Enchanted Tailor," transforms its befuddled protagonist into a citizen of Chelm, the fools' town of Jewish folklore, incorporating other comic material associated with that locale; and the third, "Bontshe the Silent," about a poor, downtrodden man brought before the Heavenly Judge after a lifetime of silence and suffering, is another author's creation entirely: it's a Peretz story. "Mendele" served as a frame character, introducing the disparate pieces and providing the third "classic" Yiddish writer some representation in the bargain, creating an organic unity for those with the knowledge to realize it.

The World of Sholom Aleichem's three-week trial run at Manhattan's Barbizon-Plaza Theater in early May was sufficiently popular to allow a return that fall for the opening of the 1953–1954 season. To stir up interest during the run, the actors had read Sholem Aleichem's will to honor the anniversary of his death: another feature attracting some notice was that a young Ruby Dee integrated the cast, playing a non-race-specific role— extremely rare for the time—an angel in "Bontshe'"s heavenly host. The show reopened at the Barbizon-Plaza on September 11, 1953, heralded by ads featuring Ben Shahn's drawing of a rabbi and a goat ("A goat was a matter of family prestige," the artist reported), for a planned seven-week engagement. That was before the reviews came out.

Brooks Atkinson, who had panned Tevye's cinematic excursion a decade and a half before, not only raved that the three mini-plays "Arnold Perl has culled out of Jewish lore are original and beautiful, and . . . are acted with remarkable sensibility," but claimed in a separate feature that these works were not "rootless make-believe," but the pure expression of folk sensibility, a practically unaltered link to a vanished place and time. Atkinson was smart enough to know the play was based on literature, not folklore; but smart enough, too, to know that the particular nature of Perl and Da Silva's success was to turn these literary efforts into "Jewish lore" for an audience that craved it. Not everyone, though, thought this was such an achievement, and thus the war over Sholem Aleichem's legacy in English-language America would begin in earnest.

Midge Decter had suspected she wouldn't like *The World of Sholom Aleichem* even before she saw it, based on Atkinson's review; but once she *had* seen it, she wrote the *Times*, she felt his "totally unwarranted praise" bespoke his—and the play's—"almost total misunderstanding" of the subject. The literature that served as the play's source, she wrote, "is very far from being 'folk,' 'devout,' or 'simple' or any of the other sweet and virtuous things your critic and others so much want it to be. It is highly complex, sophisticated with the sophistication of the aged (not the ages) and ambiguous." Decter expanded on her argument in a *Commentary* article, where she put her opposition to the play in particularly contemporary context. First, she argued, Perl and Da Silva's attempts "to quell every possible deviation from a single tone and range of gesture" were done in the service of creating "just the kind of Never-Never Land American Jews like to think they come from, quaint, not quite respectable, but abounding with a special sweetness," turning the Pale of Settlement into "a sort of spoken folk dance." The folklorization of Sholem Aleichem and his world, that is, was a response to deep-seated American Jewish desires and neuroses.

But she had a second argument, too, one that would reverberate beneath the next phase of Tevye's adventures and in some part condition many of the choices made in his adaptation. Writing that "the ghetto has always lent itself to ideological use," Decter portrayed *The World of Sholom Aleichem* as an ideological broadside: the manipulation of the past in the hands of left-wing progressives. No coincidence, she wrote, that "High School" ends with a long speech and a repeated injunction to "Strike!": "Somehow that 'Strike!' is a necessary and inevitable finale. One waits through most of the evening for it to happen." Necessary and inevitable, she insinuates, given the backgrounds of Da Silva and his company: though she limits her comments to the fact that their "political careers have left them in an acute state of professional embarrassment," her meaning's clear. Da Silva, an alumnus of the Group Theatre and a member of the famed production of *The Cradle Will Rock* during the Depression, had been blacklisted for his communist affiliations as a result of the House Committee on Un-American Activities hearings; in fact, a number of the cast members, including Jack Gilford and Will Lee (who would go on to eternal fame, if not celebrity, among my generation by playing Mr. Hooper on *Sesame Street*), had suffered a similar fate.

Decter claimed that these left-leaning types, who had somehow established "a private monopoly" over "the enterprise of folk production," have never managed to "subdue or to disguise the reprehensible politics that spark it—even in their most innocent of products." Looking at the show from over half a century's distance, Decter's argument seems overstated but not entirely flawed. The selection of "High School" out of so many Sholem Aleichem stories does seem a little less than arbitrary, and "Bontshe the Silent," whose twist ending—when granted the opportunity to ask for anything in heaven and earth as a reward for his uncomplaining suffering, he asks for a roll and fresh butter—is, in both story and adaptation, treated as savagely ironic, illustrating the disintegrating nature of mute complacence and calling for social (and socialist) activism. The same "Strike!" that Decter criticized, this time rendered through a folkloric lens.

But that folkloric lens obscures as much as reveals: subtext can be difficult to discern onstage, perhaps even more so than on the page. "Bontshe" has been misread on occasion as a paean to the virtue of martyrdom, of the suffering, persecuted silent—and in 1953, who could doubt that the Eastern European Jewish folk had suffered?—rather than a caustic evaluation of revolutionary opportunity denied. Theatergoers could mistake, or ignore, the subtext in "Bontshe," laugh at the antics of the Chelm teacher (himself transformed, in this version, from a tailor), and take the whole as a fulfillment of their desires for folk simplicity, mixed with their sentiment for reverent elegy. And that seems to be what happened: at least, it's likely that the reason the show was a hit had more to do with middle-class theatergoer acceptance than with the discovery of ideological kinship.

And it *was* a hit show. A later production had to be postponed to accommodate the play's run; a letter writer complained the management was selling seats at orchestra prices of $1.80 ($14.50 in 2010 dollars) for disguised standing-room-only tickets; the management built risers to meet the increased demand. A Chicago company opened in February 1954 at the city's Eleventh Street Theater, starring the Yiddish and English-language actor Jacob Ben-Ami; it, too, would be forced to extend its run.

A week after the Chicago opening, the New York company celebrated its 200th performance—at the time an eternity in off-Broadway circles. It finally closed in late May, after 306 performances—not bad for a work originally scheduled to perform one-fifteenth that many. There would be a Philadelphia run and a London run as 1954 turned into 1955; Ben-Ami would play Los Angeles in 1956.

As *The World of Sholom Aleichem*'s reach and reputation grew, others took up Decter's warnings. Uriel Weinreich, reviewing a newly released anthology of Yiddish literature, cautioned that the general American reader may often be "misled by frequent ill-informed descriptions of this literature as exclusively 'folk' in character" and blamed a climate in which "sentimentality or condescension pass for evaluation." But the tide was against them. Two years later, an announcement of a Sholem Aleichem anthology from the Modern Library described the author's "love and wisdom and skill" and the author himself as "a simple, wise man without hate and with God knows what patience"; a review of a new translation of Sholem Aleichem's autobiography in *The New Republic* (under the title "The World of Sholom Aleichem," no less), established the author as a Christ figure for Eastern European Jewry, who "loved his people, who knew their failings and their greatness and pretensions and struggles and heroisms, who laughed with them and sighed with them and cried with them and exulted with them and was terror stricken with them and was eternally fascinated with their every nuance of meeting whatever life had to offer them in their two thousand years of wandering across the face of the earth."

The team responsible for a good amount of that popular sentimentality had naturally been thinking about a follow-up: and, given their interest in mixing politics and sentimentality, there was an obvious candidate. Hadn't Tevye had a revolutionary daughter, after all? And so, when Perl and Da Silva's company, Banner Productions, booked the Carnegie Hall Playhouse for the 1957–1958 season, probably the most anticipated offering wasn't the children's theater on the weekends, the staged readings of work in progress by emerging playwrights on Monday evenings, or even the midnight variety shows Friday and Saturday night, including "The Best of Burlesque": it was the duo's collaboration on a dramatization of Sholem Aleichem's Tevye stories.

The previous Tevye adaptations—including Sholem Aleichem's own, as we've seen—had increasingly narrowed their focus to the Chava story, as the central fulcrum of Tevye's journey. Perl and Da Silva went another way. The two-act version of *Tevya and His Daughters* that opened at 7:45 p.m. on September 16 devoted its first half to Tevya's transformation into a dairyman and to Tsaytl's marriage, and its second to Hodl. Hodl's— and Tevya's—encounter with the appeals of revolution, then, became the evening's dramatic climax. (*The Christian Science Monitor*, in its review, archly noted that the "polemical conversations between Tevya and the idealistic Pertchik strike an ironically hollow note in view of the fact that anti-Semitism in Russia did not end with the fall of the Czar—a fact that starry-eyed revolutionaries and misty-eyed propagandists cannot admit.") While hardly shying away from the political dimension, Perl and Da Silva embraced the folklike and sentimental dimensions of the Tevye story with both arms: perhaps as a hedge against political criticism, perhaps playing to the audience, perhaps because the approach genuinely resonated with them, probably some combination of the three.

Sentimentality, though, was just as constricting an aesthetic approach as polemic, and Brooks Atkinson, who had genuinely enjoyed *The World of Sholom Aleichem*, was less enchanted with *Tevya*. His review began "Tevya, the dairyman, is a wise and lovable man who enjoys a remarkably personal relationship to God. But to judge by Arnold Perl's 'Tevya and His Daughters,' acted at Carnegie Hall Playhouse last evening, Tevya still needs to be enclosed in a play." He thought the play needed "form and movement" to create greater coherence and to "keep Tevya from drowning his character in words"; in a follow-up article a week and a half later, he advised a more stylized approach. "There must be a way," he wrote, "to make Tevya, his favorite child, live as vividly on the stage as, by all accounts, he does in the Yiddish stories. Realism in acting, the most worn of the theater's styles, cannot cope with Tevya's whimsical garrulity."

Perl and Da Silva didn't pay much attention. They had their hands full: at least in part due to the lukewarm reviews, *Tevya* was forced to close a week earlier than expected, and they needed a new tenant for the playhouse. When the dust cleared, they returned to their earlier, successful version of Sholem Aleichem, this time in a new medium.

Though Sholem Aleichem's work had gone out over the airwaves at least once before ("Home for Passover," aired on NBC in 1955 in a program produced by the Jewish Theological Seminary, used the titular story to teach "the meaning of the Passover ceremony"), *The Wonderful World of Sholom Aleichem*, as it was now known, brought the big stars to the small screen. Sam Levene, who'd originated the role of Nathan Detroit in *Guys and Dolls*, and Gertrude Berg, the star of the early hit television program *The Goldbergs*, played the parents in "High School"; the show was produced on tape by David Susskind, a giant of early television, and aired for seven days in December 1959. In introducing the show, Morris Carnovsky announced to the camera that "the world of Sholem Aleichem is everybody's world" and that "he was a man who loved people," making it perfectly clear what message the show was going to send.

Two other casting changes were noteworthy. The first, Ruby Dee's disappearance from the call sheet, spoke to the distance the medium still had to go in order to fulfill the show's promise of "gentle beauty, compassion, and social protest." The second was the appearance of Zero Mostel, one of several blacklisted actors to appear in the production, who'd recently begun climbing back into work via an Obie-winning performance in *Ulysses in Nighttown*. Atkinson, surprised to find the play more moving on television than onstage, praised Mostel as "a lyrical buffoon, prancing foolishly through the landscape."

Forces were beginning to align. A stylized version of Sholem Aleichem's Tevye, which lifted his stage presence out of exhausting loquaciousness; the free representation of Sholem Aleichem's work as folkloric memorial; Mostel's bravura performance in a Sholem Aleichem–inspired work. As the taped television show reran, to more plaudits and recognition; as Da Silva toured in a one-man *Evening with Sholem Aleichem*; as Mostel moved from strength to strength, achieving full-fledged Broadway stardom with Tony Awards for *Rhinoceros* and *A Funny Thing Happened on the Way to the Forum*; as the international literary and Yiddish community celebrated the centennial of Sholem Aleichem's birth, with Israeli stamps and Russian translations (Irving Howe keeping up the alarm, warning that Sholem Aleichem "needs to be rescued from his reputation, from the quavering sentimentality which keeps him at a safe distance"); as Maurice Schwartz, attempting to establish a center for Yiddish arts in Tel Aviv, died of a heart attack, a composer and lyricist best known for their musical about an Italian-American mayor and a book writer whose greatest success to date had been a show about Amish farmers in Pennsylvania called *Plain and Fancy* were going to take Atkinson up on his suggestions.

Scene 8

New York, 1962–1964

S heldon Harnick and Jerry Bock, lyricist and composer of the Tony Award– and Pulitzer Prize–winning musical about New York City's indomitable, diminutive mayor, were used to taking on unlikely projects. And *Fiorello!* had been an obvious Broadway choice compared to *Plain and Fancy*. But both had been successes—*Plain and Fancy* had run over four hundred performances, *Fiorello!* close to eight hundred—and at least Sholem Aleichem had a bit of a track record, with that off-Broadway success. The creative team worried; maybe the show was too Jewish for Broadway. But they persevered, cheered by producer Fred Coe's interest; anyone who'd had a hit like *A Thousand Clowns* on Broadway and was producing an Elaine May play starring Mike Nichols, the toasts of the theater scene, was bound to see it through to success. In August 1962, Coe predicted *Tevye* would debut in fall 1963; Joseph Stein, tasked with writing the book, pored through the Crown anthologies for material and inspiration.

But as summer turned to fall, trouble appeared in the form of Irving Elman, who'd planned his own Tevye musical over a decade before and still intended to mount it, complete with folk tunes. He claimed that *Tevye's Daughters*—whose title he'd changed to *As Long as You're Healthy*—would make an off-Broadway bow the same season as *Tevye*. Legal wrangling ensued. According to lawyers for Sholem Aleichem's estate, Elman's rights to use the material had expired long before. Elman countered he was using the Yiddish originals, which were in the public domain, along with the rest of the author's literary product; the estate strenuously denied *that*. And thus it went, for the best part of a year; by August 1963, not much had changed, other than Elman's title. Now it was *Sweet and Sour*.

Coe engineered a shattering one-two punch, though. First, he landed one of the hottest choreographer-directors in show business, Jerome Robbins, to direct his Tevye version; in an interview about the show, Robbins name-dropped his two monster hits, explaining that there "would be more dancing than in 'Gypsy' and less than in 'West Side Story.'" Several months later, in early 1964, came the second blow: the news that the producer was bringing on Harold Prince, the young über-producer who'd been involved with *West Side Story, The Pajama Game, Damn Yankees, A Funny Thing Happened on the Way to the Forum,* and *She Loves Me*, to share producing chores. Oh, and by March they had made a title change of their own: *Tevye* would now be known as *Fiddler on the Roof*. This was about as pedigreed as you could get, and the money followed: investors ponied up $375,000 (about $2.65 million in 2010 dollars). The show began rehearsing in June, with plans for an out-of-town debut in Detroit in July; seven weeks on the road before coming into New York in late September.

Not everything ran smoothly. During rehearsals, Robbins battled with Mostel over how broad his performance should be. (There was some subtext there: Robbins had named names to the House Committee on Un-American Activities, and Mostel, victim of the blacklist, had refused to socialize with his director when they worked together on *Forum*.) To make matters worse, Fred Coe withdrew as co-producer (though he kept a piece of the show), leaving sole duties to Prince. Not the kind of thing you want to hear about as an investor a month before your out-of-town opening. To make matters worse, a newspaper strike and heat wave in Detroit cut into promotional opportunities and seriously affected sales; and perhaps worst of all the out-of-town critics were lukewarm. *Variety*, damning it with faint praise, opined, "May have a chance for a moderate success . . . No smash hit, no blockbuster," and the *Chicago Tribune*, attacking its "clumsy symbols," "ridiculous ghost ballet," and "ineffective *Mother Courage* ending on a turntable," asserted that "the show is in trouble from title to ending." It did, however, rave about the performance of the show's lead, Zero Mostel.

Mostel, for his part, overheard two Grosse Pointe matrons whispering to each other, "I wonder how the Jews will take it?"—an additional anxiety that had haunted the show's creators since the beginning. Mostel himself had worried about the show's being too Jewish from the first time he'd read the book and heard the score; Harnick would later describe himself as "running scared" most of the time because he thought it might be too Jewish (and too serious, and too long). But not everyone shared their concerns. Seeing the show in Detroit, Sister Mary Immaculate, the executive secretary and treasurer of the National Catholic Theater Conference, immediately ordered a houseful of seats for the group's New York convention—the following summer. Asked by the box office about her act of faith—who knew if the show would run that long?—she replied, "I think it'll run forever . . . It's the most catholic—small 'c'—show I ever saw."

Sister Mary's suggestion—reformulated by Joseph Stein several years later as the credo "This isn't a play about Jewish people, it's a play about people who happen to be Jewish"—would come to be echoed by a wide variety of individuals involved with *Fiddler* over the decades and continents. But it should be noted that, in those original months and years, that universality was hard-won through a deep enough emphasis on the particulars to generate this kind of anxiety. Jerome Robbins, who would later call *Fiddler* "a celebration of my father's life and background—a thank-you note for my Jewish heritage," insisted that the company attend a series of Jewish weddings and immersed himself in Jewish books: in an interview shortly after the musical's premiere, he cast his involvement in the show as a kind of Jewish cultural return, while making it clear the religious aspect of Judaism held little appeal for him. In this, as it transpired, he and much of his American Jewish audience would be a perfect match.

But simultaneously, of course, Robbins pushed the team to search for the deep, universal themes within the stories. In adapting Sholem Aleichem, Stein fulfilled Rosenfeld's dictum of translation in reverse: instead of forcing individuals to come to terms with the deep difference of the original Tevye material, he altered the material to resonate with the audience, replacing specific phrases or customs with others less "bewildering" or "melodramatic" for contemporary theatergoers. More, he worked to establish an "over-all focus or point of view" necessary for a coherent dramatic production, which he would define several years later as the "breakdown of traditional cultural forms and beliefs of 'the shtetl,' the village community, under the buffeting of social change and hostile forces, finally leading to disintegration of that society."

Mindful, naturally, that this would be something of a downer, Stein also understood the play needed to "point up the internal strength, the dignity, the humor of that people and, like minorities today, their unique talent for survival." In doing so, it echoed another major theatrical success about Jewish strength and dignity under persecution from less than a decade earlier (though of course without the survival): the Tony Award–winning *Diary of Anne Frank*, with its famous emphasis on Frank's (somewhat bowdlerized) insistence that despite it all she believed people were good at heart. Weaving together the now conventional post-Holocaust presentation of Eastern European Jewry as sentimental, noble, and perhaps somewhat childlike, and addressing a general, universal formulation of nostalgic tradition in the face of radical, threatening change was an effective thematic strategy. And it was one that spoke to the time— Stein's side point about "minorities today" was reported in a Los Angeles paper less than a year after the Watts riots tore the city apart and spoke to the complexities of the national conversation on race; *Fiddler* premiered half a year after the Beatles played *The Ed Sullivan Show*, on which Sam Levene had performed a selection from *The World of Sholom Aleichem* a few years before. *Fiddler* was a creature of the sixties, not just the American Jewish sixties; and its universal message about the precariousness of balancing tradition and unruly change, taken in a variety of ways, was bound to resonate with the theatergoing audience.

And, judging from the box office receipts, it certainly did.

It was people like Sister Mary Immaculate—the bookers for the theater parties, the bundlers of mail orders—that swept *Fiddler* into town on wings of cash. By the day after its premiere, Prince estimated they had taken in an advance sale of $650,000, close to double their production cost (it had actually ended up costing $380,000; Prince had personally covered the overage), with reservations made by over fifty theater parties. And those numbers probably weren't counting the double line of three hundred ticket seekers clamoring at the theater box office. (The production kindly kept them hydrated with iced tea from a nearby restaurant.) Ticket brokers were apoplectically demanding seats for their usuals.

They had all, presumably, read the reviews. The *Times* critic prefaced his few criticisms with the caution that he only offered them "because 'Fiddler on the Roof' is so fine that it deserves counsels towards perfection" and that *Fiddler* helped Broadway musicals "take up the mantle of meaningfulness worn so carelessly by the American drama in recent years." And naturally, the show's authenticity, its "honest feeling for another place, time and people" came in for particular praise. The *Tribune*'s critic, who began her review by apologizing for being out of town when the show premiered, went even further (perhaps in penance for her paper's earlier negative review), creating a word picture of the audience: "All about me in that crowded theater were the older folk who did remember, come with their children and grandchildren, murmuring recognition. Having lived the originals, they know that the stories are not wise-cracks, not bright sayings of the beleaguered. They are stories created of knowledge and desperation and a dogged devotion, along with humor and the strength of acceptance that bends without breaking." The theme—that the play's human meaning was precisely concretized in its ability to authentically sum up Jewish history and dignity—was, in a generally perceptive *Times* piece by Brooks Atkinson, expanded to the work of its creative inspiration, with praise for Sholem Aleichem's "artful simplicity."

Atkinson might well have felt more comfortable, even licensed, to connect *Fiddler*'s new-won seal of authentic approval to Sholem Aleichem's ever more firmly established reputation as a pure representative of the folk by an article that had appeared in his own paper just days before, by an undisputed (if, perhaps, not indisputable) symbol of Jewish authenticity: Isaac Bashevis Singer. Singer's flourishing literary career in English over the previous decade had been tied to his identification, by himself and others, as a voice who could speak for the vanished, murdered Yiddish population and who often did so—in English, at least—by presenting them as representatives of a culture of particular morality and virtue. Singer, asked by the *Times* for "an appraisal of Sholem Aleichem and his beloved Tevye," damned his fellow Yiddish author with faint praise by adopting him as "spokesman for a people," "a genius [who could] think and feel just like an average man." Though Sholem Aleichem's son-in-law B. Z. Goldberg rose to the challenge, claiming Singer had bypassed "the greater depth and deeper meaning" of Sholem Aleichem's work (and echoing in passing an often-begrudging consensus in the Yiddish press that Singer was "an author preoccupied with sex pathology"), the number of people who read the letters section, or cared for Goldberg's message, were few.

But that message was, at least, the premise of one of the few dissenting voices. Irving Howe, in a fiercely negative review in *Commentary*, suggested *Fiddler* reflected "the spiritual anemia of Broadway and of the middle-class Jewish world which by now seems firmly linked to Broadway. Sholem Aleichem is deprived of his voice, his pace, his humane cleverness and boxed into the formula of a post-*Oklahoma* musical: the gags,

the folksy bounce, the archness, the 'dream sequences,' the fiercely ath-
letic dances." Though he praised Mostel's genius—perhaps the one universal note in all the *Fiddler* coverage—he felt even Mostel, and certainly
the creative team, was caught by Broadway's relentless gravitational
pull, "the pressure to twist everything into the gross, the sentimental,
the mammoth, and the blatant," which inevitably led to condescending,
"softened and sweetened version[s]" of their subject material. Like Decter before him, Howe also put some of the blame on American Jewry,
guilt-ridden for losing touch with their own history, then compounding
that guilt (and attempting to expiate it) "by indulging themselves in an
unearned nostalgia." Resignedly, Howe noted that "the kind of criticism
I have written serves little purpose. Those who can be persuaded must
already know, while those who cannot will be crowding the box office for
months to come." And that, of course, was inarguable.

Looking back a half century later, Howe seems to have the better of
the argument: it's much, much easier to see *Fiddler* as an authentic expression of the midcentury Broadway musical than of the actual world of the
actual Sholem Aleichem. Not only that, it's easy to see the play touching
on many of the period's intellectual and social anxieties: besides those
mentioned above, the emphasis on women's intellectualism, particularly
their reading habits—"You were reading again?" Golde asks Chava;
"Why does a girl have to read?"—took on special resonance in the age
of *The Feminine Mystique*, published the previous year. And Yente's warning about Motel and Tzeitel playing together—"From such children,
come other children"—seems more reflective of contemporary anxieties
about juvenile delinquency and "girls in trouble" rather than of a desire
to evoke shtetl living (though, of course, unwed motherhood was far from
unknown there, too).

But, at this distance, *Fiddler* also seems deeply saturated with the
memory of the Holocaust, perhaps inflected through an extremely recent
event: the Eichmann trial, which had concluded just two years before. The
pogrom that interrupts Tzeitel's wedding to end the first act is preceded
by the Constable's insistence on his "orders," an insistence expanded on

in the musical's second half, when the Constable informs Tevye the Jews must leave their village:

> CONSTABLE. I have an order here, and it says you must sell your homes and be out of here in three days . . .
> TEVYE. And you who have known us all your life, you'd carry out this order?
> CONSTABLE. I have nothing to do with it, don't you understand?
> TEVYE. (*Bitterly*) We understand.

We—and the audiences then—could clearly hear the echoes of Eichmann's claim: only following orders. These actions are clearly juxtaposed with the musical's emphasis on Tevye's capacity to break an agreement—that is, not to follow the orders established through contract—when morality, his daughters' happiness, is threatened. At Tzeitel's wedding, Lazar Wolf, disruptively, shouts, "Why should I listen to you? A man who breaks an agreement!" But it's precisely because Tevye, who has previously explained to Tzeitel that "with us an agreement is an agreement," *has* broken it that he should be listened to: he understands when such things need to be broken.

If this trading of love for law sounds a wee bit Christian, that's probably not unintentional: it was standard practice in mid-twentieth-century American Jewish culture, from Anne Frank's Broadway legacy to Singer's "Gimpel the Fool" to Malamud's *The Assistant*, to clothe Jewish victimhood in explicit or implicit Christian tropes and imagery—it was, after all, the currency of the majority culture. Tevye's explicit rejection of an Old Testamental strategy to armed resistance against the expulsions— "FIRST MAN. We should defend ourselves. An eye for an eye, a tooth for a tooth. TEVYE. Very good. And that way, the whole world will be blind and toothless"—is thus as much about presenting him as an ideal suffering servant for general American, Christian sympathies as about putting him in line with the martyr-victims of Nazi camps and ghettoes.

The musical's portrait of the banality of non-Jewish evil—after all, these characters were presented not as Nazis, but as Gentiles more generally—had to be balanced, for both philosophical and commercial reasons, with positive depictions of non-Jewish characters. This intriguingly allowed for a return to a different sort of tradition: renewing the focus on Chava as a major character in the Tevye drama. Doing so, first, helped sideline Perchik and his problematic politics. Though he displays his old fire in *Fiddler*, calling the rich criminals and arguing that "money is the world's curse," Perchik is, to use Howe's phrasing, softened and sweetened: he becomes first and foremost another Motel, a champion of romantic love, and an endearingly awkward one at that. Attempting his proposal to Hodl, he stammers that it is "a political question . . . in a theoretical sense, yes. The relationship between a man and woman known as marriage is based on mutual beliefs, a common attitude and philosophy towards society"—by which point we've discounted the content, identifying him as another egghead brought low by a pretty girl. True, the phrase "He's a radical!" appears in *Fiddler*; but the "he" in question is Tevye and the radicalism is love, which goes to show you the show's studious domestication of the political.

At least in the narrowly defined sense of the word. Because in terms of Jewish and non-Jewish relations in America, the politics were revolutionary. Balancing out the banally evil Constable is the ethically superior Fyedka, who acts, in many ways, as the musical's moral tutor. Best known, in this respect, is the episode toward the show's end, where Chava and Fyedka make their final appearance: having no intention, once married, of dissolving the marriage, they announce their plan to go into exile as well, because, as Fyedka says, "We cannot stay among people who can do such things to others." When Tevye fails to respond, Fyedka's next line, "Some are driven away by edicts, others by silence," not only prompts Tevye to tell Tzeitel to bless them, but, audaciously, presents Tevye as the moral equivalent of the expellers, shifting the Christlike mantle for the moment to Fyedka and Chava, who are willing to voluntarily enter a world of pain and suffering for the sake of others. But less frequently considered, perhaps, is Chava and Fyedka's *first* encounter. Fyedka offers Chava a book to borrow, and, when she demurs, asks her:

FYEDKA. Why? Because I'm not Jewish? Do you feel about us the way they feel about you? I didn't think you would. And what do you know about me? Let me tell you about myself. I'm a pleasant fellow, charming, honest, ambitious, quite bright, and very modest.

CHAVA. I don't think we should be talking this way.

FYEDKA. I often do things I shouldn't. Go ahead, take the book. It's by Heinrich Heine. Happens to be Jewish, I believe.

CHAVA. That doesn't matter.

FYEDKA. You're quite right. (*She takes the book.*) Good . . .

If *Fiddler*'s Tevye at times evinces an appeal that transcends his Jewishness to reach broader, Christian horizons, Fyedka does the reverse: he's not only expressing universal sentiments here, but a kind of philo-Semitism that's almost Jewish in its dimensions. (That one-liner of his, for example, sounds a little to me like young Woody Allen; the whole thing, for that matter, is a little like the pickups Allen would satirically and affectionately chronicle in stand-up routines and early films.) Fyedka is Christian, of course; and the show's liberal, universalist perspectives on intermarriage had everything to do with serving up a softball to American audiences, Jewish and non-Jewish, in the mid-1960s, increasingly comfortable with such a choice and increasingly uncomfortable with explicit opposition to it. But it didn't hurt that the suggested match was carefully structured to feel as if it participated in what we might call the "Lenny Bruce phenomenon": that certain parts of American culture were increasingly seeming Jewish, even if they weren't. *Fiddler* was a vital part of the Judaizing of American culture, and Fyedka's portrayal was an important component of that process.

There's a surprising emphasis, in the musical, on Motel's new sewing machine. On a surface level, the rhythms of industrialization were clear stand-ins for the dissolution of traditional life explicitly played out in the show's romantic elements: it's not coincidental that the sewing machine arrives in town during the very same scene that Chava tells Tevye she and Fyedka want to marry. But for an American Jewish audience, many of whom had parents or grandparents in the needle trades, the sewing machine was emblematic of a particularly American, specifically Lower East Side, experience: and the creators' decision to send Tevye to America at play's end, rather than to Israel or an undefined destination, confirmed that Tevye's story was becoming intertwined with the great American one. Tevye the dairyman was, in the end, Tevye the proto-immigrant, and his daughter's relationship, increasingly, was looking like America.

Scene 9

Everywhere, 1964–2005

Tevye's fantasy of being a rich man was, for the show's producers, investors, and stars, a fantasy no longer. Prince, who received 50 percent of the show's profit along with a managerial fee of 1 percent of the gross—plus expenses—did particularly well, though Robbins, Stein, Bock, Harnick, and Mostel all had revenue-sharing arrangements of varying sorts. Mostel's arrangement, which included a 2 percent royalty from the cast album, illustrated how the Broadway production, profitable as it was, was the tail that wagged the dog. By *Fiddler*'s third anniversary, the album had sold more original cast albums for RCA Victor than any other Broadway musical the company had recorded to date—at least a million dollars' worth—and the movie rights had been sold to United Artists for $2 million.

And then there were the touring companies and international productions. A week before *Fiddler* dominated the Tonys, winning nine (besides best musical, the winners were Mostel; Robbins twice, for choreography and direction; Maria Karnilova, who played Golde; Prince; Stein; Bock; Harnick; and Patricia Zipprodt, for costumes), a Hebrew-language production opened in Tel Aviv's Alhambra Theater, with Prime Minister Levi Eshkol in attendance. (Several months later, a kerfuffle ensued when the production's first Tevye, a thirty-six-year-old Israeli-born comedian named Bomba Zur, was replaced with the sixty-year-old Ukrainian-born Shmuel Rudensky; the Israeli reviewers, who had once characterized the play as "drowned in shmaltz" and a "banal travesty," began arguing that it was a serious work of theater. Israel, obviously, had its own debates over the meaning of authenticity.) The production would run for well over a year and be seen by over half a million people; as soon as it closed, the cast would mount a Yiddish version.

Interest in Sholem Aleichem in the Jewish state was, of course, hardly surprising. Even those who had claimed that the Zionist idea had involved *shelilat ha-galut*, "negation of the Diaspora," had hardly dismissed Diasporic culture in all its aspects, from the "national poet" Bialik outward. While the play was breaking records on Broadway, members of the cast and crew received awards from the Israel Histadrut campaign as part of fundraising efforts to build an archive for Sholem Aleichem's papers in Tel Aviv; two trunks' worth of materials would eventually be shipped from the vaults of the Irving Trust Company at 1 Wall Street, and Sholem Aleichem House would be dedicated in May 1966. At the dedication, Israel's president, Zalman Shazar, announced 1966 would be a nationwide year of Sholem Aleichem. But, as in America, *Fiddler*'s appeal far transcended any Jewish audience base. Within five years of the musical's debut, productions appeared in Helsinki, Amsterdam, Copenhagen, Melbourne, London, Oslo, West Berlin, Prague, and Tokyo (the last under the title *Yane No Ue Violin Hikki*). A particularly meaningful—and fraught—production opened in Vienna in February 1969, starring an actress who'd fled the city for Palestine after Hitler occupied it in 1938; she returned to a city whose Jewish population was a twentieth of what it had then been. The Shoah was on everyone's mind. A Viennese critic "anxiously put the question to myself whether it was permissible after the Holocaust to play such a comparatively harmless tragedy. But," he replied, echoing Stein, "the question can be answered in the affirmative. Today's Anatevka is anywhere in the world where minorities are persecuted."

Readers today might feel a bit uncomfortable with an Austrian critic's dismissal of a specifically Holocaust-related orientation—should that answer be *quite* so affirmative?—but the answer unquestionably reflected a now international consensus about *Fiddler*'s universality. Several months later, a production of *Fiddler* opened in Ankara; explaining the musical's appeal in a country 98 percent Muslim, the *Times* wrote, "Many themes such as the conflict over tradition and the oppression of a minority will strike a familiar note here." Sholem Aleichem's creation was becoming both a free-floating symbol, an Everylens for talking about universal challenges to tradition and of persecution, and simultaneously a specific, sacred form of Jewish identity, unchangeable writ.

After seeing the musical's 1,259th New York performance in 1967, theater critic Clive Barnes noted, "It is a classic. A living, breathing classic. To criticize it would be like criticizing motherhood, and, like motherhood, it's here to stay." Two and a half years later, he confirmed the sentiment: "Musicals come and go—often with an alarming frequency—but 'Fiddler on the Roof' seems to play on forever." The musical's seemingly inexhaustible legs—by the summer of 1971, approaching its eighth year, it blew by *Hello, Dolly!* to become the longest-running musical in Broadway history to date, providing a 927 percent return to investors—along with its many incarnations meant that by that point an estimated 35 million people had seen the show. For many of them, *Fiddler* served as their first, and perhaps only, encounter with Jewish history and culture, locking in an image of Jewish life and fate; for others, the show's record of success and its not insignificant artistic appeal would help shape and interpret their other impressions of Jewish culture and the people who created it. It was so strong, that is, that it would resist other efforts to redefine its subject.

At least, that's one way of explaining Norman Jewison's movie.

Jewison, a deeply talented filmmaker (often, for understandable reasons, incorrectly taken for Jewish; he's Methodist), had been riding high over the previous half decade. His work with Steve McQueen on 1965's *The Cincinnati Kid* and 1968's *The Thomas Crown Affair*, his satirical bite in 1966's *The Russians Are Coming, the Russians Are Coming*, and particularly his searingly and unusually nuanced approach to questions of race in America in 1967's Oscar-winning *In the Heat of the Night*—which marked his first nomination for best director—had demonstrated his gift for putting an individual artist's stamp on a multitude of settings and genres. So hearing he was immersing himself in the study of Jewish history and culture at YIVO and meeting with rabbis in Israel to prepare to take on *Fiddler*'s directorial reins was unalloyed good news to film lovers.

The $9 million production (about $50 million in 2010 dollars) filmed interiors in England's Pinewood Studios; Anatevka was played by the village of Lekenik, in the Yugoslav countryside outside of Zagreb. Leonard Frey, who played Motel, told the *Times* the location "got to be like a prison" and that by the third week "you had to have lists of who was talking to who," but, he allowed, "there's something special about 'Fiddler.'" What precisely that specialness was was articulated by the great Yiddish actress Molly Picon, who played Yente in the film: "This is like a document of historical significance . . . It's part of a world that's gone. What began with 'Fiddler' and the life in the nineteen-hundreds ended finally, with Hitler . . . The world we're portraying has been destroyed."

It would have been—and has been—difficult for any filmmaker to shoulder the enormous moral and aesthetic responsibilities of representing a vanished Eastern European Jewry. And the challenge was particularly difficult when it came to adapting a work that, besides having come to represent that world for American and indeed international audiences, had such fixed traditions of its own that altering them would have raised its own cries of inauthenticity. Jewison, caught between a rock and a hard place, produced a film that was both dutifully, problematically faithful and subversively, Americanesquely untraditional.

Subversively untraditional, because, as Vincent Canby noted in his review, "the gap between the reverential intention of the filmmakers and the film itself is constantly being emphasized by a kind of visual and aural grandeur that is at odds with the poverty and simplicity and faith of the Sholem Aleichem characters"; lavish production values—and, I'd add, the possibly unconscious need to make the ancestral home resonate with an upwardly mobile American Jewish population—meant that Tevye's home, for example, looks far richer than one that would have belonged to any dairyman, and, probably, to a lot of the rich men whose company Tevye aspired to join. (If you want to see a poor man's house, look at the homes in the Soviet adaptations of the 1920s; those are the kind of places Menakhem-Mendl would never want to go back to.)

And problematically faithful, because Jewison's need to stick to the material reduces some of the things that make *Fiddler* breathe the most— the stylization Atkinson suggested, fifteen years before—to pale imitations of themselves. One example should suffice: the fiddler himself. In the play, there's a moment, after the celebration of Tzeitel's engagement and Tevye's subsequent discovery of a forthcoming pogrom, where the fiddler walks onstage and dances with Tevye. On stage, it can be magical: the reality of Tevye's world and the living symbol of his life's precarious balancing act intertwined, lifting his struggles into a broader, metaphorical sphere—a stylized reminder that we're watching not authentic life, but true art. The identical scene appears in the movie; but what is so vital onstage becomes thin on screen—it just looks like Tevye is dancing with another citizen of Anatevka, and an odd, off-putting one at that. Both are too real, and so, in some sense, neither is.

A dutiful fidelity is the death of art; and though the movie was a box office hit, was nominated for eight Oscars, and won for music, cinematography, and sound (and went on to mesmerize millions of young children over the next few decades, including this one), it hardly achieved the reputation of its theatrical predecessor, serving as a custodian of its flame instead of breaking new ground. But that would be enough.

Fiddler closed in July 1972, having run for 3,242 performances. A month before, it had set the record for the longest-running Broadway performance of any sort, beating out *Life with Father*. ("Mazel tov," the *Times* editorialized.) A torch was literally passed onstage to Prince from the widows of *Life with Father*'s creators. It wasn't the only torch passing; Prince, noting "productions around the world, and stock and amateur

and school productions, and the records are selling, and the motion picture . . . playing two blocks down Broadway at the Rivoli," emphasized
the strength of the *Fiddler* machine, while acknowledging the sputtering
of its flagship version. The production had been losing between $10,000
and $30,000 a week (between $50,000 and $150,000 in 2010 dollars); Prince
had kept it alive for the record, hoping, perhaps, that the milestone would
spur a new wave of business.

Though it didn't—the show closed a few weeks later—*Fiddler* had left
an indelible imprint on the cultural landscape. A year later, for example,
sixty-four fifth and sixth graders at East Harlem's P.S. 108 performed a
reworked version of the show, singing lyrics like "Salud y suerto, to life.
/ One day pasteles and collard greens, next day plain rice and beans. /
Drink l'chaim to life. / We'll be dancing to the beat of the rhythms, /
Rhythms from the congas and tumbalies, too. / Reel and soulful rocking,
feet stomp finger-poppin', / All the things we like to do." The adapter,
a teacher at the school, said the show was "particularly well suited for
the lives of our students" because it dealt with finding joy under difficult conditions. Thousands more school productions in a wide variety
of settings lay ahead, each seeking its own relevance to its participants'
multitudinous experiences.

Fiddler would be revived on Broadway in 1990 for the show's twenty-
fifth anniversary (where its lead, Topol, addressed the "problem arising
from the fact that nearly everybody has seen 'Fiddler' in one version or
another"), and in 2004 on its fortieth (that one had its own brouhaha over
authenticity when the show cast the non-Jewish Alfred Molina as Tevye,
leading some, as Ruth Franklin put it, to go "so far as to count the Jewish names in the cast and crew"). Everyone agreed, though, that by this
point *Fiddler* had become a tradition of its own, rather than merely working in one.

And as for its source? Where was Sholem Aleichem in all this?

As *Fiddler* was riding high in 1968, Robert Kirsch published a piece
in the *Los Angeles Times* under the title "Sholem Aleichem Revival: Why
Not?," deeming the American rediscovery of Sholem Aleichem "one of the

small wonders of the age." It seemed reasonable to predict the play's success would redound to its author's benefit; Sholem Aleichem's daughter published a memoir about her father that same year, and one critic, devoting a book-length study to the author in 1974, asserted that it seemed time to reexamine his works "particularly from the American viewpoint. Sholom Aleichem is no longer the personal property of the remnants of Eastern European Jewry or their American descendants. He has emerged as a major influence in modern American fiction." That work's title— *Sholem Aleichem: A Non-Critical Introduction*—intentionally or no, bespoke the complexities of reading his work in a post-*Fiddler* world. Sholem Aleichem's creations would have an incalculable influence on American culture, and America's perspective on Jewish life. But despite a steady flow of new translations over the intervening decades—over two hundred new translations of Sholem Aleichem stories, novels, and plays between 1954 and 1988, to the point where most of his better work can be found in English in varying degrees of accuracy and aesthetic excellence—to call him a major influence in modern American fiction hardly seems accurate, compared to, say, Isaac Bashevis Singer.

This continued relegation of Sholem Aleichem to the American literary sidelines—since it's arguably the case that as a writer he received as much, if not more, general literary attention in the forties and fifties as he has in recent decades—has numerous causes, including the increasing marginality of literary fiction more generally; but I suspect that *Fiddler*'s success at identifying Sholem Aleichem's creative output with the sentimental folksiness the musical possesses has a good bit to do with it. It's ironic, as the same post-*Fiddler* period has seen the rise of a body of literary criticism in the burgeoning field of Yiddish studies that takes Sholem Aleichem's work extremely seriously. The same year the Broadway production closed, 1972, saw Dan Miron's *Sholem-Aleykhem: Person, Persona, Presence*, one of the earliest (and still one of the best) attempts in English-language scholarship to grapple with the complicated games the author plays with identity and audience. No one reading the work of Miron—or of Ruth Wisse, or David Roskies, or Khone Shmeruk, or a host of others—could fail to look at Sholem Aleichem's work and see anything less than a complex, self-conscious literary artist.

But readers of those critical works, it's fair to say, were in the distinct minority.

Scene 10

The Cloud, 2013

Some notes from the current repository of universal knowledge, conventional wisdom, idiosyncrasy, and the world's collective procrastination sink we refer to as the Internet. A few of the pages returned by a 2011 Google search on "Sholem Aleichem" reveal the way Sholem Aleichem lives now, virtually speaking.

Wikipedia comes in at the top of the rankings, of course. Entirely expected: *Fiddler* is mentioned in the second sentence of the entry. Entirely unexpected, at least to me, the notice in the disambiguation section: "For the crater on Mercury, see *Sholem Aleichem (crater)*." The article is fairly accurate, as far as it goes, though its emphases, like many Wikiarticles, are somewhat unbalanced: students assiduously copying out information for their term papers would be able to speak about his Zionism and his fear of the number thirteen, but would be hard-pressed to say anything about a single one of his characters. Perhaps accordingly, the section on "Commemoration and Legacy" is as large as "Literary Career." Less a writer, Wikipedia implies, than a personality.

A couple of websites pop up that collect witty quotes and aphorisms, presenting Sholem Aleichem in that favorite of American lights, another Mark Twain. You can tell a lot about a person's legacy from the quotes attributed to them (think about the ones you've heard put in the mouths of Oscar Wilde, or Yogi Berra), and these do similar duty. A good number are precisely the sort that might have been placed in Tevye's mouth: "No matter how bad things get you got to go on living, even if it kills you" and "The rich swell up from pride, the poor from hunger." The people's writer, the shrugging force of ironic resilience—that's how to remember him, in a dozen words or less.

The few websites that represent cultural or educational institutions bearing his name—a Sholem Aleichem College in Melbourne, a Sholom Aleichem Club in Philadelphia, the Sholem Aleichem Cultural Center in the Bronx—are lonely testaments to a different kind of vanishing world: the network of secular institutions dedicated to Yiddish culture that flourished through a significant portion of the twentieth century. Explaining their choice of name in a 1959 article, a founder of the Sholom Aleichem Club wrote that Sholem Aleichem's "literary legacy is a mainstay of the modern, humanist Jewish culture which our Club strives to uphold. It signifies closeness to the people and faith in the future good society." If *Fiddler on the Roof*, written five years later, chose to emphasize looking to the past rather than the future, organizations like the club have attempted to ensure that Yiddish culture—including Sholem Aleichem's writing—remains resonant for today's children.

It's a difficult task, and I was pleased to see that the club supports another institution that came up in the web search: the Yiddish Book Center, with which I've been involved since I interned there the summer after my freshman year of college and on whose board I now serve. The Book Center began as a recovery operation to save Yiddish books that would have otherwise been discarded as their readers passed away, their children unable to read them; having accomplished that task, remarkably, it's now become a renaissance project, making those books available to new generations of readers. When I started as an intern twenty years ago, that meant packing up crates of books to send to libraries who wanted Yiddish collections. Passing shelves and shelves of volumes written in a language I was only beginning to understand, I saw stacks of thick blue volumes: the collected works of Sholem Aleichem, dozens and dozens of copies of the multivolume set, each tantalizingly suggesting the ghost of its owner's story that, in the hands of those volumes' author, might have become another literary masterpiece.

Nowadays, most of those volumes stay on the shelves, though I used my own copy in the making of this book. Not necessarily, or not only, because of a diminishing number of Yiddish readers, but because the rising interest in Yiddish studies and Yiddish culture—and it is rising—is taking place in an Internet world, where the very nature of reading is changing. The Book Center worked for years to digitize Yiddish books, and has now made them available for free download. This seems quixotic until you learn that there've been over 200,000 downloads to date. Over a thousand of those were of works by Sholem Aleichem.

Not so many, yet. But the afterlife of Sholem Aleichem is still young.

At the end of a "Page from the Song of Songs," Sholem Aleichem wrote that "an ending, even the very best, always contains a note of sadness." Attempting to escape the terrors of an ending, he would often finish with a distracting—if enlightening—joke. Here are two we know Sholem Aleichem told himself.

The first joke. Two men, sitting on a park bench. The first one: "Life is like a fountain." His friend: "Why is life like a fountain?" The first: "Do I know?" The second requires a bit more setup. One man sells another an enormous bag full of plums; the recipient claims they're wormy and worthless. They agree to arbitration by the town's elderly rabbi. When they present their cases, the aged rabbi mumbles that he needs to see the plums first, and so they shlep the whole bag to the rabbi's house. The rabbi tastes one plum, then another, then a third, and chews and mumbles for half an hour. Finally, they ask, "Well??" The rabbi looks up and says, "What am I, some sort of plum expert?"

Sholem Aleichem was too wise, in his better moments, to claim wisdom; and too much of an expert, in his humbler ones, to claim wide expertise; but he told stories better than almost anyone. His final advice, in that same "Song of Songs" story, was that "a beginning, even the very worst, is better than the finest ending. Therefore, it is much easier and far more pleasant to tell you the story from the beginning, once and twice and even one hundred times." Sholem Aleichem's biography ended suddenly, in the middle; we'll never know what happened to Motl, or what transformations he would have wrought on his life story. But his story was, as it turned out, also a beginning; which would, in its own way, have pleased him mightily.

ACKNOWLEDGMENTS

For me, the acknowledgments page (writing one, not reading one) is always a recipe of two parts joy to two parts fear. Joy because, first, it means the rest of the book is pretty much done; second, and far more important, it's where I finally get to express that deep indebtedness and gratitude to the incredible people without whom the book couldn't possibly have been written. On the other hand, I'm always terrified I've (a) left someone out, or (b) praised with language totally inadequate to the sentiment; there's a decent likelihood of (a), and (b) is pretty much a foregone conclusion. But what would a book on Jewish themes, and especially on Sholem Aleichem, be without some mixture of laughter and tears? So here goes.

I began researching this book in Los Angeles, as a UCLA/Mellon Fellow. For the opportunity to read Sholem Aleichem on the Santa Monica boardwalk (and have *"Vos makht a yid?"* shouted at me by a roller-skating passerby), my thanks to David Myers and Eric Sundquist for their generosity and hospitality. At my home institution of Columbia, I'm indebted, as always, to the staffs of the Department of Germanic Languages, Bill Dellinger and Peg Quisenberry, and of the Institute for Israel and Jewish Studies, Sheridan Gayer and Kerren Marcus, for their unflagging efforts and constant helpfulness. My colleagues provide as congenial an intellectual environment as one could ask for; I'm particularly grateful, in the writing of this book, for the advice and support of Michael Stanislawski, Mark Anderson, Jim Shapiro, and Andy Delbanco.

I owe an enormous debt of gratitude to Agi Legutko, whose indefatigable research assistance helped inform every page of this book; and to Adi Mahalel for assisting with some important queries toward the end. Sarah Ponichtera was invaluable at tracking down some of the photographs; I thank her and the other amazing archivists and librarians at YIVO for their work. I'm extraordinarily grateful to Mikhail Krutikov for his careful reading of the manuscript and his invaluable and extensive feedback. My thanks also to Steve Zipperstein, Ruth Wisse, Adam Kirsch, Jason Zinoman, and Geri Gindea for their support and suggestions.

Working with Jonathan Rosen is taking a master class in what it means to have an editor, and, more deeply but just as truthfully, to be a writer. This book would look very different—and would be far worse—were it not for his careful attentions and invaluable commentary. My thanks also to Wayne Hoffman for some editorial suggestions at a crucial time, and especially to Altie Karper, Schocken's editorial director, for her advice, encouragement, and editorial eye. Thanks also to Susanna Sturgis, for her eagle-eyed copyediting, and Josefine Kals, for her indefatigable efforts at publicizing.

Acknowledgments

I've always considered myself unaccountably, amazingly lucky in having the family I have. My brothers, Noah and Andrew; my sisters-in-law, Sara and Rachel; my in-laws, Bob and Sherry Pomerantz, and now my nieces and nephews, Boaz, Jordana, Moses, and Delilah, provide love, support, and hand-colored birthday cards in equal measure, and I treasure them all. When it comes to my parents, Eddie and Cheryl Dauber, any given set of adjectives and adverbs simply seem utterly incommensurate, so I'll simply say this: if I turn out to be half the parent either one of them is, my son will be lucky indeed.

My son. The story of this book is also the story of the starting of a family of my own; its writing began in earnest just weeks after my wedding, and Miri went into labor just hours after the final, final version of this manuscript was emailed off. To say my wife has made these last few years happy ones would be inadequate language indeed; maybe better to say that I couldn't have imagined, before we met, that life could be as full, bright, and breathing as it is with her in it. And as for my son, to whom this book is dedicated and is, at the time of this writing, busily discovering that those things with fingers down there are connected to the rest of him: if his arrival has opened up new capacities for a peculiarly parental sort of fear, it's utterly, utterly vanquished by his provision of a new—and continually expanding—joy.

BIBLIOGRAPHICAL NOTES

Writing the story of Sholem Aleichem and of his works involves standing on many shoulders. Starting with the author's own inventive—and often invented—efforts, family members, bibliographers, and innumerable essayists and critics, particularly though not solely in Yiddish, Hebrew, and English, have attempted to illuminate hundreds of aspects of the life and grapple with the work, either in part or in full. The works cited below by no means attempt to be a comprehensive overview of the literature; they are a record, instead, of the sources I found most helpful in this book's writing. (As an example, there have been myriads of analyses of particular Sholem Aleichem stories. Most of the interpretations in this book, however, are my own, and accordingly I only cite such analyses when I found them relevant to my own thinking about the story.)

One particular aid, however, should be mentioned separately: Louis Fridhandler's indexes to the Yiddish works of Sholem Aleichem and their English translations are invaluable to any researcher interested in systematically tracking down the stories, as all of Sholem Aleichem's "Collected Works" are incomplete, and none are organized chronologically. I've taken pains to include, pace Fridhandler, both English and Yiddish citations for the stories, to allow readers of both languages to find particular tales. A general rule of thumb: If the work has appeared in English translation, I have accordingly used one of the available translations for quotation (on rare occasions altering it very slightly to bring out aspects of the work I'm talking about); if it hasn't, or if it's a letter or foreign-language criticism, the translations are my own unless it's specifically mentioned to the contrary.

Abbreviations

AV Sholem Aleichem, *Ale Verk fun Sholem Aleykhem*
AVBYL Sholem Aleichem, *Af vos badarfn yidn a land?*
AVM Sholem Aleichem, *Ale Verk*
B *Briv fun Sholem Aleykhem, 1879–1916*, ed. Avraham Lis
BOSA Irving Howe and Ruth R. Wisse, eds. *The Best of Sholom Aleichem*
CYF Ken Frieden, *Classic Yiddish Fiction*
DYFB Aleichem, ed., *Di Yudishe folksbibliotek* I
FEL Sholem Aleichem, *Felyetonen*
FOTR *Fiddler on the Roof* (published script)

Bibliographical Notes

Overture

4 "Japanese Fiddler on the Roof": http://www.youtube.com/watch?v=eGoRo -nPLOM (accessed Jan. 9, 2012).

4 Hindi and Hungarian versions: http://www.youtube.com/watch?v=DzwO36 FmqlQ (accessed March 22, 2011); http://www.youtube.com/watch?v=b3G688 WRRA4 (accessed March 22, 2011).

4 high school marching band: http://www.youtube.com/watch?v=UzvNF5rkjRI (accessed March 22, 2011).

4 sock puppet: http://www.youtube.com/watch?v=_e_X1aKLQWY (accessed March 22, 2011).

5 half of his Yiddish output: Dan Miron, "Sholem Aleichem," *YIVO Encyclopedia of Jews in Eastern Europe* (can be accessed online at http://www.yivoencyclopedia .org/; hereafter YIVO).

5 150,000 to 250,000: Estimates vary; this range taken from Arthur Aryeh Goren, "Sacred and Secular: The Place of Public Funerals in the Immigrant Life of American Jews," *Jewish History* 8.1–2 (1994): 269–305.

5 the largest public funeral: Ellen D. Kellman, "Sholem Aleichem's Funeral (New

York, 1916): The Making of a National Pageant," *YIVO Annual* 20 (1991): 277–304, 277.

6 "Sholem Aleichem" himself: See later for more discussion. On the nature of the character, compare Dan Miron, *Sholem-Aleykhem: Person, Persona, Presence* (New York: YIVO, 1972).

Chapter 1

11 163rd Street subway stop: Now called Intervale Avenue; see http://www.nycsub way.org/perl/stations?199:1641.

11 trying to recall: See I. D. Berkowitz, *Dos Sholem Aleykhem Bukh* (New York: YKUF, 1958; hereafter SAB), 11.

12 "a man's life": SAB 8.

12 "the privilege": Sholem Aleichem, *From the Fair*, trans. Curt Leviant (New York: Viking, 1985; hereafter FTF), 3.

12 Writing an autobiography: SAB 10.

12 He wrote a critic: Letter to S. Niger, May 29, 1912, in *Briv fun Sholem Aleykhem, 1879–1916*, ed. Avraham Lis (Tel Aviv: Y. L. Peretz-Farlag, 1995; hereafter B), 549.

12 Explaining the choice of name: FTF 3. Another Yiddish writer, Y. Y. Linetski, had used the same title for his own autobiography several years previously; see Jeremy Dauber, "Linetski, Yitzchok Yoyel," YIVO.

13 " 'Write your autobiography' ": FTF 4.

14 Shmulik the orphan: See FTF 9. On the character of Shmulik and his literary evolution, see David G. Roskies, "Unfinished Business: Sholem Aleichem's *From the Fair*," *Prooftexts* 6 (1986): 65–78, 73–74; see notes there for the work's textual history.

14 in 1764: Bernard D. Weinryb, *The Jews of Poland* (New York: JPS, 1972), 116.

14 a century and a quarter: "Pale of Settlement," YIVO; Anna Halberstam-Rubin, *Sholem Aleichem: The Writer as Social Historian* (New York: P. Lang, 1989), 20, 142.

15 Jewish entrance to universities: Frances and Joseph Butwin, *Sholom Aleichem* (Boston: Twayne, 1977), 24.

15 assimilating force of the military: "Military Service in Russia," YIVO; Michael Stanislawski, *Tsar Nicholas I and the Jews: The Transformation of Jewish Society in Russia, 1825–1855* (Philadelphia: Jewish Publication Society, 1983), passim; John Klier, *Imperial Russia's Jewish Question, 1855–1881* (Cambridge: Cambridge University Press, 1995), 332–349; Olga Litvak, *Conscription and the Search for Modern Russian Jewry* (Bloomington: Indiana University Press, 2006), 15–41.

15 an increasingly complicated culture war: For historical and literary overview, see Jeremy Dauber, *Antonio's Devils* (Stanford, CA: Stanford University Press, 2004).

17 Y. Y. Linetski: Borekh Tshubinski, "Linyetski, Yitskhok-Yoyl," in *Leksikon fun der nayer yidisher literatur*, vol. 5 (New York: Alveltlekhen yidishn kultur-kongres, 1963), 163–168.

17 Nochem Vevik's: FTF 7–8.

Chapter 2

19 March 2, 1859: At the time of Sholem Aleichem's birth, Russia still marked time according to the Old Style (the Julian calendar), and had not yet followed most of Europe and the world in switching to the New Style (the Gregorian calendar, thirteen days ahead); they would not do so until 1918, after the October Revolution. Calendars in his area on his date of birth would have read February 18, 1859, and his household celebrated on the 18th; but a letter written in Italy on his birthday is dated "March 2nd, 1912; according to the old style Feb. 18th, my birthday." B 119. Sholem Aleichem sometimes dated his letters or gave other dates in Old Style, and sometimes in New Style.

19 "pack of businesses": FTF 7.

19 among other endeavors: Marie Waife-Goldberg, *My Father, Sholom Aleichem* (New York: Simon and Schuster, 1968; hereafter MF), 31–32.

19 Observers: See SAB 19.

19 In the kind of historical irony: http://www.wumag.kiev.ua/index2.php?param =pgs20073/28 (accessed March 27, 2011).

20 Voronkov: The village is sometimes referred to as Voronkova.

20 "spent their happiest years": FTF 48.

20 "as small as the fine print": "Tsu mayn biografiye" (1903), in Sholem Aleichem, *Ale Verk fun Sholem Aleykhem* (New York: Forverts, 1942; hereafter AV), 2:6:273–281, 274.

20 fastidiously trying: Volf Rabinovich, *Mayn Bruder Sholem Aleykhem* (Kiev: Melukhe-farlag, 1939; hereafter MBSA), 16.

20 charity box: MBSA 15; see also Dan Miron, "Image of the Shtetl," *The Image of the Shtetl and Other Studies of Modern Jewish Literary Imagination* (Syracuse, NY: Syracuse University Press, 2000), 2; Roskies, "Unfinished Business," 68; and Israel Bartal, "Imagined Geography: The Shtetl, Myth, and Reality," in Steven T. Katz, ed., *The Shtetl: New Evaluations* (New York: NYU Press, 2007), 173–192.

20 "drag a Jewish name": MF 33.

20 Shmulik and Sholem's Voronkov adventures: FTF 61; see MF 47–48.

21 a single room: MF 34–36.

21 ascetically inclined: See Moishe Yosef Zeldin's description in Maurice Samuel, *The World of Sholom Aleichem* (New York: A. A. Knopf, 1943; hereafter *World*), 81; MBSA 20.

22 "contraband merchandise": MBSA 20.

22 "a combination": MF 37; MBSA 68.

22 a rival inn: See FTF 142.

22 "A—abusive": FTF 138. He also composed a song mocking his stepmother for his sister Brokhe's enjoyment: see MBSA 67.

22 one-eyed family maid: FTF 8.

22 "a sickness": "Tsu mayn biografiye," 275; see also MF 50–51.

23 "the rascal": FTF 9.

23 "a strange, frenzied laughter": FTF 140. For a similar anecdote involving his *kheyder* teacher, see MBSA 23.

Chapter 3

24 whitewashed walls: SAB 309.

24 the Bible: MF 50; "Tsu mayn biografiye," 277; SAB 340; I. D. Berkowitz, *Undzere Rishoynim*, 5 vols. (Tel Aviv: Hamenorah, 1966; hereafter UR), 2:72.

25 This system of elementary schooling: See "Heder," YIVO; and Shaul Stampfer, "Heder Study, Knowledge of Torah and the Maintenance of Social Stratification in Traditional East European Jewish Society," *Studies in Jewish Education* 3 (1988): 271–289.

25 "didn't understand a word": FTF 88.

25 "an extra bone": FTF 80.

25 "Preserves": "Ayngemakhts" (1908), in Sholem Aleichem, *Felyetonen* (Tel Aviv: I. L. Peretz Publishing House, 1976; hereafter FEL), 141–145.

25 "Poem from the Kheyder": Found in Sholem Aleykhem, ed., *Di Yudishe Folks-bibliotek* 1 (1888; hereafter DYFB), 241–243; English translation as "Song of the Kheyder," in Marvin Zuckerman and Marion Herbst, eds., *The Three Great Classic Yiddish Writers of Modern Yiddish Literature, II. Sholem-Aleykhem* (Malibu, CA: Pangloss Press, 1994; hereafter TGCYW), 93–94.

26 Moshe David Ruderman: FTF 81.

26 "old debt": Letter to A. B. Gottlober, dated 1888, B 226. For his part, Gottlober had encouraging things to say about Sholem Aleichem's work when he received it—perhaps in part because he was hoping for a lucrative commission from the young writer turned editor. See "Mikhtavim me-n. sokolov le-a.b. gotlober ume-a.b. gotlober leshalom aleichem," *Genazim* 4 (1971) 280–286, 285 (letter dated June 6, 1888).

26 Sholem devoured it: See FTF 146–147; MF 40–42; "Tsu mayn biografiye," 278. According to A. Gurshteyn, "Sholem Aleykhem: A kurze biografiye," in Sholem Aleykhem, *Ale Verk* (Moscow: Emes, 1948; hereafter AVM), 1:7–26, 16, the young author wrote *Daughter of Zion* at fourteen, and *The Jewish Robinson Crusoe* at fifteen.

27 Russian district school: MF 45–46; FTF 159.

27 He reminisced: Letter to Elye Barkhash, dated January 1910, B 106.

27 Turgenev, Pushkin, and Lermontov: Mentioned in FTF 167. He would read his favorite writers thoroughly, near comprehensively; he knew much of Turgenev by heart, and would later thoroughly mark up his copies of Chekhov and Gorky. MBSA 129, 139.

27 name-checks as influences: FTF 215, 231; and see his letter to Y. Kh. Ravnitski, Oct. 22, 1903, B 423. For a (very) partial list of the books in his library, see MBSA 152–153.

27 "grew sick": Letter to Y. Kh. Ravnitski, Oct. 22, 1903, B 424.

28 "our own Gogol": FTF 215. On Sholem Aleichem's interest in Ukrainian and other Russian minority cultures, see MBSA 144–146.

28 wear his hair: FTF 213.

28 *skaz*: See Gabriella Safran, "Four English Pots and the Evolving Translatability of Sholem Aleichem," in Gennady Estraikh, Jordan Finkin, Kerstin Hoge, and

Mikhail Krutikov, *Translating Sholem Aleichem: History, Politics, and Art* (London: Legenda, 2012), 114–133, 120.

28 "You must know": In Leonard J. Kent, ed., *The Complete Tales of Nikolai Gogol*, vol. 1 (Chicago: University of Chicago Press, 1985), 173.

28 "It seems": Cited in Nakhmen Mayzel, *Undzer Sholem Aleykhem* (Warsaw: Yidish-bukh, 1959), 90; for another mention, see MBSA 139. The relevant passage appears in the first part of *Dead Souls*: "And for a long time yet to come I am destined by a wondrous power to walk hand in hand with my strange heroes, to survey the whole of life in all the vastness of its onward rush, to survey it through laughter visible to the world and tears invisible and unknown to it!" Nikolai Gogol, *Dead Souls*, trans. Robert A. Maguire (New York: Penguin, 2004), 150.

29 at sixteen: MF 51; MBSA 19.

29 During Sholem's last year: MF 51; SAB 42; MBSA 30. He and Barkhash also used to steal cherries off trees together. See Melech Grafstein, ed., *Sholom Aleichem Panorama* (London, Ontario: The Jewish Observer, 1948, hereafter SAP), 190.

29 first desecration: The episode is described in FTF 165–167.

29 Pinny: See Aleichem's description of him in FTF 36–38.

29 Author: See FTF 166 and letter to Elye Barkhash, dated January 1910, B 106.

30 of all his options: FTF 202–203; MF 51; Louis Falstein, *The Man Who Loved Laughter: The Story of Sholom Aleichem* (Philadelphia: JPS, 1968), 63, 71.

30 "like a bomb": FTF 203.

30 "one angry landlady": FTF 211.

31 Quite distant: MF 57.

Chapter 4

32 a literary romance: Falstein 97; MF 63; SAB 166.

32 Loyeff's capacious library: At least part of which Sholem Aleichem would later inherit and cherish; see MBSA 153.

32 *Kol Mevaser*: The supplement first appeared on Oct. 23, 1862; see Boris Kotlerman, "Kol Mevaser," YIVO. On *Kol Mevaser*'s questionable popularity, see Olga Litvak, "Found in Translation: Sholem Aleichem and the Myth of the Ideal Yiddish Reader," in *Translating Sholem Aleichem*, 6–24, 10–11.

33 "long, heart-rending": FTF 244.

33 "On that evening": MF 67.

33 "a second home": SAB 18; see also MBSA 158.

33 Loyeff was an *arendator*: Butwin 21; Samuel 251.

34 a romantic entanglement: See particularly FTF 180–184.

34 negotiate his draft service: MF 73; Falstein 100. The move of venue was from Pereyaslav to Kaniv, right across the Dnieper from Sofievka.

34 Aunt Toibe: See FTF 250–251.

35 "a rare sort": FTF 236.

35 "It was he": FTF 252.

35 *What kind of decided*: See Hillel Halkin's translation of "Today's Children," in

Sholem Aleichem, *Tevye the Dairyman and the Railroad Stories* (New York: Schocken, 1987), 48.

35 Emerging from his room: FTF 253–256; Gurshteyn 14.

35 A brief, disastrous stint: MF 78–80; FTF 268–272.

36 "crown rabbi": "Crown Rabbi," YIVO; Isaac Levitats, *The Jewish Community in Russia, 1844–1917* (Jerusalem: Posner and Sons, 1981), 45–55; Benjamin Nathans, *Beyond the Pale: The Jewish Encounter with Late Imperial Russia* (Berkeley: University of California Press, 2002), 68; "Sholem-aleykhems a briv fun 1882," *Yidishe kultur* 35.8 (1973): 4–9.

36 "no decent man": MF 81.

36 Sholem won election: FTF 275–277; Falstein 113; MF 82.

36 "one who had eaten soap": MF 81.

36 a story he wrote: "A vort far a vort" (1915), AV 4:1:147–168, translated as "Tit for Tat" in Alfred Kazin, ed., *Selected Stories of Sholem Aleichem* (New York: Modern Library, 1956; hereafter SSSA), 212–228.

37 "What do you think": SSSA 225.

37 "I just wanted to show you": SSSA 228.

37 a different story: "Khabne" (1905), AV 3:4:137–151; translated as "The Village of Habne," in Sholem Aleichem, *Old Country Tales*, ed. and trans. Curt Leviant (G. P. Putnam's, 1966, hereafter OCT), 302–313. "Khabne" is significantly longer and lacks the autobiographical resonance of the later story.

Chapter 5

38 growing anti-Semitic sentiment: I. Michael Aronson, *Troubled Waters: The Origins of the 1881 Anti-Jewish Pogroms in Russia* (Pittsburgh: University of Pittsburgh Press, 1990), 41–43.

38 first major wave of pogroms: Aronson 44–64; John D. Klier and Shlomo Lambroza, eds., *Pogroms: Anti-Jewish Violence in Modern Russian History* (Cambridge: Cambridge University Press, 1992), 39–42.

39 "May Laws": "May Laws," *Encyclopaedia Judaica*, 2nd ed. (Detroit: Macmillan Reference, 2007).

39 a definitive answer: See Erich Haberer, "Cosmopolitanism, Antisemitism, and Populism: A Reappraisal of the Russian and Jewish Response to the Pogroms of 1881–1882," in Klier and Lambroza, 98–134, esp. 116–120; and Alexander Orbach, "The Russian Jewish Commmunity, 1881–1903," in Klier and Lambroza, 137–163, esp. 143–153.

39 certain Haskala writers: Most notably Judah Leib Gordon; see Michael Stanislawski, *For Whom Do I Toil? Judah Leib Gordon and the Crisis of Russian Jewry* (New York: Oxford University Press, 1988).

39 An 1879 letter: *Hatsefira* no. 6, 1879; a facsimile is reprinted in SAB 313.

39 "editors, thank God": "Tsu mayn biografiye," 278.

40 His first-ever published article: "Education and Its Relation to Military Service" appeared in *Hamelitz* in 1881, issue no. 51 (Dec. 29, 1881, cols. 1025–1026).

40 two further articles: Appeared in *Hamelitz* in 1882, nos. 4 (Jan. 26, 1882, col. 70) and 6 (Feb. 9, 1882, cols. 101–103). See discussion in SAB 312.

40 "by the pound": "Tsu mayn biografiye," 279.

40 "foolish": SAB 4.

40 quite an impression: For example, he gathered a crowd to read them Sholem's work aloud and carried one of the articles in his pocket for quite some time: MBSA 103–104.

40 they led to a reunion: Letter to Volf Rabinovich, Dec. 15, 1883; MBSA 76. A mid-May 1882 letter refers to an experience with Olga, so their reunion precedes that; "Sholem-aleykhems a briv," 7.

41 "God willing": FTF 168; MBSA 98. In 1915, Sholem Aleichem found a copy of the book in New York; it was apparently a description of small-town wagon drivers who united in a "trust" to battle the coming railroad. SAB 314.

41 "write the way you think": SAB 314.

42 "in my private opinion": UR 4:43.

42 wrote a relative: Letter to Hirsh Weisbord, Aug. 26, 1879, B 17.

42 Yiddish writing: See YIVO, "Aleksander Zederbaum," "Kol Mevaser."

42 "political-literary newspaper": Taken from masthead of October 1881 issue of *Yudishes folksblat*. See image at http://www.yivoencyclopedia.org/article.aspx/ Zederbaum_Aleksander; accessed April 1, 2011.

43 "the simplicity": SAB 314. On the nature of this "radical innocence," compare Dan Miron, *A Traveler Disguised*, 2nd ed. (1973; Syracuse, NY: Syracuse University Press, 1996), 17–21. In a letter to his brother at the end of 1883, he writes: "I'm now often holding a pen in hand and write one story after another in our mother tongue." MBSA 76.

43 "Two Stones": "Tsvey shteyner," in *AVM* 1:29–49; see notes on 515. The story appeared in *Folksblat* nos. 26, 28, and 30 (1883). For a closer look, see Anna Dresner, "Metziut vedimyon beyetsirato shel shalom aleichem beyidish," *Jewish Language Review* 7 (1987): 1–9.

43 "The Election": "Di vibores," in *AVM* 1:50–53; see notes on 516. The story appeared in *Folksblat* no. 38 (1883); and is translated as "The Election" in TGCYW, 77–80.

44 to hide from friends: See MBSA 105.

44 "a weekday tongue": SAB 4.

44 even the author himself: For a discussion of how the author switched back and forth between name and pseudonym in his own work, see Ken Frieden, *Classic Yiddish Fiction* (Albany: State University of New York Press, 1995; hereafter CYF), 105.

44 "the sweet familiarity": Alfred Kazin, "Introduction," SSSA, x.

44 Linetski: See Miron, *Sholem-Aleykhem: Person, Persona, Presence*.

44 "Intercepted Letters": "Di ibergekhapte briv af der post" (1883–1884), in *AVM* 1:54–146. See also Leonard Prager, "Sholem-Aleykhem's First Feuilleton Series," *Jewish Book Annual* 44 (1986–1987): 120–131. The work employs the titular literary device hoary even then—but almost certainly given new, personal energy by the author, smarting from his own intercepted letters just a few years before.

44 the first writing: SAB 316; Letter to S. Niger, May 29, 1912, B 548.

44 "by mail": "Ibergekhapte," 68–69.

44 one of the letter writers: "Ibergekhapte," 105.

45 a character has actually gone looking: "Ibergekhapte," 145.

45 Gamliel ben Pedahtzur: "A brivl tsum hern 'Sholem Aleykhem'" (1884), in *AVM* 1:487–489.

45 an exchange of letters: "Briv fun a litvak" (1884), *AVM* 1:491–495, 496–500; "An entfer dem varshaver litvak" (1884), in *AVM* 1:147–150.

45 "I have no use": FTF 153.

46 centerpiece of a sermon: "Ibergekhapte," 115–116.

46 (not terribly distinguished) poem: "Ibergekhapte," 136–137.

46 In another series: "An ibershraybung tsvishn tsvey alte khaveyrim" (1884), in *AVM* 1:165–194.

46 "To the New Year": "Tsum nayem yor" (1884), in *AVM* 2:265.

46 A postscript: "Ibergekhapte," 123.

46 another "sock puppet" letter: "Mayne briv tsu mayn fraynd Sholem-Aleykhem," also published in the *Folksblat* in 1884, in *AVM* 1:501–511.

46 "Sabbath Eve": "Erev shabes" (1884), in *AVM* 2:258.

46 "A Jewish Daughter": "A yidishe tokhter" (1888), in *AVM* 2:260.

46 "They Ask Me": "Me fregt mikh vos ikh veyn" (1888), in *AVM* 2:256.

Chapter 6

51 "My father-in-law": Letter to Eliyahu Rabinovich, June 22, 1884, B 21.

51 "a real Hasid": Letter to Eliyahu Rabinovich, July 27, 1884, B 23.

52 In early 1885: Letter to Eliyahu Rabinovich, June 10–11, 1885, B 24; MF 84.

52 lavishly decorated: MF 94, 111.

52 "city of churches": MF 26.

52 had only been reopened: Natan Meir, "From Pork to Kapores: Transformations in Religious Practice Among the Jews of Late Imperial Kiev," *Jewish Quarterly Review* 97.4 (Fall 2007): 616–645, esp. 618–628.

53 Sholem Aleichem's daughter doubted: MF 211.

53 Jewish literati: Mayzel 25, 29.

53 were living there illegally: This on the testimony of Sholem Aleichem's daughter; see MF 94.

53 it was a scandal: Letter to Eliyahu Rabinovich, Sept. 6, 1889, B 28; MF 65, 85; for Sholem Aleichem's full published account of the sordid affair, disputing the claim Loyeff had previously promised the sum to the Bohuslav poor, see Chaim Beyder, "Fustrit loyt di shpurn fun dem groysn shrayber," *Sovetish heymland* 3 (1989): 40–52. They eventually settled on four thousand rubles.

54 "The Counting-House": "Kantor gesheft" (1885), in AVM 1:250–278.

54 "half a word": "Kantor gesheft," 251.

54 *A Journey Around the World*: *Di velt-rayze* (1886), in *AVM* 1:281–342. The work, which appeared as a special supplement to the *Folksblat*, was continued in two

subsequent parts the following year under the title *Di beste yorn* (1887), in AVM 1:343–407.

55 "from this day forward": *Di beste yorn*, 403–404.

55 "Our elevated aristocracy": Letter to Y. Kh. Ravnitski, June 5, 1887, B 165.

55 *Sketches from Berdichev Street*: "Bilder fun der berditshever gas" (1886–1887), in AVM 1:409–467, 409–467.

55 "a big shot": "Bilder fun der berditshever gas," 448.

56 He offered to provide: "Bilder fun der berditshever gas," 454. Another sketch from the same year, using a theatrical metaphor, asserted disappointedly that readers were more interested in the actor (that is, Sholem Aleichem) than in the scenes his writing set. See "Fun vayte medines" (1887), AVM 1:156–164.

56 over half: Nathans, 111.

56 Shomer: See Rose Shomer Bachelis and Miriam Shomer Zunzer, *Undzer foter Shomer* (New York: YKUF Farlag, 1950), and Sophie Grace-Pollack, "Re'shito shel Shomer be-yidish," *Hulyot* 2 (1994): 69–87.

57 "cook their novels": "Ibergekhapte," 140.

57 "one of those truly interesting novels": *Di velt-rayze*, 282.

57 *Children's Game*: Kinder-shpil (1886), in AVM 2:5–107, also published in the *Folks-blat*.

58 *Sender Blank:* So the title of the first full edition in 1888; a later, revised edition referred to it as *Sender Blank and His Household: A Novel Without a Romance.* On the shifting titles, see CYF 141; for the work, see AVM 2:109–201 (1888).

58 everyone just sort of: *Sender Blank*'s history writes this process large. It was the first of a planned trilogy modeled on a massive family novel cycle by Zola, and though Sholem Aleichem seems to have written at least two drafts of the second novel, *Markus Blank the Second*, and claims he'll write *The Last of the Blanks* once he does his research on the younger generation he plans to write about, neither ever appeared; the story of the Blanks remains a blank. See letters to Y. Kh. Ravnitski, Aug. 21, 1888, B 201; to S. Dubnow, Sept. 2, 1888, B 204; and to Y. Kh. Ravnitski, June 18, 1894, B 287.

58 undercutting the suspense: See, e.g., *Sender Blank*, 190.

58 "one has to be naïve": From *Shomers Mishpet: oder der sud prisyazhne af ale romanen fun Shomer* (The Trial of Shomer; or, the Verdict of the Jury on All the Novels of Shomer) (Berdichev: Yankev Sheftel, 1888); translated as *The Judgment of Shomer* by Justin Cammy, in *Arguing the Modern Jewish Canon: Essays on Literature and Culture in Honor of Ruth R. Wisse*, ed. Cammy, Dara Horn, Alyssa Quint, and Rachel Rubinstein (Cambridge, MA: Harvard University Center for Jewish Studies, 2008), 129–185, quote on 139.

58 *Sender Blank*'s narrator fantasizes: *Sender Blank*, 181.

58 wasn't the only one: See, for the best discussion of this entire debate, Justin Cammy, "Judging *The Judgment of Shomer*: Jewish Literature Versus Jewish Reading," in *Arguing the Modern Jewish Canon*, 85–127.

59 referred to Yiddish as "garbage": UR 1:27.

59 "heartbreaking": Letter to Y. Dinezon, Dec. 27, 1887, B 170.

59 "He says": Letter to Y. Kh. Ravnitski, March 29, 1888, B 183.

Chapter 7

60 He had done his homework: Letter to A. S. Friedberg, Jan. 7, 1888, B 175.

60 1. Almost all of his novels: *Judgment*, 135.

61 "Leave the public": *Judgment*, 183.

61 "it would be": *Judgment*, 135.

61 "mercy, compassion, and pity": *Judgment*, 184.

61 "Shomer is not a belletrist": *Judgment*, 185.

61 "do away with Shomer": Letter to Y. Kh. Ravnitski, Feb. 20, 1888, B 178, translation Cammy's.

61 several portraits: See, for example, *Judgment*, 184.

62 "as if churning": *Judgment*, 157.

62 "each and every book": *Judgment*, 156.

62 by his own admission: Letter to Y. Kh. Ravnitski, Aug. 17, 1888, B 200.

62 The result: Letter to Y. Kh. Ravnitski, June 5, 1887, B 164–165.

62 "Every new work": *Judgment*, 185.

62 a potted version: See *Judgment*, 132–133.

63 for some time: He may have been inspired by a get-together of Jewish writers in Kiev in 1886; see Mayzel 30–31.

63 he first turned to Hebrew: SAB 162.

63 hash of things: See David G. Roskies, *A Bridge of Longing: The Lost Art of Yiddish Storytelling* (Cambridge, MA: Harvard University Press, 1995), 374n11.

63 he was telling: Letter to Y. Y. Linetski, March 27, 1888, B 182. His plan was for the anthology to be occasional until he received permission for a regular journal.

63 he tells a less-established writer: Letter to Y. Dinezon, April 1, 1888, B 185.

63 "gone grey": Letter to Y. Kh. Ravnitski, June 8, 1888, B 190.

64 by late July: Letters to Y. Dinezon and S. Dubnov, July 26, 1888, and Aug. 7, 1888, B 195, 198.

64 "little bundle of joy": Letter to Y. Kh. Ravnitski, Aug. 17, 1888, B 200. The planned print run was over four thousand copies; arrangements were made to sell the book through fifty subagents, "Hasidicized apostates," as he referred to them, in a variety of cities in the Pale. See letters to Y. Kh. Ravnitski, Oct. 12, 1888, 213, and to S. Y. Abramovitch, Jan. 31, 1890, B 264.

64 ways of numerating: See, for example, the eighteen-point list in the letter to Y. Kh. Ravnitski, Oct. 4, 1888, B 211–212.

64 an announcement: See *Folksblat* no. 39 (Sept. 27/Oct. 9, 1888); cf. also announcement on July 12/24, 1888.

64 more bad news: Letters to Y. Dinezon, Oct. 16, 1888, B 215, and Dec. 13, 1888, B 225.

64 went to Warsaw: Letters to Y. Dinezon, Nov. 27, 1888, B 223; Jan. 11, 1889, B 229.

64 "cheaper than borscht": Letter to Y. L. Gordon, April 7, 1888, B 187.

64 the price had risen: See letters to Y. Kh. Ravnitski, Sept. 7, 1888, B 205, and Sept. 13–14, 1888, B 207; and to Y. Dinezon, Nov. 27, 1888, B 223, and Jan. 2, 1889, B 227.

65 "On the Literary Marketplace": "Afn literarishn mark," *DYFB* 1:351–378, quote on 378.

65 "We must shoot": "Afn literarishn mark," 377.

65 "Who's paid you": Letter to Y. L. Gordon, April 7, 1888, B 187.

65 "master of our literary language": Cited in Butwin 29.

65 provided a poem: Y. L. Gordon, "A brokhe," *DYFB* 1:295–296.

65 a fawning letter: Letter to S. Y. Abramovitch, Dec. 23, 1884, B 159.

65 Abramovitch, besieged: SAB 166, 191; UR 2:91–93.

65 Linetski came to: Letter to Y. Y. Linetski, March 27, 1888, B 182; SAB 180–181.

66 demanded high rates: Letter to Y. Y. Linetski, June 12, 1888, B 191; SAB 182. Sholem Aleichem was eventually so frustrated by what he saw as a combination of resentment and greed that he broke off correspondence with the senior writer entirely.

66 got his piece: It was called *The Worm in Horseradish: The Painful Effects of My Young Polish Life.* Y. Y. Linetski, *Der vorem in khreyn,* DYFB 1: 62–92.

66 loomed throughout the editorial process: Reviewing Abramovitch's contribution to the *Folksbibliotek*'s second volume, he cut a song "fit for [the Yiddish operetta writer] Goldfaden, not for you," and refused to print his introduction to his work, feeling its critical tone was not in the author's best interests. See letters to S. Y. Abramovitch, Nov. 17, 1889, B 256, and Jan. 14, 1890, B 262; UR 1:48–49; SAB 168.

66 I. L. Peretz: See, for discussion, Ruth R. Wisse, *I. L. Peretz and the Making of Modern Jewish Culture* (Seattle: University of Washington Press, 1991), 6–17; UR 1:48.

66 "Your wish and goal": Nakhmen Meyzel, ed., *Briv un redes fun Y. L. Peretz* (New York: YKUF, 1944), 139; translation Wisse, 10–11.

67 He made the changes: See CYF 124 and *Briv un redes,* 149–151; compare Miron, *Traveler,* 59–60, 64–65, 71–74.

Chapter 8

68 "to write romances": Letter from S. Y. Abramovitch to Sholem Aleichem, June 28, 1888, in Nakhmen Mayzel, ed., *Dos Mendele Bukh* (New York: YKUF, 1959), 156–158, 157; translation taken from Cammy 99.

68 Even Haskala novels: See Sholem Aleichem's artistic manifesto in his "A briv tsu a gutn fraynd" (1889), DYFB 2:304–310.

68 "the Jewish people": *Stempenyu,* in DYFB 1:1–104 (supplement). Translated as *Stempenyu* in TGCYW, 97–180. Quote from 98–99.

69 "with his whole being": "Berditshever gas," 1:452–453.

69 "they don't live": "Mayne briv," 1:511.

69 "These are my readers?": The last entry of *Sketches from Berdichev Street* is dedicated to a set of "responses" from various "readers," notably complaints about their unsympathetic portraits in the sketches. A somewhat unrepentant Sholem Aleichem responds that, well, if the shoe fits . . . Quote from "Berditshever gas," 1:467–468. See also "Kurtse antvortn af lange fragn" (1887), in AVM 1:470–472, on the increasing desire to be left alone by readers.

69 *Sketches from Zhitomir Street*: "Bilder fun der zhitomirer gas" (1888), in AVM 1:473–486 (1888).

69 The scene's climax: "Zhitomirer gas," 1:477–478.

70 "a good, wise, honest man": Quoted in SAB 167.

70 Abramovitch's portrait: See CYF 136.

70 his own writing style: SAB 170–171. He also nicknamed Sholem Aleichem "*achastranim*," after the fleet messengers of the book of Esther, for his writing speed.

71 "one must sweat over": *Stempenyu*, 100.

71 he was twenty-nine: SAB 166.

71 telling friends: Letter to Y. Kh. Ravnitski, Aug. 17, 1888, B 200; letter to Y. Dinezon, Jan. 16, 1889, B 231; Letter to S. Dubnow, Nov. 11, 1888, B 222.

72 "Readers who are used to": *Stempenyu*, 163.

72 "a Jewish young woman": "A briv tsu a gutn fraynd"; translation Cammy's, 101.

72 "'A dull story!'": *Stempenyu*, 172.

72 "novel writing": See Anita Norich, "Portraits of the Artist in Three Novels by Sholem Aleichem," *Prooftexts* 4.3 (1984): 237–251, 249; SAB 167.

73 "that *Stempenyu* is by nature": Letter to Y. Kh. Ravnitski, Oct. 12, 1888, B 214.

73 always been interested in music: MF 141–142; SAB 135; MBSA, 25–26; Lala Kaufman, "My Father, Sholem Aleichem," *Commentary* 24 (1957): 250–253.

73 His father's inn: See FTF 169.

73 Benditsky: On this physically attractive musician, claimed as a literary model for Stempenyu by Sholem Aleichem's brother, see MBSA 189–191.

73 as a wandering tutor: See FTF 211.

73 in almost every detail: The single difference was that "it was very important to me that [my fictional Stempenyu] should leave no children after him"; in Berdichev, by contrast, Stempenyu's children lived there to that very day. See letters to Dubnow, Sept. 2, 1888, B 204; Nov. 11, 1888, B 222.

74 "a gathering place": Letter to Elye Rabinovich, Sept. 6, 1889, SAB 35.

74 Linetski, still smarting: SAB 169, 179–180.

74 "Odessa bandits": Letter to B. L. Flesker, June 7, 1890, B 267.

74 "youthful projects": Letter to M. Spektor, July 20, 1894, B 293. See also M. Spektor, "Der onheyb fun sholem-aleykhem," *Yidishe kultur* 61.11–12 (1999): 10–12.

74 Spektor: See SAB 163–165; UR 1:28–29, 48; MBSA 95. The author of the *Folksblat* article signed "S" that criticized his publishing efforts was actually the Russian-Yiddish poet S. Frug, not Spektor, as it happened; but Sholem Aleichem didn't know that.

75 lashed out: Letters to Y. Dinezon, Oct. 16, 1888, B 215; July 26, 1888, B 194.

75 Shomer: UR 2:184–185.

75 "that if it were a lady": UR 4:37.

76 Despite his prediction: Letter to Y. Dinezon, Jan. 27, 1889, B 235; Letter to S. Dubnov, Feb. 9, 1889, B 237; Letter to Y. L. Gamzu, May 8, 1889, B 239.

76 "Register of All of the Yiddish Books": See DYFB 1:469–473, esp. 472.

Chapter 9

77 "a damned illness": Letter to Y. Kh. Ravnitski, Jan. 24, 1889, B 234.

77 turned Levi down: Letter to S. Dubnow, Aug. 17, 1889, B 246.

77 in response to Levi's request: SAB 351.

78 chose to shut it down: SAB 184.

78 "blood, time, and health": Letter to Abramovitch, Jan. 14, 1890, B 262.

78 editorial attentions: See letters to Y. Kh. Ravnitski, Oct. 3, 1889, B 251–252; n.d., B 256–257.

78 "cost me a half year": Letter to S. Dubnow, July 18, 1889, B 245.

78 he famously claimed: UR 1:30.

78 his schedule: MF 15–17.

78 "There is no time": *Yossele solovey: a yidisher roman* (1889), AV 2:4:7–261, translated as *The Nightingale*, trans. Aliza Shevrin (New York: Putnam, 1985), 17.

78 "I am pregnant": Cited in MF 86.

79 Vilner Balabeysl: See letter to Y. Kh. Ravnitski, Dec. 4, 1889, B 261; J. Hoberman, *Bridge of Light: Yiddish Film Between Two Worlds* (New York: Schocken, 1991), 258.

79 the similarities: Both feature autobiographical nuggets, for example (Yosele, like his creator, also suffers from the depredations of a miserable stepmother), and both show off Sholem Aleichem's ample understanding of, and fascination with, the ins and outs of musical terminology.

79 "as far": Letter to Y. Kh. Ravnitski, Dec. 4, 1889, B 260.

79 Several years prior: See David Roskies, "Sholem Aleichem: Mythologist of the Mundane," *AJS Review* 13.1–2 (1988): 27–46.

79 "The Penknife": "Dos meserl" (1886), AV 1:5:9–32; translated as "The Penknife," in Curt Leviant, ed. and trans. *Some Laughter, Some Tears* (New York: G. P. Putnam's Sons, 1968; hereafter SLST), 113–128.

80 Critics: Criticism has generally focused on its weak father figure and the phallic connotations of the penknife, seeing in it anything and everything from an indictment of traditional Eastern European Jewish culture to a Freudian process of child development.

80 an incident from his teenage years: The young Sholem, who wants money for a violin, steals a visiting grain merchant's change purse, is consumed by guilt and troubled by nightmares, discards the purse in the river, and then changes the subject—another inconclusive ending. See FTF 171ff.

80 Simon Dubnow: In 1889, Sholem Aleichem wrote Dubnow, "You are the only writer who shows a human and sympathetic attitude to the poor Jargon. It is impossible to express the feeling of gratefulness that I owe to you." Quoted in Koppel S. Pinson, "The National Theories of Simon Dubnow," *Jewish Social Studies* 10.4 (1948): 335–358, 351.

80 "Everything took on": *Nightingale*, 100.

81 "His memory": Cited in MF 44.

81 "you are the head": Letter from Nochem Rabinovich to SA, June 8, 1887, SAB 33; MBSA 73. Sholem Aleichem had also, in recent years, supported his father in his

personal life, his business endeavors, and his medical travails, and would read him new stories at his bedside; see MBSA 44–45, 107.

82 chiding a brother: Letter to Elye Rabinovich, Aug. 17, 1890, B 29–30. His siblings often felt he assumed the parental role; see, for example, MBSA 73.

82 *A Bouquet of Flowers*: *A bintl blumen* (1888), in AVM 2:239–252 (and variant editions in 338–345). Privately circulated they may have been, though he seemed interested in finding a broader audience; discretion perhaps warring with literary ambition, he offered to provide them as a free supplement to another journal. See letters to Y. Kh. Ravnitski, Feb. 20, 1888, B 178; and March 5, 1888, B 179; letter to S. Dubnow, May 29, 1888, B 189.

82 "a sort of snare": "Afn literarishn mark," DYFB 1:355.

82 "poetry without rhyme": Letter to Y. Kh. Ravnitski, Feb. 20, 1888, B 178.

82 "I am no master": Letter to Ernestina Rabinovich, April 16, 1897; B 33.

83 "An Open Response": "Efentlekher antvort" (1887), AVM 2:266.

83 "when it comes to writing": Letter to M. Kleinman, July 3, 1903, B 410–411.

83 "The Western Wall": "Koysl-marovi," AVM 2:241–242.

84 When his friend Ravnitski asked: See letters to Y. Kh. Ravnitski and Ts. Z. Frankfeld, Jan. 15, 1886, B 160–161, and Jan. 23, 1886, B 161–163; and J. Klausner, "Sholom Aleichem the Zionist," in Sholom Aleichem, *Why Do the Jews Need a Land of Their Own?* ed. and trans. Joseph Leftwich and Mordecai S. Chertoff (New York: Herzl Press, 1984; hereafter WDJ), 13; translation partially taken from there.

84 particularly in the Hebrew press: See, particularly, the three-part article in *Hamelitz*, 1889, no. 96–98 ("Hayesh tzorekh besifrut hazhargonit?").

85 "Jargon is my love": Letters to Y. Kh. Ravnitski, June 21, 1887, B 166; Nov. 30, 1887, B 167.

85 A. L. Levinski: See UR 4:126–127; and "Mayn bakantshaft mit a.l. levinski" (1910), AV 3:6:43–50.

85 "complementary": SAP 69.

85 "Zelig Mechanic": "Zelik mekhanik" (1890), in Sholem Aleichem, *Af vos badarfn yidn a land?* (Tel Aviv: I. L. Peretz-Farlag, 1978, hereafter AVBYL), 14–39; translated as "Selig Mechanic" in WDJ 21–34.

86 "cabbages": "Selig," 23.

86 "a bit of a mitzvah": "Selig," 32.

86 "struck lucky": "Selig," 34.

86 banquet for Abramovitch: See SAB 169; UR 2:96.

Chapter 10

88 In June: Letter to B. L. Flesker, June 7, 1890, B 267.

88 "shattered friend": Letter to S. Dubnow, Oct. 2, 1890, B 268–269.

88 another letter: Letter to Y. Kh. Ravnitski, Nov. 10, 1890, B 269; UR 5:29–30.

89 Probably the explanation: See Gurshteyn 18, and his interview with the London press in " 'Sholem Aleichem' in London," *The Jewish Chronicle*, May 25, 1906,

which states that he "fell among speculators, it seems, on the Bourse," and lost over 20,000 pounds. His perspective, looking back: "I lost my money but I gained experience."

89 "what God has given": "Berditshever gas," 449.

89 Geographically: SAB 170, 194.

89 "Your friend": Letter to Y. Kh. Ravnitski, Nov. 10, 1890, B 269.

90 Natasha Mazar; Rokhl Yampolsky: MF 85, 62–63, 125; MBSA 184–185.

90 writing in Hebrew: See SAB 174; UR 2:89–90, 5:32; SAP 51, 69–70; Avner Holtzman, "Kvurat sofrim: Hatkafato shel shalom aleykhem al mikha yosef berdichevsky," *Khulyot* 9 (Summer 2005): 95–116.

91 sketches and short novels for Russian newspapers: For more on Sholem Aleichem's Russian writings—of which the majority, though not the totality, were produced in this period—see Alexander Frenkel, "Sholem Aleichem as a Self-Translator," in *Translating Sholem Aleichem*, 25–46, esp. 27–28.

91 fruitless initiatives: After Zederbaum's death in the summer of 1893, Sholem Aleichem considered creating a consortium to buy the orphaned *Hamelitz* and to publish it biweekly in Odessa, alternating between Hebrew and Yiddish; that winter, he actively targeted a backer to help fund the publication of a Yiddish paper (perhaps the first in a long line of Maecenases Sholem Aleichem would vainly pin his hopes on); and at some point, probably after 1894, he apparently attempted to ghostwrite a volume of the history of the Brodskys and their philanthropy. See letter to Y. Kh. Ravnitski, Sept. 1, 1893, B 271; letter to G. Stavitski, Dec. 8, 1893, B 275; SAB 287; *kol-mevaser*: UR 1:52; Sholem Aleichem, *Kol-mevaser tsu der yudisher folks-bibliotek.*

91 Advertisements: See, for example, *Kol-mevaser*, 47.

91 stayed furious: Letter to M. Spektor, Jan. 5, 1894, B 281.

91 reconciled: The relationship would become so warm, in fact, that Spektor would suggest they burn their correspondence so future readers would not discover it. Sholem Aleichem's response: "Why should we burn them? Let our enemies burn! On the contrary, let history read for one hundred and twenty years, how two Jewish folk writers, who were bound together without benefit of clergy, have corresponded." This hardly meant the relationship ran completely smoothly; Sholem Aleichem savaged a piece Spektor published, for example, suggesting perhaps he was drunk or temporarily insane when writing it, and presumably failed to mollify him by suggesting Spektor would see it his way once he calmed down and would slap himself on both cheeks for not consulting him before submitting it in the first place. Letters to M. Spektor, Nov. 2, 1902, B 400; Feb. 2, 1904, B 430; Feb. 4–5, 1904, B 431.

92 less than a decade later: See "Mythologist," 34.

92 Five years previously: "A farvalgert brivl fun di ibergekhapte briv fun sholem-aleykhem" (1887), AVM 1:151–155; "A tshuve fun di geherte redaktsye" (1887), AVM 1:512–514.

93 "On Londons": Translations are taken from Sholem Aleichem, "Londons," *The Letters of Menakhem-Mendl and Sheyne-Sheyndl and Motl, the Cantor's Son*, trans. Hillel Halkin (New Haven, CT: Yale University Press, 2002; hereafter MM/MC), 3-18, 3, 15, 16. This is a revised version of the stories; for the extraordinarily tan-

gled and complex textual history of *Menakhem-Mendl*, see Avraham Nowersztern, "'Menakhem-mendl' leshalom aleichem: bein toldot hatekst lemivneh hayetsira," *Tarbiz* 54.1 (1985): 105–146.

93 "From Sheyne-Sheyndl": "Londons," 7.

94 "The Counting-House": See, for example, "Kantor-gesheft," 1:262.

94 "Menakhem-Mendl": "To the Second Edition," *Menakhem-Mendl* (1910), 1.

94 "the more substantial": MF 102; Gurshteyn 20; SAP 51.

95 "since they had lived": MF 94; compare MBSA 152.

95 school to learn dentistry: MF 95, 115.

95 much of the basis: *Taknehoz* is also indebted to a Russian series, "Characters on the Stock Exchange," he had written two years before.

95 Weinreich: Max Weinreich, *History of the Yiddish Language* (New York: YIVO, 2008), 1:A234.

96 Sholem Aleichem's *Taknehoz:* "Yaknehoz" (1894), AV 3:3:31–133.

96 "Don't fly so high": "Yaknehoz," 89.

97 a variety of different jobs: See letters to Y. Kh. Ravnitski, June 7, 1894, and June 18, 1894, B 285–287.

97 *House-Friend:* Letter to M. Spektor, Nov. 23, 1893, B 273–274.

97 "Mazapevke Station": "Stantsye mazapevke" (1894), FEL 21–26.

97 "in every time": SAB 5.

97 "To 'The Dove'": "Tsu der 'toyb'" (1894), FEL 27–33; also in B 288–292.

98 "behold, a year": "Tsu der 'toyb,'" 291.

98 "Jargon and the jargonists": Letter to Ravnitski on June 7, 1894, B 285–286.

Chapter 11

99 skeptical: Letter to Elye Rabinovich, May 25, 1884, B 20.

99 "green forests": "In boyberik" (1901), AV 4:5:9–72, translated as "A Home Away from Home," in Sholem Aleichem, *Stories and Satires*, ed. and trans. Curt Leviant (New York: Yosseloff, 1959; hereafter SAS), 308–349, 309.

99 Its fruit gardens: MF 132–134, 140; Letter to M. Spektor, July 1895, B 308–309; Mayzel 57; SAP 209; MBSA 154–157.

100 "salesmen": "Home Away," 313.

100 "The story will be called": Letter to M. Spektor, Sept. 21, 1894, B 295; translation taken from Ruth Wisse, *The Modern Jewish Canon: A Journey Through Language and Culture* (New York: Free Press, 2000), 32.

100 "loved to talk": MF 144.

101 "Tevyeh-like expressions": SAP 21.

101 settled on terms: See letters to M. Spektor, Sept. 21, 1894, Sept. 26, 1894, Oct. 20, 1894, Nov. 4, 1894, Nov. 7, 1894, B 295–297.

101 copyists: MF 129–130.

101 "Please don't be offended": Letter to M. Spektor, Nov. 24, 1894, B 299. Translation taken from Ken Frieden, *A Century in the Life of Sholem Aleichem's Tevye* (Syracuse, NY: Syracuse University Press, 1997), 1.

101 "dairy products": Letter to Y. Kh. Ravnitski, July 4, 1895, B 309.

101 "were popular enough": MF 144–145.

102 "Tevye the Dairyman": "Tevye der milkhiker/Dos groyse gevins" (1894, rev. 1903), AV 5:3:15–40; trans. "Tevye Strikes It Rich," in Sholem Aleichem, *Tevye the Dairyman and the Railroad Stories* (New York: Schocken, 1987; hereafter TDRS), 3–20.

103 a few of them disappear: For a close look, and Tevye's textual history, see Khone Shmeruk, " 'Tevye der milkhiker': letoldoteha shel yetsira," in Shmeruk, *Ayarot ukerakhim: perakim biyetsirato shel shalom aleichem* (Jerusalem: Magnes Press, 2000), 9–32.

103 The historical record: MF 144; SAP 21. According to Yiddish scholar Mikhail Krutikov, a local legend suggests the existence of *two* "Tevyes": the first came into money and moved to Kiev, and his house was bought by a poor man with several daughters. Whether this resolves or complicates the question is uncertain.

103 "Tevye is a healthy Jew": Translation taken from CYF 162–163.

103 "can only be the product": *Judgment*, 142.

104 some trickiness results: Compare Michael Stern, "Tevye's Art of Quotation," *Prooftexts* 6.1 (1986): 79–96.

104 "What's my work?": "Tevye Strikes It Rich," 14.

105 "Hope": "Hofenung" (1887), AVM 2:234–238. Tevye's *also* being witty, of course; he's a master storyteller, and the precise nature of that wit changes constantly, during and across the various installments of his story. Compare Dan Miron, *From Continuity to Contiguity* (Stanford, CA: Stanford University Press, 2010), esp. 368–398.

Chapter 12

109 another Menakhem-Mendl story: "Stocks and Bonds," appearing in the *House-Friend* toward the beginning of 1896, is a variation on the previous theme (Menakhem-Mendl invests the money Sheyne-Sheyndl has sent him to help him return home after the last wipeout, with predictable consequences). "Papirlekh" (1896), AV 5:4:45–80, trans. "Stocks and Bonds," MM/MC 19–37.

109 "the first stone": "Af vos badarfn yidn a land?" (1898), in AVBYL, 14–39, trans. "Why Do Jews Need a Land of Their Own?," WDJ 49–57, 55.

109 "Dr. Pinsker": "Why Do Jews," 56.

110 "Doctor Herzl": "Der yidisher kongres in bazl" (1897), in AVBYL, 40–63, trans. "The Jewish Congress in Basel," WDJ 35–48, 36.

110 "The First Jewish World Congress": "Basel," 36.

110 "A light": "Basel," 35.

111 "Some will say": "Basel," 44.

111 "What do Jews": "Why Do Jews," 49.

111 "There is little": "Tsu undzere shvester in tziyon" (1898), in AVBYL, 119–132, trans. "To Our Sisters in Zion," WDJ 83–89, 85.

112 *Messianic Times*: Meshiekhs Tsaytn, in AVBYL, 80–118, trans. *Messianic Times: A Zionist Novel*, WDJ 58–82.

112 "too much witticism": Klausner 15.

113 *Der Yid*: See Ruth R. Wisse, "Not the 'Pintele Yid' but the Full-Fledged Jew," *Prooftexts* 15.1 (1995): 33–41, passim.

113 grumbled about the paper's name: Letters to Y. Kh. Ravnitski, Feb. 5, 1899, B 319; Sept. 9, 1899, B325.

113 "A boydem": "A boydem," (1899), AV 5:3:43–63, trans. "Tevye Blows a Small Fortune," TDRS 20–35.

113 to send his brother: Letter to Elye Rabinovich, Aug. 18, 1898, B 35.

114 he had written Spektor: Letter to M. Spektor, Nov. 6, 1896, B 315.

114 "when God looked my way": "A Small Fortune," 21.

114 "got hold of me": "A Small Fortune," 21–22.

114 "Why does": "A Small Fortune," 22.

114 "A black day": "A Small Fortune," 33.

115 "Write me": Letter to Y. Kh. Ravnitski, Feb. 5, 1899, B 320.

115 "Millions": "Milyonen," in AV 5:4:83–153 (1899), trans. as "Millions," MM/MC, 38–71.

115 "I'm through": "Millions," 38.

116 "you must be wondering": "Millions," 58.

116 "Today's Children": "Hayntike kinder" (1899), AV 5:3:67–91, trans. "Today's Children," TDRS, 35–52.

116 "A Doctor for a Bridegroom": "A khosn a doktor" (1887, rev. in 1907 as "A doktor"), AV 3:1:101–115.

116 "The Bill of Divorce": "Der get" (1888), AV 4:3:9–39. The work appeared in the first volume of Spektor's *House-Friend*.

117 "today's Jewish daughter": Letter to Elye Rabinovich, Sept. 6, 1889, B 28.

117 He even suggested: Letter to Y. Kh. Ravnitski, May 12–13, 1889, B 287.

117 Ruth Wisse has remarked: See Ruth Wisse, *The Schlemiel as Modern Hero* (Chicago: University of Chicago Press, 1971), 43.

118 "writer of the people": *Judgment*, 167.

118 "In the Book Store": "In sforim kleytl" (1899), FEL 47–53.

Chapter 13

119 "time capsule": MF 20–21.

119 A telling anecdote: MF 98–102.

119 "I need money": Letter to M. Spektor, Feb. 14, 1902, B 356–357.

120 trying to get into the act: See letter to Y. Kh. Ravnitski, dated 17 Tishrei 1899, B 326–327; letter to M. Spektor, Sept. 12, 1902, B 398.

120 "polish up": Letter to M. Spektor, 1902, B 353.

120 "Quick, brother": Letter to M. Spektor, Feb. 23, 1902, B 358.

120 money for future rent: Letters to M. Spektor, April 17, 1902, B 368; April 8, 1902, B 364–365.

121 "cash money!": Letter to S. Y. Abramovitch, April 10–11, 1902, B 365.

121 He even managed: Letters to Spektor, May 3, 1902, B 372–373; May 9, 1902, B 373–376.

121 earn over double: Letter to M. Spektor, Nov. 12, 1902, B 401–403.

121 "Hurrah!": Letter to M. Spektor, Nov. 3, 1902, B 401.

121 predicted that one day: Letter to M. Spektor, Nov. 3, 1902, B 401.

121 the *Fraynd*'s circulation: Sarah Abrevaya Stein, "Faces of Protest: Yiddish Cartoons of the 1905 Revolution," *Slavic Review* 61.4 (2002), 732–761, 735n9.

121 "Jewish Newspapers and Gazettes": "Yidishe gazetn un zhurnaln" (1903), FEL 54–59.

122 *Folksbildung*: Letter to Ravnitski and Bialik, Jan. 22, 1903, B 404–405; letter to M. Spektor, Jan. 20, 1902, B 354.

122 to prune and rewrite: The final version includes, along with *Stempenyu* and tales of Tevye, Kasrilevke, and a generous selection of children's stories, a few idiosyncratic choices, including selections from *A Bouquet of Flowers* and "Zelig Mechanic."

122 selling off some furniture: MF 149. For a detailed description of their diminished living circumstances in Kiev around this period—a middle-class third floor apartment, with room nonetheless for an office for the author to write in—see MBSA 149–153.

122 "new born": Letter to M. Spektor, April 1, 1903, B 405.

122 "God has given me": Letter to A. Schulz, May 21, 1904, B 436. See also SAP 46 and MBSA 203–205. A later press report described his public presentation particularly well: "His humorous sketches were delivered in a soft conversational voice, the clever modulation of which, together with the employment of appropriate gesture and facial play, added greatly to the effect and revealed the possession of genuine histrionic gifts. Though the audience often shook with laughter at his remarkably spontaneous humor, 'Sholem Aleichem' himself remained sober as a sexton." Description from *The Jewish Chronicle*, "'Sholem Aleichem' at South Place Institute," June 8, 1906.

123 support a new friend: He also tried to get editors to publish him. See letter to Y. Kh. Ravnitski; Dec. 30, 1898, B 318; SAB 187.

123 "What Jew": Letter to J. Engel, June 13, 1901, B 336.

123 "reflect, as in clear water": The comment appears in a 1900 essay about Warshawsky that served as introduction to a first edition of the latter's collected folk songs. See "M. M. Varshavski un zayne lider" (1900), AV 3:6:53–58, 54–55.

123 An early version: UR 1:73; SAB 58; Letter to M. Spektor, Nov. 2, 1902, B 400.

123 he wrote his daughter: Letter to Ernestina Rabinovich, Aug. 18, 1902, SAB 58.

124 *Folktsaytung* sketches: "Leytsones" (1903), FEL 60–66.

124 though still complaining: Letter to Ernestina Rabinovich, April 12, 1905, SAB 61.

124 "What can I say": Letter to Ernestina Rabinovich, March 22, 1905, SAB 60.

124 when his train: Letter to Ernestina Rabinovich, April 22, 1905, B 44.

124 might not always want: Sholem Aleichem told the tale in a feuilleton, "Sholem-Aleichem!," which castigates the press for wanting Shomerist romance when the author wants to write novels of Yiddish life. See "Sholem-Aleykhem!" (1902), AV 3:6:9–17.

124 "The Merry Company": "Di freylekhe kompanye" (1903), AV 4:3:151–209.

124 "An Honorable Profession": "A bekovede parnose" (1903, as "A naye parnose"),

AV 5:4:157–179; trans. "An Honorable Profession: Menakhem-Mendl Becomes a Writer," MM/MC 72–82.

125 "The paper wrote": "An Honorable Profession," 73.

125 flaunting its folk ties: Notes from the period suggested he planned to write three stories "without an end"—"A story with a corpse," "A story with a golem," and "A story with a goat": "The Enchanted Tailor" is clearly the story with the goat; "Eternal Life" (discussed next) is the story with the corpse. See SAB 344.

125 "stylized chapbook": Roskies, "Mythologist," 35. On his chapbooks' popularity, see Roskies, "The Medium and Message of the Maskilic Chapbook," *Jewish Social Studies* 41.3–4 (1979): 275–290, 285.

125 "The Enchanted Tailor": "A mayse on an ek/Der farkishefter shnayder" (1900), AV 4:3:9–68, trans. "The Haunted Tailor," in Irving Howe and Ruth R. Wisse, eds. *The Best of Sholom Aleichem* (New York: New Republic Books, 1979; hereafter BOSA), 2–36. The story was inspired by "an obscure chapbook by Isaac Meir Dik"; see Roskies, *Bridge*, 160.

125 "take an old caftan": BOSA 2–3.

126 "Cossack of a woman": BOSA 4.

126 "Eternal Life": "Oylem-habe" (1904), AV 4:3:213–245; trans. "Eternal Life," BOSA 43–60.

126 "strangely solitary": BOSA 45.

126 "grew in stature": BOSA 46.

127 "Whenever anyone": BOSA 60.

127 neither story has much of an ending: See Roskies, "Mythologist," 37, 45; David Neal Miller, "'Don't Force Me to Tell You the Ending': Closure in the Short Fiction of Sh. Rabinovitsh (Sholem-Aleykhem)," *Neophilologus* 66.1 (1982): 102–110.

127 "You are a young man": BOSA 54.

127 "'What is the moral'": BOSA 36.

Chapter 14

128 "The Clock": "Der zeyger" (1900), AV 1:5:65–75; trans. "The Clock That Struck Thirteen," BOSA 82–88.

128 notably superstitious: UR 2:72.

128 particularly hated the number thirteen: "The whole world can't be mad," he wrote; "if the world has assumed that a certain number is a bad thing, there is probably something in it." Cited in WDJ 206.

129 journals and newspapers: SAB 50, 85, 175; UR 2:75.

129 "Home for Passover": "Af peysekh aheym" (1903), AV 1:3:35–57; trans. as "Home for Passover," BOSA 89–102. That same year's "The Passover Eve Vagabonds" similarly compares a young boy's exile from parts of the house during Passover preparation to the Jewish Diaspora writ large; see "Di erev-peysekhdike emi-gratsiye" (1903), AV 1:6:219–231; trans. as "The Passover Eve Vagabonds," SAS 214–221.

129 "In Haste": "Bekhipozn" (1900), AV 1:3:19–31; trans. "In Haste," SSSA 162–172.

The story's title is taken from the Deuteronomic verse describing the Exodus's rapidity.

130 "Four Goblets": "Arbe koyses" (1900), AV 5:1:223–239; "Arbe koyses" (1888), AV 1:3:9–16. He was probably thinking of his father's wine business, deeply concerned with its Passover trade; see MBSA 30–43.

130 Two years later: See "Mah nishtane" (1902), AV 1:4:9–17, 11.

130 "What Is Chanukah?": "Vos iz khanike?" (1901), AV 5:1:187–208.

131 a 1900 feuilleton: "Purim" (1900), AV 5:1:211–220.

131 "the Purim of years gone by": "Purim," 211.

131 His son-in-law noted: SAB 50.

131 the recollection of that world: Case in point: the 1900 holiday story "Hannukah Money." The *gelt* the narrator and his brother collect from various family members around town isn't the real gift; the real treasures of the story are the compelling and unforgettable family portraits yielded in the process. More and more, the past was becoming valuable currency. See "Khanike-gelt" (1900), AV 1:6:29–50, trans. "Hannukah Money," SSSA 196–211.

132 "The Flag": "Di fon" (1900), AV 1:6:9–26; trans. "The Flag," OCT 76–84.

132 treads similar territory: This would become a fairly common template for Sholem Aleichem when it came to children's stories of this period, as it turned out. See, for example, "The Esrog," with a child's inexorable yearning to bite the stem off the ritual fruit used for Sukkot, and the guilt that follows ("Der esreg" (1902), AV 1:4:21–38; trans. "The Esrog," SLST 26–36), and "The Fiddle" ("Afn fidl" (1902), AV 1:5:35–61, trans. "The Fiddle," SSSA 307–323). The author himself wrote that "Fiddle" and "Penknife" shouldn't be published together "because they have one character"; letter to Y. Kh. Ravnitski and Kh. N. Bialik, June 18, 1902, B 388.

132 "Rabchik: A Jewish Dog": "Robtshik: a yidisher hunt" (1901), AV 1:5:79–94, trans. "Rabchik, a Jewish Dog" in Irving Howe and Eliezer Greenberg, *Yiddish Stories Old and New* (New York: Holiday House, 1974), 18–30.

132 "Methuselah: A Jewish Horse": "Mesushelekh: a yidish ferdl" (1902), AV 1:5:97–111, trans. "Methuselah—a Jewish Horse," OCT 87–97.

133 a real city: Sholem Aleichem once wrote a friend that Berdichev was to a Yiddish writer what Paris was to a French writer, London to an English writer, or St. Petersburg to a Russian writer. See Mayzel 44.

133 was modeled on another town: "Image," 14.

133 on the evidence: See FTF 4–5.

133 "encompass[ed]": Letter to A. B. Goldovsky, Nov. 12, 1901, B 340.

133 "not just an ordinary pauper": "Di shtot fun di kleyne mentshelekh" (1901), AV 5:2:9–17, trans. "The Town of the Little People," SSSA 28–34, 28.

133 "happy paupers": "Varshavski," 55.

134 "my muse": "Di groyse reputatsye fun di kleyne mentshelekh/Kasrilevker nisrofim" (1903, 1910), AV 4:2:9–60, trans. "The Poor and the Rich," in Sholem Aleichem, *Inside Kasrilevke* (New York: Schocken, 1948; hereafter IK), 71–118, 87.

134 "I myself": "Di groyse behole fun di kleyne mentshelekh" (1904), AV 5:2:157–210, trans. "The Great Panic of the Little People," OCT 98–135, 99–100.

134 "stuck away": "Town of the Little People," 28.

134 "twist and turn": "Town of the Little People," 32.

134 Kasrilevke sausage: "Gantz berditshev/Dos naye kasrilevke" (1901), AV 4:2:63–128, trans. "A Guide to Kasrilevke," IK 11–67, 32.

135 "the most roguish": "The Great Panic," 108.

135 "scorn the cleverest": "The Poor and the Rich," 94.

135 "The Search": "Oysgetreyselt" (1902), AV 5:2:213–221; trans. "A Yom Kippur Scandal," BOSA 37–42.

135 conservative moral conscience: for two other examples from the period, see "Tsvey shalekh-monesn" (1902), AV 5:2:87–103, trans. "Two Shalachmones, or a Purim Scandal," in *Tevye's Daughters* (New York: Crown, 1949; hereafter TD), 192–202; and "Di yorshim" (1902), AV 5:2:137–154, trans. "The Inheritors," TOC 8–20, which shows how Reb Yosifl's solutions, even when they're moral ones, can often lead, through an excess of self-sacrifice, to a kind of destruction.

135 "the rest of us": "A Yom Kippur Scandal," 42.

135 Kasrilevke only mocks: Even Methuselah, the Jewish horse, fell victim to Kasrilevke: it's where his story ends, and Kasrilevkans lead him to his death, laughing hysterically.

136 "Who of you all": "Why Do Jews," 50.

136 "common Jewish action": Cited in Antony Polonsky, "The Dreyfus Affair and Polish-Jewish Interaction, 1890–1914," *Jewish History* 11.2 (1997): 21–40, 26.

137 a throwaway joke: In 1899's "Millions," Sheyne-Sheyndl asks her husband exactly who Dreyfus is (after a local scandal where a girl asked her suitor his opinion of the Dreyfus affair, and the latter believed he was a local businessman), and Menakhem-Mendl responds with a considerably garbled version of the facts. See "Millions," 66–67.

137 "Dreyfus in Kasrilevke": "Es kon nit zayn/Dreyfus in kasrilevke" (1902), AV 5:2:61–68, trans. as "Dreyfus in Kasrilevka," BOSA 111–114.

137 "It cannot be!": "Dreyfus in Kasrilevka," 114. See Joseph Sherman, "The Irony of Faith: Sholem Aleichem's 'Dreyfus in Kasrilevke,'" *Jewish Affairs* 49.4 (1994): 35–39.

137 right on the facts: In the story's original 1902 publication in *Der Yid*, the last line can be translated as "And so it has remained until *this very day*." *Der Yid* no. 9 (Feb. 6, 1902).

139 "I talk": "Bilder fun der berditshever gas," 457.

139 "Geese": "Gendz" (1902), AV 3:4:29–44, trans. "Geese," SAS 116–128.

139 continually rehearses: Sholem Aleichem's obsessive monologists commonly have a repeated phrase or verbal tic: though they can be taken as proof of the speaking character's plausibility—real people do, like, tend to heavily fall back on certain stock phrases, you know?—they're also keys to the story's—and often Sholem Aleichem's—general themes. For another example see 1902's "Kenahore," whose title phrase is also the monologist's verbal tic. The extraordinarily common Yiddish phrase, literally translatable as "no evil eye," is repeated tens of times through the story, and shifts its meaning radically as the Kasrilevke wagon driver unspools his tale, ranging from irony to sentimentality, inviting the reader to reflect on fate in a dazzling variety of ways. "Kinahore nit" (1902),

AV 5:2:71–76. Compare Victor Erlich, "A Note on the Monologue as a Literary Form: Sholem Aleichem's *Monologn*; A Test Case," in *For Max Weinreich on His Seventieth Birthday*, (The Hague: Walter de Gruyter, 1964), 44–50, esp. 46.

139 "So I sit and pluck": "Geese," 125.

139 "The Pot": "Dos tepl" (1901), AV 3:4:9–25, trans. "The Pot," BOSA 71–81.

140 whether or not he was familiar: Compare Ken Frieden, "Sholem Aleichem: Monologues of Mastery," *Modern Language Studies* 19.2 (1989): 25–37, 36.

140 "A White Bird": "A vayse kapore" (1904), in Sholem Aleichem, *Ale Verk* (New York: Folksfond, 1917–1923), 21:47–54; trans. "A White Bird," OCT 161–167. The white bird, a symbol of transferred sin, also seems to symbolize the idea of transference itself.

140 written in a week: See letter to Y. Kh. Ravnitski, Aug. 29, 1904, B 437.

140 doubting such procedures: Besides "Three Widows," compare the monologist's complaint in "At the Doctor's," in response to previous doctors' insistence that his stomach complaints are just nerves "despite the fact that it makes no sense, logically. What connection is there between nerves and the stomach? Strange bedfellows!" (It emerges that though the patient's complaint *can* be psychologically determined—anxieties about money, and specifically how everything has become commercialized—this doctor is like all the others: a line of patients in the waiting room, putting pressure on talkers to cut down their speeches.) See "Baym doktor" (1904), AV 3:4: 95–103, trans. "At the Doctor's," SAS 175–181, quote on 177.

140 "Three Widows": "Dray almones" (1907), AV 3:4:165–212, trans. as "Three Widows," SAS 182–213.

140 "You're sadly mistaken": "Three Widows," 182.

141 "Why'd I let you": "Three Widows," 192.

141 "Well, what have you got to say": "Three Widows," 213.

141 "A Bit of Advice": "An eytse" (1904), AV 3:4:73–91, trans. "A Bit of Advice," SLST 131–144.

141 persistent visitor: See Hana Wirth-Nesher, "Voices of Ambivalence in Sholem Aleichem's Monologues," *Prooftexts* 1.2 (1981): 158–171, esp. 165.

141 "I lunged": "A Bit of Advice," 143–144.

Chapter 15

142 Kishinev: See Edward H. Judge, *Easter in Kishinev: Anatomy of a Pogrom* (New York: New York University Press, 1992), esp. 23–24, 30–32, 40–48, 72–74, 136–137. The pogrom began on Easter Sunday, which was also the final day of Passover.

142 Russian writers denounced the pogrom: Judge 88–89.

143 going so far as to write: Cited in Reuben Ainsztein, "Jewish Tragedy and Heroism in Soviet War Literature," *Jewish Social Studies* 23.2 (1961): 67–84, 67–68.

143 proposing to Sholem Aleichem: See letter to M. Gorky, n.d [1901], B 333.

143 He'd been working on the project: Letter to M. Spektor, March 30, 1902, B 362–363; letter to S. Y. Abramovitch, April 1902, B 365; Letter to Y. Kh. Ravnitski,

Sept. 10, 1902, B 397; letters to M. Spektor, Sept. 11, 1902, B 397, June 11, 1902, B 387; Gilya Gerda Schmidt, *Art and Artists of the Fifth Zionist Council* (Syracuse, NY: Syracuse University Press, 2003), 184.

143 Homel: Also known in English as "Gomel"; see Shlomo Lambroza, "The Pogroms of 1903–1906," in Klier and Lambroza 195–247, 207–210.

143 "most despicable acts": Letter to V. G. Korolenko, June 1903, B 408; MF 153–154. Korolenko had actually traveled to Kishinev and wrote a short story blaming "Christian Russia as a whole for the pogrom"; see Judge 89.

143 Chekhov confessed: Letter, Anton Chekhov to Sholem Aleichem, June 19, 1903, in Hirsh Raminik, "Sholem-aleykhem un di rusishe literatur," *Sovetish heymland* 12 (1973): 151–160, 156.

144 "terrible abomination": Letter, Leo Tolstoy to Sholem Aleichem, May 6, 1903, SAB 236.

144 "the greatest injustice": Letter to Dr. Perper, Dec. 1, 1910, B 524–526.

144 Production of *Help*: SAB 236; Letters to V. G. Tchertkov, Sept. 24, 1903, B 411–412; Oct. 14, 1903; B 422; Nov. 15, 1903, B 425–426; Nov. 27, 1903, B 426–427; Nov. 29, 1903, B 427; Dec. 8, 1903, B 428; Feb. 10, 1904, B 432.

144 a who's who: *Hilf: A Zamlbukh fir literatur un kunst* (Warsaw: Folksbildung, 1903).

144 "One Hundred and One": "Hundert eyns" (1903), AV 4:2:103–115; trans. "One Hundred and One," OCT 283–291.

145 "Does not our teacher": "Tsar baley-khayim" (1903), AV 1:5:193–200; trans. "A Pity for the Living," Sholem Aleichem, *Jewish Children* (New York: Knopf, 1926; hereafter JC), 99–105, 104.

145 written just after: Letter to M. Spektor, April 11, 1903, SAB 199.

145 "'Vengeance'": "Grins af shvues" (1903), AV 1:6:123–133; trans. "Greens for 'Shevuos,'" JC 79–88, 83.

145 in the fanciful allegory: "Kapores" (1903), AV 1:5:115–126.

145 "Lag Ba'omer": "Legboymer" (1887, different version 1901), AV 1:6:101–120; trans. "Legboymer," TGCYW 81–87.

145 "trees were people": Cited in MF 46.

146 "Two Anti-Semites": "Tsvey antisemitn" (1905), AV 4:1:151–161; trans. "Two Anti-Semites," BOSA 115–121.

146 "he was bound": "Two Anti-Semites," 116–117.

146 "Our Max": "Two Anti-Semites," 120.

147 "one of the most useful": Letter to Y. Kh. Ravnitski, Oct. 22, 1903, B 424; see also MBSA 135.

147 What about more active solutions?: See Judge 142–143.

147 "Lunatics": "Meshugoim" (1900), AV 3:5:71–134, trans. "Lunatics," WDJ 98–130.

147 "The Red Little Jews": "Di royte yidlekh" (1900), AV 3:5:9–67, trans. "The Red Little Jews," WDJ 90–130, quote on 97.

148 "Homesick": "Farbenkt aheym" (1902), AV 5:2:115–126, trans. "Homesick," WDJ 125–130.

148 two slight allegorical dramas: "A konsilium fun doktoyrim" (1903), AVBYL 198–208, trans. "Doctors in Consultation," WDJ 131–138; "Ugandiada" (1905), AVBYL 235–242, trans. "Ugandaade," WDJ 154–159.

148 "in bed": "Doctors," 131.

148 "I know it's an old remedy": "Doctors," 134.

149 "rich orphan girl": "Ugandiada," 154.

149 a scathing feuilleton: "An aseyfe fun yiko in pariz" (1903), FEL 67–73.

149 an elegiac pamphlet: *Doktor Teodor Herzl* (1904), AVBYL 209–234, trans. "Dr. Theodor Herzl," WDJ 139–153.

Chapter 16

150 didn't abandon this theme entirely: See, for example, 1902's "75,000," a long story recounting the tragic consequences of winning a lottery jackpot. The winning ticket brings chaos to all concerned; claims and counterclaims to the ticket's title are thrust back and forth—and it eventually transpires that everyone had misread the ticket's serial numbers; it wasn't a winning ticket, after all. The story's unexpected deflation is the very sound of a bubble popping. "Finf-un-zibetsik toyznt" (1902), AV 4:3:71–130, trans. "75,000," SAS 235–274.

150 replaced the pictures: Mayzel 91; MBSA 132.

151 lacquered shoes: UR 1:101.

151 "A Few Words": "A por verter vegn undzer bal-melokhe" (1889), FEL 11–20.

151 a Kasrilevke schoolteacher: "Ven ikh ben roytshild" (1902), AV 5:2:129–133; trans. "If I Were Rothschild," BOSA 129–132.

151 "everything would be run": "Rothschild," 130.

151 "I might do away": "Rothschild," 132. Another character from a story the same year attacks the capitalist system, claiming that taking interest is morally and Jewishly wrong, that the rabbis have equated it with theft, and that "he who lives off unearned money is the lowest of the low. Everyone . . . must labor in the sweat of his brow. There is no justice otherwise." "Nisht far keyn yidn gedakht" (1902), AV 5:2:53–58, trans. "May God Have Mercy," TD 141–144, 143.

151 stories on the theme: Aside from those mentioned below, in 1903 alone, see also his revision of an 1884 story, "Hekher un nidriker" (1903), AVM 1:233–249; "Eyner fun toyznt" (1903), AV 3:5:235–251, trans. "One in a Million," BOSA 245–253; and, for a perspective through the lens of the children's story, "Dos dreydl" (1903), AV 1:6:177–203, trans. "The Dreydl," SLST 65–82.

151 "An Easy Fast": "A gringer tones" (1903), AV 4:2:167–177, trans. "An Easy Fast," TD 172–179.

152 "people who found it": "An Easy Fast," 178.

152 "The Convoy": "Mitn etap" (1903), AV 4:4:53–100, trans. "The Convoy," TOC 265–300.

152 "I still could not understand": "The Convoy," 285–286.

152 "Simchat Torah": "Simkhes-toyre" (1903), AV 1:3:95–104.

152 a similar story's protagonist: "Akdomes" (1904), AV 1:3:121–131.

152 Rassel: "Dos nay-geborene, oder rasl" (1903), FEL 94–101.

152 "The First Commune": "Di ershte komune" (1904), AV 1:6:153–174, trans. "The First Commune," in Sholom Aleichem, *Holiday Tales of Sholom Aleichem* (Mineola, NY: Dover, 1979; hereafter HTSA), 76–88.

152 "those old comforting tales": "The First Commune," 77.

153 "Hodl": "Hodl" (1904), AV 5:3:95–118; trans. "Hodl," TDRS 53–69.

153 "some vague relief": MF 156.

153 some of his travel and public readings: See MBSA 205–206.

153 "Hodl," published: See Frieden, *Century*, 5n9.

154 he wrote the mock lullaby: SAB 60; Mayzel 77–78.

154 "Sleep, Alexei": "Shlof alekse" (1905, rev. 1908), AVM 2:280; Max Goldin, "Sholem aleykhem in der folkslid," *Sovetish heymland* 10 (1985): 140–144, 140. The government was not entirely unmindful of Sholem Aleichem's role in these efforts: see MBSA 135.

154 a failed scheme: See UR 1:68–75, SAB 50, 203–205; Letter to Y. Kh. Ravnitski, Dec. 7, 1904, B 440–441.

154 "the idol": Letter to the children, Nov. 15, 1904; Letter to Ernestina Rabinovich, Nov. 15, 1904, B 40–41. See also MBSA 136.

155 had been enchanted: See "Purim" (1900), AV 5:1:211–220.

155 having *Yaknehoz* staged: Letter to Hillel Malakhovski, June 28, 1894, B 292–293.

155 composed his full-length play: Letter to M. Spektor, Oct. 9, 1902, B 399; Khone Shmeruk, " 'Tsezeyt un tseshpreyt' vehahatzagot shel hamakhaze besafa hapolanit bevarsha beshanim 1905 ve-1910," *Ayarot*, 113–131.

155 finally appeared onstage: Mayzel 115; Shmeruk, " 'Tsezeyt,' " 125–126.

155 *Scattered and Dispersed*: "Tsezeyt un tseshpreyt" (1903–1906, performed 1905); AV 3:1:43–97.

155 didn't have the money: Letters to D. Frishman, April 8, 1905, April 11, 1905, B 441–442; UR 1:70–71.

156 Elysium: Jacob Weitzner, *Sholem Aleichem in the Theater* (Teaneck, NJ: Fairleigh Dickinson University Press, 1994), 5.

157 had moved to Mohilev-Podolsk: UR 1:162.

157 "the audience gave the play": Cited in MF 152.

157 "My God!": Letter to Ernestina Rabinovich, April 14, 1905, SAB 62. As it turns out, the play wasn't performed more than half a dozen times; see SAP 56.

157 a bill had announced: "Sore-Sheyndl [*sic*] from Yehupetz and Menakhem-Mendl from Mazapevke, a comedy in four acts, eight scenes, with songs. Written by S. Rabinovich (Sholem-Aleichem), translated by E. Fishzon." Letter to M. Spektor, June 7, 1903, B 408–409.

158 didn't seem to have bothered: In fact, Fishzon's play was taken from a different dramatic source entirely—the 1895 play *The Lost Soul* by the Yiddish playwright Joseph Lateiner—and simply retitled to piggyback on the popularity of Sholem Aleichem's characters. See Nina Warnke, "Going East: The Impact of American Yiddish Plays and Players on the Yiddish Stage in Czarist Russia, 1890–1914," *American Jewish History* 92.1 (2004): 1–29, 13–14, for a fuller account.

158 "Agents": "Agentn" (1905), AV 3:2:199–218, trans. "Agents—a One-Act Play," SAS 275–286.

158 "Let's be honest": "Agents," 286.

158 Four years previously: "Es fidlt nisht" (1901), AV 5:4:183–204, trans. "It's No Go," MM/MC 83–95. Sholem Aleichem uses a similar structure, played in a key of tragic innocence, in a story of tutors crafting elegant love letters to each other:

"Mayn ershter roman" (1903), AV 4:4:119–148, trans. "My First Love Affair," SAS 129–146.

158 the next installment: "Shlim-shlimazl" (1901), AV 5:4:207–219; trans. "Always a Loser," MM/MC 96–102.

Chapter 17

159 "Our task": Cited in Weitzner, 13.

159 nothing came of it: See letter to Ernestina Rabinovich, June 30, 1905, B 45; SAB 64; MF 153; UR 2:59–60; Mayzel 115.

160 literary salon: SAB 155–156; UR 1:62–64.

160 "I'm no Hasidic rebbe": SAB 158.

160 one of the "disciples": UR 1:125–130.

160 revolutionary sentiment: UR 1:93, 135, 157; MF 157.

161 the bully so pugnacious: "Getsl" (1904), AV 1:4:55–67; trans. "Getzel," JC 38–49.

161 complacent older students: "A farshpilter legboymer" (1904), AV 1:4:9–88, trans. "A Lost 'Lag Beomer,' " JC 50–57.

161 a children's story: The defeated beadle resembles a willow twig whose leaves have all been beaten off, as one does on Hoshane Rabo; thus the story's Yiddish title, "Beaten-Out Hoshanes." "Opgeshlogene hoshaynes" (1905), AV 4:4:165–189, trans. "Isser the Shamesh" and "Boaz the Teacher," SLST 161–187.

161 "Joseph": "Yoysef" (1905), AV 3:4:107–133, trans. "Joseph" in Ken Frieden, ed., *Nineteen to the Dozen* (Syracuse, NY: Syracuse University Press, 1998; hereafter *Nineteen*), 81–102.

161 "sort that likes letting their hair grow": "Joseph," 85.

161 narrator's confiding in him: And it's quite a confidence: the narrating "gent," enamored with a young woman who only has eyes for the revolutionary leader Joseph, has probably gotten the latter killed by reporting his activities to local authorities. It's very possible the gent didn't know his actions' fatal consequence; he might have just been hoping for exile, like Hodl's husband Pertchik, just getting the rival out of the way, and that his entire stuttering, self-justifying monologue, his attempts to wheedle his way onto the listener's (and the reader's) good side, is the expression of his terrible guilt. But there's another, more terrible way to read the story: the gent knew (and knows) the whole story all along; and the bumbling he displayed in his attempts to "infiltrate" Joseph's crowd to see what the fuss was all about and in his efforts to recall those attempts for the listener are just acts. The story works on both levels: it works best, in fact, if the reader is constantly shifting between approaches.

162 Strikes were breaking out: UR 1:165–166, 173–174; MF 156.

162 congratulatory telegram: Telegram to Ernestina Rabinovich, April 18, 1905, SAB 65.

162 "Do you mean to tell me": "Gimenaziye" (1902), AV 5:5:175–193; trans. "High School," TDRS 217–229, 228. The work's original title: "To the Slaughter."

162 Running home: MF 158–160; UR 1:220; SAB 66; Mayzel 63.

162   Black Hundreds: See Lambroza 224–225.

162   "cry that Jews": Letter to M. Fishberg, Oct. 21–24, 1905; B 444–445.

163   a confusing telegram: UR 1:208.

163   "the Brodskys": Letter to Ernestina Rabinovich, Oct. 21, 1905, SAB 66.

163   "This is an optimist": Letter to Ernestina Rabinovich, Oct. 26, 1905, SAB 67.

163   There was a simple Jew: Letter to I. D. Berkowitz, Nov. 23, 1905, B 50.

164   "had the means": Letter to M. Fishberg, Oct. 24, 1905, SAB 209.

164   "if we die": Letter to Ernestina Rabinovich, Oct. 26, 1905, SAB 67.

164   "Sleep, My Child": See Goldin 141.

165   put the starry-eyed optimism: UR 1:226; *The Dove*; "A grus fun der heym" (1893–1894), FEL 34–46; Letter to M. Fishberg, Feb. 23, 1906, B 451. For another early example of starry-eyed optimism, see his 1884 review discussed in Khone Shmeruk, "Sholem Aleichem and America," *YIVO Annual* 20 (1991): 211–238, 213.

165   "The main thing": Letter to M. Fishberg, Sept. 13, 1905, SAB 208.

165   Never one for second best: MF 167; Letters to M. Fishberg, Sept. 13, 1905; Oct. 8, 1905, SAB 208–209; Hoberman, 205–206.

166   "what should one do": Letter to M. Fishberg, Oct. 26, 1905, B 445–446.

166   ready cash for moving expenses: See UR 1:228; Olga Litvak, "Khave and Her Sisters: Sholem-aleichem and the Lost Girls of 1905," *Jewish Social Studies* 15.3 (2009): 1–38, 17–19, 22, 35 (quote on 22); SAB 207–208.

166   a jab at the competition: In announcing that Sholem Aleichem would "describe the pogroms for us," the *Tageblat* (Nov. 23, 1905) claimed to have heard that the *Morgen Zhurnal* had taken up a subscription for Sholem Aleichem's family, and twitted them for turning them into charity cases at the people's expense. By contrast, the *Tageblat* claimed, it would help bring Sholem Aleichem to America on its own, having cabled him 600 rubles ($300, over $7,000 in 2010 dollars) for the work.

166   Strikes were breaking out: UR 1:246; MF 165.

167   On the second night of Chanuka: UR 1:229–230, 234, 260–261.

Chapter 18

171   "benefit from the true freedom": Letter to Ernestina Rabinovich, Nov. 23–24, 1905, B 51.

171   border town of Radziwill: UR 2:8–12, 26; SAP 188.

171   Brody was a boomtown: UR 2:18, 31–37; MF 172.

172   "the students": MF 167–168.

172   All this warmth: UR 1:254–256; 2:20–23, 27–30, 38–42; MF 170; Yisroel Berkovitch, "Sholem Aleichem in rumenye," in Iza Shapira et al., *Bukareshter shriftn* (Bucharest: Criterion, 1978), 92–105.

173   Not surprising: Letter to M. Fishberg, Feb. 23, 1906; B 450–451; UR 2:44–45; MF 181.

173   artistic output: UR 2:56; "S'a lign" (1906), AV 3:4:155–161, trans. as "It's a Lie!," SLST 147–152.

173 Vilna's *Time*: UR 2:47, 62; Letter to Y. Kh. Ravnitski and Kh. N. Bialik, March 20, 1906, B 452.

173 "The Purim Feast": "Tsu der sude" (1906), AV 1:4:91–102; trans. as "The Purim Feast," TD 239–246. The story, where a recalcitrant child is forced to go to his rich, snobbish, detestable Uncle Hertz's Purim table, as the family of poor relations hopes for some recognition, might give a whiff of Sholem Aleichem's resentment about bowing to matters of financial necessity.

174 "The Guest": "Der oreyekh" (1906), AV 1:4:105–115; trans. "The Guest," BOSA 225–229.

174 "to that fortunate Jewish land": "The Guest," 227.

174 "Chava": "Khave" (1906), AV 5:1:121–140, trans. "Chava," TDRS 69–82. Scholars have suggested "Chava"'s indebtedness to several 1903 short stories by the Yiddish writer Leon Kobrin, one featuring a romance between a peasant intellectual and a Jewish girl named Khave, the other an independent and politically minded woman named Chane. See Litvak, "Khave and Her Sisters," 2. Sholem Aleichem himself had taken on the hot-button topic of conversion before—he claimed the world loved it because "the theme is a topical one" (letter to M. Spektor, Feb. 14, 1902, B 357). See, for example, "The Lottery Ticket," where a local sexton, inordinately proud of his son's intellectual achievements, nonetheless reminds his "lottery ticket" in his letters to remember that he is a Jew—a reminder that goes unheeded. See "A 'vigrishne bilyet,'" (1902), AV 4:4:9–50; partial trans. as "The Lottery Ticket," SSSA 350–371.

174 late May: UR 2:57, 62.

175 "that explains why": "Chava," 72.

175 "You know": "Chava," 73.

176 "I tell you": "Chava," 81.

176 "Once, for example": "Chava," 82. Frieden (CYF 177–178) also notes the blurring between reality and fiction here, but offers a different interpretation.

177 As late as April: SAB 214; UR 2:62, 67–68.

177 pogroms in Odessa: See Lambroza 232–233, and Robert Weinberg, "The Pogrom of 1905 in Odessa: A Case Study," in Klier and Lambroza, 248–289, esp. 267–268.

177 It had the audience: Nils Roemer, "London and the East End as Spectacles of Urban Tourism," *JQR* 99:3 (2009), 416–434, 417.

177 "what sort of a public": Letter to Israel Cohen, April 7, 1906, *Commentary* 8 (1949): 582.

177 "Colossal": Letter to the Berkowitzes, n.d., SAB 71.

177 "From the minute": *Blondzhende shtern* (1909–1910; New York: Hebrew Publishing Co., 1920); trans. *Wandering Stars* (New York: Viking, 2009), 226.

178 The familiarities: MF 176; UR 2:81.

178 "I eagerly": Letter to the children, June 16, 1906, B 54–55.

178 "everything that you read here": Letter to the children, July 6–7, 1906, SAB 73.

178 Zangwill: MF 173; " 'Sholem Aleichem' at South Place."

179 "whatever might be": "Sholem Aleichem in Manchester," *Jewish Chronicle*, July 6, 1906.

179 A mid-August meeting: UR 2:137–142, *Commentary* 8 (1949): 584.

179 Sholem Aleichem was no fan: UR 2:142–145; SAB 319.

179 "David Son of David": "Dovid ben dovid" (1906), *Di goldene keyt* 34 (1959): 18–47.

180 "Do you want to know": The introduction is reprinted in B 60–62, quote on B 60.

Chapter 19

182 "Those who know America": Letter to Natasha Mazar, Aug. 11, 1906, B 57–58.

182 ambivalence: See UR 2:162.

182 "Jews," he wrote: Letter to children, dated Oct. 16, 1906, B 63–69; MF 185–186.

184 Stella Adler: "Welcome, Sholem Aleichem!" *Morgen-Zhurnal*, Oct. 21, 1906.

184 That same Yiddish press: UR 2:166; quote MF 188.

185 ran a huge photo: "Welcome, Sholem Aleichem!"

185 The packed reception: UR 2:172–174; MF 186.

185 "one of the most famous": "A *sholem-aleykhem* for Sholem Aleichem," *Morgen-Zhurnal*, Oct. 25, 1906.

185 the banquet: "A Warm Welcome to Sholem Aleichem," *Morgen-Zhurnal*, Nov. 1, 1906.

185 When he introduced: MF 187. I rely here on the daughter's testimony, though many believe the story to be apocryphal; see Jeffrey Shandler, ed., *Sholem Aleichem in America: The Story of a Culture Hero* (New York: YIVO, 1990), 10. For Sholem Aleichem's own undoubted interest in Twain's work, see MBSA 143.

186 the papers had helpfully: "Welcome, Sholem Aleichem!"

186 The wooing: SAB 81; UR 2:170–176.

187 "From America would come": "Sholem Aleichem to the readers of the *Morgen-Zhurnal*," Nov. 4, 1906.

187 "mountains of gold": Letter to Ernestina Berkowitz, Oct. 21, 1906, SAB 82.

187 "hopefully": Letter to his Odessa friends, Nov. 4, 1906, B 453.

187 Renting an apartment: Letter to the children, Nov. 6, 1906, B 70.

187 He was so enthusiastic: Letter to the children, Nov. 12, 1906, B 72.

188 local newspaper politics: SAB 84. According to a contemporary report, "the Jewish Socialists and other radicals sulk[ed] and stay[ed] away" from Sholem Aleichem's welcome banquet, for example. See Shandler, *Sholem Aleichem*, 11.

188 The best he got: UR 2:167, 177–179, 184, 189; MF 221; SAB 355.

189 By mid-December: Letter to his friends in Odessa, Dec. 12, 1906, B 454.

189 Adler wasn't the only one: UR 2:188–191, 194; MF 210.

189 February 8: See, for example, the dueling ads placed one on top of the other in *Morgen-Zhurnal*, Feb. 6, 1907, and the *Forverts*, Feb. 7, 1907.

190 To make matters worse: UR 2:197–198.

190 "open[ed] a new world": "Sholem Aleichem's 2 New Plays," *Tageblat*, Feb. 12, 1907.

190 Other papers were less kind: MF 214–215; SAB 84; Shandler, *Sholem Aleichem*, 12.

191 "Years ago": Cited in Mayzel 119.

191 It might have been the sulfurous reviews: MF 219; UR 2:200–201; Weitzner 19–20; Shandler, *Sholem Aleichem*, 10.

191 He signed a contract: See SAB 7, 216–217; UR 2:205–206.

191 *The Deluge: Der mabl* (1907; later revised as *In shturem*), AV 2:3:7–221; trans. *In the Storm* (New York: Putnam, 1984).

192 "It was unimaginable": *In the Storm*, 148–149.

193 Writing like a demon: UR 2:208.

193 "God is a great God": Letter to the editors of *Undzer Lebn*, April 30, 1907, B 456.

193 "God wanted": "Shprintse" (1907), AV 5:3:143–163, trans. "Shprintze," TDRS 82–97, 83.

193 "reward": "Shprintze," 91.

194 The story has little to do: Sholem Aleichem had written a story about suicide two decades before, in which a character named Shprintze appears, and that might have been the seed for using the name here. See "Bilder fun der berditshever gas," Scene 3.

194 "My problem": "Shprintze," 96.

Chapter 20

195 having borrowed money: Letter to D. Kassel, June 8, 1907, B 457; MF 223.

195 Visitors to the municipal gardens: SAB 320; UR 2:217–218.

195 He had taken pains: MF 233–234; SAP 188–189.

196 Missing his family: UR 3:8, MF 226–227.

196 It almost never happened: UR 3:7; UR 2:208–209; MF 221.

197 "all the passengers": SAB 79. See also Dan Miron, "Bouncing Back: Destruction and Recovery in Sholem-Aleykhem's *Motl peyse dem khazns*," in *The Image of the Shtetl*, 181.

197 how to turn trauma into joy: A strategy old as "The Penknife" (which, like Motl, boasts a portrait of a sick father) for Sholem Aleichem, but he had been worrying over the topic in more recent works. A rabbi's young son shows incongruous joy at hearing of his sister's death in "Creature" ("Bashefenish" [1903], AV 1:5:173–189): the death and subsequent mourning rituals mean he won't have to attend school. In "The Dreydl," published that same year, the child narrator, a widow's son and thus an orphan by Eastern European standards, is given special protection from beatings and blows; and 1904's "The Littlest of Kings" begins "A lucky child, Isaac. The whole world loves him. He is everyone's darling; everyone fondles him, kisses him, showers him with endearments. . . . And they do it all because of pity. The whole world pities him, everyone feels sorry for the boy. For Isaac, the wonder child, the beautiful boy, is an orphan." "Di yungster fun di melokhim" (1904), AV 1:5:227–245; trans. "The Littlest of Kings," TD 114–127; 114.

197 "No matter where they go to": IK 99.

197 modeled on Sholem Aleichem's own brother: MBSA 11. Sholem Aleichem had an extremely close relationship with Abba and valued his talent highly: see MBSA 61–66.

198 the original emphasis: See Miron, "Bouncing Back," 182–184.

198 On board ship: UR 2:216–217.

198 the example of his brother Abba: Sholem Aleichem's brother had often partnered with his father in the latter's numerous business efforts, a dynamic possibly reflected in *Motl*. See MBSA 35.

198 first section of *Motl*: *Motl Peyse dem Khazns*, I (1907): AV 1:1:9–292; trans. *Motl*, MM/MC, 107–235.

198 packed with characters: MBSA 8–11, 192–193.

199 "satire, a sort of political creature": Letter to D. Kassel, July 12, 1907, B 458–459.

199 "The First Jewish Republic": "Di ershte yidishe republik" (1907), AVBYL, 259–337; trans. "The First Jewish Republic," WDJ 168–212.

200 "to set up a government": "The First Jewish Republic," 180.

200 "Impressions from the Zionist Congress": "Ayndrukn fun tsionistishn kongres" (1907), AVBYL, 243–258; trans. WDJ, 160–167.

200 "all these girls": "Impressions," 161.

201 "pushed one card": "Impressions," 166.

201 "fell on each other's neck": "Impressions," 162.

201 the story's more complicated: UR 2:64, 66; SAB 175, 197.

202 "and avoided": MF 228–230.

202 keeping a kosher home: A single exception: one of the children was sick, and their Kiev doctor prescribed a special diet of "breast of chicken, chopped up with a couple of eggs, fried in butter," and, on another occasion, ham. It was kept in separate areas with separate dishes; when the other children insisted on trying it, they were only allowed to eat it off paper. See MF 116–118.

202 Sholem Aleichem dropped everything: UR 3:33–34.

202 Abramovitch recited: Letter to I. D. Berkowitz, Aug. 21, 1907, B 74; SAB 86; UR 3:33–35; MF 231.

202 joked and laughed: SAB 218–220; UR 3:36–39, SAB 172.

203 "literature, Talmud": "Fir zenen mir gezesn" (1907–1908), AV 3:6:111–186, part. trans. "Once There Were Four," BOSA 254–270, 256.

203 personal tales: Abramovitch forgets the name of an Odessa hotel whose delights he extols to a stranger on a train (it turns out to be "Odessa"); Bialik, the group's sweet romantic, forgets the names of both his best friend and his fiancée when he introduces them; the caustic, profane, irascible Ben-Ami, frustrated by trying to arrange a passport, can't remember his own name.

204 The *Tageblat* never published: SAB 87, UR 3:44–46.

204 the *Amerikaner* was giving him problems: UR 3:47–48; SAB 296; Miron, "Bouncing Back," 185–187.

204 finances got so dire: UR 3:49.

204 "they never did such a thing": Letter to M. Spektor, Jan. 23, 1908, B 463–464.

204 in such financial trouble: SAB 86; UR 1:141–142, 3:76–83; MF 156.

205 Two new New York publishing houses: They had been office boys for the Tushiya Press, which had been putting out volumes of Sholem Aleichem's work for years based on an arrangement long ago rendered inoperative.

205 "others have earned": Letter to Natasha Mazar, Feb. 11, 1909, B 93–94.

205 "might be a 'joke'": Letter to R. Breinin, Feb. 17, 1908, SAB 222.

205 false starts and minor efforts: UR 2:220; see, however, the one-act *Mentshn* (Ser-

vants), which passed the censor in July 1908, with its intriguing commentary on the possibility or impossibility of changing class identity. *Mentshn* (1908), AV 3:1:119–150.

205 a first full attempt: UR 3:53, 58, 66, 70–72.

206 *The Treasure: Der oytser* (1908; later retitled *Di goldgreber*); *Di tsukunft*, Oct.–Dec. 1927, 555–687.

206 traced the play's history: UR 3:116; Sholem Aleichem, *Ketavim Ivriyyim*, ed. Khone Shmeruk (Jerusalem: Bialik, 1976), 106.

206 a meditation on the differences: Delphine Bechtel, "America and the Shtetl in Sholem Aleichem's *Di Goldgreber* [The Golddiggers]" *MELUS* 17.3 (1991–1992): 69–84, 75–76.

206 On February 21: MF 234; UR 3:89–90.

207 preened: Letter to V. Weisblat, Feb. 22, 1908, B 467; letter to Tashrak, March 5, 1908, B 468–469; UR 3:89–90, 110.

207 Adler's natural role: Weitzner 41.

207 The play fared even worse: UR 3:96–108, 112–113; SAB 87.

208 "Five Letters": "Finf oysyes" (1908), FEL 146–148.

208 "An Early Passover": "A frier peysekh" (1908), AV 1:3:151–168; see also UR 3:127.

Chapter 21

209 "The land of Ivan": SAB 89; UR 3:120; UR 3:125; Letter to I. D. Berkowitz, May 14, 1908, SAB 89.

209 "Either say good-bye": "Elye hanove" (1908), AV 1:4:119–124, trans. "Elijah the Prophet," SLST 21–25, 24. The story is also another lovely evocation of how parents' mild warnings can loom large in the echo chamber of a child's head, given as it is to imagination and terrors, a theme Sholem Aleichem had sounded since "The Penknife."

210 "Beareleh": "Berele" (1908), AV 5:1:91–105. For another clear-eyed look at some of Russia's problems, see 1908's "Three Little Heads," a Dickensian look at three little children—the heads of the title—who live in a blighted landscape, where they don't even know what trees look like when they grow or how vegetables work, and the older brother tells the younger two tales of America and of Paradise. "Dray keplekh" (1908), AV 1:4:135–143; trans. "Three Little Heads," SSSA 333–338.

210 "diamond lockets": SAP 210. See also SAB 259–260; MF 236; UR 3:136.

210 Muranov theater: SAP 210.

211 mindful of this issue: Letter to *Hamelitz*, May 7, 1889, B 238–239; Letter to B. L. Flesker, Oct. 14–15, 1889, B 253–254.

211 "afraid of murders": Letter to Spektor, June 23, 1908, B 471; UR 3:139.

212 potentially fatal operation: According to the Yiddish writer Peretz Hirschbein, a virtually identical thing happened to Bialik; one wonders whether both writers encountered the same (con?) man. See Jeffrey Veidlinger, *Jewish Public Culture in the Late Russian Empire* (Bloomington: Indiana University Press, 2009), 152.

212 Olga: UR 3:136, 138–141; SAB 261.

212 Toward the very beginning: MF 237, 241. Other accounts have him collapsing at the train station.

212 "Baranovitch station": "Stantsye baranovitsh" (1909), AV 5:5:41–59, trans. "Baranovich Station," TDRS 152–163, quote on 163.

212 They organized volunteers: UR 3:147, MF 238–239; SAB 261.

212 he wrote Spektor: Letter to M. Spektor, Fast of Gedaliah 1908; B 472; SAB 90; MF 238.

213 his illness had sidelined him: SAB 266, 340, 342–343; UR 3:145; "Czernowitz Conference," YIVO.

213 "light, sun": SAB 265.

214 the author's twenty-fifth jubilee: MF 239–241, UR 3:145–146.

214 Some Warsaw supporters: UR 3:155–157; MF 243; SAB 262–263.

214 satires of the medical profession: See, for example, "In di varembeder" (1903), AV 4:5:75–118; trans. "To the Hot Springs," SAS 350–378; and letter to Berkowitzes, March 1, 1913, B 132.

215 "a spot in Italy": "Fun der rivyere" (1909), AV 3:4:215–220; trans. "From the Riviera," SAS 303–307, 303.

215 "as medicine was to learn": MF 247.

215 Awakened by the sunlight: Letter to Natasha Mazar, Nov. 14, 1908, B 83–84; MF 247.

215 writing his daughter: Letter to Ernestina Berkowitz, Oct. 23, 1908, SAB 90–91.

216 "Wonders of the World!": Letter to Odessa friends, Dec. 6, 1908, SAB 224.

216 The only medical instruction: See MBSA 164.

216 He dedicated: UR 3:163–165.

216 "Shmuel Shmelkes": "Shmuel shmelkis un zayn yubileum" (1908), AV 4:1:203–237.

217 "for not having sufficiently prized him": "Dr. Theodor Herzl," 139–140.

217 Dinezon: UR 3:174.

217 the festivities were appropriate: SAB 264; MF 241–242; UR 3:175–176.

218 The honoree: Letter to M. Spektor, Oct. 21, 1908, B 473; Letter to G. Levin, Nov. 12, 1908, B 477; Letter to M. N. Sirkin, Dec. 6, 1908, B 481.

218 as the fall went on: Letters to Natasha Mazar, Dec. 7, 1908, Jan. 15, 1909, Jan. 25, 1909; B 86–87, 90–91; Letter to G. Levin, Nov. 23, 1908, B 478–479.

219 suffering from insomnia: Letter to G. Levin, Nov. 23, 1908, B 479.

219 "by saving": Letter to Y. Dinezon, Erev Rosh Hashanah 1908, B 473.

219 deepened reader interest: SAB 266, UR 3:221.

219 "such poor, small": Letter to Natasha Mazar, Dec. 7, 1908, B 87.

219 "simply put, revived the dead": Letter to Y. Dinezon, Jan. 15, 1909, B 489; SAB 268; UR 3:224; MBSA 165.

219 The subsequent settlements: Letter to Natasha Mazar, Feb. 11, 1909, B 92–94. Krinski was the final holdout.

220 The editions were soon a great success: SAB 268–270, 272; UR 3:224–225, 227, 233. MF 244–245; Letter to G. Levin, March 27, 1909, B 499–500.

220 writing habits: UR 3:178, 193–194, 207–209.

221 Ever since the word had spread: Letter to G. Levin, Jan. 15, 1909, B 489; UR 3:161, 198–199; SAB 271–272; letter to Israel Cohen, Jan. 14, 1909, *Commentary* 10 (1950):381.

221 "that he merited": Letter to Ben-Ami, March 21, 1909, B 497.

221 "Tevye Leaves for the Land of Israel": "Tevye fort keyn eretz-yisroel" (1909), AV 5:3:167–195; trans. "Tevye Leaves for the Land of Israel," TDRS 97–116.

221 Readers weren't the only ones surprised: SAB 51; MF 147.

222 "sells herself": "Tevye Leaves for the Land of Israel," 100.

222 "a steal": "Tevye Leaves for the Land of Israel," 101.

222 "Don't go comparing me": "Tevye Leaves for the Land of Israel," 103.

222 "where all the old Jews": "Tevye Leaves for the Land of Israel," 110.

223 "What's the point": "Tevye Leaves for the Land of Israel," 106.

223 "I only wish": "Tevye Leaves for the Land of Israel," 98.

223 Another farce: "Blintses" (1909), AV 1:3:171–197.

223 another Kasrilevke tale: "Tsvey toyte" (1909), AV 4:2:181–199; trans. "Two Dead Men," SSSA 74–88.

223 "The Pair": "Dos porfolk" (1909), AV 1:5:129–153, trans. "The Pair," SSSA 12–27.

223 a pair of turkeys: See letter to A. L. Levinski, Dec. 27, 1908, B 485.

223 "Pages from the Song of Songs": "Shir-hashirim" (1909–1911), AV 5:1:9–74; trans. "A Page from the 'Song of Songs'"; "Another Page from the 'Song of Songs'"; "This Night"; and "Final Pages from the Song of Songs"; JC 9–19; 89–98; 241–268; OCT 35–48.

223 "my health does not permit me": Letter to Sh. Rapaport, July 13, 1909, B 507.

224 "Many waters": Song of Songs 8:7.

224 more were planned: Sholem Aleichem had apparently intended to have eight chapters, including ones set on Tisha B'av, Rosh Chodesh Elul, Sukkot, Chanukah, and Purim.

224 modeled on Sholem Aleichem's wife's niece: MF 124.

224 "everything, everything": "A Page," 12.

224 "You need not": "A Page," 18.

225 "Don't press me": "Final Pages," 48.

Chapter 22

226 "The Goldspinners": "Di goldshpiners" (1909), AV 5:2:225–244, trans. "The Goldspinners," HTSA 54–67.

226 confessed in March: SAB 269; letter to Frug, March 5, 1909, B 493.

226 A resurgence: Letter to Ba'al Makhshoves, March 21, 1909, B 496; letter to Ayzmans, March 22, 1909, B 498.

226 left Nervi: Letter to Dinezon, May 15, 1909, B 501; SAB 271; UR 3:237.

226 "The whole art": Letter to "a good friend"; July 1, 1909, B 503; Letter to Ravnitski, n.d., B 502; UR 3:261.

227 It was a good time: UR 3:253.

227 a satiric feuilleton: "Iber a nomen" (1909), FEL 149–175.

227 producing stories: See "Goles Datshe" (1901), AV 4:5:9–72; trans. "A Home Away

from Home," SAS 308–349; and "Der daytsh" (1902), AV 4:3:133–147; trans. "The German," TD 281–291.

228 "whole gang": Letter to M. Spektor, Aug. 21, 1902, B 391.

228 "Third Class": "Drite klas" (1902), AV 5:5:295–303; trans. "Third Class," TDRS 279–284.

228 "Before long": "Third Class," 283.

228 "Burnt Out": "A nisref" (1903), AV 5:5:231–242, trans. "Burned Out," TDRS 247–255. See Dan Miron, "The Pleasure of Disregarding Red Lights: A Reading of Sholem Aleichem's Monologue 'A Nisref,' " in *Arguing the Modern Jewish Canon*, 201–231, esp. 201–205, for more on the two waves of tales.

228 how hard it was to get a foothold: See, for example, "Funem prizev" (1902), AV 5:5:197–211; trans. "The Automatic Exemption," TDRS 229–238. There, a narrator's son who should be automatically exempt from the draft keeps receiving call-up notices thanks to bureaucratic mix-ups. The story isn't only, or even primarily, about military service and the long reach of the government; it's about the constant shifting of identities and the problems that causes.

229 "Types, encounters": SAB 295; Letter to N. Zablodovski, Sept. 12, 1909, B 510–511. See also Miron, *Image of the Shtetl*, 261.

229 "bought himself a notebook": "Tsu di lezer" (1911), AV 5:5:7–8, trans. "To the Reader," TDRS 135–136, 135.

230 "solely [by] seeing": "Konkurentn" (1909), AV 5:5:11–21, trans. "Competitors," TDRS 136–143, 137. For other examples, see the same year's "Taken," which adds an overtly political element and plays on the confusion between two uses of the title word: accepting Jews into Russian schools despite the difficulties of quotas, and impressment into the army. "The Happiest Man in All Kodny" is happy not, as the narrator speculates, because he has won the lottery, or enrolled his son in a *gymnasium*, or made a good match for his daughter; it's because, despite opposition from a fellow Jew, he has managed to retain the services of a distinguished Gentile professor to examine his ill son. "Tsugenumen" (1909), AV 5:5:63–68; trans. "Eighteen from Pereschepena," TDRS 163–166; "Der gliklekhster in kodne" (1909), AV 5:5:25–38, trans. "The Happiest Man in All Kodny," TDRS 143–152.

230 "The Man from Buenos Aires": "Der mentsh fun buenes-ayres" (1909), AV 5:5:71–88, trans. "The Man from Buenos Aires," TDRS 166–177.

230 "I'm kind of a middleman": "The Man from Buenos Aires," 171.

230 51 percent: Victor A. Mirelman, "The Jewish Community Versus Crime: The Case of White Slavery in Buenos Aires," *Jewish Social Studies* 46.2 (Spring 1984): 145–168, 150–151.

230 "Not in etrogs": Halkin's translation employs the image of Chanukah candles.

230 since he gets a story: A similar relationship, in 1910's "A Game of Sixty-Six," has a con man trying to lure the narrator into the popular card game, telling several stories in the course of doing so; the narrator, who at the tale's end innocuously asks what this "sixty-six" is that the card shark keeps talking about, proves himself to be the con man. "A zeks-un-zekhtzik" (1910), AV 5:5:155–171; trans. "A Game of Sixty-Six," TDRS 207–217.

231 "Cnards": "Knortn" (1912), AV 1:3:201–222; trans. "Cnards," SSSA 410–425.

231 "the Slowpoke Express": "Der leydikgeyer" (1909), AV 5:5:105–109, trans. "The Slowpoke Express," TDRS 184–186.

231 doubtful possibility: See "The Miracle of Hoshana Rabbah," where an argument over the engine's workings between a Jewish local coming to look at this new-fangled train and a priest already there leads to the primal suspenseful scene of the early twentieth century: the runaway train. True, in the end, the train eventually runs out of coal, and thus steam—as does the argument between Jew and non-Jew. But it's hardly an idyllic ending; the priest has jumped off long before. "Der nes fun hoyshane-rabe" (1909), AV 5:5:113–126, trans. "The Miracle of Hoshana Rabbah," TDRS 186–194, 194.

232 "The Wedding That Came Without Its Band": "A khasene on klezmer" (1909), AV 5:5:129–137, trans. "The Wedding That Came Without Its Band," TDRS 194–199. For a slightly different approach to these stories, compare Leah Garrett, "Trains and Train Travel in Modern Yiddish Literature," *Jewish Social Studies* 7.2 (2001): 67–88, 79–81.

232 That early fall: UR 3:270–271.

233 "to end my trilogy": Letter to the editors of the *Naye Velt*, Sept. 10, 1909, B 509.

233 Its basic idea: Khone Shmeruk, "Kokhavim toim," *Ayarot*, 80–112, 81–84.

233 "Both would go": *Wandering Stars*, 69.

233 "traveling": *Wandering Stars*, 134.

234 "Never, never": *Wandering Stars*, 414.

234 "apparently there is no happiness": *Wandering Stars*, 422.

235 "with already-written reviews": *Wandering Stars*, 364.

235 "filled mostly with short notices": *Wandering Stars*, 279.

235 "old pieces": *Wandering Stars*, 283.

235 "the same pregnant women": *Wandering Stars*, 239, 281.

235 "a world": *Wandering Stars*, 37.

235 "didn't recognize": *Wandering Stars*, 210.

236 "hard-won fruit": *Wandering Stars*, 184.

236 "jolly clown": *Wandering Stars*, 41.

Chapter 23

237 was sufficiently ill: SAB 94.

237 "Once more": Letter to Olga Rabinovich, Dec. 17, 1909, SAB 96; ellipsis in original. He often employed a pet name, Bibe, for her; see MBSA 160.

237 rectified its one flaw: SAB 95, 105; UR 4:78–79.

238 "I write a great deal": Letter to the Kaufmans, Jan. 11, 1910, SAB 96.

238 Despite Spektor's hopes: UR 4:22–24, 58, 60, 66.

238 "A Mighty Uproar": "Afn himl a yarid" (1911), FEL 180–190.

238 a generation of mass readership: For a close look at this phenomenon in all its complexity, including the growth of libraries, literary societies, public readings, and more, see Veidlinger, *Jewish Public Culture*, esp. 24–164; on Sholem Aleichem's popularity—far and away greater than that of any other Yiddish writer—see 99–101.

238 In 1906: David Shneer, "Who Owns the Means of Cultural Production? The Soviet Yiddish Publishing Industry of the 1920s," *Book History* 6 (2003): 197–226, 202.

239 Fiscal realities: UR 4:63–65.

239 "*very* interested in plays": Letter to August Schulz, Oct. 1, 1903; B 414.

239 the founding of a new press: UR 3:230–232.

240 "in any case": Letter to Y. Pinus, Jan. 3, 1910, B 513. See also SAP 53.

240 They were, to put it mildly: UR 4:72–73, 75; MF 251, 254.

240 "laughing off the trauma of history": David G. Roskies, *Against the Apocalypse: Responses to Catastrophe in Modern Jewish Culture* (Cambridge, MA: Harvard University Press, 1984), 163.

241 Other volumes: UR 4:75, MF 251; SAP 56; Litvak, "Found in Translation," 21.

241 he still couldn't find: UR 4:69–70.

241 He got sick: Letter to M. Gorky, April 22, 1910, B 521; SAB 272, UR 4:82, 86–87.

241 writing an old friend: Letter to Elye Barkhash, n.d., SAB 42.

242 soon he was sending: UR 4:82, 89, MF 251.

242 In a series of letters: Letters to Misha, Dec. 30, 1908, B 88; Jan. 23, 1909, B 89; Dec. 17, 1909, B 103; Jan. 22, 1910, B 104–105.

242 "The King of Spades": "Kenig pik" (1910), AV 3:3:221–235. See Leonard Prager, "Sholem-Aleykhem's *Kenig-Pik* 'King of Spades,'" *Jewish Language Review* 2 (1982): 7–20, for an account of its complex textual history and linguistic play.

243 "Shraga": "Shrage" (1911), AV 3:2:239–261.

243 "What do I care": "Shrage," 243.

243 Badenweiler summer days: UR 4:93–95, 110; SAB 98; MF 257.

243 a regular home: UR 4:113–119, 151, 160–165; MF 251.

244 a sweet confection: "Vi sheyn is der boym!" (1910), AV 3:6:21–28.

244 "Auto-da-Fe": "Oyto-da-fe" (1910), AV 3:6:31–40.

245 "Breakfast?": "Oyto-da-fe," 39.

245 "It's good you've reminded me": Letter to D. Frishman, Nov. 22, 1910, B 524.

246 The newspaper switch: UR 4:169–174.

246 "Gitl Purishkevitch": "Gitl purishkevitch" (1911), AV 3:4:223–234, trans. "Gitl Purishkevitch," OCT 139–148.

247 "owes everything": "Gitl Purishkevitch," 139.

247 "write [the town] up": "Gitl Purishkevitch," 148.

247 readers regularly asked him: UR 4:175.

248 the subject of some disagreement: UR 4:181–182.

248 *Marienbad*: *Maryenbad* (1911), AV 4:5:121–192, trans. Sholem Aleichem, *Marienbad* (New York: G. P. Putnam's, 1982).

248 "bitter taste": *Marienbad*, 157.

248 "it's a new world": *Marienbad*, 87.

249 The previous winter: Letter to E. Barkhash, January 1910, B 106; UR 4:197.

249 Tenth Zionist Conference: UR 4:189, 201–203, 207–208.

249 With summer ending: UR 4:210.

Chapter 24

250 influenza: Letter to S. Y. Abramovitch, Nov. 25, 1911, B 538.

250 that October: UR 4:214–216.

250 "which is, for me, a remarkable occurrence": Letter to S. Y. Abramovitch, Oct. 15, 1911, B 535–536.

251 the resulting standoff: Sholem Aleichem thanked Frishman in a satiric letter for his "brilliant idea," writing "the upshot: that Sholem Aleichem is leaving the *Haynt* and the straitened budget has shrunk by 200 rubles a month and what will happen next?" Letter to D. Frishman, Dec. 14, 1911, B 541.

251 the first two entries: "Men iz zikh moykhl" (1911), AV 4:4: 193–223, partial trans. "The Day Before Yom Kippur," TOC 319–328; "Me hulyet" (1911), AV 4:4:227–259, partial trans. "The Merrymakers," TD 162–171.

251 "Times have changed": "The Merrymakers," 163.

252 "there are ritual murders": Letter to Amphiteatrov, May 23, 1911, B 533.

252 "I was holding my sides": Letter to D. Frishman, May 28, 1911, B 534.

253 Censorship became so severe: UR 4:251–253.

254 named the character Rabinovich: UR 4:221–222.

254 *The Bloody Hoax*: *Der blutiker shpas* (1912–1914), trans. *The Bloody Hoax* (Bloomington: Indiana University Press, 1991).

255 "they could build a case": *The Bloody Hoax*, 204.

255 "it was fated": *The Bloody Hoax*, 290.

255 "the end of the tragicomedy": *The Bloody Hoax*, 366.

255 "out of love": *The Bloody Hoax*, 372–373.

256 "sad, tragic story": *The Bloody Hoax*, 39.

256 "they won't triumph": *The Bloody Hoax*, 165.

256 Sholem Aleichem was informed: UR 4:253.

257 "There are so many Yiddish writers": Letter to the children, Feb. 8, 1912, SAB 100–104, 104.

257 "On Account of a Hat": "Iber a hitl" (1913), AV 5:1:243–254, trans. "On Account of a Hat," BOSA 103–110.

257 "Twenty times": "On Account of a Hat," 108.

257 "'How does it feel'": "On Account of a Hat," 110.

258 a snappy modern dresser: UR 2:76.

258 And five years before *that*: "A farshterter peysekh" (1901), AV 1:6:75–97, trans. "The Ruined Passover," SAS 287–302.

258 his share of train mishaps: Letter to Ernestina Rabinovich, March 22, 1905, SAB 60.

258 After the 1905 pogroms: Letter to Ernestina Rabinovich, Oct. 26, 1905, SAB 67.

259 "Reb Yosifl": "Kasrilevker moyshev-zkeynim" (1902, rev. 1910), AV 4:2:131–140, trans. "Epilogue: Reb Yozifil and the Contractor," IK 119–127.

259 whose plot: See Nathan Ausubel, *Treasury of Jewish Folklore* (New York: Crown, 1948), 127–128.

259 "The Squire's h'Omelette": "A negidishe prezhenitse" (1904), AV 3:4:67–69, trans. "The Squire's h'Omelette," *Nineteen*, 54–56.

259 nested narratorial boxes: See David G. Roskies, "Inside Sholem Shachnah's Hat," *Prooftexts* 21.1 (Winter 2001): 39–56.

260 "that this true story": "On Account of a Hat," 103. A very similar ploy appears a few years earlier, in the tales of the Slowpoke Express: see "The Slowpoke Express," 186.

260 stern missives: Letter to S. Niger, April 12, 1912, B 545–546.

261 serial's growing success: UR 4:232, 247–250.

261 responding to a critic's claim: Letter to Ba'al Makhshoves, July 28, 1912, B 550–551.

261 Another source: UR 5:52–53.

261 Olga became ill: Letter to Y. Dinezon, May 6, 1912, B 548; letter to Dobin, June 5, 1912, B 549.

261 By sheer coincidence: SAB 353.

261 "Purchased Eternal Life": "Gekoyft oylem-habe!" (1912), FEL 201–204.

262 and doesn't disagree: The embrace from out of the darkness and the kiss can also be symbols of a blessed death—Moses, recall, merited having his life ended by a divine kiss.

262 Montreux: Letter to the Berkowitzes, Dec. 23, 1912, B 124; SAB 106, 108, 109; UR 5:62.

262 Finishing the novel: Letters to Ernestina and to the Berkowitzes, Dec. 27, 1912, Jan. 4, 1913, Jan. 7, 1913, SAB 108–109.

262 Not to write: Letter to S. Niger, Jan. 10, 1913, B 557–558.

262 "the pain": Letter to I. D. Berkowitz, Jan. 18, 1913, B 128.

263 Hiding the news: Letters to Niger, Jan. 17, 1913, B 560; Jan. 18, 1913, SAB 245; UR 5:64.

263 "since I've lived long enough": Letter to Y. Kotik, Feb. 5, 1913, B 561–562; SAB 111–112.

263 could only sleep: Letter to I. D. Berkowitz, Feb. 24, 1913, B 130.

263 Zuckerkandl, diagnosing: Letter to I. D. Berkowitz, Feb. 26, 1913, B 131; SAB 110.

263 his reception: Letter to Berkowitzes, Feb. 28, 1913, SAB 113; Letter to S. Niger, March 31, 1913, SAB 246.

263 They returned to their old haunts: Letter to Y. Kotik, March 3, 1913, B 562; letter to Tschernowitz, March 12, 1913, B 563; letter to the children, March 4, 1913, B 133; UR 5:68; SAB 115–116.

264 he wrote at the end of January: Letters to Y. Kotik, Jan. 28, 1913, B 560; Jan. 6, 1913, B 555; Jan. 10, 1913, B 556.

264 negotiations failed: SAB 111.

264 Sh. Shriro: UR 3:218; SAB 266, 292.

265 naturally enthusiastic: Letters to Shriro, April 5, 1913, April 6, 1913, April 30, 1913, July 20, 1913, July 23, 1913, B 564–569, 576–577; UR 5:70–73.

266 The peripatetic businessman: Sholem Aleichem had written an adventure of Menakhem-Mendl's in America in 1903; it didn't make it into the canonical collection of stories. See Shmeruk, "Sholem Aleichem in America," 218–220.

267 "to write about": Sholem Aleichem, *The Further Adventures of Menakhem-Mendl* (Syracuse, NY: Syracuse University Press, 2001; henceforth *Further*), 5.

267 "if you were clear": UR 5:73–76.

267 overarching, central insight: See, for example, *Further*, 8, 28, 36–37.

267 "what you write me": *Further*, 75, 92.

267 "Do you think": *Further*, 31.

267 Abramovitch worried: SAB 170.

267 "*You*, Dinezon": Letter to Y. Dinezon, June 9, 1913, B 573. Sholem Aleichem, though friendly, had become somewhat disappointed with Dinezon's increasing role as a "water-carrier" for Peretz; see MBSA 139.

268 "is brewing with schemes": *Further*, 167.

Chapter 25

269 Much of the summer: UR 5:78–81; SAB 276, 302.

269 "many objects": MF 103. See also MBSA 150.

270 thriving émigré Jewish community: See David N. Myers, " 'Distant Relatives Happening onto the Same Inn': The Meeting of East and West as Literary Theme and Cultural Ideal," *Jewish Social Studies* n.s. 1.2 (1995): 75–100, 87.

270 his first public reading: UR 5:84–85, 91, 95–97.

270 "The sensation": SAP 200–202.

270 "There are, they say": *Further*, 122.

271 The first Russian movie houses: Hoberman, passim; quote from Hoberman, 14.

271 apologized to his son-in-law: Letter to I. D. Berkowitz, Oct. 28, 1910, SAB 98.

271 "shows such comic pictures": Letter to Tamara Berkowitz, Jan. 10, 1914, SAB 116.

271 helping a few unaccompanied minors: SAB 360.

271 of the 123 movie theaters: Hoberman, 26.

271 "The World Goes Backwards": "Di velt geyt tsurik" (1913), 1:4:187–191.

272 appearance of Beilis films: See Hoberman, 28–29.

272 Toward the end of 1913: Letters to A. Vorkal, Dec. 6, 1913, Dec. 8, 1913, B 582–583; Weitzner 96–98.

273 "only such an artist": Letter to J. Adler, Jan. 20, 1914, B 584.

273 While reworking: SAB 246.

273 "Lekh-Lekho (Get Thee Out)": "Lekh-lekho" (1914), AV 5:3:199–220, trans. "Lekh-Lekho," TDRS 116–131.

274 easy, if dramatic, fix: UR 5:98–99.

274 focus that same perspective: See 1910's "A Country Passover," where a family who'd lived in their village for generations in happy coexistence with their neighbors can feel threatened by those neighbors' changed attitudes (thanks to the anti-Semitic press), especially when their children's disappearance to play around Passover time practically turns into a blood-libel-inspired mob; by 1913, Sheyne-Sheyndl is reporting, only half comically, the possibility of a blood libel in Kasrilevke. See "A peysekh in dorf" (1910), AV 1:4:163–178, trans. "A Country Passover," SSSA 339–349; *Further*, 18.

274 "A pogrom is a pogrom": "Lekh-Lekho," 122.

274 "I just hope you realize": "Lekh-Lekho," 122.

274 mandating that Tevye sell his house: In an abandoned section of the story, later published separately under the title "Vekhalakloykes," Tevye again triumphs

through talk, challenging the previous era's would-be pogromists via a shared text, the book of Psalms, to repeat a tongue-twisting set of words including the story's title; their failure dissipates their violent impulse. Perhaps one reason Sholem Aleichem abandoned the section was that shibboleths were always the province of separating Jews from other Jews (as the provenance of the word from the book of Judges makes clear), and separation is the province of the later setting in the story, not the earlier one. Only there do words become impossible. Additionally, the fragment illustrates that Tevye's books *do* have power, after all, in this world and not just the next; and the fragment's disappearance, with its suggestion that such victories are impossible in the world as Sholem Aleichem now saw it, speaks volumes. "Vekhalakloykes" (1914, rev. 1916), AV 5:3:223–230, trans. "Tevye Reads the Psalms," OCT 27–32.

275   "the minute": "Lekh-Lekho," 129.

275   "What do you say": "Lekh-Lekho," 129–130.

275   "*I am not worthy*": "Kotonti," TGCYW 227.

276   with a deep love for his God: Notably, "Vekhalakloykes" was originally published under the title "We Have a Strong God."

276   the best-known version: This discussion is taken from the version published in AV 3:3:167–235; for a discussion of the changes and manuscript version, see Wolitz 534n6; Weitzner 74–77; Frieden, *Century*, 8.

Chapter 26

281   a financial necessity: UR 5:101.

281   in the aftermath: Letter to M. Spektor, Feb. 17, 1914, B 588.

282   "what can you do": Letter to Moshe Borotshin, Shushan Purim 1914, SAB 118–119.

282   "Who knows": Letter, April 5, 1914, to Berkowitz and Kaufman, B 141, SAB 131.

282   "Afikomen": "Afikoymen" (1914), 5:1:153–171.

283   "The illness": SAB 280. See also MBSA 215.

283   "A language": Letter to *Undzer Bruder*, Oct. 27, 1911, B 536–537.

284   The question came down to banquets: UR 5:109–110; SAB 280–281.

284   One Sabbath: UR 5:112; SAB 355; MF 264.

284   "Warsaw"; "Sholem Aleichem summer": Letter to Shriro, May 25, 1914, B 595; MF 264; UR 5:113; SAB 213.

285   after ending his tour: Letter to M. Spektor, June 20, 1914, B 595–596; UR 5:116–119, 121–122; MF 267–270; SAP 191 (which has a slightly different account of the rent negotiations); MBSA 170.

286   The train stations: UR 5:127–156; SAB 143, 354; MF 271–273.

289   "wasteland": Letter to M. Kaufman, Sept. 1, 1911, B 112.

289   "I've traveled": "Sholem Aleichem tsu zayne lezer in Amerike," *Sholem aleykhems verk, 6 vols.* (New York: Tageblat, 1912), 1:9–10.

289   While Sholem Aleichem was stranded: UR 5:154–169; SAB 124.

291   "Hard to Be a Jew": "Shver tsu zayn a yid" (1914), AV 3:3:9–164; trans. "It's Hard to Be a Jew," SAP 235–266. See UR 5:157.

291 "stupid and ridiculous": "Hard to Be a Jew," 266.

291 "If *this* doesn't": UR 5:158.

291 "One Thousand and One Nights": "Mayses fun toyznt eyn nakht" (1915), AV 3:5:137–232, partial trans. "The Krushniker Delegation," BOSA 232–244.

291 "innumerable stories": "Mayses fun toyznt eyn nakht," 141.

292 "Kishinev wasn't worthy": "The Krushniker Delegation," 241.

Chapter 27

293 second arrival: UR 5:170–171, MF 281; "Sholem Aleichem Arrives," *Tageblat*, Dec. 2, 1914; *Forverts*, Dec. 3, 1914.

293 Harlem had cemented: SAB 124; UR 5:171; MF 284–285.

294 He made the rounds: UR 5:174–175.

294 On December 14: UR 5:175–176, 184; MF 286–287; Kellman 281; Letter to Natasha Mazar, Dec. 15, 1914, B 145.

295 The author weighed: UR 5:169–170, 178; MF 288.

295 gave another reading: SAB 356; UR 5:179–180.

295 "In a million years": *Further*, 48.

296 "Progress in Kasrilevke": "Kasrilevker progres" (1914–1915), AV 4:1:11–84, trans. "Progress in Kasrilevke," SAS 17–67.

296 The news: SAB 125; UR 5:190–192.

297 his expenses outpaced: SAB 122–123, 356; UR 5:184–188; MF 290; SAP 215.

298 "Do you still live?": Letter to S. Y. Abramovitch, May 28, 1915, B 601–602.

298 His brother: SAB 125; UR 5:188–189, 199; MF 38; MBSA 73.

298 the one who gave with a broad hand: According to his brother, he would even, when he was flush, occasionally make sure to take money with him when he went out walking in case he had the opportunity to give someone financial assistance. MBSA 163.

298 He had never appreciated: SAB 358–359; UR 2:204.

298 "Berl-Ayzik": "Berl-Ayzik" (1915), AV 5:2:247–254; trans. "On America," SAS 230–234.

299 "swell from hunger": "On America," 230–231.

299 "Mister Boym": "Mister boym in klazet" (1915), AV 3:2:283–289.

299 "Mister Green": "Mister grin hot a dzhab" (1915), AC 3:4:245–249, trans. "Mr. Green Has a Job," SLST 233–236.

299 "A Story About a Greenhorn": "A mayse mit a grinhorn" (1916), AV 3:4:253–259, trans. "The Story of a Greenhorn," SLST 243–248.

300 made his head spin: Letter to Y. Faler, Dec. 5, 1910, B 527; Miron, "Bouncing Back," 188–189.

300 His careful investigation: UR 2:14–15.

301 film scenario: SAB 144.

301 He first stayed: SAB 144–145; MF 292–293.

301 "Write about American Judaism": Letter to Y. Opatoshu, April 27, 1915, B 599–600.

302 Victor Studios: UR 5:195–196.

302 "Paradise": "Oylem-habe" (1915), AV 3:2:265–280, trans. "Heaven," SAP 226–235.

302 *The Jackpot*: "Dos groyse gevins" (1915), AV 3:1:153–256, trans. Kobi Weitzner and Barnett Zumoff, *The Jackpot* (New York: Workmen's Circle Education Department, 1989).

302 was really about Americans: UR 5:196.

302 almost all of Pereyaslav: In fact, Sholem Aleichem seems to use a lottery agent's periodic presence, absence, and eventual death in his memoir as a symbolic stand-in for the ebbs and flows of his and his family's fortunes.

302 "a satire by some joker": *Jackpot*, 40.

303 He worked hard: Weitzner III; SAB 125.

303 complaining: Letters to Emma and Misha, April 15, 1915, July 7, 1915, B 147; letter to Natasha Mazar, Sept. 2, 1915, B 149; UR 5:194–195, 198–199; MF 295–296; SAB 126.

304 No cable arrived: SAB 147–150; UR 5:200.

304 Misha had died: Letter to Natasha Mazar, Oct. 29, 1915, B 154.

304 In the interim: Letter to Emma and Misha, Sept. 15, 1915; B 150–151.

304 The 17th: SAB 128–129, 150; UR 5:202–203; SAB 360.

306 never quite gotten the hang: Though he would use its practice of incorporating many common American words into Yiddish sentence structures in a number of satirical stories like "Mr. Green Has a Job" and "A Story About a Greenhorn," another story from his first visit, "Otherwise, There's Nothing New," unfavorably contrasted the violence to the Yiddish language in America with the violence to Russian Jews after the constitution. Satire, obviously, but Sholem Aleichem's discomfort with Americanized Yiddish might have meant that the satire didn't just go in one direction. Or, perhaps, it simply meant he was getting too old to adapt. "Nishto keyn nayes" (1907), AV 1:3:141–148; trans. "Otherwise, There's Nothing New," SLST 237–242.

306 "Comfort?": Letter to Polinkovskis, Jan. 8, 1911; B 529–531.

307 "it would come out": Letter to Kaufmans, Sept. 21, 1915, B 151–152.

307 "About my spiritual-creative life": Letter to Liali, Oct. 14, 1915; B 153.

307 He had been steadily: Letter to the Kaufmans, Dec. 2, 1915, B 154; UR 5:209–210; MF 301.

307 as the year came to a close: Letter to the Kaufmans, Jan. 29, 1916, B 155; MF 302 (which casts the financial arrangements slightly differently than other sources); UR 5:211.

308 "he is one of the world's greatest writers": "Introducing Sholem Aleichem of New York," *The World Magazine*, Dec. 26, 1915. In this sketch and the next week's introduction, the characters are depicted as "the real prototypes of Potash and Perlmutter," ethnic Jewish characters from a recent Broadway hit; *The World Magazine*, Jan. 2, 1916.

309 Sholem Aleichem reveled: Letter to Kaufmans, Jan. 29, 1916, SAB 130–131.

309 He had no such complaints: MF 304. For Cahan's illustrations, see "Off for America: The Story of a Yiddish Family Exodus," *The World Magazine*, Jan. 2, 1916. The "authorized translation" was by Marion Weinstein, the secretary to Herman Bernstein, the editor of the *Tog*, who had taken Sholem Aleichem on a tour of the

Lower East Side during his first visit. See *The World Almanac and Encyclopedia 1907* (New York: Press Publishing Co., 1906), 22.

309 the Motl adventures: *Motl Peyse dem khazns, tsveyter teyl* (1916), AV 1:1:9–228., trans. MM/MC 237–318.

311 "There are thousands": MM/MC 267.

311 "All Kasrilevke": MM/MC 289.

Chapter 28

312 The additional income: SAB 150, 123; UR 5:213.

312 On March 4: UR 5:214; MF 310.

313 an American adaptation: "Fir kashes fun an 'amerikan boy'" (1916), AV 1:4:15–17.

313 home for Jews and not Jewishness: Another Passover-themed work that year, translated as "The Holiday Kiddush," concerns a self-professed "numbskull" whose inability to recite the liturgically complex holiday kiddush ruins his father's plans for his engagement. Some matches, perhaps between the father's and children's culture, are ruined by ignorance. "Kidalto vekidashto" (1916), AV 1:5:249–256, trans. "The Holiday Kiddush," OCT 65–72, 65.

313 "even more": SAB 48.

313 "many languages": Letter to Z. Gabay, n.d. [1911], B 529.

314 "What's the problem?": Letter to Liali, April 25, 1907, B 76.

314 a letter to Misha: Letter to Misha, Nov. 27, 1908, B 84; letter to Ravnitski, Feb. 2, 1899, B 319.

314 "From Passover to Sukkot": "Fun peysekh biz sukes" (1915), AV 4:1:187–199, trans. "From Passover to Succos, or The Chess Player's Story," TD 247–256.

314 "It's enough": "From Passover," 256.

315 "The Malicious Matza": "Di geferlekhe matze" (1916?), AV 1:4:201–204, trans. "The Malicious Matza," OCT 278–280.

315 "Haman and Mordechai": "Homen un mordkhe" (1905, rev. 1916), AV 1:3:225–237.

316 On March 25: He also contributed an allegorical feuilleton to the *Bazaar Gazette*, resurrecting his old characters Reyze and Pinny from earlier political pamphlets to discuss the mass suffering that had resulted from the war. SAB 131–133, 257; UR 5:214; MF 310; letter to Menakhem, March 24, 1916, B 603.

316 "But what can I do": Letter to Kaufmans, April 17, 1916, B 156.

316 an article on Bialik: "Mayn bakantshaft mit kh. n. biyalik" (1916), AV 3:6:101–107.

316 practical joke: Sholem Aleichem had always been fond of slightly barbed practical jokes. He once sent his new son-in-law on a wild goose chase to give his personal regards to a Berlin leather manufacturer, who when finally discovered had never heard of the author; another time, in the early days, after introducing the critic David Frishman to another intellectual as Finkelshteyn, he asked the intellectual his opinion of Frishman. UR 4:42, 5:216–217.

317 The doctors: See UR 5:220; MF 310–312; SAB 357; SAP 351.

317 His mood rallied: UR 5:223; SAB 370; SAP 176.

317 one observer: SAP 176.

317 The next night: SAB 150, 189, 371; SAP 177.

318 into the early hours: UR 5:224–227.

Epilogue

Scene 1

In addition to the sources below, this discussion is indebted to Goren, "Sacred and Secular"; Kellman, "Sholem Aleichem's Funeral"; and MF 315–316.

319 rabbi Jacob Joseph: "Death of Chief Rabbi Jacob Joseph," *New York Times*, July 29, 1902; "Riot Mars Funeral of Rabbi Joseph," *New York Times*, July 31, 1902.

319 "the Jewish people in microcosm": Cited in Kellman 295.

321 Yiddish theaters had shuttered: *New York Times*, "East Side Mourns Jewish Mark Twain," May 14, 1916.

321 Mt. Nebo Cemetery: Sholem Aleichem had asked for a temporary burial until such time as he could be reburied in Kiev. In 1921, the plan was abandoned and the body was reinterred in the Workmen's Circle, Mount Carmel Cemetery, with Sholem Aleichem the first occupant of a newly established Honor Row. See David G. Roskies, *The Jewish Search for a Usable Past* (Bloomington: Indiana University Press, 1999), 129.

321 Estimates: "Vast Crowds Honor Sholem Aleichem," *New York Times*, May 16, 1916 (100,000); Seth Wolitz, "The Americanization of Tevye or Boarding the Jewish Mayflower," *American Quarterly* 40 (1988): 514–36, 514 (over 250,000); Delphine Bechtel, *MELUS* 17.3, (1991–1992): 69–84 (50,000); Falstein (30,000); Sanford Pinsker, *The Schlemiel as Metaphor: Studies in Yiddish and American Jewish Fiction* (Carbondale: Southern Illinois University Press, 1991) (over 150,000); and Goren (between 150,000 and 250,000).

322 a member of the New York Republican delegation: William Stiles Bennett was also a former member of the United States Immigration Commission. See Andrew R. Dodge, *Biographical Directory of the United States Congress, 1774–2005* (U.S. Congress, 2005), 642.

322 "the greatest": This and subsequent quotations are taken from the *Congressional Record*, 53 Cong. Rec. 11 (1916), 7907–7908.

322 Isaac Siegel: Dodge 1910.

322 *New York Times* editorial: "A Touching Appeal to Children," *New York Times*, May 18, 1916.

322 its story: "Aleichem Begs to Lie with Poor: Will of Noted Writer Says His Ambition Is to Rest Among Plain Jewish Laborers," *New York Times*, May 17, 1916. This English-language version of the will is taken from its appearance in the *Congressional Record:* 53 Cong. Rec. 11 (1916), 7907–7908.

323 very little of his work: Aside from the material in the *World*, discussed above, see Helena Frank, *Yiddish Tales* (New York: JPS, 1912) and *Stempenyu* (London: Methuen, 1913).

Scene 2

324 Carnegie Hall: "2,500 Jews Mourn Sholem Aleichem," *New York Times*, June 18, 1916.

325 among other languages: See, for example, a discussion of an early German translation in Jeffrey A. Grossman, "Sholem Aleichem and the Politics of German Jewish Identity: Translations and Transformations," in Jerold C. Frakes and Jeremy Dauber, eds. *Between Two Worlds: Yiddish-German Encounters* (Leuven, Belgium: Peeters, 2009), 81–110.

325 Helena Frank: UR 2:156–157.

325 "the transmigrated soul": Letter to Israel Cohen, Dec. 2, 1908, *Commentary* 10 (1950): 380.

325 "its special echo": Frank, 6. See, for general discussion, Jeffrey Shandler, "Reading Sholem Aleichem from Left to Right," *YIVO Annual* 20 (1991): 305–32, and Rhoda S. Kachuck, "Sholom Aleichem's Humor in English Translation," *YIVO Annual* 11 (1956/1957): 39–81.

325 Hannah Berman: Letter to Y. Dinezon, May 6, 1912, B 548.

326 "Shalom Aleichem": *New York Times*, "Books and Authors," Sept. 5, 1920. A new edition of the work, at times incorrectly identified as "a novel of Jewish life," was released near the beginning of 1922; "Books and Authors," *New York Times*, Jan. 29, 1922; "Latest Books," Feb. 19, 1922.

326 "Like many Americans": Shalom Aleichem, *Jewish Children*, trans. Hannah Berman (New York: Bloch, 1937), v.

Scene 3

Sources consulted for this section throughout include Shneer, "Who Owns the Means of Cultural Production?"; Jeffrey Veidlinger, "Let's Perform a Miracle: The Soviet Yiddish State Theater in the 1920s," *Slavic Review* 57.2 (1998): 372–397; Veidlinger, *The Moscow State Yiddish Theater* (Bloomington: Indiana University Press, 2000); Lois Adler, "Alexis Granovsky and the Jewish State Theatre of Moscow," *The Drama Review: TDR* 24.3 (1980): 27–42; Gennady Estraikh, "Soviet Sholem Aleichem," in *Translating Sholem Aleichem*, 62–82; Mikhail Krutikov, "A Writer for All Seasons: Translating Sholem Aleichem into Soviet Ideological Idiom," in *Translating Sholem Aleichem*, 98–112; and Weitzner, *Sholem Aleichem in the Theater*. On the critical approaches to Sholem Aleichem, see the special issue of *Prooftexts* 6.1 (1986), "Sholem Aleichem and the Critical Tradition," especially David G. Roskies's introduction there. See particularly Max Erik, "*Menakhem-Mendl* [A Marxist Critique]," 23–41; and Meyer Wiener, "On Sholem Aleichem's Humor," 41–54. See also Sh. Werses, "Shalom Aleichem: chamishim shanot bikoret," in *Bikoret Habikoret* (Tel Aviv: Agudat hasofrim, 1982), 165–197.

327 among many other institutions: Most notably, the infrastructure behind the massive anniversary celebrations of Sholem Aleichem, especially the tenth anniversary of his death in 1926 and the eightieth anniversary of his birth in 1939. See Estraikh 67–73.

328   would later prove influential: Chagall himself refused to see *Fiddler on the Roof*, seemingly afraid it would misrepresent the Vitebsk of his childhood. See Stephen J. Whitfield, "Fiddling with Sholem Aleichem: A History of *Fiddler on the Roof*," in Jack Kugelmass, ed., *Key Texts in American Jewish Culture* (New Brunswick, NJ: Rutgers University Press, 2003), 105–125, 106.

328   "invent[ing]": Roskies, "Introduction," 2.

329   "rejection": Erik, *"Menakhem-Mendl,"* 23.

329   "that the prevailing social conditions": Wiener, "On Sholem Aleichem's Humor," 53.

329   A gossipy squib: "With the Producers and Players," *New York Times*, May 17, 1925.

329   Alexander Arkatov: Hoberman, 46.

329   *Wandering Stars*: *Blondzhende stern* (1927), dir. G. Gricher-Cherikover (VUFKU: USSR).

329   "idealiz[ing] the pathological": Hoberman, 128.

330   adaptation of *The Deluge*: *Der mabul* (1925), dir. Yevgeni Ivanov-Barkov, Boris Vershilov, Ivan Pyriev (Sovkino: USSR).

330   "petty bourgeois psychology": See Eric Goldman, *Visions, Images, and Dreams: Yiddish Film Past and Present*, rev. 2nd ed. (Teaneck, NJ: Holmes & Meier, 2011), 33. See also Hoberman, 97–100.

330   *Laughter Through Tears*: *Durkh trern* (1928, rereleased with sound 1933), dir. G. Gricher-Cherikover (VUFKU: USSR). See Goldman, 37–40; Hoberman, 129, 140.

330   "We find here": Cited in Hoberman, 140.

331   *Yidishe glikn*: *Yidishe glikn* (1925), dir. Alexander Granovsky (Goskino: USSR)

331   "the funniest writer": Cited in Estraikh, 74.

Scene 4

333   The gatherings and concert benefits: *New York Times*, May 14, 1917, "Honor Sholem Aleichem"; Dec. 30, 1917, "Various Musical Events"; May 26, 1918, "News of Music"; May 27, 1918, "Honor Aleichem's Memory."

333   Schwartz's own story: See, for general discussion on Schwartz and the Yiddish Art Theatre, Nahma Sandrow, *Vagabond Stars: A World History of Yiddish Theater* (New York: Limelight, 1977), 251–274; "A New Yiddish Theatre: Playhouse, Which Opens Thursday, Is Goal of Maurice Schwartz's Career," *New York Times*, Nov. 7, 1926.

334   "for a theater": Quoted in Sandrow, 262.

334   would have strongly resonated: See Wolitz, 520.

334   "the public": *Forverts* review, cited in Weitzner, 105.

335   Olga Rabinovich laid the cornerstone: "Lay the Cornerstone for Yiddish Theatre," *New York Times*, May 24, 1926.

335   there were others: Muni acted in *Hard to Be a Jew*, about anti-Semitism and the blood libel, in 1920; there were also productions of *The Gold Diggers* and *The Great Fortune*, satires about wealth and their consequences in 1922 and 1927, and a dramatic adaptation of *Stempenyu* in 1929. "Yiddish Plays Announced," *New York Times*, Sept. 26, 1921; "Theatrical Notes," *New York Times*, Jan. 9, 1927; "Yiddish Theatre's Plans," *New York Times*, Sept. 7, 1928.

335 A warm 1922 appreciation: Rebecca Drucker, "At the Yiddish Art Theater," *New York Times*, Jan. 29, 1922.

335 "atavistic and parochial": "Audience Enjoys 'Stempenyu' Hugely: Yiddish Art Theatre Gives Old-Fashioned Play from Sholom Aleichem's Novel," *New York Times*, March 29, 1929.

335 their overblown running times: See, for example, "The 'Great Fortune,'" *New York Times*, Dec. 9, 1922; "Audience," *New York Times*, March 29, 1929; "Actors' Odyssey Told in 'Roaming Stars,'" *New York Times*, Jan. 25, 1930.

335 "art was forgotten": "Audience," *New York Times*, March 29, 1929.

335 "continuous racket": "Give Gold Diggers at Jewish Theatre: Players Present a Lively Interpretation of Sholom Aleichem's Comedy: Built on a Novel Plot: Draws Humor from Amusing Situations in Search for Hidden Treasure," *New York Times*, Dec. 3, 1927.

336 There were some failures: "Yiddish Art Theatre Is to Move Uptown," *New York Times*, May 22, 1931; "Again the Yiddish Stage," *New York Times*, Sept. 6, 1931; "North of Second Avenue," *New York Times*, Sept. 24, 1931; "Theatrical Notes," *New York Times*, Oct. 2, 1931; "Mr. Schwartz of 2nd Ave.," *New York Times*, Oct. 4, 1931.

336 Licking his wounds: "Again the Jewish Stage," *New York Times*, Sept. 25, 1932.

336 Schwartz had been involved: Goldman, 14–15, 28–29.

336 while touring in Vienna: "Second Avenue's Season," *New York Times*, Sept. 22, 1935; "Second Avenue Moves to Broadway," *New York Times*, Sept. 13, 1936.

337 While in Warsaw: Hoberman, 237; Goldman, 111.

337 He knew the superficial problem: "Screen News Here and in Hollywood," *New York Times*, July 11, 1939; "Written on the Screen," *New York Times*, March 30, 1939; "Outside of Jericho," *New York Times*, July 30, 1939; Hoberman, 53–54.

338 "If you don't think": "The Screen in Review," *New York Times*, Dec. 22, 1939.

338 The biggest problem: Hoberman, 304–305; Frieden, *Century*, 11–13.

338 *Tevye: Tevye der milkhiker* (1939), dir. Maurice Schwartz (Maymon Films: US).

338 "scenes which are obscene": Cited in Hoberman, 309. For other negative reactions, see Whitfield 114–115.

339 *Gone With the Wind*: Hoberman, 312; "News of the Screen," *New York Times*, Dec. 13, 1939; "News Here and in Hollywood," *New York Times*, Dec. 21, 1939.

Scene 5

The account here is taken from Avrom Sutzkever, *Fun vilner geto* (Moscow: Der Emes, 1946), 112–117, quote on 117; see also Joshua Starr, "Jewish Cultural Property Under Nazi Control," *Jewish Social Studies* 12.1 (1950): 27–48.

Scene 6

340 By April 1943: See Anita Norich, "Harbe sugyes / Puzzling Questions: Yiddish and English Culture in America During the Holocaust," *Jewish Social Studies* 5.1–2 (1998–1999): 91–110, 101–102.

340 "a small, teeming world": *New York Times*, "His World Was Rich," April 4, 1943.

340 Samuel's book: See Shandler, "Reading Sholem Aleichem," 7, 13.

340 "the ghetto": *Chicago Daily Tribune*, "Story Teller of Ghetto and His Honesty," May 2, 1943.

341 "the mirror of Russian Jewry": Maurice Samuel, *The World of Sholom Aleichem* (New York: Schocken, 1943), 5–6.

341 "could write a *Middletown*": Samuel 6–7.

341 "some millions": Samuel 6–7.

341 "part of their life": Samuel 329–330.

342 Though the book: "Books—Authors," *New York Times*, March 30, 1944; May 2, 1944; "Maurice Samuel, Jewish Writer," *New York Times*, May 5, 1972. It received the Anisfield Prize as the best book on racial relations of 1943.

342 when the *Times* announced: *New York Times*, "Books and Authors," May 11, 1946; "Books—Authors," *New York Times*, May 15, 1946, May 16, 1946.

342 Orville Prescott's *Times* review: "Books of the Times," *New York Times*, June 24, 1946.

342 "interesting and colorful": "Beloved Humorist," *Washington Post*, June 30, 1946.

342 one startling review: William Barrett, "The Promise and the Pale: A Gentile View of Jewish Irony," *Commentary* 2 (1946): 208–211.

343 Ben Hecht: "Tales of Capering, Rueful Laughter," *New York Times*, July 7, 1946.

343 extensive use of translators' license: "What was entirely right and simple and flavorsome in Yiddish," they write, "completely missed fire when translated literally." "Foreword," TOC, viii.

343 "the quality": "The Blessings of Poverty," *The New Republic*, July 22, 1946.

344 best-seller list: "The Best Sellers," *New York Times*, Aug. 25, 1946, Sept. 8, 1946.

344 Frances Butwin: Her husband had died when *The Old Country* was in proofs. See Joseph Butwin, "Tevye on King Street: Charleston and the Translation of Sholem Aleichem," *American Jewish History* 93.2 (2007): 129–156, 132.

344 indifferent reviews: *New York Times*, April 14, 1948; "More Magic from the Pen of S. Aleichem," *Chicago Daily Tribune*, April 25, 1948; Stephen Seley, "Sholem Aleichem and the Emancipated," *Commentary* 5 (1948): 480–482.

344 Crown's announcement: "Books—Authors," *New York Times*, Dec. 30, 1948.

Scene 7

344 "a part of the life": "Introduction," TD, xvii.

344 "the movement and mutter": "Humor That Is Poignant," *New York Times*, Jan. 23, 1949.

345 "A folk-poet": Alexander Klein, "Ghetto Laughter," *The New Republic*, April 4, 1949.

345 The precincts of folkdom: Of course, Sholem Aleichem's work was not the only effort in this regard. The year 1952 saw the publication of a complementary work that presented shtetls "as instances of a single ideal type presented in the present tense, as if it still existed . . . much of [which] is an exercise in avoidance in its portrait of a way of life that [its author] knew to be darker and more complex

than the bright, Chagall-like hues in which he painted it." On the complex story behind this deeply influential book—Mark Zborowski's *Life Is With People*—see Steven J. Zipperstein, "Underground Man: The Curious Case of Mark Zborowski and the Writing of a Modern Jewish Classic," *Jewish Review of Books* (Summer 2010): 38–42, quotes 38, 42.

345 Sophie Maslow: "City Dance Group Gives 2 Novelties,"*New York Times*, Dec. 17, 1949; "The Dance: A Record"; *New York Times*, June 4, 1950; "Maslow's Dances Given at Festival," *New York Times*, Aug. 19, 1950, "The Dance: Premieres at New London," *New York Times*, Aug. 27, 1950.

345 the actor Sam Jaffe: "Script Intrigues Sam Jaffe," *New York Times*, Oct. 7, 1949; "Guild Subscribers Show Gain of 4,663," *New York Times*, Nov. 18, 1949; "News and Gossip Gathered on the Rialto," *New York Times*, Dec. 11, 1949.

345 "There's a likelihood": " 'The Enchanted' in Debut Tonight," *New York Times*, Jan. 18, 1950.

346 they couldn't get to everything: "Economy Guides Shepard Traube," *New York Times*, May 24, 1950; " 'Texas' to Suspend Run for a Month," *New York Times*, July 10, 1950; "Miller Is Revising 'Enemy of People,' " *New York Times*, Aug. 28, 1950; "Equity Discusses Loyalty Blacklist," *New York Times*, Sept. 23, 1950.

346 In April 1953: At the same time, some other works of his were published in translation, which failed to make the same impression. See, for example, 1952's *Wandering Star* [*sic*] ("Books and Authors," *New York Times*, June 12, 1952; "Uncommon Bohemians," *New York Times*, July 13, 1952; Irving Howe: "An Unknown Treasure of World Literature: Who Will Make Sholom Aleichem Available?" *Commentary* 14 [1952]: 270–273, 272); and 1953's *Mottel the Cantor's Son* ("Books and Authors," *New York Times*, March 23, 1953; "Books of the Times," *New York Times*, April 16, 1953; Norman Podhoretz, "Sholom Aleichem: Jewishness Is Jews," *Commentary* 16 [1953]: 261–263.)

346 "the fabled bookseller": "Da Silva in Aleichem Work," *New York Times*, April 3, 1953.

347 three-week trial run: " 'Sholom Aleichem' Opens Tonight," *New York Times*, May 1, 1953; "Actors to Read Aleichem Will," *New York Times*, May 13, 1953; "Michael Abbott to Offer Comedy," *New York Times*, May 20, 1953.

347 integrated: See R. L. Hilliard, "Integration of the Negro Actor on the New York Stage," *Educational Theater Journal* 8 (May 1956): 97–108; E. Austin Gerlyn, "The Advent of the Negro Actor on the Legitimate Stage in America," *Journal of Negro Education* 35.3 (1966): 237–245, 244.

347 "A goat": "Ben Shahn Illuminates," *New York Times*, Aug. 30, 1953.

347 planned seven-week engagement: " 'Sholom Aleichem' Is Back," *New York Times*, Sept. 11, 1953.

347 Brooks Atkinson: "At the Theatre," *New York Times*, Sept. 12, 1953.

347 "rootless make-believe": "Three Short Plays: 'The World of Sholom Aleichem Makes Art Out of Simple Things About People," *New York Times*, Sept. 20, 1953.

347 "almost total misunderstanding": "Drama Mailbag," *New York Times*, Jan. 31, 1954. A letter for the defense came from, of all people, Sholem Aleichem's son-in-law B. Z. Goldberg (unidentified as such in the letter), acknowledging Eastern

European Jewry's lack of simplicity while asserting the play's complexity—particularly the Sholem Aleichem section, praised for its "tension, agony, and redeeming humor." "Drama Mailbag," *New York Times*, Feb. 14, 1954.

348 "to quell": Midge Decter, "Belittling Sholom Aleichem's Jews: Folk Falsification of the Ghetto," *Commentary* 17 (1954): 389–392.

349 a hit show: "Two Shows Clash on Opening Date," *New York Times*, Sept. 23, 1953; "Drama Mailbag," *New York Times*, Nov. 8, 1953, Nov. 22, 1953.

349 A Chicago company: "New Kanin Play to Open Tonight," *New York Times*, Jan. 7, 1954; "Ella Logan Seen in Stage Return," *New York Times*, Jan. 30, 1954; "Hail Ben-Ami as Master in a Folk Drama," *Chicago Daily Tribune*, Feb. 15, 1954; "Theater Notes," *Chicago Daily Tribune*, Feb. 21, 1954.

350 200th performance: "Playgoers Lured by Water Sprite," *New York Times*, Feb. 20, 1954.

350 It finally closed: "Levin to Put On Play by Stevens," *New York Times*, April 16, 1954; "News and Gossip Gathered on the Rialto," *New York Times*, May 2, 1954, May 23, 1954.

350 There would be a Philadelphia run: "New Stage Group in Debut Tonight," *New York Times*, Nov. 9, 1954; "Yugoslavs to See 'Porgy and Bess,' " *New York Times*, Dec. 9, 1954; "London Sees 'Aleichem,' " *New York Times*, Jan. 12, 1955; "Ben-Ami Premiere Draws Full House," *Los Angeles Times*, April 5, 1956.

350 "misled": "A Story to Tell," *New York Times*, Nov. 28, 1954.

350 "love and wisdom": "In and Out of Books," *New York Times*, Nov. 4, 1956.

350 a new translation: "Books—Authors," *New York Times*, March 25, 1955.

350 "loved his people": "The World of Sholom Aleichem," *The New Republic*, May 16, 1955.

350 Banner Productions: "Walker Musical Assembles Staff," *New York Times*, April 22, 1957.

351 The two-act version: "Aleichem Stories Opening Tonight," *New York Times*, Sept. 16, 1957; Wolitz 524–525.

351 "polemical": "Tevya and His Daughters," *Christian Science Monitor*, Sept. 21, 1957.

351 *Tevya*: Perl and Da Silva reached out to leading Jewish actors like Joseph Buloff and Sam Jaffe, but when the cast was announced, Tevya, as they spelled it, was played by Mike Kellin (né Myron), who'd been nominated for a Tony the year before for the Rodgers and Hammerstein musical *Pipe Dream*. "News and Gossip of the Rialto," *New York Times*, June 23, 1957; "House Shortage for Plays Is Felt," *New York Times*, Aug. 1, 1957; "5 Join Cast of 'Tevya,' " *New York Times*, Aug. 16, 1957.

351 "Tevya, the dairyman": "Theatre: Tevya's Family," *New York Times*, Sept. 17, 1957.

351 in a follow-up article: "Fun with Words," *New York Times*, Sept. 29, 1957.

352 was forced to close: "Theater Sought for Ewell Play," *New York Times*, Nov. 11, 1957.

352 gone out over the airwaves: "Television: Faith," *New York Times*, April 4, 1955.

352 brought the big stars: "Miss Berg, Levene in 'Play of Week,' " *New York Times*, Nov. 14, 1959; "N.B.C.-TV Plans Daytime Specials," *New York Times*, Dec. 5, 1959.

352 "gentle beauty": "TV: Aleichem's 'World,'" *New York Times*, Dec. 15, 1959.

352 "a lyrical buffoon": "Theatre: Finest TV Show," *New York Times*, Jan. 6, 1960.

352 the taped television show reran: "7 Prior Shows Set by 'Play of Week,'" *New York Times*, Aug. 31, 1960; "Sentiment, Wit Mark TV Plays," *Chicago Daily Tribune*, May 16, 1960; "TV 'Play of Week' Slated for Reruns Beginning in June," *New York Times*, March 9, 1962.

352 Da Silva toured: "Musical Planned on Religious Sect," *New York Times*, Jan. 30, 1960.

353 celebrated the centennial: "News of the World of Stamps," *New York Times*, Jan. 18, 1959; "Yiddish Writer Hailed in Russia," *New York Times*, March 8, 1959.

353 Irving Howe: "The Sholem Aleichem Centenary," *The New Republic*, March 7, 1960, 24–25.

353 Maurice Schwartz: "Maurice Schwartz, Actor, Dead; Founder of Yiddish Art Theatre," *New York Times*, May 11, 1960.

Scene 8

353 Fred Coe's interest: "Aleichem Stories Inspire a Musical," *New York Times*, Aug. 20, 1962.

354 Irving Elman: "ANTA Series Lists O'Casey Works," *New York Times*, Sept. 26, 1962.

354 And thus it went: "Laurence Harvey Returning to Broadway in Fall," *New York Times*, Aug. 6, 1963.

354 "would be more dancing": "Robbins to Direct 'Tevye,' A Musical," *New York Times*, Aug. 29, 1963.

354 über-producer: "News of the Rialto: The Busy Prince," *New York Times*, Jan. 12, 1964.

354 a title change of their own: "The Rialto: Brisson and Burrows," *New York Times*, March 29, 1964.

354 out-of-town debut: "Musicals Given Longer Tryouts," *New York Times*, June 20, 1964.

354 There was some subtext: Whitfield, 109.

354 Fred Coe withdrew: "Stage's 'Hamlet' Becomes a Film," *New York Times*, July 3, 1964.

355 newspaper strike: "Detroit Responding to 'Fiddler on the Roof,'" *New York Times*, Aug. 8, 1964.

355 "May have a chance": "A Robust 'Fiddler' Approaches Its 3d Birthday," *New York Times*, Sept. 4, 1967.

355 "clumsy symbols": "Zero Mostel Great in 'Fiddler on the Roof,'" *Chicago Tribune*, Aug. 14, 1964.

355 Grosse Pointe: "It's a World Sholom Aleichem Never Dreamed Of," *New York Times*, March 20, 1966.

355 "running scared": Cited in Wolitz, 525.

355 "I think it'll run forever: "A Robust 'Fiddler' Approaches Its 3d Birthday," *New York Times*, Sept. 4, 1967.

355 Jerome Robbins: "Robbins: He Kicks Up a Temperamental Storm," *New York*

Times, Nov. 1, 1964; see also Whitfield 109, which mentions a formative childhood trip to Poland.

356 "bewildering": " 'Fiddler' Had to Be Revamped to Play," *Los Angeles Times*, May 15, 1966.

357 *Ed Sullivan Show*: Picture, *New York Times*, Aug. 21, 1960.

357 Prince estimated: "Fiddler Scores Year's First Hit," *New York Times*, Sept. 24, 1964.

357 The *Times* critic: "Theater: Mostel as Tevye in 'Fiddler on the Roof,' " *New York Times*, Sept. 23, 1964.

357 "All about me": "On the Aisle," *Chicago Tribune*, May 23, 1965.

358 "artful simplicity": Atkinson did caution that the "folk materials of Sholem Aleichem's stories are so full of nuances and religious subtleties that anyone who is not a Jew must be cautious about discussing them." The warning itself speaks worlds about sacred license (does anyone, after all, preface their review of Shakespeare by apologizing for their lack of Elizabethan Englishness?). "Critic at Large: Artful Simplicity of Sholem Aleichem Captured in 'Fiddler on the Roof,' " *New York Times*, Oct. 6, 1964.

358 "an appraisal": "Sholem Aleichem: Spokesman for a People," *New York Times*, Sept. 20, 1964.

358 B. Z. Goldberg: Letter, *New York Times*, Oct. 11, 1964.

358 Irving Howe: "Tevye on Broadway," *Commentary* 38.5 (November 1964): 73–75.

359 "You were reading again?": Joseph Stein et al., *Fiddler on the Roof* (New York: Limelight Editions, 1964; hereafter FOTR), 10.

359 "From such children": FOTR 13.

359 "orders": FOTR 100.

360 CONSTABLE. I have an order: FOTR 140.

360 "Why should I listen": FOTR 93.

360 "with us": FOTR 63.

360 "FIRST MAN. We should defend ourselves": FOTR 141–142.

361 "money is the world's curse": FOTR 61.

361 "a political question": FOTR 106.

361 "He's a radical!": FOTR 97.

361 Best known: Wisse, *Arguing the Modern Jewish Canon*, 62.

361 "We cannot stay": FOTR 150.

362 FYEDKA. Why?: FOTR 87.

Scene 9

363 the album had sold: "A Robust 'Fiddler' Approaches Its 3d Birthday," *New York Times*, Sept. 4, 1967; "United Artists Reported Close to Acquiring 'Fiddler on the Roof,' " *New York Times*, Jan. 26, 1966.

363 A week before: " 'Fiddler,' 'Roses,' Gilbert Miller Win Tonys," *New York Times*, June 14, 1965.

363 Hebrew-language production: "Tevye Delivers a Hit to Tel Aviv," *New York Times*, June 9, 1965; "Now, Israel Has a Jewish Tevye," *New York Times*, Jan. 23, 1966.

364 The production would run: "'Fiddler' in Hebrew Ends Longest Run in Tel Aviv," *New York Times*, Sept. 2, 1966.

364 Interest in Sholem Aleichem: "Writer's Daughter to Present Awards," *New York Times*, Nov. 18, 1964; "Aleichem Works Going to Israel," *New York Times*, Dec. 21, 1961; "Papers of Sholom Aleichem to Get a Home in Israel," *New York Times*, March 15, 1964; "Israel Remembers Life in the 'Shtetls' of Eastern Europe," *New York Times*, May 16, 1966; "Aleichem Notes Going to Israel," *New York Times*, March 20, 1968.

364 productions appeared: "'Fiddler,' Aged 2, Is Getting Bigger," *New York Times*, April 22, 1966; "'Fiddler' Will Play in Japanese," *New York Times*, June 30, 1967; "'Fiddler on the Roof' Wins Warm Reception in Prague," *New York Times*, Feb. 22, 1968.

364 Vienna: "Israelis Starred in Viennese 'Fiddler' Draw Enthralled Yet Uneasy Throngs," *New York Times*, Feb. 26, 1969.

365 Ankara: "Some Ankara Housing an Overnight Thing," *New York Times*, Sept. 6, 1969.

365 Clive Barnes: "Theater: Reappraisal," *New York Times*, Sept. 28, 1967.

365 "Musicals come and go": "Theater: A Reappraisal," *New York Times*, Feb. 28, 1970. Someone else who was here to stay: Bette Midler, who played Tzeitel in the Broadway production during this period, from 1966 to 1969. See Whitfield, 116.

365 seemingly inexhaustible legs: "'Fiddler' Is Saying Hello to a Record," *New York Times*, July 21, 1971.

365 Norman Jewison's movie: *Fiddler on the Roof* (1971), dir. Norman Jewison (MGM: USA).

366 The $9 million production: "Tevye's Suffering Enacted for Movie," *New York Times*, Jan. 5, 1971.

366 Canby noted: "Screen: 'Fiddler' On a Grand Scale," *New York Times*, Nov. 4, 1971.

367 "Mazel tov": "'Fiddler' Is History," *New York Times*, June 17, 1972.

367 Prince, noting: "Fiddler, 3,225 Performances Old, Tops Long-Run List," *New York Times*, June 18, 1972.

368 had been losing: "'Fiddler' Ends Sunday With Record of 3,242," *New York Times*, June 27, 1972; "'Fiddler' Bows Out After 3,242nd Show," *New York Times*, July 3, 1972.

368 A year later: "Different Tune for 'Fiddler' in Barrio," *New York Times*, June 21, 1973.

368 *Fiddler* would be revived: "'Fiddler' Celebrates 25 Years of Tradition," *New York Times*, April 8, 1990; "On Stage," *New York Times*, June 22, 1990; "Theater: Sunrise, Sunset," *New York Times*, Nov. 18, 1990; "'Fiddler' Returns, with a Heritage of Its Own," *New York Times*, Nov. 19, 1990; "A Cosy Little McShtetl," *New York Times*, Feb. 27, 2004.

368 "so far": "Shtetl Shtick," *New York Times*, Feb. 29, 2004.

368 Robert Kirsch: "Aleichem Revival: Why Not?" *Los Angeles Times*, Aug. 7, 1968.

369 "particularly from the American viewpoint": Sol Gittleman, *Sholom Aleichem: A Non-Critical Introduction* (The Hague: Mouton, 1974), 8.

369 over two hundred: See Shandler "Reading Sholem Aleichem" 4.

Scene 10

370 Wikipedia: http://en.wikipedia.org/wiki/Sholem_Aleichem.

370 A couple of websites: http://www.brainyquote.com/quotes/authors/s/sholom
_aleichem.html; http://thinkexist.com/quotes/sholom_aleichem/.

371 Sholem Aleichem College: www.sholem.vic.edu.au.

371 Sholom Aleichem Club: http://www.sholomaleichemclub.org/.

371 Sholem Aleichem Cultural Center: http://shul21.org/.

371 "literary legacy": http://www.sholomaleichemclub.org/history.htm#name.

371 Yiddish Book Center: www.yiddishbookcenter.org.

372 free download: http://www.yiddishbookcenter.org/books/search.

372 The first joke: SAB 275–276.

INDEX